THE CISTERCIAN ABBEYS OF TIPPERARY

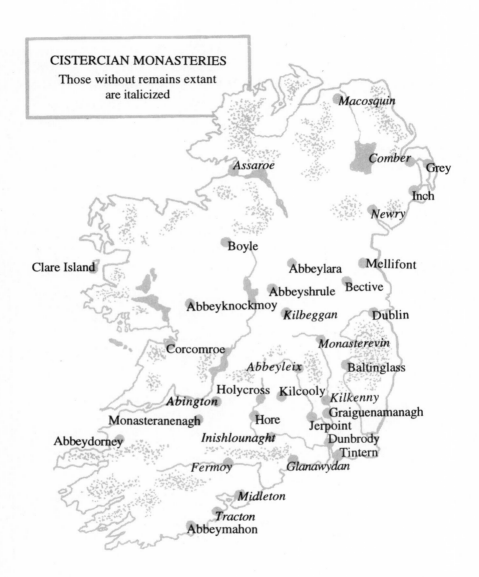

CISTERCIAN MONASTERIES
Those without remains extant
are italicized

Macosquin

Assaroe

Comber

Grey

Inch

Newry

Boyle

Clare Island

Abbeylara

Mellifont

Abbeyshrule

Bective

Abbeyknockmoy

Kilbeggan

Dublin

Corcomroe

Monasterevin

Abbeyleix

Baltinglass

Holycross

Kilcooly

Kilkenny

Abington

Graiguenamanagh

Monasteranenagh

Hore

Jerpoint

Abbeydorney

Inishlounaght

Dunbrody

Tintern

Fermoy

Glanawydan

Midleton

Tracton

Abbeymahon

Map of Ireland including the medieval Cistercian abbeys of Tipperary:
Holy Cross, Inis(h)lounaght, Kilcooly and Hore Abbey.

THE CISTERCIAN ABBEYS
OF TIPPERARY

Colmcille Ó Conbhuidhe, OCSO

edited by
Finbarr Donovan

FOUR COURTS PRESS

Published by
FOUR COURTS PRESS LTD
Fumbally Lane, Dublin 8, Ireland
e-mail: info@four-courts-press.ie
and in North America by
FOUR COURTS PRESS
c/o ISBS, 5804 N.E. Hassalo Street, Portland, OR 97213.

A catalogue record for this title
is available from the British Library.

ISBN 1–85182–380–8 hbk
ISBN 1–85182–381–6 pbk

Printed in Great Britain by
Antony Rowe Ltd, Chippenham, Wiltshire

CONTENTS

LIST OF ILLUSTRATIONS

EDITOR'S PREFACE

The two books Fr Colmcille wished to complete before his death were 'The Parish of Collon and the Cistercian Order' and 'Cistercian Abbeys of Co. Tipperary', representing two great loves of Clonmel-born Fr Colmcille – Mellifont abbey and Co. Tipperary. He had also hoped to publish a revised and shortened edition of *The Story of Mellifont Abbey*, and to write a history of Collon, Co. Louth. The present work is an attempt to complete the Tipperary book. Fr Colmcille told me that he had planned to use the individual studies already published, viz.: 'The Cistercian Abbey of Inishlounaght,'[1] 'The History of Holy Cross Abbey,'[2] 'Kilcooly Abbey,'[3] 'The Abbey of the Rock of Cashel.'[4]

I wish to thank the editor of the *Clonmel Nationalist* and the editors of *Citeaux*, the *Old Kilkenny Review* and the *Journal of the Clonmel Historical and Archeological Society* for their permission to use the above studies. Fr Colmcille was aware of the need to integrate the four studies and to eliminate duplication. This I have attempted to do. Some duplication remains; to remove it completely a more drastic re-write would have been required.

Fr Colmcille had intended to have a section on the abbey of Owney included in this volume. He considered this appropriate because the abbey was founded by Theobald Walter, the king's butler of Ireland, from whom were descended the Butlers, who later became earls of Ormond and Ossory. I have confined the work to the abbeys of Co. Tipperary proper as being a natural association.

In the case of Holy Cross, Fr Colmcille had begun to work on a first draft based on his original newspaper articles; that draft was not found. He had also started a second draft which was to include footnotes on source material. I have attempted to do some 'reverse re-engineering', to use a computer software phrase, in order to supply some source references, albeit quite inadequate by Fr Colmcille's standards.

Of the many virtues which Fr Colmcille possessed in abundance, his friends will have recognised his intellectual honesty and courage, underpinned by a strong faith and lightened by a sense of humour. Two quotations from his other works are relevant to this volume and I feel that Fr Colmcille would have included some such observations if he had produced the book. The first quotation is:

> A certain writer once prefaced a historical work with the following remark: 'To men of candid minds it will not be necessary to offer an

1 *Journal of the Clonmel Historical and Archeological Society*, 1955-6, pp 3-52. 2 *The Nationalist*, Clonmel, 17 June–9 October 1978. 3 *Old Kilkenny Review*, 1984-5, pp 55-63; pp 177-82. 4 *Citeaux* 12 (1961) 307-20.

apology for speaking the truth.' This preface is not intended as an apology, for we presume our readers will expect to find truth in the pages of a book which professes to deal with history and the story of the Irish Cistercians is essentially history. If truth is an essential element in history of any kind it is especially so in ecclesiastical history. It is intended in these pages to give a picture of the lives and times of the men with whom the story is concerned, and we have tried as far as possible to draw out information from the most authentic sources. Covering a period of five hundred years, it traces the vicissitudes of the Irish Cistercians during that period, and thus covers the beginnings, the expansion, the decline and the suppression of the Order in Ireland. It will readily be understood that in a story so complicated, covering as it does such a long period of time, a great amount of detail had to be omitted. It will also be evident that in any narrative which aims at giving a trustworthy, factual picture of Cistercian life and religious organisation during the centuries surveyed in this book, there must be light and shade, the darker side of the picture being presented as well as the brighter side. The story is necessarily complicated by the impact of the Anglo-Norman invasion on an already well-organised and expanding Order in the institute in its later years had its origin in this racial strife so utterly opposed to Christian charity and to natural justice.[5]

The second quotation, which applies to this work, is:

In writing this story every effort has been made to avoid all flights of fancy and to keep strictly to the facts. Theory has sometimes to be substituted for fact but in all such cases the available evidence for and against has been laid before the reader. Future writers may demolish these theories but they cannot change the facts. Original sources have been consulted as far as possible and no attempt has been made to gloss over less edifying aspects of the story. To do so would be an outrage on historical truth. To set down in these pages the truth, and only the truth, has been the constant endeavour of the writer. Religion can never be served by falsehood, and suppression of the truth in historical matters is in effect the uttering of an untruth. Following the advice of Pope Leo XIII in the Constitution *Saepe numero* (18 August 1883), we have endeavoured to 'state facts with truth and candour', and have to the best of our ability tried to 'go to the fountain-head for information'. We have especially kept in mind the advice given by the same Pope Leo when, writing in the

5 Extract from a draft paper by Fr Colmcille.

Constitution aforesaid, he warned writers to bear in mind above all things that 'the first duty of a historian is never to venture on a false statement; next, never to shrink from telling the truth; so that his writings may be free from all suspicion of favour or malice'.[6]

To make this work more self-contained and to preserve some of Fr Colmcille's unpublished research I thought it appropriate to add a General Introduction section as well as a number of appendices, using previously published material as well as both some unpublished lecture notes and research notes of Fr Colmcille. The sources for this were as follows:

Chapter 1: chapter 1 of *The Story of Mellifont*, supplemented by some unpublished notes on the chronology of the Irish Cistercian houses.

Chapter 2: unpublished lecture notes.

Chapter 3: unpublished research notes supplemented by material from *The Story of Mellifont*.

Chapter 4: unpublished lecture notes, supplemented from material from Fr Colmcille's article, in *Citeaux* 16 (1965) 144-160 and Prof. G. MacNiocaill's book *Na Manaigh Liathe in Eirinn* (Dublin, 1959), 'a pioneer work of great value', to use Fr Colmcille's own words. MacNiocaill's book was also the main source for the lists of the abbots.

Appendices: unpublished lectures and chapter 2 of *The Story of Mellifont*.

The Epilogue was adapted from the Epilogue in *The Story of Mellifont*.

Some additional material was added, based on the last four volumes of the *Calendar of Papal Registers* which have been published by the Irish Manuscripts Commission since 1978.

The present state of the architectural remains of the four Tipperary abbeys varies enormously. It ranges from Kilcooly, still in private hands and well preserved, to a partially reconstructed Holy Cross, to a decayed ruin of Hore abbey, and finally, with little or nothing of Inishlounaght remaining. In the appendices I have endeavoured to give some idea of the ruins in the last and this century as viewed by scholars such as Archdall, John O'Donovan, Canon Power and finally the authoritative observations of Roger Stalley in his magnificent work, *The Cistercian Monasteries of Ireland*. In a 'Note on Conservation' (p. 251) Stalley has this to say:

While antiquarian interest in Cistercian monuments increased steadily after 1790, very little was done to arrest their disintegration

---

6 *The Story of Mellifont* (Dublin, 1957), pp xxiii and xxiv..

and decay. Collapses of walls and towers were occurring at regular intervals. During the first half of the nineteenth century one person to take an active interest in preservation was Dr Charles Wall, a Senior Fellow of Trinity College, Dublin, who purchased the ruins of Holycross in 1833. He has been described as a 'genuine scholar, whose five volumes on Hebrew orthography brought him some reputation in his day'. He also deserves to be remembered for his enlightened moves at Holycross, where he repaired the east window and restored parts of the nave. The arcades on the south side were reinforced and arches were erected over the adjacent aisle, alterations which admittedly were more classical than Gothic in spirit. About 1874, the vaults of the chancel of Monasternenagh fell, the last major catastrophe on a Cistercian site before the formal establishment in 1874-5 of the National Monuments Branch of the Office of Public Works. By 1900 the Commissioners of Public Works were responsible for twelve Cistercian abbeys and today only four out of the twenty-one Cistercian ruins are not listed as national monuments, either in the north or south of the country (Abbeydorney, Abbeylara, Abbeymahon and Abbeyshrule). In their early years the Commissioners carried out a number of vital rescue operations, such as the construction of 'flying' buttresses at Grey abbey in 1908, which saved the nave from collapse. But not all their achievements at this time were without blemish. Many sites were cleared of 'rubbish' in a fashion the make the modern archaeologist wince and Mellifont was excavated in the 1880s without serious recording of what was found. Conservation methods also left much to be desired. At Grey abbey, repairs were executed with a lavish display of concrete, the crudity of which is still obvious today. The 1909 report of the Commissioners explained with bland optimism that 'the newness in the appearance of the concrete and cement pointing is wearing off and the new work will soon be of the same colour as the old'. Since 1922, however, Cistercian ruins have for the most part been scrupulously maintained by the ancient monuments departments, both north and south.

I would like to thank the abbot of Mellifont, Revd Fr Bernard Boyle OSCO and his community for their generous help, hospitality and permission to do this work in honour of Fr Colmcille. I also wish to thank Fr Laurence OSCO of Mellifont abbey, Fr Flannan OSCO of Mount St Joseph abbey, Roscrea, and Liam Ó Duibhir for their encouragement and help. To Professor Roger Stalley special thanks are due for permission to use material from his *The Cistercian Monasteries of Ireland,* which is an account of the history, art and architecture of the Irish Cistercians from 1142 to 1540.

LIST OF ABBREVIATIONS

AFM	*Annals of the kingdom of Ireland by the Four Masters*, ed. J O'Donovan, 7 vols, Dublin, 1848-51.
AH	*Archivium Hibernicum.*
ASOC	*Analecta Sacri Ordinis Cisterciensis.*
BSD	*Books of Survey and Distribution*, ed. R.C. Simington, 4 vols, IMC, Dublin, 1944-67.
Brady	W.M. Brady, *The Episcopal Succession in England, Scotland and Ireland A.D. 1400 to 1875*, 3 vols, Rome, 1876-7
Canivez	*Statuta Capitulorum Generalium Ordinis Cisterciensis*, 8 vols, ed. J.M. Canivez, Louvain, 1933-41.
CDI	*Calendar of Documents relating to Ireland 1171-1307*, 4 vols, ed. H.S. Sweetman and G.F. Handcock, 1875-86, 5 vols, PRO, London, 1875-86.
COD	*Calendar of Ormond Deeds, 1172-1603*, 6 vols, ed. Edmund Curtis, Dublin, 1932-43.
Comment. Rinucc.	*Commentarius Rinuccinianus, ... 1645-9*, 6 vols, ed. Stanislaus Kavanagh, Dublin, 1932-49.
CPI	*Chartae, Privilegia et Immunitates, ... 1171-1395*, Rec. Comm. Ire., Dublin, 1889.
CPR	*Calendar of entries in the Papal Registers relating to Great Britain and Ireland, papal letters.* 14 vols., ed. W.H. Bliss, J.A. Twemlow and Charles Johnston, PRO, London, 1893; 4 vols, ed. M.J. Herren and A.P. Fuller, IMC, Dublin, 1978-94.
CS	*The Civil Survey*, ed. R.C. Simington, 10 vols, IMC, Dublin, 1931-61.
DS	Down Survey.
Extents	*Extents of Irish monastic possessions, 1540-1541*, ed. Newport B. White, IMC, Dublin, 1943.
Fiants	*Calendar to fiants of King Henry VIII to Elizabeth.* In *Reports* 7-22 of the Keeper of the Public Record Office of Ireland, Dublin, 1875-90.
FNMI	*Facsimiles of the national manuscripts of Ireland*, ed. J.T. Gilbert, 4 vols, Dublin, 1874-84
Harl. Chart	Harleian Charter, 75 A 4 and 75 A 5, British Museum
Hartry	Malachy, Hartry, *Triumphalia Chronologica Monasterii Sanctae Crucis in Hibernia*, ed. D. Murphy, Dublin, 1891.
HC	Harris *Collectanea*, Nat. Lib. Ireland, 19 folio vols, especially vols xiii and xiv.

Hoberg	H. Hoberg, *Taxae pro communitas servitiis*, 1949.
IER	*Irish Ecclesiastical Record.*
IMC	Irish Manuscripts Commission.
IMED	*Irish Monastic and Episcopal Deeds,1200-1600*, ed. Newport B. White, Dublin, 1936.
Janauschek	P.L. Janauschek, *Originum Cisterciensium*, Vienna, 1887.
JAS I	*Calendar of Irish Patent Rolls, James I*, Dublin, 1830.
KC	King's *Collectanea*, Mss. F.1, 15, 16 (TCD)
MH	M. Archdall, *Monasticon Hibernicum*, London, 1786.
Morrin	*Cal. of Patent and Close Rolls of Chancery in Ireland*, ed. J. Morrin, 3 vols, Dublin, 1861.
OS	Ordnance Survey
OSL	Ordnance Survey Letters, by John O'Donovan and others, in the RIA. Reproduced from the originals under the direction of Revd M. O'Flanagan, typescript, 42 vols, Bray, 1927-35.
RDC	*Repertory to the Decrees of Chancery*, PROI, 1a/49/63.
Registrum	'Registrum Epistolarum Abbatis Stephani of Lexington', *Analecta Sacri Ordinis Cisterciensis* 2 (1946) 1-118.
RIA	Royal Irish Academy.
Rot. Pat.	*Rotulorum patentium et clausorum cancellariae Hiberniae calendarium*, vol. 1, pars 1, Hen. II–Hen. VII, ed. E. Tresham, Dublin, 1828.
Spic. Ossoriense.	*Spicilegium Ossoriense … to the year 1800*, ed. P.F. Moran, 3 vols, Dublin, 1874-84.
Tax. I. Cist.	'Taxation of the Irish Cistercian Houses', *Citeaux* 15 (1964) 144-160.
VM	A. Theiner, *Vetera monumenta Hibernorum et Scotorum*, Rome, 1864.

PART ONE

General Introduction

1. THE FOUNDATIONS

The Cistercian Order takes its name from the monastery of Citeaux in Burgundy. It is a reform of the Benedictine Institute and originated in an attempt to go back as far as possible to the literal observance of the Rule of St Benedict. The story of Cistercian beginnings has been told many times and in many ways, but in no way so briefly and withal so clearly as by the founder of the Order himself, St Stephen Harding, who, in his *Exordium Parvum*,[1] has left us an authentic account of the small beginnings from which a great Order was to develop. In order not to weary the reader I propose in this chapter to summarise the account of the founding of Citeaux contained in the *Exordium Parvum*.

In the year 1098, Robert, abbot of Molesme, came, in company with certain brothers of that monastery to the papal legate, Hugh, archbishop of Lyons, beseeching him to aid them by the apostolic authority which he possessed in their purpose of regulating their lives according to the holy rule of St Benedict. The legate gave them letters in which he authorised them to retire to some place which the goodness of God would point out to them that they might there serve the Lord together with those who, according to the rule and by common consent, they had determined to join with them.

Returning to Molesme they chose as their companions those who wished to keep the rule, and, twenty-one monks in all, set out on their journey to the desert of Citeaux. This was a wild forlorn spot, covered with dense thickets and briars and frequented only by wild beasts. The men of God were all the more pleased with this place because it was inaccessible to men and so, cutting away the briars and thickets, they began at once to build their monastery having first obtained the consent both of the bishop of the diocese (Chalons) and the lord of the place.

The duke of Burgundy, in whose territory Citeaux lay, heard of the labours and the holy purpose of these religious men, and, we are told, was much pleased at their holy fervour. He was quite willing, therefore, to help them in any way possible, and, asked to do so by a letter from the legate, finished at his own expense the monastery begun by them, bestowed on them an abundance of lands and cattle, and for a long time continued to supply them with all their daily needs. Meanwhile the abbot was given the

---

[1] Two translations of the *Exordium Parvum*, as it is called, were made into English. The first, by Denis Murphy sj, appeared as part of the introduction to his edition of Malachy Hartry's *Triumphalia Chronologica Monasterii Sanctae Crucis in Hibernia*, which was published in 1891; the second was made by Robert E. Larkin and was published for the first time in 1953 by Louis J. Lekai, S.O.Cist, in his book *The White Monks* (Okauchee, Wis. 1953). All authorities agree in attributing the original to St Stephen Harding.

pastoral staff by the bishop, a sign that he was now invested with abbatial authority, and so the monks were established in Citeaux in accordance with the sacred canons, and the monastery itself became an abbey.

Now, the monks of Molesme, after departure of Robert and his companions to the desert of Citeaux, had elected a certain Godfrey to be their abbot. He, however, did not wish to continue in the abbatial office but wanted Robert to return to his former charge, and with this end in view he sent certain of the monks to Rome to ask the pope that Robert might be restored to his old house. The pope hearkened to their appeal and commanded the legate to restore Robert to the community at Molesme if it could be done, while at the same time allowing those monks who had chosen to dwell in the desert to remain there in peace. It would appear from the pope's letter on this occasion, that the monks of Molesme had appeared at the council, which had been convened in 1099 to condemn the system of investiture, and had raised a great clamour there.

On receiving the pope's letter the legate wrote to his very dear brother Robert, bishop of Langres, in the following terms:

We have thought it necessary to notify to you what we have determined on in the conference lately held at Pontansille about the business of the church of Molesme. There came into our presence there with your letter, monks of Molesme, showing the abandonment and destruction of their place which had been brought on them by the removal of Robert the Abbot, and earnestly asking that he should be given back to them to be their father, since they thought that by no other means could peace and quiet be restored to the church of Molesme, and the vigour and prosperous condition of the monastic order re-established; and in our presence Brother Godfrey, whom you set over the same church and abbot, said that he would give up his place willingly to Robert as to his father if it was our pleasure to restore him to the church of Molesme. Having heard the petition of the monks of Molesme and having read carefully the letter of our Lord the Pope on this subject addressed to us and leaving the whole to our will and decision, and having taken the advice of many religious men summoned together, as well as of others who were then with us, in accordance with your request and theirs we have decreed that he shall be restored to the church of Molesme; yet so that, before he returns, he shall go to Chalons and give back the pastoral staff and the care of the abbey into the hands of your brother the bishop of Chalons, to whom he made his profession like other abbots; and that he shall set free from their profession and obedience the other monks of the New Monastery who made their profession and promised obedience to him as abbot; and in this way he shall be absolved by the bishop from the profession made to him and to the church of Chalons. We have also given permission to all the brethern of the New Monastery who came with him to return with him to Molesme when he leaves the New Monastery, on this condition, however, that henceforth no one shall presume to solicit or to receive any other, unless as far as the blessed Benedict enjoins that the monks of the New Monastery should be received. And when he shall have done what is laid down above, we give him over to you, that you may restore him to the church of Molesme as its abbot. If, however, through thoughtlessness,[2] a thing not uncommon, he abandons this same church at any future time, no one shall be appointed in his place during the lifetime of the said Abbot Godfrey withough our consent and yours and that of the said Godfrey, all which we ratify by apostolic authority. And as regards the altar furniture and the other things which the aforesaid Abbot Robert took with him from the church of Molesme when leaving it, and came with to the bishop of Chalons and to the New Monastery, we have ordained that all should remain in the possession of the brethern of the New Monastery except a certain breviary which they shall keep until the feast of St John the Baptist, in order to copy it, with the consent of the monks of Molesme.

So it was done. Abbot Robert set the monks free from the promise of obedience they had made to him, while the bishop of Chalons set the abbot free from the promise made to the bishop and the church of Chalons. Robert returned to Molesme, bringing with him some other monks who, says the writer of the *Exordium*, did not like the desert.

It became necessary after Robert's departure that a new abbot should be elected to take his place and the choice fell on

a certain brother, Alberic by name, a man of letters, sufficiently instructed in things sacred and profane, a lover of the rule, who had filled the office of prior for a long time both at Molesme and here, and who had laboured much and long to bring about that the brethren should come hither from Molesme, and who, for the part he took, had endured many reproaches, imprisonment and stripes.

Alberic was a man of foresight, and looking to the future he with the advice of his brethren sent two monks to Rome, beseeching the pope to

2 Dr Larkin translates: 'if ... he should in his usual fickleness', and this seems to bring out the meaning better than Fr Murphy's version. The legate seems to hint here of a want of stability in Robert's character.

take the community under the protection of the Apostolic See. These brethren, furnished with sealed letters from Hugh, archbishop of Lyons, Walter, bishop of Chalons, and the Cardinals John and Benedict of the Roman Church, presented themselves before Pope Paschal who, approving of the purpose of the new community, took the monks of Citeaux under the immediate protection of the Holy See by letters dated 19 October 1100.

The monks of Citeaux now commenced their new life in earnest. What manner of life this was and what were the ideals placed before themselves by these monks we learn from the *Exordium Parvum*:

> Henceforth the abbot and his brethren, mindful of their promise, strove all of them to establish and keep the Rule of St Benedict in that place. They rejected whatever was opposed to the rule: habits with ample folds, furs, linen shirts, hoods, drawers, combs and bedspreads, mattresses, various kinds of dishes in the refectory, lard, and all else opposed to the Rule.

Not only did these early Cistercians reject the innovations in matters of food and clothing which had in the course of time come to be accepted as something normal by the majority of monks, but they even went so far as to reject every kind of ornament or superfluity in their churches. The norm of conduct in future was to be the purity of the Rule, and whatever was not to be found therin was to be discarded. Hence they turned their backs completely on the manorial system renouncing all bakeries, mills, farmhouses, serfs and other feudal sources of wealth. They rejected in similar fashion the possession of private churches and the incomes from such churches, as well as altarages, offerings, burial dues, and all tithes. Their lands were to be situated in places remote from the haunts of men and were to be used for the purpose of their own communities and exploited by their own work, the system of rents and revenues, serfs and tenants, being altogether abandoned by them; for their aim was to earn their bread by the labour of their own hands. Moreover, since they realised that without the help of lay brothers they would be unable to fulfill perfectly the precepts of the Rule, they decided to admit such brothers into the community, treating them like themselves in life and in death excepting that they would not have the status of monks. For this reason, too, they decided to employ hired labour when necessary, and whenever they would have farms and engage in agriculture they determined that such farms would be managed by the lay brethren so that in this way the monks would be left free to dwell within the cloister and to attend to the duties of the choir.

After the death of Abbot Alberic, his prior, Stephen Harding, an Englishman, was elected abbot in his place, and he may be said to have been the founder of the Order known from its mother house of Citeaux as the Cistercian Order. It was under the direction of Abbot Stephen that regulations were laid down regarding the furniture of the church and he too was the author of the famous *Charter of Charity*, the primitive constitution of the Cistercian Order, which is the basis of the modern constitutions of both the Strict and the Common Observances. The appointment of Stephen and the regulations introduced by him are thus described in the *Exordium Parvum*:

> The man of God, Alberic, having practised fruitfully regular discipline in the school of Christ for nine years and a half, went to the Lord, glorious in his faith and virtues and therefore deservedly to be blessed by God in life everlasting. He was succeeded by a certain brother Stephen by name, and Englishman by race, who had come with the others from Molesme and was a lover of the Rule and of the new place. During his time the brethren and this same abbot forbade the duke of that country or any other lord to hold court in that church as they were wont to do heretofore on solemn feasts. Moreover, lest anything might remain in the house of God (in which they desired to serve God devoutly day and night) which would savour of pride or superfluity or which might at any time corrupt poverty, the guardiam of virtue, which they had chosen of their own accord, they resolved to use no crucifixes of gold or silver but only of painted wood; no candlesticks except one of iron; no thuribles unless of copper or iron; no chasubles except of wool or linen without gold or silver embroidery; no albs or amices unless of linen without silk gold or silver. They rejected altogether the use of palliums, copes, dalmatics and tunics, though they kept silver chalices, not golden, but when possible gold plated; the silver tube (for communion), gold plated if possible; and stoles and maniples of silk only without gold or silver. They also ordered that the altar cloths should be made of unembroidered linen and that the cruets should have on them no gold or silver.

St Alberic died in 1109 and for the next three years the new monastery of Citeaux suffered much poverty as well as from the dearth of numbers, while death wrought havoc as a result of a contagious disease which sorely afflicted the brethren. It seemed as if the little community was doomed to extinction when God at last intervened, sending the monastery an influx of vocations. In the year 1112 came the advent of St Bernard with thirty companions and thenceforth the future of the new monastery was assured. Foundations began to be made and the *Charter of Charity* was composed and confirmed by apostolic authority in 1119. St Bernard went forth to found the abbey of Clairvaux and soon the new abbot became famous throughout Europe as the greatest man of his time. Cistercian monasteries multiplied 'beyond number,' and among the many monasteries founded from Clairvaux by the care and devotion of its great abbot was the house of Mellifont in Ireland, the cradle of the Cistercian Order in this country. The beginnings of Mellifont are described below:

In the year 1140 Maelmhaodhog Ó Morgair, one-time archbishop of Armagh and then bishop of Down, and better known as St Malachy, set out for Rome accompanied by five priests and a number of inferior clerics. His purpose was to petition the pope for the palliums for the new archbishops of Armagh and Cashel. Attracted by the fame of St Bernard he turned aside to visit Clairvaux, and such was the impression made upon him by the holy abbot and by the community that he would fain resign his pastoral care and end his days as a simple monk in Clairvaux. On his arrival at Rome he did indeed petition the pope to allow him to become a Cistercian but the Holy Father would not hear of it. The Irish church still required the presence of the holy bishop who was the guiding light of the reform, and the pope sent him back to Ireland to continue his great work as legate of the Holy See.

Malachy paid a second visit to Clairvaux on his way back to Ireland and, since he could not become a Cistercian himself, he left four of his companions behind him to be trained by St Bernard in the Cistercian life with a view to introducing the Order into Ireland at a later date. Among these young novices was Gillacrist (Christian) Ó Connairche, later to be the first abbot of the Irish foundation of Mellifont. Malachy had no sooner arrived home than he set about gaining further recruits for the new Order and shortly after his return was able to send another batch of Irishmen to join the original group at Clairvaux. These brought with them a letter addressed to St Bernard and a staff as a present for the venerable abbot from Malachy; for from the moment of the first meeting between these two men they became joined in the closest bonds of friendship, a friendship which endured as long as life itself and was not ended even by death.

Though the letter written by Malachy on this occasion has not been preserved we are enabled to form an opinion of its contents from the tenor of Bernard's reply. It seems that Malachy was desirous of bringing the Cistercians to Ireland at the earliest possible opportunity and had requested the abbot of Clairvaux to send two of the Irish brethren home to prepare a place for the new community. Bernard could not agree to this. Writing to Malachy he gives him reasons for not doing as the latter wished:

Amongst all the many worries and troubles by which I am distracted, your brethren from a distant land, your letter, and your gift of a staff supports my weak body, and your brothers serve God humbly. I have accepted all, all have given me pleasure, and all work together for my good. With regard to your wish that I should send you two of the brothers to prepare a place, I have discussed it with the brethren and we are agreed that it would not be well for them, until they are better equipped to fight for the Lord. When they have been instructed in the school of the Holy Ghost, when they are clothed with strength from on high, then they will return to their father to sing the songs of the Lord no longer in a strange land but in their own.

Do you in the meantime, with the wisdom given you by the Lord look for and prepare a site similar to what you have seen here, far removed from the turmoil of the world. The time is not far distant when I shall be able with God's grace to send you men fashioned anew in Christ Blessed forever be the name of the Lord by whose gift it has come about that we have sons in common whom your teaching has planted, my exhortations have watered, and to whom God has given increase ...[3]

Acting on the suggestion of St Bernard, Malachy chose a secluded glen about five miles north-west of Drogheda as the site most suited for the proposed monastery. Far removed from the haunts of men was the wild and rugged glen theough which flowed the waters of the Mattock, a tributary of the Boyne. In the days of St Malachy it must have been a wild and desolate spot indeed, for even at the present day, though surrounded by pleasant hills and fertile pastures, it retains a certain picturesque and wild aspect which suggests to the imagination that it must, on the first coming of the monks, have been something like the original Clairvaux as depicted by William of St Thierry – 'a place of horror and vast solitude'.[4] It lay within the limits of the kingdom of Airghialla whose king, Donnchadh Ua Cearbhaill, was a friend of St Malachy and a powerful patron of the reform movement in the Irish church, and who may be considered as one of the founders of the new monastery. He it was who gave the lands on which the abbey was to be raised to the Cistercian Order and supplied the materials for the building, both wood and stone. He is also credited with having supplied the monks with agricultural implements for the work of cultivating the lands thus acquired and with books for the use of the choir.[5]

3 Letter 383. This and all the other quotations from St Bernard's letters made in this book are from the English translation, *Letters of St Bernard* (London, 1953), by Bruno Scott James, unless the contrary is stated.   4 William of St Thierry, friend and biographer of St Bernard of Clairvaux, was a Benedictine abbot who later became a Cistercian. He was the author of the first book of the *Vita Prima* from which the extract here quoted ' a place of horror and vast solitude', has been taken (*Vita Bernardi*, PL 185:225-266, I, v. 25).   5 So a note in the Antiphonary of Armagh, dated 1 January 1170.

The date of foundation of the new monastery is variously given as 1140 and 1142, the latter date being the commonly accepted one.[6] The pioneer community seems to have been made up of two elements, namely, the Irish monks who had been left behind at Clairvaux by St Malachy and trained under the supervision of St Bernard, and a certain number of French monks. As it was customary among the Cistercians to send thirteen monks on every new foundation, the abbot and twelve monks in imitation of Christ and his twelve apostles, we may assume that this procedure was followed also in the case of the new Irish foundation. In this case the Irish monks formed a fourth of the community, the remaining three fourths being French. At a later stage more Irish monks arrived from Clairvaux, consisting apparently of the second batch of postulants sent to that monastery by St Malachy on his return to Ireland.[7]

The first Cistercians to arrive in Ireland brought with them a letter from Bernard of Clairvaux to his friend Malachy:

> I have done what you commanded, if not as it should have been done, at any rate as it could have been done at the time. The calls on me have grown so many that I have been scarcely able to accomplish the little that I have done. I have sent you these few seeds that you see before you. They may suffice for the sowing of a small part of that field where Isaac had gone to meditate when Rebecca was brought to him by the servant of Abraham, to be happily united to him for ever after. Scorn not this seed that I have sent to you, for in it I find fulfilled in our day those words of the Prophet: 'Except the Lord of hosts had left us seed, we had been as Sodom, and we should have been as Gomorrah,' I have sowed and now it is for you to water, then God will give the increase. I greet the saints who are with you and humbly commend myself to your prayers and theirs.[8]

Work on the building of the new monastery seems to have begun immediately, for in 1144 we find St Bernard writing to St Malachy to con-

---

6 'MCXLII. Mellifons Fundatur' (*Chartularies of St Mary's Abbey, Dublin*, ed. J.T. Gilbert, London, 1884, no. 255A, i, p. 279). The annals of the same abbey bear a like testimony: 'MCXLII. Fundatur Abbatia Mellifontis, Donato, Rege Urgallie terras et posessiones donante, Malachia episcopo procurante, ad quam regendam Bernardus, Abbas Clarevallis, misit Conventum de illis quos Malachias in Claravalle ad addiscendum ordinem reliquerat, et postea miserat, dato eis in Patrem Fratre Christiano, adiungens de suis quanti sufficerent ad numerum Abbatie, que conceipt et peperit quinque filias ...' (Annals of St Mary's Abbey, Dublin, MS. E.3, 11, TCD, printed by Gilbert in his *Chartularies*, op. cit., ii, p. 262). 7 This is implied in the words used by Bernard addressing Malachy in a letter brought to Ireland early in 1144 on the occasion of the return of Robert to Mellifont: 'I commend to you my sons who are yours too ...' (Letter 385). The reference here seems to be to the second group of Irish postulants who appear to have returned to Ireland on this occasion with Christian Ó Connairche and Robert. 8 *Letters of St Bernard*, no. 384.

gratulate him on the progress being made. Nevertheless the work did not proceed too smoothly, at least in the beginning, and dissensions arose between the Irish and the French monks. It has been supposed by some writers that the trouble arose as a result of the insistence of the French on having the new monastery constructed after the model of Clairvaux which followed the plan adopted by all Cistercians houses, and the opposition offered by the Irish monks to a monastery of this type which differed altogether from the traditional Irish abbey. This, though pure surmise, affords a likely enough explanation of the quarrel between the two groups. The Irish were conservative and were inclined to hold fast to the traditions of their ancestors. So attached were they to old ways that they continued to favour the old Irish type of monastic establishment long after the introduction of the Cistercians; and even as late as 1228 we find complaints being made to Rome and to the general chapter of the Cistercian Order that the Irish monks had in many places abandoned their monasteries and built for themselves 'miserable huts' of clay and wattle outside the monastic walls.[9]

Whatever the cause of the trouble between the Irish and French elements in the new monastery, it seems to have been sufficiently serious to lead to the withdrawal of many, if not all, of the French monks from the enterprise. It took all St Bernard's powers of persuasion to prevail on a certain monk Robert, who seems to have been the architect or builder-in-chief of the new house, to return to the post which he had deserted. The whole work of the foundation appears to have been brought to a standstill at least for the time being, and Malachy wrote an urgent appeal to Bernard for the return to Ireland of Robert. Eventually Bernard succeeded in persuading Robert to return and with him came Gillacrist Ó Connairche, bearing a letter to Malachy from which we quote the following relevant extracts:

> I commend to you my sons, who are yours too, and I do so all the more earnestly for their being so far away from me. You know how, after God, I put all my trust in you by entrusting them to you, because it seemed wrong to refuse your prayers. Do all you can to open your heart to them and cherish them. Never on any pretext let your care and ardour for them flag or fade, never allow to perish what you hand has planted. I have learned from your letters and from those of my brethren that the house flourishes exceedingly both in temporal and in spiritual things. With my whole heart I

9 Letter from the abbot of Citeaux to Pope Gregory IX written probably about September 1228 (Register of Stephen of Lexington, ii) and a letter from Abbot Stephen Lexington himself to the abbot of Citeaux and the general chapter (Letter XXXI) which may be dated about June 1228.

render thanks to God for this, and my congratulations to you. But because there is still need for vigilance in a new country among a people little accustomed to the monastic life and unfamiliar with it, I beg you in the Lord not to remove your care from them until the work you have so well begun has been perfectly finished. Concerning the brethren who have returned I would have been well content for them to remain with you. But perhaps those natives of your country who are little disciplined and who found it hard to obey observances that were strange to them, may have been in some measure the occasion of their return.[10]

It is evident from certain passages in the above that St Bernard considered that the cause of the trouble between the French and Irish monks was due, at least in great measure, to a want of discipline on the part of the latter. He points out that the Irish are as yet but little accustomed to the monastic life. This may seems to us a strange observation on the part of St Bernard, for we have been accustomed to think of the Irish church as preeminently a monastic one. We have heard so much of the island of saints and scholars, and have so long been accustomed to associate those saints and scholars with the monks and the monastic schools of Ireland, that it almost takes our breath away to hear St Bernard refer to the Irish as being unfamiliar with and little accustomed to the monastic life. Yet we must remember that the long centuries of the Danish wars had resulted in the relaxation of the bonds of ecclesiastical discipline. The monasteries themselves had to a great extent become laicised, and it may be said that the older Irish monasticism was by this time in a state of almost universal stagnation.

St Bernard's letter continues: 'I have sent back to you my very dear son Christian, having instructed him as well as I could in the observances of our Order, and I hope that in future he will be more careful about them.'

Some authors infer from the words of St Bernard quoted above that Christian, that is Gillacrist Ó Connairche, came to Ireland with the first contingent of monks in 1142 but was found not to be as well instructed in the Cistercian observances as might be desired and so, when the French monks abandoned the new foundation, was recalled to Clairvaux that he might there take up once more his religious training and, having completed it, return to Ireland at a later date. He returns now with Robert and it is possible that some more of the former deserters returned with them. Bernard, indeed, complains of the difficulty in finding men willing to go on the Irish foundation, and we may suppose that the experiences of the French monks who took part in the pioneer venture did not encourage many of them to return a second time.

---

10 *Letters of St Bernard*, no. 385.

Do not be surprised that I have been able to send many with him (Christian), for I could not find many suitable mem who were willing to go, and I was loath to oblige them to do so against their will. My dear brother Robert acceded to my request this time like an obedient son. It will be your business to help him in the buildings and other things necessary for the well-being of your house. I would also suggest that you persuade those religious who you are hoping will be useful to the new monastery that they should unite with their Order, for this would be very advantageous to the house, and you would be better obeyed. Farewell, and always remember me in Christ.[11]

Despite the differences which had arisen between the Irish and French brethern at this early stage of the new foundation the work of construction seems to have gone on with but little interruption and the new monastery was already sufficiently advanced in 1152 to allow of the holding there of the famous synod of Drogheda which the Annals of St Mary's Abbey, Dublin expressly declare was convened at Mellifont, as the new abbey was called.[12]

The new monastery suffered a great loss in 1148 by the death of St Malachy. Again making his way to Rome to seek the palliums he broke his journey at Clairvaux where he arrived about the middle of October. He was not long there when he was forced to take to his bed, struck down by fever. There he died in the arms of St Bernard soon after midnight on 2 November in the fifty-fourth year of his age. St Bernard's biographer relates that when saying mass for the repose of Malachy's soul on the following day, the holy abbot, instead of saying the collect for the faithful departed at the postcommunion, sang that for a canonised bishop; it was an instance of a saint canonizing a saint.[13] Writing to the Irish Cistercian

---

11 As the last sentence in Letter no. 385 is somewhat ambiguous and susceptible of more than one translation we subjoin here an alternative version from the pen of Fr Ailbe J. Luddy OSCO. 'One more suggestion I will offer ... It is that you should employ your influence to persuade men of exemplary life and such as may be expected to prove worthy religious to enter the community. People will readily follow your counsel; and so you will promote most effectually the interests of the house.'   12 'MCLI. Christianus, Episcopus Lysmorensis, tocius Hibernie Legatus, in Mellifonte consilium celeberrimum celebravit ...' The description which follows in the annals and the purpose for which the synod of Mellifont was convoked make it clear that there is here question of the assembly usually known as the synod of Drogheda or the synod of Kells. There really were, it would seem, two synods, or to speak more exactly, two sessions of the same synod, the first being held in Kells and the second in Mellifont, called by the annalists, Drogheda. The Annals of St Mary's Abbey, Dublin, are the only ones which identify the Drogheda of this synod with Mellifont. For the whole question of the synod of Kells (and Drogheda or Mellifont) see Aubrey Gwynn's papers in IER 77 (5th series), 'The centenary of the synod of Kells,' and the papers by Thomas Gogarty in the IER 12 (5th series) 122.   13 *Vita Prima* (S. Bernardi) IV, iv, 21. The author of this book (as well as of the third and fifth books) of the *Vita Prima* was Geoffrey of Auxerre of whom it has been said that as a biographer of St Bernard 'he stands supreme in a class apart' (William Watkins, *St Bernard of Clairvaux*, Manchester, 1935, p. 376).

communities afterwards to console with them on the death of Malachy, Bernard begged them not to begrudge his abbey of Clairvaux the holy bishop's body, considering that they had been privileged during many years to enjoy the grace and glory of his living presence.[14]

When the new abbey was at last completed and the great stone buildings erected, which were a cause of wonder to the natives, the consecration of the abbey church took place in the year 1157.

Mellifont abbey had made great progress in the years which had elapsed between the first coming of the Cistercians to Ireland in 1142 and the consecration of the abbey church in 1157. While Mellifont was still in course of building the first foundation was made from the new house in 1145. This had become necessary by the enormous inflow of recruits for the Order in Ireland who could no longer be housed in the mother abbey. A new colony was therefore sent forth to establish a daughter house in the kingdom of Meath. Like its mother house the second Irish Cistercian abbey was situated in the valley of the Boyne near the town of Navan (An Uaimh) and was named *Beatitudo Dei* or *Monasterium de Beatitudine* (Bective). It was founded and endowed by Ua Maeleachlainn, king of Meath. In the course of the eight years which followed no less than six additional foundations were made from Mellifont, Innislounaght or Suir, about 1147, Boyle in 1148,[15] Mainistir-an-aenaigh (Maigue) and Baltinglass in 1148, Kilbeggan in 1150 and Newry in 1153.[16] In the following year, 1154, the monastery of Maigue gave birth to a daughter of its own, Odorney in Kerry, the first granddaughter of Mellifont. Moreover, there was founded in Dublin in 1139 a Benedictine monastery of the Savignian Congregation and this monastery, known as St Mary's abbey, adopted the Cistercian rule in 1147 with all the other houses of the Congregation, so that in little more than a decade the original Cistercian foundation in Ireland had increased and multiplied. With the foundation of Fermoy in 1170 from Inishlounaght there were eleven houses in the Order in Ireland before the coming of the Anglo-Normans.

In the year 1171 the small abbey of Glenawydan (Vallis Caritatis) was founded in what is now known as the parish of Monksland in Co.

---

14 *Letters of St Bernard*, no. 386. **15** This abbey was originally founded at Grellachdnaih but moved to Drumcanny c.1150, to Bunfinnay in 1158 and finally to Ath-da-Iorg on the river Boyle where the permanent settlement was made in 1161. **16** That Suir abbey was one of the earliest foundations is clear from St Bernard's Life of St Malachy where he tells us that the latter presented the monastery with its first lay brother. Dr Lanigan (*Ecclesiastical History of Ireland*, Dublin, 1822, iv, chapt. xxvii, 10) considered that the abbey of Suir was, in all probability, the oldest of all the five Cistercian monasteries mentioned by St Bernard as existing in Ireland in his time with the exception, of course, of Mellifont. It is not certain, however, whether the original abbey of Suir was on the same site afterwards occupied by 'Abbey Inishlounaght.' We later find Suir a daughter house of Maigue and this may be explained by a refoundation of the abbey in the time of Donal Ó'Briain, king of Thomond. Possibly the original foundation had fallen on evil days and the community had dwindled as happened in other cases.

Waterford.[17] Being insufficiently endowed and never having more than a small community it was unable to exist as a separate entity and was eventually suppressed by the general chapter in 1228. The next foundation was that of Assaroe in Co. Donegal (1178) which was followed in quick succession by Jerpoint, Chore abbey (Middleton) and Holy Cross abbey in Cos. Kilkenny, Cork and Tipperary respectively. Chore was founded in 1180, Holy Cross about the same time or perhaps in 1181. Jerpoint, which seems to have begun its existence as a house of Black Benedictines, adopted the Cistercian discipline in 1180 and its foundation is reckoned from that year in the official Cistercian tabulae.[18]

Within the decade following the foundation of Holy Cross abbey no less than eight new houses came into existence: Dunbrody, Co. Wexford, in 1182, Abbeyleix (Co. Laois) and Kilcooly (Co. Tipperary) in 1184, Killenny (Co. Kilkenny) in 1185,[19] Inch or Inishcourcy (Co. Down) in 1187, Abbeymahon (Co. Cork) and Rosglas alias Monasterevan (Co. Kildare) in 1189, and Knockmoy abbey which was founded by Cathal Crobhdhearg, king of Connacht, in 1190. There were only three foundations between 1190 and 1200, Grey abbey, Co. Down (1193), Corcumroe (Co. Clare) founded by the king of Thomond in 1195, and Comber (Co. Down) founded in 1199. During the period 1200-1205 there were four foundations, Tintern (Co. Wexford) and Abbeyshrule (Co. Longford) in 1200, Duiske (Co. Kilkenny) in 1204 and Owney (Co. Limerick) in 1205. The monastery of Abbeylara, popularly known as Granard, was founded in 1214. Four years later came Macosquin in Co. Derry (1218) and the great era of foundations ended with the abbey of Tracton, Co. Cork, in 1224. For more than half a century no more Cistercian houses were founded until in 1272 the monastery of Cashel (Hore abbey) replaced an earlier Benedictine foundation in the archiepiscopal city. This abbey, an off-shoot of Mellifont, was the last abbey of the order to be founded in Ireland during the middle ages.

Of the monasteries listed above Glenawydan and Killenny were suppressed by the general chapter. The lands of the former were first assigned to Dunbrody but were later restored to Inishlounaght which still held them when the monasteries were dissolved in 1539. The lands of Kilkenny were annexed to the abbey of Duiske and formed part of the possessions of that abbey until the dissolution. One other abbey, which had but a brief existence, was that of Flumen Vivus (Abbeystrowery, Co. Cork), a daughter house of Abbeymahon. It seems to have died out at an early date, for a statute of 1281 decreed its restoration. If this decree was actually carried

17 The name Glengragh has been given to this abbey since the seventeenth century. It is an attempt to translate the Latin name (*Vallis Caritatis*) into Irish and was never the nams of the abbey nor of the place in which it was situated. 18 See 'The Origins of Jerpoint Abbey, Co. Kilkenny', *Cîteaux* 14 (1963) no. 4. 19 Ibid.

into effect the monastery must have failed a second time. It was no longer in existence in 1539 and, indeed, apart from one reference in the statute of 1281 nothing is known of the house or its history, nor has any record been preserved of the date of the original foundation. In the extent made at Cork in February 1541 of the abbey de Fonte Vivo (Abbeymahon) Abbeystrowery is described as a 'cell called Manistre Inshorrye' and stated to be in 'Manartynaghes country' (MacCarthy Riabhach's country).

Two others supposed abbeys may be mentioned, Abbeyfeale in Co. Limerick and the monastery on Clare Island, Co. Mayo. Although many writers have classified Abbeyfeale as a Cistercian house and daughter of Maigue, no evidence has ever been offered in support of the statement. The statutes of the general chapter make no reference to such an abbey nor does the name appear on the tabulae of the order. It is, of course, possible that there was a grange or cell of Maigue here at one time, but even that cannot be proved. The Irish name (Mainistir na Feile) and its English rendering show that there must have been some kind of monastic establishment here at one time, but that is all that can be said with certainty. Much the same applies to the monastery on Clare Island. It is unlikely that it was ever a Cistercian house in the strict sense; it was probably a grange or cell of the abbey of Knockmoy among whose possessions it was listed at the dissolution of that abbey. References have sometimes been made to a Cistercian monastery at Kilfore (now Kilmonaster) near Lifford, Co. Donegal. Here again the name 'monastery' is a misnomer. There was, in fact, an extensive grange there which belonged to the abbey of Assaroe and is mentioned in medieval documents as the grange of Cillifori, commonly called St Mary's monastery. There is no evidence to show that this grange ever had the status of an abbey. However, since a decree of the general chapter implies that Irish Cistercian houses had been suppressed, it is quite possible that some of the granges attached to various abbeys were originally separate monasteries which for one reason or another had failed to develop and had to be suppressed by the general chapter.

2. CISTERCIAN LIFE

In all Cistercian houses of the period there dwelt the *monachi* and the *conversi* (the monks and lay brothers) enjoying alike all the advantages of the religious state but differing in their functions and employments. Both shared the same general way of life and the same manual labour, but the principal work of the monk was the celebration of the liturgical office, the work of God as St Benedict terms it, in choir. For that reason the monks were generally employed at manual labour near the monastery while the lay brothers worked on more distant parts of the monastic land especially on the granges tending sheep and cattle as well as in the cultivation of the soil. Some of the brethern were employed within the precincts of the monastery itself at the dairy, the bakehouse, the brewhouse, the mill and the various workshops of the monastery.

The Cistercian day was a long one. It normally began at two hours after midnight except on the great feasts when the monks rose earlier. Rising from their straw pallets and slipping on their shoes, for they slept fully clothed, they went to the church by the night stairs which led directly from the dormitory of the monks into the southern transept of the church. A fine example of the night stairs is to be seen to this day at Holy Cross abbey. In the church the monks took their allocated places and commenced the canonical hour of Vigils at the signal of the abbot. They sang the psalms standing in choir, facing each other, with their hands crossed upon their breasts. Much of the night office was sung in darkness, for books were scarce and a goodly part of the office, expecially the psalms, was recited by heart. We are told that the sweet chanting of the early Cistercians struck some of their contemporaries as something supernatural. Many of the early Cistercians at Mellifont and some of its earlier daughter houses had been trained to the monastic life under St Bernard at Clairvaux and had brought with them to Ireland some of the fervour and devotion which reigned in that abbey; and the effect of their monastic offices offices on those who flocked to hear them must have been great indeed. A contemporary account speaks of the monks of Clairvaux as they sang the praises of God purely and fervently, and describes their 'lingering and carefully pronunciation of the words of the psalms, showing how sweet to their lips were the praises of God, sweeter than even honey to their mouth'.

The second canonical hour of the day was that of Matins or Lauds which was supposed to commence about daybreak and consequently was sung at a later hour in winter than in summer. As soon as there was full daylight the hour of prime was sung and this was always followed by Chapter at which the abbot explained the Rule to the assembled monks and novices and on certain days publicly accused themselves and each other of faults against the Rule, afterwards kneeling to receive a penance from the abbot. After Chapter the monks went to work. The common work varied from the season. Winter and summer much work had to be done in the fields; in winter trees were felled, brushwood grubbed up and burned and the ground cleared for cultivation. With spring came an extension of farming activities; ploughing, sowing, harrowing and all the various activities of the farm had to be carried on; and as the year wore on the work grew heavier until it reached peak point at the harvest. It has been remarked of the Cistercians that their labour was good hard work by which they gained their livelihood and with the help of their lay brothers supported themselves and gave abundant alms to the poor. Since they did not use serfs in the years of their first fervour, they employed hired labour when necessary and thus gave employment to the people in the neighbourhood; while their guest houses received rich and poor alike, affording shelter, comfort and refreshment of body and soul to travellers and pilgrims and the hospital, which was a feature of Cistercian houses in the early years of the Order, looked after the sick poor.

During the harvest season it often happened that the whole community went out into the fields, the sick and weak only excepted. In such times the canonical hours were usually recited in the fields by the community. This has drawn from one modern writer the remark that 'few things are more remarkable that this mixture of all the details of spades and forks, haymaking and reaping, with the meditation and constant prayer of the Cistercians'. The sight of men of every degree, freeman and serf, noble and commoner, working side by side and sharing the hardships and labours of the day without distinction of persons had a powerful effect on public opinion and helped to break down the universal prejudice which then existed against manual labour, which was looked upon as something demeaning, fit only for serfs and peasants. In the Cistercian system manual labour was as much a necessity as a choice, for the early Cistercians, setting before their eyes the primitive ideal traced out by St Benedict, determined to earn their livelihood by the labour of their own hands, and for this reason repudiated all sources of income which derived from possession of churches and cemeteries, tithes, rents from lands, villeins and serfs, and indeed all sources of income which did not involve personal labour on the part of the monks. It must not be forgotten, however, that manual labour in the eyes of the founding fathers of Cîteaux was but a means to an end, not an end in itself. The Cistercian was something more than a glorified farm labourer. Monks laboured with their lands and by so doing they might have the wherewithal to live and might be able to provide out of their abundance for the poor. They also accepted manual labour as the common lot of all men and the penance imposed on fallen man by God himself. They saw in manual labour, then, a powerful means of sanctification; their labour was bound up with their prayer and to pray and to labour for God was their ideal. There was, indeed, a danger that devotion to labour as one of the means of serving God might deteriorate into devotion to work as a means of accumulating material wealth, and that zeal of the work of God in its widest sense might be transferred into the vice of avarice and cupidity, resulting in the neglect of the service of God and one's neighbour. That this was a real danger the course of events was to prove, for one of the causes assigned by historians for the subsequent decline of the Cistercian Order was the great and indeed excessive wealth of the medieval Cistercians. The lavish hospitality for which the Order was so well noted may also have contributed to the decline, for it strained the resources of many houses to the utmost. The danger signs were apparent early on and Dom David Knowles in his great work, *The Monastic Order in England*, remarks that the evidence of the statutes of the Cistercians general chapters themselves goes far to substantiate the charge of avarice brought by Gerald of Wales and Walter Map against the white monks. The Cistercians sometimes developed their possessions into great ranches and converted arable land into sheep pastures, destroying entire hamlets and villages and ejecting the population from their holdings in the process.

After the morning work had ended the canonical hour of Terce was sung in the abbey church and the conventual mass followed, those of the brethren who communicated doing so at this mass. mass was followed by the canonical hour of Sext after which the monks went to the refectory for dinner, which was taken about midday and was the first meal of the day. In the winter season the conventual mass was sung before the brethren went to work and the hour of Sext was said after work, dinner being postponed until after the canonical hour of none which was celebrated about two o'clock. During the fasting season which lasted from 14 September until Easter this was the only meal of the day, but in Lent this single meal was not taken until after vespers. Besides the long winter fast and the Lenten season all Wednesdays and Fridays outside paschal time were fast days on which only one meal was served; the food itself was coarse and scanty, meat never being served in the common refectory. It was, however, allowed to the sick and weak and those who took their meals in the infirmary refectory away from the other brethren. The drink served at table was the ordinary drink of the country – wine in Italy, France and parts of Germany, beer or ale in the more northerly part of Germany, in Flanders, Britain and Ireland. Fish and eggs seem to have been allowed but were not always available owing to the difficulty of procuring them. As the early Cistercians refused to serve flesh meat, even to their guests, fish was a very important item of food in the monastery and almost every Cistercian monastery had its fishponds or if it was sited near a river its fisheries and fishing weirs. The charter granted to Holy Cross abbey by Donall Ó Briain, for instance, mentions fisheries and the Civil Survey of 1654 shows that there were 'four Eele fishings' on the river Shewer as well as'one fishing' in Bellacumusk and Killeenene.

In matters of dress as in other matters the Cistercians returned to the original simplicity of the Rule of St Benedict. Their garments were to be simple and poor consisting of undyed wool obtained from their own sheep. The habit consisted of a tunic of undyed wool, a black scapular for work which was worn over the tunic and confined with a leather girdle and a cowl of undyed wool to be worn in choir and at other functions. Shoes and stockings were worn by all and the laybrothers wore habits made of the same material but in this case the material was russet brown.

After supper in summer or after vespers in winter came a period of quiet and recollection towards the close of which the entire community assembled in the reading cloister (or in cold climates in the chapter house) to listen to the reading aloud of some devotional book. One of the favourite books used in this public reading was the *Collations* of Cassian, treating of the lives of the fathers of the desert, a book recommended by St Benedict himself as suitable reading matter for this time of the day. At a later period a light repast was allowed the monks during this reading to temper the austerity of the long fast and in course of time the term collation came to mean, not the reading, but the repast itself. At the end of the reading the abbot gave the signal at which all arose and, headed by the abbot, proceeded to the church in single file. The great bell to the abbey was tolled solemnly as the priest sang the prayer of compline, the monks' night prayer, before retiring to bed. This is one of the most beautiful prayers in the monastic breviary, calling down, as it does, blessings on the house and on all who dwell therein. At a later period the solemn singing of the *Salve Regina* was added, a custom still in vogue – after which the brethren spent some time in private prayer and then at the signal of the abbot, rose and left the church in order of seniority. As they left the church in single file each monk bowed profoundly to the abbot, who, standing at the door, sprinkled him with holy water. As soon as each monk received the holy water he drew his hood over his head and proceeding to the dormitory removed his shoes and lay down on his straw pallet, fully dressed to take his well earned rest

One of the main sources of our knowledge of the interior life of any order is the spiritual teaching enshrined in the writings of the master of the spiritual life in that order. As far as the Cistercians of Ireland are concerned no such literature exists. Such intellectual activity as manifested itself among the Irish Cistercians seems to have been confined to two fields, the compilation of hagiographical literature and of monastic annals. Only fragments of the annals now remain and these do not throw any light on the interior spiritual life of the monks of the middle ages. Undoubtedly the works of the Fathers of the Church and of various ecclesiastical and monastic authors, including those of the Cistercian school, were copied assiduously in the monasteries to provide matter for the *lectio divina* of the monks. No doubt the Scriptures as well as the liturgical books needed for divine service were also copied, but with these we are not concerned here. None of these throw any light on the interior life or the spirituality of the Irish Cistercian monks. Dr Myles Dillon was of the opinion that in the

Irish-speaking monasteries there was a good deal of literary activity in the vernacular, and he considers that the great resurgence of Irish literature in the thirteenth and fourteenth centuries accompanied as it was by numerous translations or works then popular on the continent was due to the Cistercians. That the impetus may have come from the Cistercians is likely enough, but it would seem to me that these translations were the work rather of the Franciscans and of laymen rather than of Cistercians. It seems beyond question that the Book of Leinster, the greatest of our twelfth century manuscript collections, owed its inspiration to the Cistercian bishop of Kildare, Finn Ó Gormain, who was for many years abbot of Newry. It is possible that Finian was not a Cistercian at all, but an abbot of a native Irish foundation in Newry before the Cistercians arrived there. It is possible, too, that the Cistercians had a hand in compiling the numerous lives of the Irish saints which made their appearance in Latin and Irish about the second half of the twelfth century and became popular reading matter in Irish monasteries. As 'Lives', indeed, they are of little value though they are filled with topographical information and contain abundant illustrations of the manners and customs of the Ireland of that period. The bulk of the devotional literature of the medieval period, however, seems to owe nothing to the Cistercians. Where authors or translators have left us their name they prove to have been members, not of the Cistercian Order, but of one or other of the medicant orders, particularly the Franciscans. Other anonymous authors may well have been laymen. The most popular translation of all, that of the *Meditationes Vitae Christi* was the work of a secular choral canon of Killala, Tomás Ó Bruachain by name. A fifteenth-century translation of the *Instructio Pie Vivendi* has come down to us only in a single manuscript which suggests, perhaps, that it had a rather limited circulation; and since the original is thought to have been the work of a Cistercian nun and is eminently suitable for monastic communities, it is possible that the translator, too, was a Cistercian. A copy of the *Meditationes Vitae Christi* found hidden in the wall of Hore abbey, Cashel, in the nineteenth century testifies to the kind of reading favoured by the Cistercians of Cashel. It is evidence also of the fact that despite the widespread religious decadence of the age some, at least, of the monks still practised *lectio divina*.

Unlike the Benedictines, the Cistercians were not noted for literary work, at least in the early years. Their work *par excellence*, apart, that is, from the work of God, was heavy field labour, and the poverty of the early foundations necessitated, while the ideals of the young Order demanded, that the work performed by serfs in other monasteries should at Citeaux be performed by the monks themselves, shared, it is true, by the laybrothers, and supplemented when necessary by the labours of hired men. Nevertheless the intellectual life was not wholly neglected, and this is true even of the early days when St Stephen Harding ruled the Order. There may not have been much scope for its exercise in the Citeaux of those days, for other and more pressing labours took up the time of the community; but in so far as it was excercised at all it was excerised in a surprisingly thorough manner. Quality, not quantity, was the watchword here.

> However strict and uncompromisingly ascetic Abbot Stephen was amidst all the hardships of life, Citeaux became under his regime a unique centre of monastic learning. It is difficult to conceive how a small community in a remote monastery managed to accomplish such difficult tasks as a large scale liturgical reform, the collection of authentic hymns and Gregorian melodies, the revision of the Bible and the composition of a constitution of admirable wisdom and foresight ... Abbot Stephen himself made a significant exception in the application of his programme of stern simplicity: he remained an ardent lover of beautiful books, and the manuscripts copied in the early days of Citeaux belong to the most lavishly illuminated codices of the whole century. modern Cistercian historian.[1]

The copying of books does not, of course, pertain strictly to the intellectual life, but the revision of the Bible and of the liturgical chant certainly does. Beginning with St Bernard, a school of Cistercian writers made its appearance, and from the twelfth to the fifteenth century some 335 Cistercian authors are enumerated. Even in the twelfth century the Order produced no less than ninety-five writers of distinction. All this happened in spite of a prohibition against the writing of books issued by the general chapter. This prohibition was not, however, absolute. It did not prevent the writing of books provided the permission of the chapter was first obtained. In practice, as David Knowles pointed out, the rise of St Bernard in the Order and the encouragement he gave to literary work by others, besides the fact that he was himself a literary genius of the first class, offset to a great extent any deterrent effect the prohibition by the general chapter might have had.[2]

Though a school of Cistercian writers made its appearance in England at an early stage, there is no sign of any such development in Ireland. Apart from the Latin annals which seem to have had a common source in some Cistercian house, possibly St Mary's abbey, Dublin, and from the Irish *Annals of Boyle*, also it would appear of Cistercian origin,[3] there is no trace of any literary activity among the Irish Cistercians of medieval times. Indeed we hear mention of only one Irish Cistercian during the whole

---

1 Lekai, op. cit., p. 148. 2 Knowles, *The Monastic Order in England* (Cambridge, 1940), p. 643. 3 Fr A. Gwynn points out that *The Annals of Boyle* were begun as Cistercian and continued as Premonstratensian annals.

medieval period who in any way contributed to sacred learning. This was Henry Crump, a monk of Baltinglass and a professor of theology at Oxford; the same who won some notoriety for maintaining publicly at Oxford that the Friars were contrary to the General Council of Lateran and that Pope Honorius was persuaded to confirm their institutes through pretended and false dreams. He was compelled to abjure his statements and was later attacked by William Andrew, the Dominican bishop of Meath, for teaching heresy regarding the real presence of Christ in the Eucharist.[4]

In 1245, the general chapter of the Cistercian Order directed that in every country one monastery should be selected where aspirants to the priesthood might pursue their studies under qualified professors, though it also allowed schools to be set up in the different abbeys for the same purpose. There is no record of any such school in Ireland, but after the foundation of the college of St Bernard (now St John's) at Oxford for students of all the Cistercian Order, the monasteries of Ireland, as well as those of England, Scotland and Wales, were expected to send their students there, each monastery sending a certain number in proportion to the size or the community. How this worked out in practice for Ireland it is impossible to say. Likely enough it was observed within the limits of the Pale and perhaps in the great Anglo-Irish lordships, but it was probably disregarded outside those areas. Nevertheless, even outside the Pale it is probable that some students were found, if only occasionally, to pursue their higher studies at Oxford, for a decree of 1445 ruling, that Irish students should have equal rights and privileges with those of England, would seem to refer to those of the Irish nation and distinct from the Anglo-Irish who were of the English nation and always so styled themselves.

3. LAY BROTHERS, MANUAL WORK AND GRANGES

LAY BROTHERS

The early Cistercians having as their aim a return to the primitive and literal observance of St Benedict's Rule rejected altogether as a source of revenue everything that seemed to them opposed to the purity of that rule. On the one hand they rejected all the usual sources of income then

---

4 He was said to have taught that Christ's body in the Blessed Sacrament was only a looking-glass to his body in Heaven.

accepted by the vast body of monks, while on the other hand they appeared to their contemporaries as innovators with the introduction of lay brothers. This institution the Cistercians brought to the highest point of development since it became not merely a useful adjunct but an essential element of the monastic life, without which in the circumstances of the time the whole Cistercian economy would have been impossible.

As long as the Cistercians retained their primitive ideals the lay brotherhood flourished but when those ideals vanished the lay brothers vanished with them for the brothers were then no longer necessary to the Order. Indeed, for the decadent Cistercians of the late medieval period there could be no place for the lay brothers since there was no place for manual labour. All the sources of income rejected by the primitive Cistercians were accepted by their degenerate successors, and the effect was disastrous for the Order.

These early Cistercians had no tenants. They had no villeins or serfs. Unlike the secular lord who had his army of serfs to labour for him, the Cistercian relied upon the labour of his own hands. What was the attitude of the Cistercians to serfdom? We must remember that most of the agricultural labour in those days was done by serfs and that this was the practice even on the monastic estates. The Cistercian banished the serfs from his land or rather emancipated them. Many of the Cistercian lay brothers, as well as their hired labourers, were undoubtedly drawn from the serf class. The serf was an essential part of the feudal system and even the Church had its own serfs. In refusing to have serfs the Cistercians were not only turning their backs on what was a universal institution; they were also asserting the dignity of man. In Ireland, the serf class was greatly augmented by the reduction of numbers of the free tenants to the status of serfs after the Norman invasion. Some of the grants made by Irish kings and others to certain Cistercian communities even as early as the second half of the twelfth century contain references to the lands 'with their men', the men in this case being the *adscripti glebae, betaghs* or serfs. Such grants show that in Ireland some at least of the Cistercian houses became feudalised at an early date. The possession of serfs by the Cistercians was, at that period, an exception, being opposed not only to the statutes of the Order but to the general practice. Outside the Order it was common, most bishops, abbots and priors having their serfs or *hibernici*. In departing from this universal custom the founders of Citeaux set a noble headline which was not generally followed. Instead of retaining serf in bondage they took the to themselves as brethren and fellow workers in Christ's vineyard. They, like St Benedict before them, made no distinction between free and unfree but looked on all alike as the common children of our heavenly Father. Deprived of the services of serfs and tenants, and bound by their rule to devote a large part of each day to the service of God in the church, the Cistercians had in some way to make provision for carrying on all the work inseparable from the maintenance of a self-supporting community. The answer to the problem was found in the introduction of the lay brethren into the Order.

The lay brethren were, according to the *Exordium Parvum* to be treated exactly like the choir monks in life and death. Though they retained their lay status and were not considered *monachi* they were in the fullest sense religious, just as much so as their brethren of the choir. They made their vows like the latter but did not receive monastic tonsure nor embrace the clerical state. Hence, not being bound to the divine office they were free to continue their labours at times when the *monachi* had to go to the church to sing the canonical hours. Very full information regarding the status and role of the lay brothers in the Cistercian Order is contained in the *Usus Conversorum* said to have been written by St Stephen Harding himself, and in the *Regula Conversorum* composed at a later date by a monk of Clairvaux. The statutes of the general chapter also abound in references to the lay brothers and afford much material for a study of their varied activities. And truly their activities were varied. Some of them dwelt in the monastic enclosure while others were scattered in the granges. In the monastery itself the western range of buildings contained the *Domus Conversorum*, the lay brother's dwelling quarters, and in the workshops of the abbey they plied their crafts and exercised their trades. Among them were shoemakers, cobblers, saddlers and harness makers, tanners, fullers, weavers, clothmakers and tailors, masons, bricklayers, carpenters, plasterers, thatchers, blacksmiths, brewers, millers, bakers, dairymen, and, of course, the cook, without whom the whole life of the monastery would come to a standstill.

Notwithstanding the various trades and crafts exercised by the lay brothers in the monastery the majority of the lay brethren were engaged in ordinary agricultural pursuits, in tilling the soil, sowing the crops, herding the cattle and sheep, looking after the swine and performing the many other tasks that fall to the lot of the farmer. They did not, of course, replace the monks altogether, for the latter were not dispensed from labouring with their own hands, but they set themselves especially to the tasks that had to be performed on the more distant parts of the farm and in the granges, and so left to their brethren of the choir the work that lay within easy reach of the abbey. In the early years of the Order the number of lay brothers was very great. A note in the Antiphonary of Armagh dated 1 January 1170, and referring to the death of Donnchadh Ua Cearbhaill, king of Airghialla, one of the founders of Mellifont, states that there were then three hundred lay brothers in that house. This may appear an enormous number for one monastery, and it it possible that the writer of the note exaggerated. Nevertheless we must remember that many brothers would be required for the work on even a single one of the monastic granges and the granges of Mellifont were numerous and of more than average size. They were, moreover, scattered over a very extensive territory. Each of these granges had its own farm buildings, with a dormitory, refectory and calefactory for the brothers who dwelt there.

There was also an oratory on the grange. Most of these brothers slept on the granges, returning to the monastery only on Sundays and on the greater feasts of the Church. The number of lay brothers attached to a monastery might then be very great without causing any undue congestion in the monastery proper.

The labours of the lay brethren were of immense service to the Order and helped to win for it that renown which it achieved by reason of its agricultural activities. These activities included the raising of the crops necessary to supply the community with food and the raising of surplus crops for the market. A certain amount of this surplus produce may have found its way overseas, for there was quite a large trade in agricultural produce between Ireland and England in those days. A large amount of Irish agricultural produce also went to the Continent, but in time of war the kings of England took measures to ensure sufficient provisions for their campaigns in Scotland and France, and the quantity of agricultural produce as well as of livestock that was sent across the water during the thirteenth and fourteenth centuries to provision the king's armies can only be described as enormous. The Cistercians, like all other agriculturalists, contributed their own quota.

The agricultural exports from Ireland to England during the thirteenth century included wheat, barley, oats, malt of wheat, malt of oats, flour, oatmeal, peas, beans, onions, honey, hay, and beer, besides cows, pigs, sheep, and carcases of salt beef. These were often exported in immense quantities, On 17 January 1246, the king ordered the justiciar of Ireland to purchase 3,000 quarters of wheat, 8,000 quarters of oats, 2,000 hogs, 5,000 quarters of lime and 300 tuns of wine. The wine, of course, though purchased in Ireland, came from abroad, but all the rest were Irish in origin.[1] In December 1298 the king commanded the justiciar to provide among other supplies from Ireland, 8,000 quarters of wheat (6,000 of these to be in bolted flour without bran, placed in safe and dry barrels), 10,000 quarters of oats, 2,000 quarters of ground malt, 500 carcases of salt beef, 1,000 fat pigs and 20,000 dried fish.[2] These figures give some idea of the flourishing state of agriculture in Ireland in the thirteenth century and enable us to realise what an amount of work must have been put into farming operations. Among the farmers of those days the Cistercians held a leading place and there can be no doubt that by their efficiency and the use of the most

1 CDI, i, no. 1245. 2 Idem.

up-to-date methods, as then known, they contributed much to improve the quality of an to increase the production of agricultural goods.

Besides the cultivation of the soil there were other agricultural operations carried on by the Cistercians which deserve some mention here. These included the raising of livestock – sheep, cattle and horses in particular – the development of the woollen industry which played an important part in the trade of the middle ages, the development of the dairying industry which has always been of prime importance in Ireland along with the fattening of cattle, and the marketing of the monks' surplus goods and livestock. The Cistercians moreover introduced into Ireland, as into other countries, new and improved methods of agriculture. We are not to suppose, however, that the Irish knew little or nothing of agriculture before the coming of the Cistercians, as some writers seem to imagine. Indeed, much nonsense has been written about agriculture, or rather the want of agriculture, in pre-invasion times. From some of the accounts given one would suppose that the Irish were altogether a pastoral people and even to a certain extent a nomadic people. Nothing could be farther from the truth.

All our literary and archaeological evidence as well as the testimony of the ancient laws of Ireland points to the fact that although the Irish were a pastoral people in the sense that the raising of cattle formed the principal source of their wealth, they were also cultivators of the soil, and that from the earliest period. Most of the native crops now in use were cultivated in pre-Norman times. The modern root crops were for the most part unknown though the parsnip and carrot are both mentioned in the ancient literature. Leeks and onions were grown as well as a kind of cabbage described in the *Vision of Mac Conglinne* as 'boiled, leafy, and brownwhite', while water-cress was eaten raw just as we eat lettuce at present. This, of course, grew wild and was a favourite dish with poor people. But the most general crop in pre-Norman days was the corn crop which included wheat, barley, rye and oats, the latter being reckoned the most important since it was used both for animal feeding and human food. The oatmeal was used both for the making of bread and porridge, the latter dish being a favourite one among the ancient Irish. Wheaten bread was also used, of course, and both barley bread and rye bread are mentioned in the literature.

The corn was cut with the reaping hook or sickle (corran) and specimens of this useful implement dating back to the bronze age are to be seen in the National Museum. The Irish reaping hook was a small implement and the cutting of an acre of corn must have been a slow and laborious task. In later ages the stalks were cut off at the bottom as in modern times but there is some evidence that in the very early period the grain-bearing tops alone were cut off and the straw left behind to be dealt with later.

Agriculture has developed comparatively slowly through the ages and it is only in modern times that there have been any sweeping changes in the implements used in farm work. Up to quite recently, indeed, most of the implements in use in the pre-Norman period were still in use. The sickle, scythe, flail, shovel, spade and plough all ante-dated the Norman invasion, and even the various cars and wagons used on the farm in our own days had their prototypes in more ancient forms. Even such a specialised vehicle as the modern Irish hay-cart with its low platform and its winding gear is but a development of the older two-wheeled cart, and has been remarked as 'an interesting development of the versatility which the Irish have shown in developing the two-wheeled cart, their primary mode of transport'.[3] Various types of cars were also used in ancient times, including solid-wheeled, spoke-wheeled and slide-cars, all of which may still be seen today in various parts of the country. With the coming of the Cistercians new and improved methods were introduced though even these were primitive enough when judged by our standards. Yet the methods then introduced may be said to have continued in vogue almost to modern times; for apart from a new change in the agricultural system from the thirteenth to the nineteenth century, when the invention of the reaper and binder, the cast-iron plough, and the improvement of the threshing machine which had been first invented in 1785, made possible a revolution in the methods of labour so great that the present-day conditions differ far more from the conditions in which our great-grandfathers worked than did their conditions from those of the early middle ages.

The cultivation of green vegetables was especially fostered by the Cistercians. The monks grew beans, peas, cabbage, kale, parsley, lettuce and onions very extensively. The older grain crops were also grown on a large scale by the Cistercians. Morover, the monastic communities, at least in the early days, were completely self-supporting. The monks were clothed in the wool from their own sheep and fed with the produce of their own soil. Their beasts of burden and other farm animals were raised on their own land. Even the monks' drink was home produced, consisting generally of beer or ale brewed by the monastic brewer in the abbey brewhouse. Great herds of cattle and sheep were kept by the monks and the rearing of cattle became in time the principal industry by which the Cistercians supported themselves. Much of the work on the granges was concerned with cattle raising though tillage also had a prominent part, and we often meet with references to the oxen which were used for drawing the plough, a custom which had come down from remote times when, in early Irish history, we read of both horses and oxen being employed for this purpose.

3 E.E. Evans, *Irish Heritage* (Dundalk, 1942), p. 98.

Though details unfortunatly are lacking there are passages in the State Papers and the Statute Rolls which suggest that the rearing of cattle must have been carried on, on a very extensive scale in some of the houses. The same applies to the dairying industry. Of cows alone we find mention of six hundred in Mellifont, that being the number taken by William Marshal, earl of Pembroke, from the monastery lands to maintain the king's army in the war against Hugh de Lacy. Six hundred cows were taken, but we may presume that not all nor even the greater part of the cows of Mellifont were included in that number, for it would scarcely be in the king's interest any more than it would be in the interests of the monks themselves to have the abbey of Mellifont impoverished by such exactions. When we consider the amount of labour involved in the maintenance of such large herds of cattle and sheep as well as in the cultivation of large areas of arable land to produce the various crops required for their suste-nance, not to speak of the crops required to produce the food necessary to feed the monks themselves together with their guests and hired labour-ers and the poor of the surrounding districts for whom they were expected to have a special care, we shall not wonder at the large number of lay brethren to be found in some abbeys. But we do wonder that even then they were able to get through all the work that had to be done on the monastic farm. The ordinary farm work, it must be remembered, had to go on throughout the year from seedtime to harvest, and the means at the disposal of the community for engaging in these labours were not by any means comparable to what the modern Cistercian can employ.

The rejection by the Cistercians of serfs and even of tenants was part of the movement to restore the Benedictine tradition that the monks should live by the labours of their own hands. Gradually the Cistercians began to adopt the manorial system which their founders had rejected and the entanglement in feudal obligations began. Serfs began to make their appearance on Cistercian granges and with the advent of the serfs came the gradual disappearance of the lay brotherhood. The lay brethren had been originally introduced into the Order to help their brethren of the choir but not to replace them at manual labour. However, at a fairly early period a tendency began to manifest itself in certain houses of the order to leave the manual labour to the lay brethren while the choir brethren began to devote themselves exclusively to the service of the church. Even so fervent and holy an abbot as the venerable Arnulph of Villiers, who was very devoted to the lay brothers and was much loved by them, showed this tendency very strongly, insisting that the proper place for the monk was the church and the cloister to the exclusion, as it would seem, of manual labour. Such a view is a distinct break with Cistercian tradition. Yet Abbot Arnulph lived and died within a century of St Bernard's lifetime; so it is evident that even in that comparatively short space of time not only had the original Cistercian ideal become to a certain extent blunted but that St Bernard's successors had come to accept as the genuine Cistercian ideal something which was, in fact, very different.

When did these various symptons of economic change and of departure from the traditions of the primitive Cistercians first make their appearance in Ireland? In the foundation charter of Rosglas, which dates back to 1189, certain lands with their appurtances 'and with the men belonging to the same lands' were granted to the community by the king of Offaly. That the men thus designated are the serfs belonging to the land is certain. We cannot however deduce from this that the Irish Cistercians had already adopted or were then in process of adopting the feudal system. In all probability the serfs thus granted were freed by the monks after the lands had come into possession of the community, and it may be that some of them aftrwards became the hired men of the abbey or were even to be found among the lay brothers. The foundation charter of Duiske mentions the monks, 'their men' and their tenants. Here the phrase 'their men' almost certainly means the serfs. The mention of tenants as well as serfs in this charter is significant of the direction in which the Order was tending at this period, the first decade of the thirteenth century. In the year 1208, the general chapter made a radical change in the traditional economy by permitting the renting of lands on certain conditions. This was indeed a new departure, for up to then the capitular fathers had always insisted (following the tradition of Alberic and Stephen) that the monks should cultivate their own lands by their own labour assisted if necessary by that of their hired men. The decree of 1208 thus marked a big break with the old Cistercian ideal. This decree, which permitted the leasing only of such lands as were either less useful or too far distant to allow of convenient cultivation was indeed abrogated in 1214. The tide had set in, however, and the right to lease land was granted again in 1220. On the occasion of the visitation made by Stephen of Lexington the right of the Cistercians to acquire churches as well as the letting of lands to tenants was already recognised as certain references in the regulations made by the abbot-visitator testify.

From the end of the twelfth century, side by side with the economic changes went a growing dissatisfaction on the part of the lay brothers. The system of leasing land continued to gain ground and with the introduction of serf labour and the acceptance of tenants on the monastic land the practice of having the granges worked by the lay brethren began to be abandoned. A feeling grew up among the lay brethren in many monasteries that they were no longer wanted. One sign of the growing discontent was a series of revolts and conspiracies as a result of which the reputation of the Order suffered considerably. In 1302 the old system was ended once and for all by a bull of Pope Boniface VIII allowing all Cistercian lands that had not been hitherto subject to tithes to be free of tithes thenceforth even though nor worked by the monks but by serfs or tenants. This bull, which has been described as a 'momentous change in Cistercian economic policy' met with the approval of the general chapter in 1303. From then on the decline in the lay brotherhood became progressively rapid, the number of *conversi* growing snaller and smaller although, in spite of all their vicissitudes, they were never wholly eliminated from the Order. To the economic causes just mentioned was added the havoc wrought by the terrible 'Black Death' while the founding of the mendicant orders had an adverse effect on the recruitment of the Cistercian lay brotherhood, the new orders attracting great numbers of young men who would otherwise have gone to the Cistercians. By the fifteenth century the lay brothers had almost vanished from the Irish houses and we find no mention of them in the monastic 'extents' of 1540. By that time the Irish Cistercians had become great landowners having as their principal sources of income the tithes, altarages and oblations of the various churches impropriated to the abbeys and the rents of a numerous tenantry. With the change over from tillage to pasture in the fourteenth century serfdom began to die out, the serfs themselves becoming tenants. Indeed some of the lay brothers themselves had been transformed into tenants living on the monastic lands before the end of the thirteenth century, as we learn from a statute of the general chapter of 1262. These tenants generally paid their rent not in money but in kind or in services. Some gave so many days reaping, others carted turf, others again mended roads, while others provided cocks, hens, hogs, claves, and so forth. Those holding weirs or pools had to supply a certain amount of fish from the same – we read of a tenant who held a salmon-weir and an adjacent pool and who was obliged to give the monks half of the salmon caught in the pool and four out of every five caught in the weir. Tenants who held mills were generally bound to give certain measures of grain to the monastery. In the course of time money payments took the place of services though in some cases services and payments in kind continued right down to the suppression of the monasteries in the sixteenth century. Among the customs noted as in vogue in the manor of Mellifont at that period was that by which each tenant and cottager in Tullyallen had to give a hen at Christmas to the abbey of Mellifont.

MANUAL WORK

The very nature of the Cistercian reform made manual labour a necessity and the circumstances in which most of the early foundations were made ensured that this aspect of the Benedictine life would assuredly not be neglected. The restoration of manual labour to its former importance in the monastic *horarium* was indeed one of the outstanding achievements of the Cistercians. Yet their devotion to manual labour should not blind us to the fact there was another aspect of the monastic life more important by far which might easily be neglected as a result of this very devotion to the more material prescriptions of the Rule. The Cistercians attained a not undeserved fame as scientific agriculturalists but it has to be remembered that men did not enter the monastic state simply to indulge in agricultural activitites; though the founders attached great importance to manual labour as one of the pillars of the monastic life they were well aware of the dangers which could come from over-indulgence in this respect. One of the causes of the later decline of the Order was, in fact, the widespread activities of the monks in the realms of industry and commerce. Monastic milling, we are told, became a commercial enterprise,[4] and in some localities the Cistercians had a monopoly of this industry.[5] In other regions wine was produced in wholesale quantities for the markets and complaints were made in some cases that the Cistercians produced wine purely for profit.[6] The abbey of Eberbach in the Rhineland which sold about 53,000 gallons of wine a year wholesale could boast of possessing the largest wine cask in the world, the 'Giant Barrel of Eberbach',[7] of which it was written,

> What is there to prevent the cask of Eberbach, than which there is none larger in the world, from being included among the miracles of antiquity? It may truly be said that it is a sea of wine and a pool of Bacchus from which nectar flows day and night.

The entrance of the Cistercians into the commercial arena led to various undesirable results. There was keen rivalry between the secular merchants and the Cistercians and the monks were often charged with unfair competition. Moreover, the great success of the Cistercians in the reclaiming of wasteland and woodland for cultivation and in the exploitation of their farm lands by means of the admirable system of granges, cultivated by the lay brethren for the most part, resulted in a great increase of wealth on the part of the Order. Monasteries which had once been poor and struggling now found themselves prosperous; and with the reclaiming of the waste lands to conquer. In more than one country they earned a reputation for avarice, and many of the attacks made by their contemporaries on the wealthy Cistercians were based on the fact that only too often the territorial expansion of the already large monastic estates was achieved at the expense of the neighbouring population, oeading in some cases, as in England to the destruction of villages and the eviction of the inhabitants.[8]

4 Leckai, op. cit., p. 220. 5 Ibid. 6 Ibid., p. 216. 7 The 'Giant Barrel of Eberbach' was 28 feet long, 9 feet high and had a capacity of 26,000 gallons. 8 Knowles, op. cit., pp 350-1.

We mention the foregoing facts only to show that however admirable the aim of the Cistercians in resoring manual labour to its proper place in the monastic *horarium*, it carried with it dangers of its own. The spectacular achievements of the Cistercians in the domain of agriculture and industry might easily lead us to forget that these were, after all, but of secondary importance, and, if carried to excess, could result in great evils. The monastic life was above all a life of prayer, and everything was so arranged as to contribute to the promotion of that life of prayer in the monastery. The Cistercian monk was a contemplative and all the Cistercian observances had to subserve this end. Manual labour itself was the original penance imposed by God on mankind after the Fall and it was suited in a special manner to that God from whom he had departed by the sloth of disobedience.[9] It served as a great preservative against idleness and for this reason St Benedict enjoined it on the sick and aged who were to be given some type of work suited to their condition: 'Let the work or employment that is laid or weak or delicate brethren bu such as may neither leave them idle nor yet overwhelm them by the weight of their burthen so as to cause them to lose heart. And their weakness must also be taken into account by the abbot.'[10]

Manual labour was also the ordinary means proposed by the Cistercians for the support of their communities who were to earn their bread by their own labours, and though such labours would vary according as the circumstances of the place and the time demanded, the normal labour for Cistercians was the cultivation of the land and the rearing of cattle. Provided that this practice of manual labour did not become an end in itself but was kept strictly subordinate to the 'one thing necessary', it would be a powerful aid to the individual monk in striving for his sanctification.

The chief work of the monk was not, however, the cultivation of the monastic lands but the sanctification and salvation of his own soul. He came to the monastery to give himself to God and to live a life of contemplation, and hence it is that St Benedict requires of the novice in the first place that he truly seeks God. It was for this reason that the founding fathers of the Cistercian Order ordained that the monasteries should be built in places far removed from the haunts of men and the tumult of thw world. The rule of silence, too, which loomed so large in the Cistercian life was intended to further this end by leaving the monk free to speak to God; for, if not altogether impossible, it is certainly extremely difficult to hear the voice of God and to converse with him in the midst of tumult. If the monk practised silence it was that he might withdraw from the conversation of men in order to enjoy the conversation of God with the soul.

9 Rule of St Benedict, Prologue. 10 Ibid., chap. XLVIII.

GRANGES

The early Cistercians as a general rule had no tenants. Unlike the secular lord they had no villeins or serfs, relying as they did on the labour of their own hands and those of their *conversi* to work their extensive estates. If more help was needed they had recourse to hired labour, for it was not until the first fervour of the new order had commenced to cool that serfs and tenants began to make their appearance. This was a gradual process; and though it was already creeping in early in the thirteenth century, the direct exploitation of their estates by the monks and *conversi*, aided by whatever hired labour was deemed necessary, continued by and large till the closing years of that century. The early Cistercian communities, unlike their Benedictine contemporaries, did not normally possess a number of scattered manors, farms, fields and tenements in various parts of the country. Each community normally held a single blockof land in the midst of which stood the abbey. Some Cistercian estates had comparatively small beginnings and grew more extensive with the course of time; others were of great extent from the earliest days. Those foundations which dated from the twelfth or early thirteenth centuries frequently included great expanses of forest, moor and wasteland, much of which had to be cleared to fit it for cultivation and this often entailed drainage on a large scale in marshy areas.

The extent of an estate might vary from a few thousand acres in the case of the smaller abbey to 40,000 or more in the case of the greater ones. Nine of the greater abbeys, ranging from 20,000 to 40,000 acres in extent, contained between them about fifth eight per cent of the total amount of land held by the Cistercians in medieval Ireland. Typical examples of the smaller monastic estate were those of Bective (Co. Meath) and Inch (Co. Down), the possessions of which amounted to some 4,400 acres and 5,795 acres respectively. The abbey which had the smallest estate at the time of the dissolution of the monasteries was that of Abbeyshrule (Co. Longford) the landed possessions of which amounted to only 2,822 acres. Slightly larger were the estates of Chore abbey (Co. Cork) and Hore abbey (Cashel, Co. Tipperary) which amounted to 2,845 acres and 2,969 acres respectively. The lands of Mellifont, amounting in all to between 40,000 and 50,000 acres, 33,000 of which formed a solid block of land around the monastery proper, may be taken as the outstanding example of the greater monastic estate.

The earliest Cistercian settlements were normally made on large tracts of what was practically undeveloped land, much of which may have been covered by forest, and the early charters testify to the presence on many of the monastic estates of moorland, marshland and wasteland as well as of forest This land the Irish Cistercians, like their brethren on the Continent, usually proceeded to divide up into what they called 'granges', the number of which varied according to the extent of the monastic possessions. In Cistercian usage the word 'grange' had a twofold meaning. In the narrow sense it signified a *grangia* or granary and, by extension, a group of farm buildings; but in its wider and specifically Cistercian sense it meant an estate or farm, more or less consolidated, and normally worked by the monks or *conversi* with the assistance, where necessary, of hired labour. The Cistercian granges, therefore, were really farms, each of which had its own farm buildings as well as dormitory and refectory for the use of the *conversi*. The brothers assigned to a particular grange were placed under an official called a *grangemaster* and lived and worked on the grange, returning to the monastery only for the greater feasts. In the early days of the order it was laid down as a strict rule that no grange should be more than a day's journey from the abbey, but this rule soon fell into abeyance. Up to the year 1255 the celebration of mass was not customary in granges and, indeed, was even forbidden. But since by that time many of the granges were situated at a considerable distance from the monastery this rule was being disregarded and so, in 1255 Pope Alexander IV authorised the celebration of mass at granges which were far from the abbey or the parish church. That the custom of saying mass at the granges had already been in existence for some time when that permission was given is clear from contemporary documents. And although it is true that the order had for a long time tried to prevent the erection of altars at granges, a regulation made by Abbot Stephen of Lexington during his visitation of the Irish houses in 1228 prescribed the celebration of mass at the granges of Duiske abbey by chaplains specially appointed for that purpose.

The grange was the farming unit of the Cistercian system and formed the basis of all land planning. Granges varied in number and size from monastery to monastery. The area of the average grange has been variously estimated. Henry Pirenne, in his *Economic and Social History of Medieval Europe*, has estimated that the average grange was from five hundred to seven hundred acres in extent; but T.A.M. Bishop, writing in the *English Historical Review*, was of opinion that the average Cistercian grange contained between three hundred and four hundred acres of arable land. The difference between these two estimates is, perhaps, more apparent than real; for Dr R.A. Donkin has pointed out that the total area of a grange with about four hundred acres of arable land might well approach one thousand acres, and indeed the granges of many of the Irish monasteries approximated nearer to the higher than to the lower figure. On the granges of the twelfth and early thirteenth centuries forests were cleared, land drained and cultivated, and the foundations laid of the flourishing agriculture for which the Cistercians became renowned. In those early days much hard work was necessary to reclaim land from the wild and bring it under cultivation, and due credit must be given to those who turned what was once a wilderness into a smiling paradise. When we find ourselves inclined to be critical of the vast size of some of the early monastic estates we should remember this; and we should also recall how primitive were the agricultural methods employed in the middle ages compared to those of modern times. It took a considerable time to develop such great acres, and although the process of development commenced with the very foundation of the monastery, it usually continued over a long period, and in the case of most of the Irish houses was probably not completed until well into the thirteenth century or even later. Only a comparatively small portion of the whole area comprised in many of these monastic estates could be success-fully cultivated, and the cultivated portion was generally scattered over the estate, forming those numerous granges of which we have been writing. Despite the rule already mentioned that granges should be no more than a day's journey from the abbey many of our Irish monasteries had granges situated at a considerable distance form the abbey site. Boyle abbey, for instance had granges in Cos. Sligo and Leitrim and Galway as well as in Co. Roscommon. One of its granges lay about forty-five miles from the abbey while some of the others were between twenty-five and thirty miles distant. Inquisitions taken after the dissolution of this abbey indicate that at that time the monks held eighteen granges, including a grange near the abbey itself which was probably the 'home farm' of the monks. It would, of course, be impossible to deduce from the number of granges enurmerated in a sixteenth century document how many granges were worked by the monks in the early days of the abbey's history. It is certain that in many monasteries, lands which had been developed as granges in the early period no longer appeared as granges in the surveys made at the time of the dissolution. On the other hand the name 'grange' had become attached in some cases to lands that had never been granges in the sense explained here. Owing to the great dearth of documentary evidence it is not possible to give anything like a detailed account of the Cistercian grange in Ireland such as has been done for England by R.A. Donkin. The charters bear witness to the process by which the monks built up and con-solidated their granges during this period. Whether such consolidation was effected with or without the displacement by eviction of the population already settled on the lands is a question which cannot be decided without further evidence. In mountain areas like Glencullen it is unlikely that there was any widespread displacement of the population to make way for the grange of the monks. These mountain lands were to a great extent moor-land and forest, and can scarcely have supported a population of any size when the monks took them over. But the rich lands in the plain had been occupied by Irish or Norse-Irish before the coming of the Normans and it is probable that some displacement of population was inevitable in that area. If such a displacement took place, and if it was on a large scale, no mention of it occurs in any contemporary source, nor can it be inferred from the charters themselves that the consolidation of lands by which many of the Cistercian granges were built up was, in fact, accompanied by whole-sale evictions of the kind carried out by the English Cistercians in Yorkshire, for instance, where whole villages are said to have been wiped out and even parish churches in some cases levelled to the ground. The complete silence of all contemporary documents would suggest that what-ever may have been the state of affairs in England there was no wholesale displacement of people in Ireland as a result of the consolidation of Cistercian granges. Indeed there is evidence that early in the thirteenth century tenants were already being accepted by the Irish Cistercians and even serfs were not unknown before the close of the twelfth century. Once the monks had accepted gifts of populated land two courses only were open to them: either to keep the letter of the rule by reducing villages and populated centres to the status of granges, which meant in practice the expulsion of the tenants, but on the other hand allowed the monks to develop the land by the labours of their own hands and to fulfill the con-dition imposed by their rule of living removed from the world; or to disre-gard the rule in this particular and allow the tenants to remain on the land. By following the latter course of action they did not incur the odium they would undoubtedly have incurred had they resorted to the process of evic-tion. Since the monks of St Mary's abbey are known to have possessed serfs at the time the Normans first appeared in Ireland and since there were ten-ants on some of the monastic lands in the early years of the thirteenth cen-tury, it is probable that, contrary to the legislation of the general chapter and the primitive *Consuetudines,* the lands thus consolidated were devel-oped as granges with the assistance of serf labour. The chartularies show that in many cases the men belonging to certain lands were transferred with those to the order.

4. SOME HISTORICAL ASPECTS OF CISTERCIAN LIFE IN MEDIEVAL IRELAND

The purpose of this chapter is to discuss certain aspects of Cistercian life during the period 1200-1539. Naturally there are large areas of the canvas which must be left untouched owing to limitations of time and space. Due to the great dearth of original source material we know next to nothing of the ordinary day-to-day life of the Irish monks. From the evidence of the surviving sources we may conclude that for much of the medieval period the obstacles to community life were such as to make it extremely difficult, if not actually impossible, to achieve the ideal set before themselves by the founding fathers of the order. This applies in particular to the first half of the thirteenth century, the second half of the fourteenth century and practically the whole of the fifteenth century. Many and various causes contributed to this state of affairs, but the principal ones may be summed up in the words of a report submitted by John Troy, abbot of Mellifont, to Jean de Cirey, abbot of Citeaux. This report bears no date, but a reference therein to the death of Walter Champfleur, abbot of St Mary's, near Dublin, shows that it must have been written after January 1497/8. Describing what he terms the 'ruin and desolation of the whole order in Ireland', John Troy informs the abbot of Citeaux that for a full hundred years no one from the more remote districts has visited his Father Abbot, and for this reason very many of the monasteries, being left without a visitator and recognizing no superior, have, abbots and monks alike, 'gone over completely to the rebels'.

In this report the abbot of Mellifont lists some of the principal causes of the sad state of the order in Ireland, namely, the ceaseless wars waged between the two races in Ireland arising from the hatred begotten in consequence of the original conquest, the system of provisions and commends by the Holy See, the excessive oppression practised by the nobles, the pensions and tributes paid by monasteries for the support of provisors and commendatory abbots contrary to the rights of the incumbents, as well as similar pensions and tributes for the support of the said incumbents against the provisors and commendatory abbots. In consequence of such exactions the order was in straitened circumstances and large sums of money for these and other purposes had to be poured out. Laymen had in many cases taken over the revenues of the monasteries so that the monks had not wherewith to live and were compelled to wander around in search of the very necessaries of life. Consequently hospitality was no longer practised, divine worship was neglected, and many of the monks, throwing off the religious habit, lived among the nobility while the provisors and commendatory abbots took no care of the goods of the house except to plunder them for their own use. Many of these abbots were not even ordained and scarcely visited their houses once a year. Lettered laymen entered into occupation of the abandoned abbeys as abbots and, having neither habit nor tonsure, seized by main force the revenues and income of the house. Hence the abbot of Mellifont found it necessary to inform the abbot of Citeaux that there was scarcely a monastery in the whole of Ireland in which the divine office was sung according to note or the monastic habit worn except the abbey of Mellifont itself and that of the Blessed Mary, near Dublin. He complained vehemently of those abbots of the order who, without any knowledge of the religious life or instruction in the regular observances of the order were, from being seculars, promoted to rule abbeys when they had scarcely been clad in the habit and were even appointed reformators and visitators.The report passed the most severe strictures on such men who 'having no care for the divine worship or for regular observances, blinded by avarice and by worldly pleasures, and given up to the vain display of superiority, drag down their subjects with themselves and plunge them into the same pit'.

From the consideration of these matters the abbot turns his attention to the visitation and reformation of the monasteries. He had already mentioned early in his report the grave losses and heavy expenses incurred by abbots who visited abbeys situated among those whom he terms the 'wild Irish' who not only do not observe the rule of the order but are guilty of practices about which, for the honour of religion, he will be silent since the deeds perpetrated by them do not bear mention and to speak of them would be to disparage our religion. As joint-reformator with Abbot Walter of Dublin he had practical experience of the difficulties encountered in carrying out such visitations and begs to be excused from making any more of this kind. He points out that it was in consequence of the intolerable labours entailed in such visitations that the late Abbot Walter, then an old man, took ill and died. Abbot Troy then describes his own experience. He generally met with a hostile reception from the monks and describes the provisors and commendatory abbots, supported by armed men, retiring to the battlements of the churches and belfries from which vantage points they meet the advances of the visitator with showers of javelins, arrows and even stones, driving him by force from the monasteries. 'Therefore,' he concludes, 'I beseech Your Paternity to relive me of the care and burden of a visitation and reformation of this kind.'

I have summarised in the foregoing passages the principal points made by the abbot of Mellifont in his report on the state of the order because, although that report deals with conditions existing at the close of the fifteenth century many of the complaints made therein show a state of affairs which was but a recurrence of what had happened at various times during previous centuries. If we take some of the principal points made by the abbot, and review some of the events recorded in Irish Cistercian history from 1200 to the close of the fifteenth century this will be apparent. The ceaseless wars between the two races in Ireland had a lamentable effect not only on the Cistercians but on all the religious orders. Hand in hand with this went the deliberate policy of discrimination practised by the Crown and the Anglo-Norman church authorities against the native Irish in the matter of promotion to ecclesiastical benefices and the later policy of prohibiting religious houses situated in those parts of Ireland occupied by the English from receiving native Irishmen to profession. In the first quarter of the thirteenth century Connacht in particular was in a state of utter chaos and the monasteries suffered in consequence. Priests were stripped, churches pillaged, and women and stock found therein were carried off 'without regard to saint or sanctuary'. These depredations were often carried out by mixed armies of Gael and Gall. In the year 1202 the armies of Cathal Carrach Ó Conchubhair, William de Burgo, the two sons of Domhnall Mór Ó Briain and the Mac Carthaigh of Desmond swept through Magh Luing where they occupied the monastery of Boyle for the space of three days and are said to have polluted and defiled the whole monastery. The annals state that the mercenaries of the army and the women were billeted in the hospital of the monks as well as in the cloister and indeed throughout the monastery, the monks and conversi being confined to the dormitory of the monks and the house of the novices. The monastery itself suffered severely at the hands of the soldiery, much of it being damaged and part of it burned. On the third day fighting broke out between the various elements in the army and the king of Connacht and many of his followers were killed. The monastery came under attack again in the years which followed and in 1235 was attacked and looted on the night of Trinity Sunday when the soldiers broke open the sacristy and looted all its valuables, mass-chalices and altar cloths. The conduct was deplored by the leaders of the army who returned all the articles they could find and paid for the rest

Many other abbeys besides Boyle suffered from military occupation or hostile attacks. These attacks did not always come from warring armies; sometimes they were due to neighbouring lords who harboured designs on the monks' property which they raided and despoiled without scruple. Sometimes, too, the officials of the king of England himself were the men responsible. On one occasion William Marshal, the earl of Pembroke, took no less then 600 cows from Mellifont to maintain the king's army in the war against Hugh de Lacy. Letters of protection from the king and from the pope were of little avail. Even on their way to the general chapter the abbots were not safe, and it is recorded that in 1216 while on their way through England they were attacked by the English ''nd the choice of them slain'. Boyle abbey seems to have been singled out as a victim more often than any other house. In 1284 the lands of the abbot and convent around Corrshliabh were ravaged and devastated by the Anglo-Norman armies, and in 1296 the abbey itself was again occupied by a mixed army of Gael and Gall for the space of four days and four nights during which time they made frequent incursions into Magh Loirg, destroying much corn and property throughout the entire district.

The early years of the fourteenth century brought new dangers to the monasteries, many of which were by this time greatly impoverished and burdened with debts. Since the middle of the thirteenth century the Irish kings had been sporting heavy-armed mercenary troops from the Western

Isles of Scotland, men of mixed Irish and Norse descent known as Galloglaigh, and with the advent of these soldiers the tide of battle began to turn in favour of the Irish. In 1315 came what is generally known as the Bruce invasion during which the monastery at Dublin was burned. About the same period (as we know from archaeological evidence) Mellifont itself was burned but it is impossible to say whether this was the result of accident (as in the case of the Dublin abbey) or was an act of war. Boyle abbey was again attacked as were many other churches, and all Magh Loirg is stated by the annalist to have been 'beggared and bared'. The abbey itself was profaned and its cattle and corn looted. According to the annals of Connacht the cattle and corn and even the very altar-cloths were given to the galloglaigh for wages due to them. In the same year St Mary's abbey, Dublin, shortly before its destruction, was the scene of a sharp struggle in the guest-house when Richard de Burgo, Red Earl of Ulster and father-in-law of Robert Bruce, was arrested in his room. During the struggle seven of his retainers were killed and the room was set on fire. Two years later the abbey of Corcomroe was occupied by the army of Diarmaid O Briain and the Clann Toirdhealbhaigh. On their way to the monastery they commenced a great cattle drive, collecting together all the beasts that came their way until they reached the lands of the monastery where they left their stolen cattle within the precinct. They slept that night in the monks' dormitory enjoying what the historian of the wars of Turlough (Caithreim Thoirdhealbhaigh) calls 'the soft luxury of those most comfortable cubicles'. We are not told where the monks slept that night but, after the battle had ended the following day, it fell to the lot of the Cistercians to succour the wounded and bury the dead on both sides. It can be readily understood that monasteries situated, as so many of the Irish monasteries then were, in the very battle line, were constantly harrassed and oppressed by one or other of the contending armies and, of course, shared in the general desolation which war brings in its train. In such circumstances we cannot expect that community life will proceed on its even way unruffled. In fact it would be surprising if the generally unsettled state of the country were not reflected to a greater or lesser extent in the Cistercian communities which felt the impact of these events in many and various ways.

The Bruces passed away, but the Irish resistance to English rule continued to grow and the territories held by the English in Ireland continued to shrink. The effect of the wars on the monasteries may be gauged from the fact that the general chapter in 1357 found it necessary to decree that since it was not possible safely to make the visitation of the Irish houses because of the wars in those parts the abbots of the said houses could be summoned by their father abbots or their commissaries to come with the seniors of their communities to some neighbouring and safe monastery, there to receive the benefit of visitation. We have no evidence as to how far this decree was effective. Abbot Troy's statement more than a century later that for a full hundred years the Irish monasteries in the more remote parts of Ireland had ceased to have communication with Mellifont would suggest that by and large the decree failed in its purpose. In fact the only recorded instance of an effort to put the decree into effect occured in 1495 when Abbot Troy himself, wishing to fill a canonical vacancy at Boyle and being unable for stated reasons to come to that monastery, commanded the prior, the cellarer and certain other brethern to come to Mellifont, there to elect an abbot in his presence. The decree of 1357 shows the state to which the order had been reduced in consequence of the ceaseless wars. It is a frank confession of the breakdown in the system of regular visitation. It suggests that the monasteries in Ireland were out of touch not only with the general chapter but with one another, As early as 1202, the monasteries had begun to be affected in a grave way by the wars between Irish and English. Some improvement had taken place by the middle of the century but at the end of the century the position was deteriorating again, and in 1306 we find the abbot and convent of Duiske asking the general chapter to petition the faithful for alms for the monastery, 'then reduced to a lamentable state of dissolution by hostile incursions'. By the middle of the same century these wars, still in progress, were proving a formidable obstacle to the carrying out of the regular visitation of many of the houses. That matters had not improved by the end of the century appears from the fact that in 1377 the abbey of Assaroe was burned down and twenty-one years later was invaded by Niall Ó Neill with his army, when it is stated to have been plundered. A party of O'Donnells people gave battle to the raiders and many were slain and wounded. That was in 1398, and in the same year Maelruanaidh Mac Diarmada of Magh Loirg took away all the food he found in the abbey of Boyle to his own stronghold on the Rock of Loch Cé.

The pattern in the fifteenth century was much the same. In 1476 the English of Meath made an incursion into the Annaly where they burned to the ground the abbey of Flumen Dei (Abbeyshrule) and plundered the fields and corn crops of the surrounding country. The English were not the only destroyers of monasteries and churches. A Cistercian abbot and bishop was even worse. At this time the Annaly was torn by civil war between different factions of the ruling dynasty, the O'Farrells. The abbey of Granard (more correctly Abbeylara) was ruled by Richard O'Farrell who alienated much of the monastic property and so dilapidated the resources of the house that the monks were compelled to wander about the countryside in search of food and shelter. Abbot Richard was later promoted bishop and received a dispensation to hold the abbey *in commendam*. As bishop he showed even less consideration for the monks than as abbot, going so far as to expel some of the community. The abbey was

GENERAL INTRODUCTION 55

ruled later by another O'Farrell, William, who like Richard was in turn promoted bishop and allowed to hold the abbey in commendam. When he finally gave up the commend it was given to another O'Farrell who represented a rival branch of the dynasty. In 1496 the Cistercian bishop William proclaimed himself chief or king of Annaly and from that time acted in both capacities. The state of the diocese in consequence has been described by Dean Monahan in his *Records relating to the Diocese of Ardagh and Conmacnoise*.

> He [the bishop] insisted on his rights. He assembled his forces, assailed and reduced to absolute ruin his oppponents, together with the remnant of the little city of Ardagh. The cathedral shared in the general destruction so that only the walls remained and one altar canopied by the azure vault of heaven. There were only four houses remaining in the city, all built of wood, and scarcely any inhabitants. There was neither sacristy nor belfry nor bell. The vestments and altar ornaments are described as hardly sufficient for mass, which was rarely offered up, there being only one priest in the entire district.

We are no longer surprised, in view of the state of affairs revealed by the annals, the statutes of the general chapter and other authentic documents, at the statement of Abbot Troy that divine worship was neglected in the monasteries, hospitality no longer practiced and the monks compelled to wander abroad seeking the wherewithal to live. The papal registers and the statute rolls of Ireland amply confirm this picture of the impoverishment of the monasteries as a result of war and various other evils. We may cull a few references here: In 1411 we are informed that the abbey of Granard (Abbeylara) is in a bad state, because of the wars and other calamities while the convent was too impoverished to repair them. Six years later the goods of the same abbey are said to be alienated and dilapidated while the monks, formerly numerous, wander forth for the necessaries of life. At Jerpoint, the cloister, dormitory, belltower and other offices were said to be in much need of repair in 1442 and almost a century later we learn that the chancel of the church had already been thrown down before the suppression of the house. In 1444 Kilcooly is described as having been almost completely destroyed by armed men, so that the abbot and two monks had to go to England in search of food and clothing. A few years later the property of Knockmoy is said to be dilapidated and alienated.

In some monasteries the bad state of the house was due to internal mismanagement or the quarrels of rival abbots or aspirants to the abbacy. In 1459 it is complained that the abbot of Duiske does not reside in person; spends the revenues of the house on his sons and daughters and other laymen. The situation did not, apparently, improve with time for in 1468 we find the monks pawning two chalices and a bible belonging to the house, and they were still in pawn in 1471. In 1469, Magonius O'Gallagher, abbot of Assaroe, is described as a notorious fornicator who has dilapidated the goods of the monastery and commmitted simony and other excesses. In Tracton (1463), the abbot could not keep up his state and that of the convent, repair its buildings or bear its other burdens because of the abundant hospitality given to all without distinction. The abbot of Tintern is described in 1470 as being much wasted in consequence of the efforts of two rival abbots to enlist the support of laymen to forward their claims. Those claimants, we are told, freely granted their lay supporters, leases, pensions, tithes and lands for terms of years whereby the divine service of the abbey was lost in as much as no sufficient convent could be found or had in it to the honour of the divine service of God. In the abbey of Suir, too, rival claimants vied with one another for the abbacy. One, an Augustinian friar, was actually provided by the Holy See but resigned within a year. Another, a monk of the house, elected by the convent and confirmed by ordinary authority was set aside by the Holy See as an intruder and the abbey was finally secured by Diarmuid O'Heffernan, a monk of Holy Cross who may or may not have been the same Diarmuid whose appointment to Holy Cross itself had been set aside on the grounds that he had immediately succeeded his own father, Fergal O'Heffernan, as abbot of that house. Diarmuid was deposed from the abbacy of Suir because of various specified excesses and crimes and provision was made to William O'Donoghue, son of a former abbot, who, after ruling for some years, was himself deposed to make way for Maurice O'Heffernan, the son of another Cistercian abbot. Among the many charges made against William was that of neglect of divine worship, and it was alleged that, owing to this neglect, the church of the monastery was in great part in ruin and fallen. A former daughter house of Suir, Fermoy, was also plagued by the curse of rival abbots, one of whom deposed the other and seized power himself with the help of armed men. To this intestine rivalry was added the impact of the wars then unceasingly waged throughout the land, so that the abbot and convent complained to the Holy See in 1467 that their resources were so slender that the convent could not be fittingly maintained therewith, nor could they keep up hospitality or provide for the repair of the church, cloister, dormitory and refectory of the house which, 'by reason of wars and other misfortunes which in times past afflicted these parts are in great part threatened with ruin'. It may be added here that much of the dilapidation and neglect of which complaint is made in so many cases arose from the mode of life of so many of the abbots and their natural desire to make provision for their own children in the first instance.

Mention has been made of the oppression of monasteries by powerful neighbours. A few instances may be given. In 1223 Pope Honorius III issued letters of protection to the abbot and convent of Mellifont and ordered sentence of excommunication to be pronounced against those who irreverently despoiled the goods, possessions or houses of the said abbot and convent or of their men, or detained unjustly legacies bequeathed them by the dying. In 1268 the statutes of the general chapter accuse a petty king of interfering in the affairs of the abbot and convent of Assaroe by intruding an abbot into the monastery. No name is mentioned but the person referred to is probably Domhnall Ó Domhnaill, king of Tir Chonaill from 1258 to 1281. In 1428, the abbot and convent of Newry were forced to complain to the archbishop of Armagh that the followers of Art Magennis and Ardghal O'Hanlon were attempting to seize the lands and goods of the monastery. Two complaints were made to the Holy See in 1450, one from the abbot and convent of Duiske, the other from the abbot and convent of Abbeydorney.

The abbot and convent of Duiske complained that James Butler, earl of Ormond and certain other nobles, whom they named, as well as certain clerics whom they did not name, of the dioceses of Ossory and Leighlin,

> more cruel than Pharaoh ... do not fear to subjugate the said monastery to their jurisdiction and temporal rule as if it were their own patrimony, (compel) the abbot and convent ... to give and pay them feudal dues, stipends, tallages, commons, private subsidies, collections, protection money, compel the men and subjects therof to wars at their own expense and to give and pay fines and many other penalties, exactions and servitudes which they have been wont to exact and receive from their own lay subjects, and to undergo all other lay burdens, and other wise fear not to afflict the said monastery and its subjects with divers taxations and to impose the same upon them ... by reason of which things all the buildings of the monastery are threatened with ruin.

The complaint from Abbeydorney was couched in the same language but was directed against James Fitzgerald, earl of Desmond, and Patrick Fitzmaurice. The appeal to the pope was effective, at least for some years. On the death of the earl of Desmond, however, the oppression of the house commenced anew under his successor so that there was another appeal in 1467 warning as the oppressors this time Thomas Fitzgerald, earl of Desmond, and Thomas Fitzmaurice, who was the earl's marshal in those parts.

Mellifont, too, had its ups and downs. In 1307 mention is made of 'the intolerable controversies and contentions continually had between many monks with very many hired men-at-arms from the desire of obtaining the highest place, that each of them would be abbot by ousting his adversary as well as by conspiracies with other abbots by those desirous of such honour, each one in turn with his accomplices'.

Many other houses were involved in such controversies at that time so that the general chapter had deposed many abbots in consequence. When Roger Boley became abbot of Mellifont in 1471 the house was said to be on the brink of ruin. By 1486 its temporal prosperity had been restored and this tempted the powerful lords in the neighbourhood to begin to oppress the community. They, with their following of manservants and boys and various others are said to have maliciously and forcibly entered on the lands and possessions of the abbey and to have cut down, appropriated and laid waste crops, trees, plantations, woods, weirs, fisheries and meadows. A provincial council of Armagh, held at Drogheda in 1495, addressed letters to all ecclesiastics throughout the province touching the complaints made by the abbot and convent and threatening most severe penalties, including excommunication, on all who should in future be guilty of the oppression and exactions complained of. The nobles were accused of extorting

> illegal and detestable exactions ... demanding as their right provision and lodging for themselves, their horses and servants, food for their men, provender for the horses, fleshmeat, bread, ale, and all kinds of delicacies desired by them or pleasing to them which they expect to be given ... to them for nothing ... they exhort it from the said tenants and vassals against their will and despite their resistance by means of threats, terrorism, fury, forcible taking of pledges, savage floggings of men and women and other devilish and unchristian ways ...

REGIONAL COUNCILS OR CHAPTERS

During the Great Schism of the West (1378-1417) the breach between the Irish abbeys and the general chapter seems to have been complete. Only once during the entire period is there mention of an Irish house in the statutes of the general chapter and that was in 1411 when the schism had almost run its course. In 1402 a papal mandate addressed to the abbots of Mellifont and Dublin empowered them to convoke a chapter, general or particular, of all abbots, priors, provosts and other prelates of the order in Ireland with faculties to elect two visitators to visit, corract, reform and preside over elections. The order in Ireland was released from obedience to the abbot of Citeaux while the schism lasted.

National or regional chapters were nothing new in Ireland. The policy of holding meetings or councils of abbots goes back at least to 1228 as we know from the Register of Stephen of Lexington who convoked a council of abbots in Dublin and held another later in Tintern to discuss the problems confronting him in dealing with the complicated Irish situation. In 1248 a statute of the general chapter authorised the abbots of Mellifont, Dublin and Duiske to convoke the abbots of Ireland as often as was found necessary and according as the business to be transacted demanded, in order to take common counsel to defend the common liberties of the order against the growing ill-will and hostility manifested in many parts of the world towards the priviledges and immunities of the order. In 1357 the general chapter felt it necessary to allay the scruples of 'some simple souls' by pointing out that the excommunication inflicted on abbots who convoked or took part in regional assemblies did not apply to meetings of abbots in Ireland or elsewhere which were convoked to discuss the affairs of the monasteries and, in particular, to defend the liberties of the order, provided that no ordinances or statutes were enacted in such assemblies.

We have no evidence concerning the total number of such councils or chapters of abbots held between 1226 and the dissolution of the monasteries in the sixteenth century and, indeed, such references as we have to councils of this kind are mostly incidental and are few in number. This is not surprising in view of the dearth of original documents. There is evidence of a meeting of abbots at Tullaherin in Co. Kilkenny on 29 May 1288, at Castledermot in Co. Kildare on 15 May 1289 and on 23 May the same year at Jerpoint. A public 'convocation' at Kilkenny in the parish church of St Mary's in 1468 presided over by the abbot of Holy Cross (Matthew O'Mulryan) and a monk of Mellifont (Roger Boley, later to become abbot of that house) was concerned with the visitation and reformation of the order in Munster and Leinster and was convened by authority of the general chapter. We have a detailed report on a council of abbots and other superiors held a Skreen on 7 and 8 June 1496. This council was convoked by the abbots of Dublin and Mellifont acting in their capacity of joint reformators of Irish Cistercians. The fact that houses in the Irish parts of Munster and Ulster, in the province of Connacht and in the territories of the earl of Desmond were not even summoned to this meeting indicates a distinct cleavage in the order in Ireland and a fairly general breakdown in organization.

DECAY

In the early decades of the thirteenth century many of the monasteries had become so impoverished that they could no longer support a community and had to be suppressed by the general chapter. We read in the Register of Stephen of Lexington that houses which at their foundation had been endowed with twenty carucates of land had not even three carucates in 1228 while monasteries originally possessing eighty had by that time only fifteen. Many of the monks were living outside the cloister and in at least one case the visitator had seen an abbot's seal pawned in a public house and had redeemed it. Many of the abbots were wanting in the basic virtue of obedience and led the rebellion against the higher superiors in what became known as the Mellifont Conspiracy.

Relations between monks and people were not always good. In Cashel two monks were attacked as they prayed in the church, one being slain before the altar, the other beaten to death by the citizens. A *conversus* who was present was driven out and thrown into the river. At Holy Cross not far away, lands were alienated and the monks were dispersed in various places. The king of England took advantage of this to command the abbot of Mellifont 'to cause men of English race to the extent of half the convent' to be put into the abbey on the grounds that the losses suffered by the monastery were due to the Irish monks 'as commonly happened where houses were placed under their rule'. The incidents at Cashel and Holy Cross occurred in 1290 and 1297 respectively. Some years later (1307) a similar complaint is made against the abbot of Maigue who is accused of alienating the tenements and goods of the abbey in hatred of the English tongue, to maintain that no monks of England shall dwell there as was accustomed. The slaying of the monks at Cashel may have been due to the resentment of the citizens of that town at the fact that a long-established Benedictine community had been banished by the Cistercian archbishop to make room for a community of Cistercians from Mellifont. The complaints concerning Holy Cross and Maigue suggest, perhaps, resentment on the part of the English at the undoing of the Lexington settlement of half a century earlier and the restoration of the *filiatio Mellifontis*. The explanation of the alienation of lands in Maigue and Holy Cross is a simpler one. In the south of Ireland, especially, the monasteries were heavily in debt between 1275 and 1320. The monks could not fulfill the contracts they had made with Italian bankers and merchants to deliver a certain number of sacks of wool over a certain specified term of years and the Italian creditors sought security. As security some abbots handed over churches and lands or even, in some cases, Holy Cross was one instance, entire manors, and this rather than 'hatred of the English tongue' was the explanation of what happened at Holy Cross and Maigue.

That this, indeed, is the explanation is confirmed, I think, by the fact that not only native Irish houses but such foreign houses as Owney and Duiske from which the natives were barred were alienating lands and churches in exactly the same way. In 1295, for example, the abbot of Owney gave the Riccardi of Lucca the church of Thurles and two chapels as security for £1,000. The Riccardi foreclosed on the mortgage and leased the chapel to the abbot for forty marks a year. Already in 1299, the abbey of

Duiske, 'the English abbey' as it was called, was in debt to the same company and the abbey of Baltinglass which by then must have become almost entirely English in composition was in the same plight. Before the middle of the fourteenth century the Cistercians had abandoned the wool trade and the economy changed from sheep raising to one of rents. Thenceforward the monks turned more and more to the rentier system and the working of the granges by the brothers was abandoned. The *conversi* themselves felt they were no longer wanted and growing discontent on their part led up to a series of revolts and conspiracies as a result of which the reputation of the order suffered considerably. By the end of the century the conversi had practically vanished from the scene. The monks too declined in numbers because of the Black Death and possibly owing to a dearth of vocations. As the communities contracted the number of servants increased until by the end of the fifteenth century there were probably more servants than monks in most of the houses. Many years ago Fr Ambrose Coleman OP pointed out that the conclusion is forced upon us from contemporary evidence that the old monastic orders were generally in a state of stagnation and decay at this period. Yet, although that observation is profoundly true there were certain changes even in the monastic orders. The remains of many Cistercian abbeys bear evidence to those changes.

This diminution in the number of monks was not confined to Ireland. In almost every country and abbey the same phenomenon could be observed. In Ireland, indeed, the number of monks was only a fraction of what it once had been. If we accept an entry in the Antiphonary of Armagh at its face value the Mellifont community was at one time composed of 100 monks and 300 *conversi*, making a total of 400 religious. By the year 1228, the number had fallen to 110 of whom fifty were monks and sixty were conversi. By the year 1493 it was scarcely more than twenty and by 1539 had fallen to fourteen. There were then no *conversi*. The position in the Dublin house was somewhat similar except that there was a slightly bigger community there than at Mellifont.

Figures regarding other monasteries are hard to obtain, but it may be inferred from certain documents in the Ormond collection in the National Library of Ireland that the average number of monks in the important abbey of Jerpoint did not exceed half a dozen during the whole period from 1513 to 1540. If we could suppose that the number of monks who received pensions at the dissolution of the monasteries was the equivalent of the actual number of monks in the monasteries at the time we should have to conclude that many of the smaller houses had only a handful of monks while some even of the greater houses were in no better plight. Assuming that all the monks did, in fact, receive pensions we should be forced to the conclusion on the available evidence that the abbey of Granard, for instance, held only six monks, the abbey of

Inishlounaght only five and Kilcooly abbey and Hore abbey no more than two each. These figures may, of course, be correct. If the surrender in all these cases was signed by every member of the community they certainly are correct. There is a divergence of opinion among historians on this matter, and we cannot say with certaintly whether or not every member of the communities above named did, in fact, sign the surrender and receive a pension. Nevertheless the probability is that they did. The king's commission for the dissolution of the Irish religious houses lays down expressly that while those who 'contumaciously refuse to surrender their houses' are to be apprehended and punished, those who 'willingly surrender' are to be assigned competent pensions and to have the liberty of 'exchanging their habits and of accepting benefices under the king's authority' as, indeed, they did in Mellifont. In most cases it seems probable that in practice, at any rate, the number of pensioned monks represented the actual number in the community, for there is no case recorded of the apprehension or punishment of even a single monk for refusal to comply with these conditions. On the other hand, only 21 of the 33 abbeys then in existence are named in the Extents of 1540-1. It would appear that in the case of seven of the twenty-one the survey was made not on the site but at some other place else and there is no evidence that the king's officers succeeded in getting actual possession of these abbeys at that time. The houses in question were those of Maigue, Tracton, Fermoy, Chore, Abbeymahon, Abbeyshrule and Kilbeggan, and it is significant that none of the monks or abbots of these houses figure on the pension lists. Besides these houses there were the abbeys lying in territories completely outside English control; these included Boyle, Assaroe, Knockmoy and Macosquin, and we have no means of estimating the number of monks in these houses.

We are able to judge the relative economic value of the various Irish Cistercian Houses from two tables for 1460 and 1479 (see below). The 1460 table comes from a register kept at Citeaux, now preserved in the Archives de la Cote-d'Or at Dijon (MS II H 1159). The 1479 table is found in a manuscript of Sir James Ware (MS. Rawlinson B484 f.255), now in the Bodleian Library, Oxford. Unfortunately Hore abbey is one of three Irish houses apparently missing. There were four taxation assessments, based on the total to be extracted. The sums were mentioned in *florins de compte* which would be equivalent to the *livre tournous*. There is no indication that the sums of money were actually paid. In 1454, the general chapter found it necessary to complain that the English Welsh and Irish houses, despite the fact that they were well off, contributed nothing to the support of the order. In 1456 the abbot of Dublin was empowered to demand, levy and revenue the contributions owed by these houses and to enforce payment *secundam taxam in rotulo per idem Capitulam super hoc confecto* Inishlounaght is on 18v of MS II H 1159, as is Holy Cross. Kilcooly is on 19v. There is a possibility that Hore abbey (*de Rupe*) is Casale on 13v. It is valued at £15 which is the precise contribution imposed in the abbey of *Rupis Cassilis* in MS Rawl. B484.

RAWLINSON TABLE

Inishlounaght	xviij*lb*	xv*s.*
Holy Cross	xiij*lb*	x*s.*
Kilcooly	xviij*lb*	xv*s.*
Hore	xv*lb.*	

DIJON TABLE

	Moderate	*Mediocre*	*Duplex*	*Excessive*
Inishlounaght	18. 15*s.* 0*d.*	25. 0*s.* 0*d.*	37. 10*s.* 0*d.*	50. 0*s.* 0*d.*
Holy Cross	13. 10*s.* 0*d.*	18. 0*s.* 0*d.*	27. 0*s.* 0*d.*	36. 0*s.* 0*d.*
Kilcooly	18. 15*s.* 0*d.*	25. 0*s.* 0*d.*	37. 10*s.* 0*d.*	50. 0*s.* 0*d.*
Hore (?)	15. 0*s.* 0*d.*	20. 0*s.* 0*d.*	30. 0*s.* 0*d.*	40. 0*s.* 0*d.*

Professor G. Mac Niocaill gives the income from land *c.*1539 as follows:

	Income	*Percentage of total valuation*
Inishlounaght	£28. 12*s.* 11*d.*	88%
Kilcooly	£15. 15*s.* 7*d.*	34%
Hore (Cashel)	£18. 1*s.* 8*d.*	68%

He gives the income from benefices *c.*1539 as follows:

	Income	*Percentage of total valuation*
Kilcooly	£29. 6*s.* 8*d.*	64%
Hore (Cashel)	£8. 12*s.* 4*d.*	25%

He also gives some of the following valuations of the Tipperary Cistercian Houses in the fifteenth century:

INISHLOUNAGHT		*Source*
1439	40 marks	AH 12 (1946) 16-7
1463	49 marks	AH 12 (1946) 19, and CPR 11, p. 186
1464	60 marks	AH 12 (1946) 21
1474	95 marks	CPR 12, p. 414
1476	80 marks	CPR 13, p. 531
1492	80 marks	CPR 14, p. 30

HOLY CROSS   *Source*
1448   20 marks   CPR 10, p. 389
1490   50 marks   CPR 14, p. 256
1492   50 marks   CPR 14, p. 300

KILCOOLY   *Source*
1450   16 marks   CPR 10, pp 511-2
1464   16 marks   CPR 11, pp 505-6
1498   20 marks   AH 20 (1957) 30

HORE (CASHEL)   *Source*
1459   24 marks   CPR 12, p. 12
1486   25 marks   Obligationes Cassell, 1 Ch. 15.

APPENDICES

IRISH CISTERCIAN ABBOTS

In considering the Cistercian abbot in medieval Ireland, it is necessary to state that the abbot here depicted is not the ideal abbot whose character is delineated in the Rule of St Benedict, but the very human and often very imperfect abbot revealed to us in the historical and judicial documents of Church and State in Ireland in so far as such documents are available to us. The great drawback of such documents is, of course, that they depict primarily the public life of the abbot and have very little to say, except by inference, of the abbot as ruler of his monastery and father of his community. These documents tell us practically nothing of his work as the wise physician of souls depicted by St Benedict, the master chosen for his wisdom of doctrine, learned in the law of God, whose duty it was to teach and instruct his disciples not merely by word of mouth but more especially by the good example of his own life. The picture we get from contemporary historical and legal documents, whether of Church or State, is necessarily one sided, and that fact must be borne in mind when reading this appendix.

The surviving documents show clearly that the medieval Irish abbot figured prominently in the public life of his time. This involvement of the abbot in public affairs had already begun before the close of the twelfth century and was to continue and to increase right up to the dissolution of the religious orders in Ireland under Henry VIII in 1539. The Cistercian reform, as we know, aimed, at a return to the primitive simplicity of the

Benedictine Rule, and that rule lays down in no uncertain terms the kind of man the abbot ought to be, as well as his position in the monastery. In the second chapter of the Rule of St Benedict it is stated that the abbot is believed to hold the place of Christ in the monastery. Elsewhere (chap. 63) he is reminded that he is called lord and abbot, not because he has taken it upon himself, but out of reverence and love of Christ. He is told, therefore, to be mindful of this and show himself worthy of such an honour. In treating of the election of the abbot, St Benedict reminds the brethren that he who is to be appointed should be chosen for the merit of his life and the wisdom of his doctrine (chap. 64). He is to be learned in the law of God that he may know whence to being forth new things and old; he must be chaste, sober and merciful, ever preferring mercy to justice that he himself may obtain mercy. He is to hate sin and love the brethren; and even in his corrections he should act with prudence and not to go too far, lest while he strives too eagerly to rub off the rust the vessel be broken. He is warned to keep his own frailty ever before his eyes and remember that the bruised reed must not be broken. This does not mean that he should suffer vices to grow up; but that prudently and with charity he should cut them off in the way he shall see best for each. In all he commands, whether concerning spiritual or temporal matters, he is to be prudent and considerate. In the works he imposes he is to be discreet and moderate so that he may not cause his flock to be overdriven (chap. 64). He is to be both a father and a shepherd and should follow the example of the Good Shepherd who, leaving the ninety-nine sheep on the mountains, went back to seek the one which had gone astray, on whose weakness he had such compassion that he deigned to place it on his own sacred shoulders and so carry it back to the flock (chap. 27).

St Benedict leaves his disciples in no doubt as to who is the master in the monastery. The abbot is the master both as a teacher and a disciplinarian. He is the master who is to teach more by the example of his life than by word of mouth; but he is also the master who must be obeyed and who must sometimes show 'the dread character of the master' in reproving, correcting and chastising the negligent, the undisciplined and the hard of heart. The abbot stood at the head of the community and his power was supreme, subject only to the Rule and the Law of God. Because of the responsibility which power brings and the grave temptation to abuse power, especially when it is absolute, the abbot is warned to remember always the name by which he is called and to make his actions correspond therewith. He should study to be loved rather than feared and should remember that it befitted him rather to make himself useful to the brethren than to rule over them. Even in giving orders he was to be considerate, showing discretion and kindness; and he was so to arrange all things that strong souls might desire to do more while the weak might not be discouraged. Finally he is reminded more than once that he must give an account to God of his judgements and of all his deeds and that he himself must observe the rule in all things.

Although the Cistercian reform was based on a return to the primitive observance of the Rule, the reformators, drawing on the experience of the centuries that had passed since St Benedict's day, deliberately limited the abbatial authority as conceived by that saint. In order to preserve the spirit they found it necessary to make certain changes in the letter of the Rule. These changes resulted in a highly centralised system of government which subjected the abbot to certain checks and restraints aimed, at preventing the abuse of power which had brought ruin to the Congregation of Cluny. Although the abbot was still supreme in his own house his power was no longer absolute; for he himself was subject not only to the Rule of St Benedict but also to the constitutions of the order laid down in the *Carta Caritatis* as well as to the decrees and definitions of the general chapter. He was moreover subject to an annual visitation of his house by the abbot of the mother house and so was checked by a number of restraints not envisaged in the Rule of St Benedict. His power, therefore, was by no means absolute, and although theoretically he was elected for life he could be, and in fact frequently was, deposed by the general chapter or by the Father Immediate if he abused his power or failed to carry out his duties in a satisfactory manner. Despite all this, and notwithstanding the vigilance of the general chapter, the abbot developed in the course of time on lines not envisaged either in the Rule of St Benedict or in the *Carta Caritatis* and, influenced perhaps by the part played by St Bernard in the public affairs of his time, came eventually to play an important role in secular life.

In Ireland, this development had already begun before the close of the twelfth century. Within a decade of the foundation of Mellifont, the first house of the order in Ireland, its abbot, Gilla Crist O Conairche, had become the first of a long line of Irish Cistercian bishops. He had been created bishop of Lismore in 1150 by Pope Eugenius III who had been his fellow novice at Clairvaux, where both had been trained by St Bernard. Consecrated by Eugenius himself and appointed by him permanent legate for all Ireland, he returned to Ireland with Cardinal Paparo with whom he presided over the great synod of Kells in 1152. This synod, which seems to have opened at Kells and concluded at Mellifont (Drogheda) gave the Irish hierarchial system the form it has substantially retained to the present day. The part played by the abbot of Mellifont in that synod shows that already the new order was making itself felt in the public life of the Irish Church. Before the close of the same century at least ten Cistercian bishops had occupied Irish sees and with the invasion of Ireland by the Anglo-Normans we find the Cistercian bishops foremost in supporting the new regime which, incidently, had the wholehearted support of the pope.

Once again Gill Crist O Conairche presided over a national synod, this time the synod of Cashel, convened by the royal reformator, Henry II of England. Closely associated with Gilla Crist in this synod was Ralph, abbot of Buildewas in England, who was one of the three English representatives sent by the king to call the bishops together and to assist at their deliberations. He was also the Father Immediate of the abbey of St Mary, near Dublin. Thus the English as well as the Irish Cistercians were represented at this synod which among other things forced the Irish church to abandon its ancient observances and adopt those of the church of England while at the same time confirming the Anglo-Norman conquest of Ireland and swearing fealty to the king of England as lord of that land.

With the decade following the synod of Cashel Gill Crist O Conairce had resigned his see and retired to the abbey of Kyrie Eleison in Kerry, where he died in 1186. Meanwhile five other Cistercians had been appointed to Irish sees between 1172 and 1182, while three more sees came into Cistercian hands between 1182 and 1189. Thus between 1150 and 1199 ten Irish sees were ruled by a longer or shorter period by Cistercian bishops. The status of the tenth is not known but it is very likely that he, too, was an abbot. Three of the bishops had been abbots of Mellifont, two had been abbots of Boyle and one each, abbot of Baltinglass, Jerpoint, Monasterevan and Newry. The first Cistercian archbishop of Cashel, Muirgheas Ua hEnna, who was made papal legate in 1192, had later fallen into disgrace and retired to the abbey of Holy Cross where he died in 1206. It is not improbable, therefore, that he was originally a monk of that house and may even have been abbot there before his promotion to the episcopacy. A simple monk at that period would scarcely have been sufficiently well known to merit appointment to such an important position in the ecclesiastical hierarchy. The prominent part played by Cistercians in contemporary ecclesiastical affairs is strikingly illustrated by the fact that, from 1185 at least until 1238, four successive archbishops of Cashel were Cistercian monks; and although the Cistercian succession was temporarily interrupted by the election of the Dominican friar David Mac Cellaigh Ua Gillapatric in 1238, he was succeeded in 1253 by another great friend and benefactor of the order, David Mac Cearbhaill, who himself took the Cistercian habit in 1269 and ruled for the last twenty years of his life as a Cistercian bishop. He it was who brought the Cistercians from Mellifont to Cashel in 1272, thus becoming the founder of the last daughter house of Mellifont. Of the seven archbishops who ruled Cashel from 1200 to 1300 all but two were Cistercian; and it was largely due to the rigorous efforts of these archbishops in bringing to the notice of the Holy See the wrongs inflicted by the Anglo-Norman administration on the Irish Church and people, that the pope was moved to issue a scathing denunciation of the iniquitous customs introduced by the Normans with the aim of discriminating against the native Irish. Writing to his legate, the pope commanded him to see that these customs were completely abolished and to compel the English, even by ecclesiastical censure, if needs be, to allow the Irish to enjoy equal rights with themselves.

During the whole of the thirteenth century the Irish Cistercians were active in the affairs of the Church and no less than thirty monks of the order ruled over Irish sees between 1200 and 1300. These Cistercians bishops included men of Anglo-Norman as well as of Irish race. Apart from the bishops the abbots themselves were now beginning to take a leading part in public life and their involvement in public affairs did not stop at the religious sphere. Wedded as it was to the cause of ecclesiastical reform, the order was used by the pope to carry out papal policy and thus were abbots brought more and more into prominence in public life. This involvement, though confined at first to ecclesiastical affairs gradually extended to secular life and lead eventually to the involvement of the abbots in the whole feudal system. By the end of the century the Cistercian abbot had become a feudal lord and by the middle of the following century had, in many cases, come to take his place in the parliaments and councils of the king as a peer of the realm in Anglo-Norman Ireland. Not all Cistercian abbots were summoned to parliament and the grounds on which any of them were summoned are far from clear. It has been stated that only those prelates who were tenants in chief of the king and held their lands of him in barony were bound to attend the *Curia Regis* and were vested with the dignity of parliamentary barons. Since the Cistercians held their lands not in barony but in frankalmoign – in free and perpetual alms – they should not strictly have been bound to attend parliament at all.

We have little information about the attendance of Cistercian monks at parliament before 1375 but we do know that the abbot of Owney did attend before then.[1] By 1375 the following Cistercian houses were summoned: Tracton, Dublin, Duiske, Jerpoint, Monasterenagh, Mellifont, Dunbrody, Tintern and Baltinglass. It should be noted, as is evident from the location of these houses, that the parliament was no more than the parliament of the Anglo-Norman colony. It should also be noted that medieval parliaments were not democratic and there were no political parties. The parliament was summoned relatively infrequent for example, eleven parliaments are recorded between 1366 and 1382, and was held in different parts of the country for example, Kilkenny in 1360, Ballyhack, Co. Cork, in 1372, Clonmel in 1381, Cork in 1382, Kildare in 1385.[2] Some of the councils or parliaments met in the chapter-room of the Cistercian

1 H.G. de Vancheke OSB, 'Abbots in Anglo-Norman Parliaments', *North Munster Antiquarian Journal* 15 (1972) 42-50.   2 H.G. Richardson and G.O. Sayles, *Parliaments in Medieval Ireland* (Dundalk 1964) and *Parliaments and Council in Medieval Ireland* (Dublin, 1947).

abbey of St Mary's in Dublin, still to be seen off Capel Street in Dublin. Although up to eleven Cistercian abbots were summoned to attend subsequent parliaments, the abbot of Holy Cross is not named in any of the writs of parliamentary summons nor is there any evidence to show that he ever attended the councils or parliaments as a spiritual peer. The abbot was commissioned in 1374, 1376 and 1382 to collect a clerical subsidy for the state but this does not imply that he was a baron of parliament. It appears that in some cases daughter houses were represented in parliament by their mother houses and as the abbot of Maigue was the original *Pater Abbas* of Holy Cross and the abbot of Mellifont subsequently assumed this office, Holy Cross was represented by one or other of these abbots. Sir James Ware does not include the Holy Cross abbot among the thirteen who were numbered among the peers of parliament: neither does Malachy Hartry, who was unlikely to omit any of the temporal achievements of Holy Cross, mention any parliamentary involvement by the abbots nor indicate that the abbot was ever known as the 'earl' of Holy Cross. If the abbot did not attend the Anglo-Irish parliament he did attend the palatine court of the earl of Ormond, the court of the liberty of Tipperary.

Whatever about the honour attaching to the dignity of a baron of parliament it is quite certain from the available evidence that many if not most of the abbots on whom the duty of attending parliament devolved looked upon it as a burden rather than a privilege, and many sought to be excused from attending. It was of course an expensive privilege and often entailed absences from the monastery on the part of the superior which led to the neglect of his monastic duties. In 1375 the abbot of Jerpoint asked to be excused on the grounds that the abbot of Baltinglass, his Father Immediate, who himself attended the parliament, represented his daughter house as well as his own. On this occasion the abbot's plea was accepted and he was freed in perpetuity from the obligation of attending parliament. Nevertheless we find the abbot of Jerpoint summoned again in the year 1382. The number of abbots attending the parliament continued to drop with the passing of time. The abbot of Duiske does not seem to have been summoned in 1378 while in 1380 the abbot of Tintern is missing from the list as well as the abbots of Duiske and Jerpoint. Although the abbot of Jerpoint was back again by 1382 the attendance continued to drop for by them the abbot of Maigue had ceased to attend. During the course of the fifteenth century the attendance decreased still further until at last only the abbots of three houses – Dublin, Mellifont and Baltinglass, continued to attend. These last three seem to have continued to sit in parliament until the final suppression of the religious houses in the sixteenth century.

The presence of an abbot at the sittings of parliament meant that he had to be absent from his house for a greater or lesser period during the time parliament was in session, and this absence was occasionally used by refractory monks to organise a conspiracy against the abbot with a view to oust him from office. A case in point is the attempt by a Welsh monk with the connivance of certain Irish abbots and a disaffected monk of Mellifont to remove the abbot of that house from office by means of a pretended 'visitation' of the monastery while the abbot, Richard Contour, was attending a parliament in Dublin. The abbots of Jerpoint and Tintern issued a summons ordering the abbot of Mellifont to present himself before them on 29 May 1533, at a visitation to be held by·them in Mellifont. At the time they issued this summons they were well aware that the abbot could not come owing to his parliamentary duties; they were also aware of the fact that the regular visitation of his abbey had already been carried out by the abbot of Bective at Easter. In the event they came to Mellifont and, in the course of their pretended 'visitation', deposed the abbot and appointed in his place the Welsh monk Lewis Thomas who had some six years earlier assisted the abbot of Bective to make a canonical visitation at Mellifont. The two abbots purported to depose Abbot Richard Contour notwithstanding the fact that the latter had appealed to the abbot of Citeaux against the action of the pretended visitators. The deposed abbot then sought letters of protection from the archbishop of Armagh. The outcome of the affair was that Richard's title to the abbacy of Mellifont was upheld and confirmed by an ecclesiastical court of inquiry held in the following year.

A more extraordinary case was that of the abbot of Dunbrody who, when summoned by writ to come to parliament was reluctant to come in his own person because of the danger of the ways. He did, however, send his proctor to answer for him in the parliament and the latter was received and admitted in due course. The abbot himself underwent a change of heart later, and decided that he would after all attend the parliament despite the fact that he had already sent his proctor. The rest of the story is best summarised from *The Statute Rolls of Ireland*. The abbot, we are told,

> peaceably reposing himself in his chamber the night before he should begin his journey to the said parliament, Dom John Balle, Dom Thomas Sutton, Dom Nicholas Furlong, apostates, William Robertson Sutton and William Davyson Sutton of the county of Wexford, and Thomas Comerford of Waterford, with divers others unknown, with force and arms against the peace of our sovereign lord, entered the chamber of the said abbot and there took him prisoner.

To make a long story short, the parliament issued a proclamation against the kidnappers of the abbot ordering them to set him at large and to restore to him the goods and chattels they had taken from the abbey. This was to be done within eight days on pain of forfeiture of all their lands, rents, possessions, goods and chattels to the king.

By the middle of the fourteenth century the Cistercian abbot in Ireland had become a great temporal lord exercising secular as well as ecclesiastical jurisdiction over great tracts of land. The abbot and convent had their tithes, altarages and other feudal revenues or sources of revenue. They had their tenants and their courts. These courts were of various kinds. In the first place there was the manorial court to which the tenants and vassals had to come to plead and receive judgement. Here justice was administered and disputes between tenants and vassals of the lord abbot were settled; for the abbot as lord of the manor was judge over all his vassals and presided over the manorial court, called the court-baron, either in person or by his steward, the court being composed of all the free tenants or freeholders of the manor. When, as sometimes happened, the possessions formed a seignory of several manors held under one lord this seignory was known as the honour and had an honorial court. Many of the larger monasteries were, in fact, composed of several such manors and consequently had their monastic manorial courts. One of the earliest functions of the court-baron was the overseeing of *frankpledge* and its attendant jurisdiction. By *frankpledges* were meant the free men who were mutual pledges for the good behaviour of one another. The jurisdiction attendant on *frankpledges* was concerned with the preservation of peace and various offences against the common good and when exercising these powers the court-baron came to be known as the *court-leet*. The court-leet was held within the manor and a year and was a court of record, that is to say, its proceedings were efficiently recorded and it had the power to fine and imprison. It had not only the right but the duty to present by jury all crimes committed within the jurisdiction and to punish the same. Besides the courts-baron and the courts-leet monasteries, which had the right to hold a fair had also a court known as the court-merchant which was used both for the settling of trade disputes and for trying strangers. All these courts pertained to the abbot's function as a feudal lord, charged with administering feudal justice. But the abbot was not only a secular lord; he was also endowed with ecclesiastical jurisdiction over his religious subjects and in this capacity had his ecclesiastical court to which his lay vassals were not subject. Since monks and clerics were not generally subject to secular courts in medieval Ireland they had to be brought before a secular court he could plead exemption from the jurisdiction of such a court and would, on the fact of his exemption being proved, be delivered to his abbot to be dealt with by the abbot's court. Cases of this kind are on record and two instances concerned with Cistercian monks may be mentioned here.

In 1277, two monks of St Mary's abbey near Dublin who at the time were dwelling on the abbey grange at Portmarnock were arrested and brought before the chief justiciar charges with the murder of John Comyn, lord of Kinsealy. During the trial in Dublin castle the abbot appeared before the court and demanded that the monks should be handed over to him as his subjects. When it was proved to the court that they were indeed the abbot's subjects they were delivered to him to be tried by his court. In the event they were convicted of the murder and sentenced to perpetual imprisonment in the monastic prison in chains and on bread and water. Monasteries like Mellifont and Dublin had two prisons: one for delinquent monks and the other for delinquent lay people. All abbeys might not have a secular prison, but the prison for the religious was legislated for by the general chapter itself. A strong and secure prison was ordered to be erected in each abbey of the order for the incarceration of thieves, incendiaries, forgers, murderers and other criminals. These prisons were used not only for the incarceration of criminals but also for the insane. The same abbey of St Mary near Dublin provides us with an example of the treatment of the insane at the period while also recording another clash between secular and ecclesiastical jurisdiction in which the abbot on the one hand and the king's official on the other were involved. A certain Brother William who had been showing some signs of mental aberration for about two months became completely insane and committed a felony, which led to an attempt by the authorities to arrest him. The abbot resisted, claiming that Brother William as a monk and his subject should be detained in the monastic prison; but the king's sergeant insisted and the outcome was that William was delivered up by the abbot under protest. The case eventually came before the chief justiciar in Dublin castle where the abbot appeared in person to claim William as his subject. The claim was allowed and the justiciar directed that the accused monk should be transferred from the prison of Dublin Castle to that of St Mary's abbey. This was done, and the unfortunate Brother William spent the remainder of his life in chains in the monastic prison.

With the growing involvement of the Cistercian abbot in public life he ceased to live as heretofore in the midst of his monks. In the monastery itself it became the recognised custom for the abbot to have his own quarters as well as his own household or establishment of servants and retainers, and the income of the monastery was divided between the community and the abbot. This gave rise to many evils, for the status of the abbot as a great secular lord made the abbatial office a rich and tempting prize to be striven for and won by ambitious men who had little or no concern for religion except as a means of worldly advancement; and in fact by the middle of the fifteenth century the order in Ireland was plagued by the activities of such men. Not that such men formed the majority of monastic superiors at any time; but in general the lord abbot of the late medieval period was far removed in temperament and outlook from the abbot of St Bernard's day. In many cases he was a man of worldly outlook in whom spiritual fervour was sadly lacking even though in his public or secular role he might be a talented administrator and an energetic promoter of the material well-being of his community. Of course it could and sometimes did happen that an abbot could be at one and the same time a fervent religious man and an able administrator of the monastic property while occupying a prominent position in the public life of the time. Such an abbot was Walter Champfleur, abbot of St Mary's abbey outside Dublin, whose holding the office of treasurer and keeper of the great seal under Edward IV and Richard III did not prevent him from working hard and perseveringly in the cause of monastic reform during the period of his abbacy. But this was exceptional.

A report sent by John Troy, abbot of Mellifont, to the abbot of Citeaux sometime after January, 1498, describes what he terms the 'ruin and desolation' of the entire order in Ireland at that time. The report makes sad reading. Among the causes of the ruin which had overtaken the order in Ireland the abbot enumerates the ceaseless wars waged between the two races arising from the hatred begotten as a result of the original conquest, the excessive oppression of the nobles; the pensions and tributes paid by the monasteries for the support of provisors and commendatory abbots contrary to the rights of the incumbents, as well as similar pensions and tributes for the support of the said incumbents against the provisors and commendatory abbots. In consequence of such exactions the order was in straitened circumstances and large sums of money for these and other purposes had to be poured out. Laymen had in many cases taken over the revenues of the monasteries so that the monks had not wherewith to live and were compelled to wander abroad in search of the very necessities of life. As a consequence divine worship was neglected, hospitality was no longer practised, and many of the monks, throwing off the religious habit, lived among the nobility while the provisors and commendatories appointed by the Holy See took no care of the monastic goods except to plunder them for their own use. Hence the abbot complained that there was scarcely a monastery in the whole of Ireland except the abbeys of Mellifont and Dublin in which the divine office was sung according to note or the monastic habit worn. He complained especially and vehemently of those abbots who, with out any knowledge of the religious life or instruction in the regular observances of the order were, from being seculars, promoted to rule abbeys when they had scarcely been clad in the habit, and were even appointed 'reformators' and visitators.

The state of affairs disclosed by the abbot of Mellifont in his report is confirmed by the papal registers, the statute rolls of Ireland, the statutes of the general chapter, the Irish annals and other authentic documents of the period. In some cases the evidence shows that the bad state of certain monasteries was due to internal mismanagement or even to the quarrels of rival abbots or aspirants to the abbacy. Complaints were made that the abbot did not reside in person in his monastery; in one case he was stated to have spent the revenues of his house on his sons and daughters and other laymen. The abbot in this case was the abbot of Duiske and the year was 1459. His house appears to have been much impoverished and the situation did not improve with time for in 1468 we find the monks pawning two chalices and a bible belonging to the house, and these articles were still in pawn in 1471. Rival claimants to an abbacy had no hesitation in enlisting the support of laymen to promote their interests and freely granted such allies leases, pensions and tithes for terms of years to the grave loss of the community. Reference to the ruinous an dilapidated state of the monastic buildings is made frequently in the papal registers; various causes are mentioned as responsible for this widespread dilapidation and ruin among which may be noted the impoverishment of the monasteries by wars and other calamities, the abundant hospitality given to all without distinction, the excessive exactions of the nobility who compel the abbot and convent to pay them feudal dues. From the abbey's tenants and vassals they extort 'illegal and detestable exactions ... demanding as their right provision and lodgings for themselves, their horses and servants ... and all kinds of delicacies ... which they expect to be given ... to them for nothing'.

When the second synod of Cashel compelled the Irish to substitute the forms and observances of the Anglican church for their own native traditions one of the inevitable sequels was the adoption in Ireland of the royal *conge d'elire*, which required that before an episcopal or abbatial election the electors should inform the king of the vacancy and seek and obtain licence to elect before proceeeding with the election. Meantime during the interval which elapsed between the death, resignation or deprivation of the bishop or the abbot and the assent of the king to the election of his successor and the confirmation of the same, the revenues of the see or abbey came into the king's hand and were administered by the king's officials. When the election had been at length confirmed it was the custom to issue a royal writ ordering the restoration of the new bishop or abbot of the temporalities of the monastery. This right of interference with abbatial elections was unknown to the Cistercians since, unnlike the majority of religious houses in Ireland, they held their lands, not of the king, but in *frankalmoign*, that is, in free and perpetual alms, being bound by no ties of any kind to the Crown; the Cistercians were therefore free from all outside interference in their elections and their temporlities did not come in to the king's hand during the vacancy of an abbey. We may sum up here the Cistercian legislation concerning the election of abbots as set down in the

Carta Caritatis, the fundamental constitution of the order, and developed during the following centuries.

When any house of the order became vacant by the death, resignation or deprivation of the abbot, the *Pater Abbas*, that is the abbot of the mother house, took full charge of the administration of the vacant abbey until such time as a new abbot was elected; and a day having been appointed for the election, all who had a right to vote were summoned, and in the presence of the *Pater Abbas* and fortified by his advice and counsel, chose their new abbot. According to the primitive practice of the order the monks themselves were to elect their abbot either from their own community or from any other house of the order. Later on, the right of taking part in the election was extended, in the case of a mother house, to the abbots of the daughter houses while a further development allowed the brethren to choose their new abbot not only from the monks of the daughter houses but even from the abbots thereof. The custom of having electors nominated beforehand from the community, which seems to have existed already before 1228 (it was used by Stephen of Lexington in 1228 and made it possible for him in most cases to ensure the election of the candidate favoured by himself) was confirmed by the papal constitution *Parvus fons* in 1265. This constitution freed the Cistercians from the obligation of observing all the forms of election decreed by the Fourth General Council of the Lateran and confirmed the electoral processes proper to the Cistercian Order out of respect, as it states, for the simplicity of the Cistercian usage. The papal constitution also provided that before the election, the prior, subprior and cellarer of the vacant house should come to an agreement concerning the electors whom the said prior, after they had agreed upon them, should nominate in chapter. In order to safeguard freedom of election it was provided that the *Pater Abbas* or visitators should not name any of the electors, nor give any command to the electors thus created, either strictly to enjoin on them in public to make provision for the vacant monastery according to their consciences and in good faith. Nor should the *Pater Abbas* of any community claim for himself the right of naming the electors before they were named in chapter; nor should he summon to himself any of those gathered together to elect; nor in any way intimate his will by word, writing or sign, to all or any one of them. He was forbidden to impede the election in any way, openly or secretly, which would take away the liberty of the electors. he was bound to confirm the person elected provided he was suitable and sifficient and if he acted contrary to those instructions he was to be severely punished. Finally he was forbidden to remove any official from office or to expel anyone from the monastery as long as it remained without an abbot.

From the terms of the Clementine Constitution, *Parvus fons*, it is clear that the custom of nominating electors had already existed in the order before 1265 when the constitution was promulgated. It seems clear also that many of the ordinances mentioned above were prompted by the desire to eradicate certain abuses which had become associated with the exercise of this custom. The ordinances regulating the functions of the *Pater Abbas* in connection with such elections were clearly designed to prevent the abuse by him of the electoral system so as to impede de facto the freedom and the liberty of the elector. That the system was open to abuse is evident. The numerous references in the *Register of Stephen of Lexington* to the creation, by the doughty abbot, of new abbots throughout Ireland and the details given there of the elections carried out in Mellifont, Dublin and Inishlounaght show that the system of election by electors nominated for the purpose was then in vogue. Had it been otherwise, it would scarcely have been possible for Stephen to boast that, in such purely Irish houses as Jerpoint and Mellifont and Inishlounaght then were, English or Anglo-Norman abbots could have been elected by the unanimous vote of the monks. In the case of Inishlounaght, the Register states expressly that the electors were nominated and this was very probably the case at Jerpoint. Other references in the same register show that in certain cases lists of names were drawn up by the visitator and that no one was eligible for election unless his name was on the approved list In one case, at least, that of St Mary's abbey, near Dublin, the right guaranteed the community by the *Carta Caritatis* of electing their abbot from any house of the order was taken from them by the visitator, for by his decision the choice of the electors was limited to the personnel of four English abbeys.

In the election ordered to be held at Boyle the voters were presented with a list containing only four names – two Irish and two English. Any one of the four candidates named on the list might be elected but no other. Since all such lists were drawn up by the visitator who clearly intimated to the monks the men he wished to have elected, it is difficult to understand how these elections could be described – in the words of the visitator himself – as 'absolutely free, without the use of any compulsion or threats'. In some cases indeed the man to be elected had been decided upon long before the monastery was visited. Stephen, for instance, wrote to the abbot of Furness asking him to send to Ireland one of his monks whom he could appoint abbot of Suir; and some months later a monk of Furness, presumably the man he had asked for, was unanimously elected abbot by the *electoribus nominatis*. It is clear that the manner in which elections were carried out in Ireland during the visitation of 1228 conformed, neither to the canons laid down by the Fourth Council of the Lateran, nor to the principles of the Cistercian *Carta Caritatis*. Neither were they in conformity with what was later prescribed in the Clementine Constitution which, as we have seen, laid down the principle that the visitators should vote according to their consciences. To round off the legislation concerning the election of abbots, the general chapter in 1276 issued a decree which prescribed that the designation of the monks to whom the election was to be committed by the prior, subprior and cellarer, should be made with the counsel of the seniors of the house and especially of the confessors. The intention of the general chapter was undoubtedly to take precautions lest, by the indiscriminate choice of electors, an unworthy person might be elected to the abbatial office. Nevertheless one may be pardoned for thinking that the inclusion of the confessors in this decree was to say the least, imprudent, and, in fact, was liable to endanger the secrecy of the confessional.

As far as it is known, the system of election described here survived in the Irish houses (or at least in some of them) until the dissolution of the monasteries in the sixteenth century. Provision was also made for election by compromise, and the last recorded election in Mellifont, before the dissolution of the house was, in fact an election by compromise, the official record of the process being still in existence. Long before the dissolution of the monasteries, however, the elective system had fallen into disuse in the majority of the Irish houses, having been replaced almost entirely by the system of papal provision. Whatever the merits in theory of the system by which the pope reserved to himself the right of appointing abbots to religious houses instead of allowing the monks freely to elect their own superior, as was enjoined by the rule of St Benedict and the constitution of the Cistercian Order, the terrible abuses which resulted from this practice and the disastrous consequences not merely to the monastery itself but to the entire order, justifies us in holding that to this pernicious practice more than to any other single factor, was due the spiritual and material ruin which overtook the order the fifteenth century. In some monasteries, Mellifont and Dublin, to name but two, the abbot was still elected by the community according to the laws and usages of the Cistercian Order as modified by the Clementine Constitution; but by and large the electoral system had given way to the system of papel provision; and even in those houses, rapidly dwindling in numbers, in which the electoral system had not fallen into abeyance completely, it sometimes alternated with the system of papal provision, if the two systems did not actually run concurrently, in which case the abbot elected by the convent was more often than not displaced by the rival to whom provision, had been made of the abbey by the pope.

The abbots appointed by papal provision instead of by the free choice of the community as the rule required were known as provisors. The system of papal provision began to operate in Irish Cistercian houses for the first time during the schism (1378-1417) and by the end of the fifteenth century had superseded the elective system in many if not in most of the houses. These provisors were to become the curse of the order. Many of them were prepared to go to any length in order to obtain the abbey of their choice and were not too scrupulous in the means they used to oust a rival. Some of these abbots had been Cistercian monks at the time of their appointment; some were monks or friars of other orders; others again were secular priests or clerics and many were mere laymen. We have not anything like a full list of the abbatial succession in most of the medieval Cistercian monasteries in Ireland.

John Troy, abbot of Mellifont, in a report to the abbot of Citeaux vehemently complains of appointments made to the office of reformator of the order of men who from the being seculars were promoted to rule abbeys by papal provision without any knowledge of the religious life or instruction in the regular observances of the order. He had in mind particularly the case of William O'Dwyer, abbot of Holy Cross, whom he elsewhere described as an impetrator and provisor, as indeed he was, and whose appointment to the office of reformator seen after he had been made abbot by papal provision he considered nothing short of a disaster for the order. O'Dwyer was a typical example of the ambitious impetrator and provisor, a man plainly unfit to rule the order, and a typical product of the system which threatened in the expressive words of Abbot Walter Champfleur to 'extinguish whatever little glimmer of religion still remained' in Ireland. We find frequent mention in the papal registers of a class of abbots called intruders, so called because they had been unlawfully intruded into abbeys to which they had no canonical title. The intruder was generally, but not always a religious who intruded himself into the abbatial office by force, often with the help of hired men-at-arms, and made himself abbot *de facto*. It could and indeed did happen that two or even more rival abbots made their appearance in a house: one provided by the Holy See, another elected by the convent and confirmed by the ordinary authority in the order, and a third setting himself up as a rival to both! It is probable that many of the abbots denounced in the papal registers as intruders were, in fact, men who had been elected and confirmed in accordance with Cistercian usuage and so were, in the eyes of the monks at lease, the true abbots.

The most notorious class of abbots were the abbots *in commendam*, as they were called. These were not really abbots at all but men-often bishops, who, because the revenues of their benefice were too scanty to maintain them in a state befitting the dignity of their office, received a dispensation to hold an abbey *in commendam*, drawing all the revenues of but permorming none of the duties of the abbot. Some of the abbots *in commendam* in this country were members of the ruling families in the territories in which the abbeys were situated or, perhaps, members of the family of the founder, but many were bishops who, before their elevation to the episcopal rank had been abbots and sought to retain the revenues of their abbeys to augment the episcopal revenues which they did not consider sufficient to keep them in a manner befitting their state. They differed from the provisors insofar as the latter, if not Cistercians at the time of their provision, had at least to take the habit and make profession of the rule while the former had no connection with the order or the monastery except to draw the revenues. The total number of abbots of whom there is record, from 1400 to the dissolution of the monasteries, was 253. Of these, 35 were abbots *in commendam*, 85 were 'provisors', 21 were said to be 'intruders' of one kind or another while the remainder had been elected and confirmed in the regular way. The number so elected gradually decreased until at the end of the fifteenth century most of the abbots present at a regional council could be described by the abbot of Mellifont as men who owed their promotion to provisions made by the Holy See; men, to use the words of the same abbot, who took no care of the goods of the house except to plunder them for their own use

As we have already seen, a number of the Irish Cistercian abbots took their seats in parliament as peers of the realm. Some were also justices of the peace while others acted as agents for crown officials of the highest ranks. Two of the abbots of Dublin, as has been noted attained to the highest position in the State under the lord deputy – keeper of the great seal – while part of the State archives was housed in their monastery and the king's council met and deliberated in the chapter house of the abbey (which, is still in existence). It was in that chapter house that the son and heir of the earl of Kildare, Thomas Fitzgerald, commonly known as 'Silken Thomas', threw down the sword of state on the table and went into open rebellion against the English crown on hearing the rumour that his father and six uncles who had been imprisoned in the Tower of London by order of the king had been executed. The rumour in fact was false but the rebellion resulted in the attainder and death of the unfortunate Silken Thomas himself and the fall of the house of Kildare, the most powerful of all the Anglo-Irish families. The abbot's close involvement in the public life of the period sometimes led him into devious political courses as happened in 1487 when the abbots of Mellifont and St Mary's, Dublin, were included in the Lambert Simnel campaign. The Anglo-Irish bishops and practically all the great Anglo-Irish lords, with the notable exception of the Butlers, and the clergy of the pale, and the two Cistercian abbots named above, took a prominent part in the proceedings. Mustering an army the Anglo-Irish nobility landed in England where, unfortunately for their cause, they were completely overthrown by the forces of Henry VII, many of their leaders losing their lives in the battle of Stoke near Newark where Lambert Simnel himself was captured. In the following year the new lord deputy, sent to Ireland by Henry VII, received the fealty and homage of the discomfited supporters of the Yorkist cause and proclaimed, a full pardon to all Simnel's chief supporters. Among those pardoned on this occasion were Walter Champfleur, abbot of St Mary's of Dublin, in whose abbey the fealty and homage of the former rebels had been received by Sir Richard Edgecumbe and the full pardon proclaimed, under the great seal, and John Troy, abbot of Mellifont. It is quite certain that these two abbots, like the vast majority of the Anglo-Irish and English of Ireland really believed that Simnel's claim to be Edward, earl of Warwick, was genuine. In supporting his coronation, therefore, they did so under the impression that they were aiding in the coronation of the true king of England in opposition to the usurper who then occupied the throne.

Abbot Butler in his work on Benedictine monachism has painted a picture of the feudal abbot which is as true of the medieval Cistercian abbot as it is of his Black Benedictine brother.

> Naturally and inevitably they were caught up into the feudal system and became feudal lords, exercising the functions, enjoying the priviledges, bearing the burdens, sharing the rank of the feudal barons. They had their courts; they attended parliament, and consequently had their London houses; they frequently were engaged on business with or for the king. The pope commissioned them to hear ecclesiastical cases and appeals ... and the king employed them on missions to the Holy See and to other soverigns. At the abbey too they had their own quarters separate from the community, and their own establishment; and the income of the monastery was divided in fixed proportions between abbot and community, each having their own obligations towards the upkeep of the house. The abbot was not a 'Lord abbot' for nothing, This was no courtesy title. The 'Lord abbot' was not only a lord of parliament, but was as truly a lord of the serfs and vassals, the tenants and retainers throughout his abbey lands, as the baron and earl who were his peers and his next-door neighbours.

Although Abbot Butler is speaking specifically of the Black Benedictine abbot in the passage quoted above, the description in most particulars is literally true of the Cistercian abbot in medieval Ireland. Such an abbot was my lord abbot of Mellifont and my lord abbot of the house of the Blessed Mary near Dublin, with the nine other Cistercian abbots who ranked as lords of parliament. These abbots were lords of vast domains, that of Mellifont exceeded fifty thousand acres, that of Baltinglass thirty thousand, that of Dublin twenty thousand, and this vast domain, vast by our standards, was populated by tenants and vassals of various degrees as well as serfs.

The abbot's convent drew a large rental from the numerous tenantry. The abbot might even exercise his lordship over a number of towns and villages, holding the power of life and death over his secular subjects of which the manorial pillory and the gallows were grim reminders. These latter powers formed part of the very extensive liberties and immunities and privileges of a secular nature with which some of the greater abbots, such as those of Dublin and Mellifont, were endowed by the king of England in the period between the Anglo-Norman conquest of Ireland and the destruction of the Irish monasteries under Henry VII. One of the most extensive grants of this kind was that made by the king to the abbot and convent of Mellifont on 28 September 1348. By this charter the monks were granted in perpetutity free warren in all their demesne lands in Callan, Ballymascanlan, Salterstown, Culboyg, Grangegeeth, Monknew-town, Ballyfeddock, Fernaght, Sleubroght, and their granges of Oldbridge, Staleen, Rosnaree, Knowth, Doe, Gulboyle and Newgrange in the counties of Meath and Oriel. They were also permitted to build a prison at their own expense in any one of their manors in Co. Meath, wherever they should deem it most expedient, to have in perpetuity to themselves and their successors. In this prison were to be confined malefactors and felons indicated in the monks' lands as well as such of the king's enemies as might happen to be apprehended in the marches of the same lands, there to be detained until justice could be done on them according to the law and custom of those parts. They were to have in all their lands and fees various privileges including *Infangthef* (that is, the privilege granted the lord of the manor to judge thieves captured on his own lands) and *Outfangthef* (that is, the privileges whereby the lord of the manor was empowered to bring to judgement in his own court any man dwelling in his manor and taken for felony in another place out of his fee: in fact more or less what we call extradition to-day).

In the town of Callan, Ballymascanlan, etc., as well as in the granges already mentioned, amounting in all to ten different places in the coun-ties of Meath and Louth, the abbot was empowered to have a gallows, a pil-lory and a tumbrill and all the other liberties already enjoyed by the abbot and convent of St Mary's abbey near Dublin. Besides having custody and assay of weights and measures in their own lands the abbot and convent were given permission to acquire a house in Dublin and one in Drogheda or in the suburbs therof as a dwelling and residence for the abbot and his successors and his (or their) household in coming to parliaments or other councils or assemblies which might be summoned or held there. From *The Statute Rolls of Ireland,* we learn that by 1479 the abbot of Mellifont had, or claimed, to have 'all manner of ecclesiastical jurisdiction and the correc-tion of whatsoever persons, as well ecclesiastical as secular, within the precincts of the lands and possessions belonging to the aforesaid house', and the king in the following year (out of love for the Cistercian Order as the statute roll records) granted to the abbot and his successors the right of apprehending excommunicated persons such as was wont to be exercised by bishops. This meant in practice that should anyone be excommunicated by the abbot and not make satisfaction to God and Holy Church within a month after such excommunication, then, if the abbot certified this fact to the chancery, a writ should be directed to the sheriff or to another royal offical to seize the excommunicated person and to keep him in prison without bail until due satisfaction should have been made. Eight year later, by a decree dated 28 September 1487, Pope Innocent VIII granted to all the abbots of the order jurisdiction over all their tenants, vassals, subjects and servants even to the extent of freeing their subjects from all jurisdiction, superiority, correction, visitation, subjection and power of archbishops, bishops and their vicars, etc., and subjecting them immediately to himself and to himself and to the Holy See. This was the apex of the abbot's power. The ascent (if so it may be termed) had been a gradual process extending over centuries. The descent was rapid. Fifty-two years later came the quarrel between Henry VIII and the pope culminating in the breach between England and Rome and the dissolution of the religious orders in England and Ireland. The Cistercian communities were suppressed with the others; the abbots were pensioned off, the monks dispersed and the vast landed possessions of the order confiscated. *Sic transit gloria mundi.*

IRISH CISTERCIAN LANDS

The findings set forth here rest in the main on the evidence supplied by the monastic extents, that is to say, the surveys of the monastic possessions made by the Commissioners appointed by the Crown at the time of the dissolution of the Irish monasteries, as well as the surviving records (admittedly scanty) of individual monasteries. The Inquisitions of the sixteenth and seventeenth centuries (Exchequer and Chancery), the fiants of Henry VIII, Edward VI, Philip and Mary, and Elizabeth I, the patent rolls of Chancery in Ireland from Henry VIII to Charles II, and certain subsidiary sources including a mass of seventeenth- and eighteenth-century documents which are invaluable in identifying many of the monastic lands under their modern designations.

Considerations of time and space make it impossible to give a detailed account of the process by which the lands held by each monastery on the eve of the dissolution have not only been identified but have been equated with specific lands on the modern ordnance map. In many cases these lands have changed their names more than once, while lands which formed single units in the sixteenth century have, by a process of subdivision, become groups of separate townlands all bearing distinct names.

Hence it seems desirable to give here a more detailed explanation of the sources listed already. This will serve to illustrate the process by which it has been possible to show on the modern map the bulk of the lands held by the Cistercian Order in Ireland at the dissolution of the religious houses in the sixteenth century.

Although the great mass of Irish Cistercian documents including monastic archives, cartularies, registers, liturgical books, account books, rentals, etc, has long since perished, a small number of manuscripts survive. These include two chartularies of St Mary's abbey, Dublin, the register of Dunbrody abbey, Co. Wexford and an *ordinarium* from Monasterevan containing, inter alia, a copy of a charter granted to that abbey in 1289. A number of deeds and charters pertaining to the abbeys of Duiske, Jerpoint, Killenny, Holy Cross, Inishlounaght and Owney are preserved among the Ormond Deeds in the National Library, Dublin, which also houses the Drogheda Papers containing original charters and deeds from Mellifont abbey. A few original charters from other dissolved abbeys have survived, as well as copies of others, the originals of which have disappeared. The more important of the monastic deeds in the Ormond collection have been printed *in extenso* by Dr Newport White in his compact volume *Irish Monastic & Episcopal Deeds* while the chartularies of St Mary's abbey, Dublin, with the annals of that houses and the register of Dunbrody together with additional material which included the surveys made in 1540-1 of the possessions of these two abbeys, have been edited by John T. Gilbert in two volumes, *The Chartularies of St Mary's Abbey, Dublin.*

Some Irish Cistercian charters had been enrolled in the great charter rolls of the kings of England. These are now preserved in the Public Record Office, London, and abstracts or translations of the more important ones have been published in the *Calendar of Charter Rolls* (five volumes) and the *Calendar of Patent Rolls* (England). Others again have been preserved in whole or in part in copies transcribed into two great complications known as *King's Collectanea* and the *Harris Collectanea* which are lodged in the Library of Trinity College, Dublin, and in the National Library of Ireland, respectively. The TCD *Collectanea* dates from the last quarter of the seventeenth century while the *Harris Collectanea* dates from the middle of the eighteenth century and incorporates in volume xiii of its nineteen folio volumes practically the whole of the TCD *Collectanea*. Other volumes, particularly volume xiv, also contain some scattered Cistercian material. It should be noted that reference to individual abbeys and to abbey lands are met with in various medieval sources such as the *Patent and Close Rolls* (English as well as Irish), the *Pipe Rolls*, the *Justiciary Rolls*, the *Statute Rolls of Ireland,* and various other compilations.

Our most important source for the landed property of the Irish Cistercians at the time of the dissolution of the monasteries is the series of surveys made in the period 1540-1, following the dissolution. These surveys were made by virtue of a commission issued to Sir Anthony St Leger and others in 1540. Of the thirty-three houses of men, then in existence only twenty-one are mentioned in the published *Extents*. Even for those so listed all the details are not given. For four of them (Abbeyshrule, Kilbeggan, Monasteranenagh and Monasterevan) no particulars at all are given while the figures for Abbeyleix are incomplete. This last abbey did not, in fact, surrender until 1550, and we obtain a more correct estimate of its possessions from later grants of its properties and from four paper copies of inquisitions taken in 1550 and 1551, comprising in all eighteen sheets, part of the Ormond Deeds, now lodged in the National Library of Ireland. A note of the rents of this abbey preserved in the same collection and dated May 1535 gives additional information. For Abbeyshrule, too, we must rely on grants made of the property at a later date as well as on inquisitions taken at various times. The Abbeylara extent published in White's *Extents of Irish Monastic Possessions* is also very meagre, and not until we consult the grant made by Queen Elizabeth I to Sir Richard Nugent of the monastic possessions of this house do we get any real details of their extent.

For all the foregoing abbeys, as well as for others not dissolved until a later period, Mervyn Archdall supplies details in his *Monasticon Hibernicum*. Archdall, who wrote in the eighteenth century, seems to have copied from the originals, then extant, in the office of the auditor-general and chief remembrancer, and the details supplied by him are of great assistance in filling the gaps in Dr White's volume on the monastic extents. The Public Record Office, Dublin [National Archives] contains a number of transcripts and calendars of chancery and exchequer inquisitions made by the Record Commissioners (1810-30). These inquisitions, particularly the exchequer ones, afford quite an amount of information concerning monastic land and cover every county in Ireland. The transcripts of the exchequer inquisitions have never been published but they may be consulted at the Public Record Office, and are far more informative and helpful concerning the extent of the monastic possessions at the time of the dissolution of the monasteries than are the chancery inquisitions. Two volumes of the latter have been published – those, namely, for Ulster and Leinster. Those for Munster and Connacht were never printed and all the originals perished in the destruction of the Four Courts during the Civil War of 1922. However, two sets of manuscript calendars are in existence, one in the PRO, Dublin [National Archives] and the other in the Royal Irish Academy and may be consulted by the student. There is, therefore, no dearth of material for the study of the possessions of the Irish Cistercians at the period of the dissolution of the monasteries in Ireland. The *Patent Rolls* have already been mentioned. It should be pointed out here that although the printed Calendars of Patent Rolls of Henry VIII, Edward VI, Philip and Mary, Elizabeth I and Charles I are more notable for what they omit than for what they contain; nevertheless, in view of the fact that the originals have for the most part utterly perished, they do provide us with a certain amount of information otherwise unobtainable. One set of patent rolls deserve special mention, those of James I, contain a mass of information relating to the dissolved abbeys and includes abbeys which were not actually dissolved until the conquest and the plantation of Ulster in the early seventeenth century. They embody numerous inquisitions of monastic property and the grants themselves include detailed lists of lands under a variety of names and spellings with an alias in cases where a particular parcel of land had more than one name at any one time or at various times. Although the originals have perished in the flames of Civil War a *Calendar of the Patent Rolls of James I* had been published before their destruction, and this calendar, though not at all perfect, is a veritable mine of information for the purpose of our study.

Substitutes of various kinds for original records destroyed in 1922 or earlier may be found in abundance and include the *Ferguson Collection* of transcripts of old exchequer records in the Public Record Office of Ireland, the *Lodge Collection* of transcripts mainly from Patent Rolls in the PRO and the *Record Commissioners' Transcripts* which include the inquisitions already mentioned as well as transcripts and calendars of ancient records from the time of Henry III onwards, especially patent rolls, plea rolls and memoranda rolls, all of which merit serious investigation. A certain number of the original Crown Patents, which had been preserved in private hands for centuries, and include grants of monastic lands, has come with other material into the possession of the Irish Land Commission. Many of these patents are now lodged in the PRO [National Archives], while others remain in the Records Branch of the Land Commission. The Records Branch of that Department contains a great mass of material including rentals, mortgages, fee farm and other grants, abstracts of title, leases, and various other deeds and papers relating to estates which originated in grants made by the Crown of the lands of dissolved religious houses. The patent rolls in particular give the names of the grantees who acquired possession of these land together with the conditions on which they received their grants, the term of years for which they held the lands of the Crown and the rents they paid to the Crown therefor. Most of the grantees continued to hold the lands thus acquired until the middle of the seventeenth century. At that period those of them who were Catholics lost their lands which, under the Cromwellian and Restoration 'settlements' passed into English Protestant hands. The documents connected with the Commonwealth, Restoration and Williamite governments during the period 1641–1703 are, therefore, of prime importance in tracing the subsequent history of many of the former monastic lands. They are also important – and indeed indispensable – for the satisfactory identification of the medieval lands and their equation with the denominations of the Cromwellian and post-Cromwellian eras as depicted on the *Down Survey* maps of the seventeenth century and the ordnance survey maps of modern times. Indeed the importance of the Cromwellian and post-Cromwellian material can scarcely be overestimated. Although much has been lost much still remains. This last includes what is left of the *Strafford Survey* of 1636, the *Civil Survey* of 1654, the *Down Survey* of 1655 and the fine series of records known as the *Books of Survey and Distribution* which in their original form must have been compiled during the period 1562-1588, and to which were added particulars relating to the forfeited estates of 1688 and the sales of the forfeited lands in 1703. The Books of Survey and Distribution comprise in all twenty volumes, cover every county in Ireland and are based on the various surveys already mentioned as well as on a great number of official records of various kinds. Every parcel of land set forth therein bears a particular number which corresponds to a number attached to the same denomination on the map of the Down Survey so that by comparisson of one with the other we can determine exactly on the map what parcel of land belonged to a particular proprietor the number of acres of land contained therein, the name of the original 'Irish Papist' proprietor who held the land in 1641 as well as that of the new Cromwellian or Williamite grantee who supplanted him and various other details which need not be mentioned here.

The Civil Survey of 1654, in which the Books of Survey and Distribution as well as the Down Survey are in part based, gives us not only the names of the proprietors of 1641 with their qualifications ('Irish Papist' or 'English Protestant'), but indicates also the titles by which they held their lands, whether by descent from their ancestors, by patent from the Crown, or by purchase. These particulars can often be extremely useful in affording a clue as to whether any particular parcel of land is confiscated monastic land or not. This can be illustrated by one example out of many: in volume 1 of the Civil Survey we find on page 64 particulars relating to the parish of Holycross in Co. Tipperary. 'The tythes of this parish', we are informed, 'are an intire rectory and impropriat conferred many yeares past upon the earle of Ormonds Ancestors by pattent from the Crowne'. In all but one of the denominations named as part of this parish from page 64 to page 66 the earl is said to be the inheritor of the said lands by patent from the Crown or by patent from the Crown conferred on his ancestors by way of descent. The one exception to this is the denomination of 'Beakstowne and Ballycormock'. Here, then, is a clear case for investigation. Fortunately, we have not far to go to find the patent which is preserved among the Ormond Deeds. It is dated 3 October 1563 and

bears the great seal of Ireland. This patent grants to Thomas Butler, earl
of Ormond, the site, ambit and precinct of the late monastery of the Holy
Cross in Co. Tipperary, the lands of the said monastery in Holy Cross and
elsewhere, and the rectories, churches or chapels of Holy Cross, Ballycahill
and Templebeg with all their tithes, oblations, altarages and obventions,
pertaining to the said rectories, churches or chapels. On page 66 of the
same volume of the Civil Survey the proprietor of 'Beakstowne and
Ballycormock' is stated to be Theobald Purcell who held the lands in fee
'by descent from his Ancestors as we are informed.' And rightly were the
Commissioners so informed; for the medieval *Red Book of Ormond* shows
that these lands were held by the Purcell family *in capite* of Edmund Butler
as far back as 1328. The tithes of the denomination of 'Beakstowne and
Ballycormock' were not held. The Civil Survey is our evidence for the fact
that these tithes, great and small, belonged in 1540 to the impropriate rectory of Holy Cross of which the earl of Ormond was proprietor, 'conferred
upon him by his ancestors by patent from the Crown.' How the said tithes
came to belong to Holy Cross abbey in the first instance may be read in Dr
Newport White's volume of *Irish Monastic and Episcopal Deeds* (pp 22-3)
which calendars two deeds relating to the appropriation to Holy Cross
abbey by Richard (Ó hEidighenin), archbishop of Cashel in the year 1430.

For the purpose of this study use was made of composite maps of Cos.
Tipperary and Carlow which were the only two composite maps available
at that time. These maps were drawn for the Irish Manuscripts Commission by Mr Robert Johnston under the direction of Dr Robert C.
Simington, the learned editor of the Civil Survey and of such of the Book
of Survey and Distribution as have been published. These maps, representing the superimposition of the Down Survey on the original ordnance
survey maps of 1839-43, show the respective boundaries of territorial units
and contrast old and new place names. Without the help of such composite maps or, failing that, a comprehensive study of the Down Survey, the
Civil Survey, the Books of Survey and Distribution and the Ordnance
Survey, this appendix could never have been written. For the purpose of
this study all the sources mentioned above had to be used and the boundaries of the Down Survey maps had to be plotted on the Ordnance Survey
maps in the case of areas not contained in the counties of Carlow and
Tipperary. For those two counties, of course, the composite maps already
referred to were available so that the labour involved was much less and
the time saved was considerable. The Down Survey, carried out under the
direction of Sir William Petty, was so called because the lands were plotted
or laid down on paper by admeasurement. The Strafford Survey which
preceded both the Civil Survey and the Down Survey was also based on the
actual admeasurement of the lands surveyed but was by no means as precise as the Down Survey, and only a few fragments now survive of the maps

so plotted. Petty's survey was a very thorough one and was carried out in what was for those days a very scientific manner so that Petty has been called with some justice 'he world's first exact geographer'. The Civil Survey, on the other hand, was based on estimates and was essentially a descriptive survey. It was based on the sworn testimony of the native inhabitants of the areas surveyed, mostly the landowners of 1641 who were formed into juries for that purpose. It recorded not only the tenures, Gaelic as well as Norman, by which the lands were held, but gave detailed descriptions of the lands as well as an account of their amenities, and it rendered phonetically into the English of the period a great wealth of place names. Since it is unlikely that the boundaries of denominations noted in the monastic extents of the sixteenth century had undergone any significant change before 1641, it is probably safe to say that in most cases the boundaries noted in the Civil Survey and shown also on the Down Survey maps which, of course, can be plotted on the modern ordnance map with reasonable accuracy, represent the boundaries of the same denominations as they existed at the time of the dissolution of the religious houses. In this way it has been possible to ascertain with reasonable certainty the bounds of many if not most of the monastic lands.

At the end of the middle ages, then, there were in Ireland thirty-three houses of Cistercian monks. There had at one time been other houses in existence which had either died out or had been suppressed by the general chapter and/or reduced to the status of granges. There had been at least two houses of nuns, neither of which seems to have survived until the dissolution of the monasteries. It would appear from references in the *Register of Stephen of Lexington,* abbot of Stanley and later abbot in turn of Savigny and Clairvaux, that there had been numerous houses of nuns, or perhaps houses in which monks and nuns formed a joint community, in the early decades of the thirteenth century; but these houses had given rise to such abuses and scandals that the abbots were absolutely forbidden to receive any more nuns, while the nuns already established in or near houses of monks were banished to more distant locations. The thirty-three houses of men were distributed over the four provinces, the great majority being in Leinster and Munster. On the eve of the dissolution there were Cistercian monasteries in twenty out of thirty-two counties and in twenty-two out of twenty-six dioceses. Many of these abbeys had lands in more than one county so that the landed possessions of the order in Ireland were more extensive than the distribution of the abbeys would suggest They extended in fact to twenty-eight of the thirty-two counties and comprised, at a moderate estimate, almost half a million acres of land.

Of the thirty-three abbeys which existed at the end of the middle ages thirteen were located in Leinster, twelve in Munster, six in Ulster and two in Connacht. Every county in Leinster, but two, had a least one Cistercian abbey. Cos. Kilkenny, Longford and Wexford had two each, while only Cos. Carlow and Offaly had none. The lands belonging to those abbeys, on the other hand, were distributed over eleven of the twelve counties of that province, the county of Offaly being the only county in the whole province which had beither abbey nor land belonging to the order.

In Munster five out of the six counties had Cistercian abbeys. Tipperary and Cork had four each, Limerick had two, and Clare and Kerry had one each. Waterford had no abbey. There had been one there in the early part of the thirteenth century which had been suppressed in the year 1228 by the general chapter. The lands belonging to the suppressed abbey remained in the possession of the Order which also held lands in the north of the county adjoining Tipperary. All these lands in Co. Waterford, with the exception of a small parcel containing about forty-eight acres, amounted in 1539 to approximately 5,000 acres and formed part of the possessions of the abbey of Inishlounaght in Co. Tipperary. The forty-eight acres forming the exception were the remnants of a more extensive estate held by Dunbrody abbey, Co. Wexford, at an earlier period.

In Ulster there were six abbeys, four of which were located in Co. Down and one each in Cos. Derry and Donegal. The landed possessions of these six abbeys extended beyond the boundaries of the counties just mentioned and included lands in Armagh, Antrim and Fermanagh.

Although there were only two Cistercian abbeys in Connacht their lands were very extensice and were distributed over the whole province. One of the reasons for this would appear to have been the inclusion of many monastic estates belonging to pre-Cistercian Irish communities, some of which had died out before the coming of the Cistercians to Ireland. There is good reason to believe that much of the land granted by Cathal Crobhdhearg, king of Connaght, to the abbey of Knockmoy in Co. Galway was former monastic land; and indeed there is some evidence that similar grants had been made by other provincial kings of kings of Tuatha in various parts of Ireland. I may mention in this connection that among the monasteries which received land of this kind were, besides Knockmoy, those of Baltinglass, Jerpoint, Monasterevan and Kilbeggan in Leinster; Holy Cross, Kilcooly, Owney, and Inishlounaght in Munster; Comber, Assaroe, Macosquin and Inch in Ulster; and Boyle and Knockmoy in Connacht. Besides the lands held by the two last-named abbeys in Connacht, one of the Munster houses (Corcumroe, Co. Clare) and the important abbey of St Mary's, outside Dublin, also held lands there, the combined acreage of the lands held by Dublin and Corcumroe amounting to close on 3,800 acres.

The distribution of Cistercian lands in Ireland at the dissolution of the monasteries province by province and county by county is as follows:

In the province of Leinster the total land held by Cistercians amounted to 199,541 acres, distributed as follows:

Co. Carlow	7,167 acres	Co. Louth	23,360 acres
Co. Dublin	17,079 acres	Co. Meath	25,759 acres
Co. Kildare	16,284 acres	Co. Westmeath	7,902 acres
Co. Kilkenny	32,710 acres	Co. Wexford	30,758 acres
Co. Laois	11,056 acres	Co. Wicklow	14,383 acres
Co. Longford	8,093 acres		

In the province of Munster the total landed possessions of the Order amounted to 103,528 statute acres, distributed as follows:

Co. Clare	5,387 acres	Co. Limerick	40,336 acres
Co. Cork	20,524 acres	Co. Tipperary	28,438 acres
Co. Kerry	3,583 acres	Co. Waterford	5,170 acres

In the province of Ulster the total lands held by the Irish Cistercians amounted to 60,538 statutes acres, distributed as follows:

Co. Antrim	1,018 acres	Co. Donegal	18,195 acres
Co. Armagh	6,208 acres	Co. Down	32,992 acres
Co. Derry	1,801 acres	Co. Fermanagh	324 acres

Finally, in the province of Connaght the landed possessions of the Order amounted to 63,050 statute acres and were distributed as follows:

Co. Galway	37,727 acres	Co. Leitrim	796 acres
Co. Mayo	780 acres	Co. Roscommon	14,003 acres
Co. Sligo	10,524 acres		

This gives a grand total for the whole of Ireland of 427,447 statute acres. We have not got full details of some of the possessions and further research may reveal that the above figure is an underestimation. It should also be mentioned that in this paper account has not been taken of certain lands, admittedly not very extensive, held by some English Cistercian houses in Ireland. It should also be pointed out that the figures given in this work relate exclusively to the lands actually held by the Irish Cistercians at the time the monasteries were dissolved. All the available evidence goes to show that much of the monastic properties had been reduced by dilapidation and alienation between the thirteenth and the sixteenth centuries, and in the fifteenth century in particular. That the monastic estates as a whole underwent a great development in the twelfth and thirteenth centuries is shown by the available evidence. The ravages of war and pestilence, however, had their effect on the Order and led in many cases to the breakdown of discipline and the wasting of the temporal possessions. In the course of time much land was alienated and Mellifont itself was brought to the verge of ruin in the fifteenth century not only by reason of the great extortions practised by the nobility who oppressed the tenants and vassals of the abbot and convent and did not scruple to invade, unjustly occupy, depopulate, devastate and lay waste the lands and possessions of the community, but also by reason of the conduct of some of the abbots themselves who made grants of fees, annuities, rent charges, leases and offices to various people including their friends and relations for half their value and sometimes, indeed, for nothing. Many of the houses were in straitened circumstances in consequence of such dilapidation of monastic property. Nevertheless, as the figures given show, the amount of land held by the Order in Ireland on the eve of the dissolution was still considerable. The dissolution of the monasteries marked the end of an apoch. The fallen abbeys with their vast landed possessions eventually found their way into the hands of the king's favourites. Many of the leading Irish Catholic families, Gaelic as well as Norman, shared in the monastic spoils; but ill-gotten gains have a way of disappearing and most of the families thus enriched by the plunder of the monasteries lost not only the abbey lands but, with them – their own hereditary possessions in the great confiscation of the following century.

IRISH CISTERCIAN ARCHITECTURE

The English monastic historian Dom David Knowles has pointed out that 'the Cistercians, as planners, had two great advantages over their predecessors: they had a detailed code of observance, to which all were bound under penalties to conform; and they could set out their monastery upon a virgin site'. He also pointed out that the transference of an abbey in its early years from one site to another is extremely frequent. Boyle is a good example of this in Ireland. Knowles goes on to remark: 'Sometimes this transference took place almost at once; elsewhere after two or three, or even after ten or twenty years. Sometimes the new site was less than a mile from the old sometimes one or five or twenty miles separated them.'

Knowles explains how their sites were chosen.

> From a study of a number of Cistercian sites and ruins it is possible to ascertain what the planners sought. One rule was almost universal, one commodity was essential, and one circumstance decisive. The church stood upon the highest point of the site, a fairsized

stream of water was needed for drainage and power, and the drainage must be available at particular points of the monastic buildings. In addition, a sheltered site was desirable. The ideal terrain was therefore a level space of land, sloping almost imperceptibly from north to south towards a stream forming its southern limit or, failing a stream, facilities for leading over the site an artificial current of water. When the abbey (as at Tintern and Buildwas) could not easily be placed to the north of the stream the planners did not hesitate to set the cloister to the north of the church, while in exceptional cases they were prepared, as at Rievaulx, to swing the church and the whole complex out of the traditional orientation in order to get water for their drains. The Cistercians indeed, were almost from the beginning skilled water engineers. In addition to the network of channels and drains of running water that flowed beneath all the offices of the monastery, pure spring water was piped to the house, sometimes from a distance of a mile or more, and distributed throughout the buildings with a complexity and lavishness rarely if ever exceeded by even the wealthiest abbeys of black monks.

The Cistercian monastery in Ireland followed the general plan of Cistercian monasteries everywhere. Ruins of some of these monasteries may still be seen in many parts of Ireland. It should be noted that the introduction of the continental type of monastic building into Ireland was a revolutionary event which was received with mixed feelings. Many of the early Cistercians in Ireland were disciples of St Malachy who had himself been reared in the Irish monastic tradition which differed in many important respects from that of Citeaux. The Irish monasteries of the native tradition were for the most part composed of detached cells or huts grouped round a church or oratory. The huts themselves were normally built of clay and wattle but in districts where stone abounded and where wood was scarce the huts were round beehive-shaped cells of stone as may still be seen on Sceilg Mhichil and in some other places. This characteristic Irish style formed a stark contrast to the massive stone buildings of the Cistercians and was regarded with disdain by the French monks who came to Ireland with the first Irish Cistercians. There was a clash of two traditions and this may have been one of the causes leading to the withdrawl from Mellifont while the abbey was still in course of construction of the architect Robert and some other French monks. That in many places the Irish continue to cling to their own tradition is certain. Even as late as 1228, Abbot Stephen of Lexington noted that the Irish monks had abandoned the fine stone monasteries and taken to living in groups of three of four in little huts outside the abbey walls. These wretched huts may well have scandalised Stephen; but to many of the native Irish the stone monasteries of the Cistercians must have seemed more like splendid mansions than the dwelling places of men dedicated to a life of humble poverty.

Some monasteries were built and ready for completion in quite a short time. Others took many years to complete. Mellifont, founded in 1142, was the scene of a great synod in 1151 and its church was consecrated in 1157. Boyle, on the other hand, after some changes of site, was finally located in 1161 on the river whose name it bears. Yet the abbey church of Boyle was not consecrated until almost sixty years later, to be exact, in the year 1220. It took many years to build a monastery; it took but a few hours to destroy it by fire which was the fate reserved for more than one Cistercian houses including Dublin, Mellifont, Assaroe, Abbeyshrule and, in part at least, Boyle.

All Cistercian monasteries were built according to a uniform plan, and whereever that plan was departed from it was either owing to the fact that local circumstances made it impossible or impracticable to adopt the traditional arrangement or that the monasteries in question were built before their communities had adopted the Cistercian reform. Thus in Ireland Hore abbey is an exception to the usual plan since it has its church on the south instead of on the north side of the quadrangle. A modern example of the same type of departure from the traditional Cistercian arrangement is Mount Melleray abbey. In the case of Hore abbey the divergence from the Cistercian plan is generally explained by the fact that Hore was at first a Benedictine foundation and only later adopted the Cistercian observance. In the case of Mount Melleray the nature of the site made it impossible to follow the Cistercian usage and so we find the church on the wrong side. Mount St Joseph abbey, near Roscrea, shows the typical Cistercian plan in full use in modern times.

Though the normal Cistercian plan envisages the church on the north side, it would not be correct to say that there are no examples of medieval Cistercian abbeys to be found having the church on the south side. As a matter of fact there was a large group of English monasteries in which the church was invariably situated on the south side of the quadrangle. Most of these abbeys, however, were originally of Savignian foundation, and as the Congregation of Savigny did not unite with the Cistercian Order until 1147, such churches cannot be considered typically Cistercian. Even when they conform in architectural style to the Cistercian ideal they still do not represent the traditional Cistercian plan which was accustomed to place the church on the north side.

In Ireland all the medieval Cistercian monasteries with the exception of Hore abbey (and possibly the original abbey of St Mary's near Dublin) were planned on traditional lines, so that, allowing for some minor deviations from this plan, we may study them all by studying one. Naturally enough the fact that all the abbeys, with the exceptions noted, follow the same general plan does not prevent them from differing in various particulars of architectural detail, and most, if not all, of the Irish Cistercian churches have been influenced to some extent by the native Irish tradition, this influence being noticable to a greater or lesser degree. Here again Mellifont may be reckoned an exception, but this is explained by the fact that Mellifont abbey was the first of the Irish Cistercian houses to be built, and that it was built under the personal supervision of the French architect sent over by St Bernard, and was, moreover, modelled on the contemporary abbey of Clairvaux, the details of which it was intended to reproduce. As Christopher Brooke has stated, 'The Cistercians achieved a unique degree of uniformity, partly by the centralised organisation of their order, partly by their deliberate efforts in this direction; partly, no doubt, by recruiting expert masons among their early lay brothers.'

The monastery was constructed in the form of a quadrangle round an open space, the church being on the north side. Opening on this central space was the cloister, an arcaded gallery with a lean-to roof communicating with the different parts of the monastery. The northern walk of the cloister, which generally extended the length of the nave of the church as far as the southern transept, was provided with benches for reading and was called the reading cloister. Here the brethern assembled each evening before compline to listen to the public reading over which the abbot presided, and here during Lent the regular reading was performed according to the Rule of St Benedict. The eastern walk of the cloister extended southwards from the angle of the nave and the southern transept along the entire length of the east range of buildings. Nearest to the church was the sacristy, then came the library, the chapter house, the parlour where the monks engaged in necessary conversation with their superiors, and the *scriptorium* or community room. The monks' dormitory was generally located on the second floor over the chapter house and was connected directly with the church by a staircase known as the night stairs since it was used by the monks for the purpose of coming from the dormitory to the church for the night office.

Turning west at the end of the eastern cloister one found oneself in the southern cloister which ran alongside the south range of the monastic buildings. This range contained the calefactory or warming room at its eastern end, the refectory or dining hall of the monks, generally known as the *Frater*, in the centre, and the kitchen at the western end. Opposite the door of the refectory was located the *Lavabo* which opened out of the cloister. A fine example is still partially preserved at Mellifont. Here was the washing fountain at which the brethren performed their ablutions and washed their hands before entering the refectory for meals. The west range of the monastery extended from the church on the north to the kitchen on the south, or even beyond the kitchen. This range included the *Domus Conversorum* or lay brothers' quarters with the various storerooms and the cellarer's room; and a corridor reserved for the use of the lay brethern, called the corridor of the lay brethren, was to be found in many Cistercian abbeys running parallel to the western cloister, between it and the west range of buildings. The dining hall of the lay brethren was located in the *Domus Conversorum* while their dormitory was overhead. Lay visitators were not allowed into Cistercian churches and the naves were dedicated to the lay brothers. It is believed that the lay brothers could not normally see the high altar. A chapel for the use of externs was sometimes erected outside the enclosure. Sometimes a second quadrangle contained additional buildings such as the novitiate and the infirmary, as well as the various workshops; but more often than not these were built somewhat apart from the monastery, as was the guest-house.

Dom Knowles has pointed out that

> The Cistercians, like the black monks, were accorded certain dispensations from the meatless diet of the Rule by the Cistercian pope, Benedict XII, in 1336. Unlike the black monks, however, the Cistercians had no tradition of previous semi-official relaxations, and therefore had no room in existence to serve as a meat-eating refectory. They accordingly constructed a *misericord*, usually a square room of moderate size, near the infirmary, whither service could come from the infirmary kitchen.

He also outlined the evolution of the infirmary:

> The infirmary seems often to have been the last essential part of the complex to be given permanent form. The founding monks were presumably as a rule young and vigorous; early Cistercian traditions had little respect for the physician, and it was long before the elderly monks retired to the infirmary for their declining years as did their black brethren. Even when built, the first infirmaries were often of wood and were not replaced by stone erections for thirty or forty years; the twelfth-century infirmary hall resembled that of the black monks in being a building of three aisles, its roof supported by two rows of posts or columns, and containing a fireplace. This was often rebuilt *c*.1300 on a larger scale, with an adjacent chapel and a second fireplace. The next stage was for the aisles to receive partitions and become a row of cubicles. Finally, in the early part of the fifteenth century at latest, the hall was broken up internally into rows of private chambers in two storeys, often each having its own fire. The Cistercian infirmary rarely developed into a cloister,

but of all the components of the white monks plan this shows the lease fixity in its sitting.

Most medieval monasteries contained a special and distinct group of buildings set apart for the use of the abbot and known as the abbot's chambers, these buildings being often connected with the guest-house. Dom Knowles also outlines the evolution of the abbot's lodging

> The second member of the complex to show constant evolution was the abbot's lodging. The constitutions prescribed that the abbot should sleep in the dorter, and in early days he certainly did so. The first move was to a small sleeping chamber at the northern or transept end of the room; this was abandoned, in the second hald of the twelfth century, for a larger room, adequate for use in inter-viewing as well as for sleep, on the east side of the dorter near its southern end. This, as opening upon the dorter or rere-dorter, might be held still to fulfil the letter of the law. The accomodation in this position developed rapidly.

There were, in addition to the buildings here described, the mill and the farm buildings. In early Cistercian churches towers were not allowed, but in later times they were added, and large and massive central towers became a distinguishing feature of Cistercian architecture. In medieval times the unsettled state of the country led to the building of strong towers, suitable for defensive purposes and often surmounted with battle-ments, for many of the monastic buildings were constructed to withstand the attacks of marauding armies. In spite of the fact that the middle ages are sometimes called the Ages of Faith, scant respect was shown to the churches and monasteries in those disturbed times, and we read often enough of the sacking or burning of an abbey after its capture by one or other of the many armies which were continually marching through the land.

The first permanent monasteries of the Cistercian Order were built for the most part between the second and fourth decades of the twelfth cen-tury, those which existed before that period being generally only tempo-rary structures of wood or rough stones. This first outburst of building activity on the part of the Cistercians coincided with the change-over from the massive barrel-vaulted, rounded-arch, so-called Norman type of archi-tecture, to the lighter ribbed-vaulted, pointed arch, Gothic style. Many of the Cistercian churches were of great size, this being necessary owing to the very large communities housed by the greater abbeys, but all were noted for their extreme simplicity of design and absence or ornament; and the harmony of their proportions as well as the gravity and austerity of the style combined to produce churches or surpassing beauty which inspired what amounted to a revolution in architecture and led ultimately to the abandonment of the Romanesque in favour of the Gothic throughout Western Europe.

There are two types of Cistercian churches to be seen in Ireland, one aisled, the other aisleless. In some cases an original aisled church had the aisles removed at a later period. Thus in Jerpoint the south aisle seems to have been removed 'and the space thrown into the cloister' about the fifteenth century. The abbey church was divided according to Cistercian custom into four distinct sections. First, at the east end of the church came what was known as the presbytery; this was the chancel where was situated the principal altar of the church, the floor being raised at least one step above the level of the rest of the church. The tower sprang from the junction of the nave and transepts, resting on four massive piers, and was generally strong and squat. West of the chancel arch was the choir of the monks and behind this was the retro-choir or choir of the sick. Behind this again was the choir of the lay brethren. These various divisions were usually partitioned off one from the other by screens of stone or wood, reaching in some cases to the roof and provided with a doorway in the centre. Behind the stone screen which separated the lay brothers' choir from the choir of the sick were usually placed two altars, one at either side of the central doorway. The foundations of this screen with the space for the two altars may still be seen at Jerpoint, while the screen itself still exists in Holy Cross.

In some of the Cistercian churches the *sedilia* were stone and usually very ornate, while in others they were probably of wood. In speaking of *sedilia* we must distinguish those in the presbytery from those in the choir. The *sedilia* in the presbytery had three stalls for the use of the celebrant, deacon and subdeacon at high mass. They were situated on the epistle side of the altar, between the altar and the chancel arch, and were often very beautiful. The most magnificent example remaining is that at Holy Cross of which an eminent authority has said that 'the workmanship is particularly good and the whole design perhaps the finest of its kind in Ireland'. The *sedilia* in the choir were the stalls of the abbot and prior, the former on the south, the latter on the north side of the choir. The remains of two exquisitely carved *sedilia* are to be seen in Kilcooly, that of the abbot being the more elaborate.

Most of the Irish Cistercian churches were rebuilt at a later period so that many of them contain examples of work ranging from the twelfth to the fifteenth and even to the sixteenth centuries. The oldest of the Irish Cistercian monasteries was certainly Mellifont, but until recently there was little to be seen of the remains of this historic abbey beyond the mere foundations of the church (very little of which belonged to the original

twelfth century structure), the thirteenth-century *Lavabo* and the beautiful fourteenth century chapter house. The excavations which commenced
in 1953 have brought to light not only the foundations of the original
twelfth century church but an entire crypt of the same date extending
under the western end of that church. The foundations of the twelfth century cloister have also been uncovered as well as portions of the (fallen)
cloister arcade. These are by far the oldest specimens of such work extant
in this country. Like most of the other Irish Cistercian churches that of
Mellifont underwent large scale reconstruction in the thirteenth, fourteenth and fifteenth centuries. Indeed it may be said to have been entirely
rebuilt in the thirteenth century following on what appears to have been
a disastrous fire, the cause of which is at present unknown. The available
evidence goes to show that this fire occured midway in the thirteenth century and that the church was rebuilt on the old foundations though the
chancel was extended and the transepts widened and extended at the
same time. The glorious *Lavabo*, part of which still remains, probably dates
from this period and is said to be 'the only example of such a building surviving in situ in the British Islands'.

Though Bective abbey also belongs to the twelfth century no remains
of the original buildings are extant. The earliest surviving buildings of this
monastery seem to date from the late twelfth or early thirteenth century.
Baltinglass, another early foundation, seems to have likewise undergone
reconstruction at a later period. Though founded within six years of the
coming of the Cistercians to Ireland the remains of the nave date only
from the late twelfth century. Among other interesting features brought to
light during excavations made in 1931 were some Irish Romanesque bases
to transept piers.

Perhaps the finest Cistercian monastery of medieval times which
remains to us is Holy Cross abbey. The whole eastern section of this abbey
is comparatively new, being the result of extensive reconstruction work
undertaken in the late fourteenth and early fifteenth centuries, and it has
been well described as the most complete and perfect example extant in
Ireland of the work of the period. In most of the rebuilding which took
place at this period the more austere and plain lancet windows of the earlier Cistercian churches gave way to decorated or flamboyant Gothic, while
this period also saw the introduction of the massive towers and the tesse-
lated pavements, the tiles for which, it would appear, were manufactured
at Mellifont.

We have ample evidence, for instance, that many monasteries underwent extensive repairs, some being practically rebuilt during the fifteenth
century. Dr Leask who spent the best part of a lifetime studying the ruins
of our old abbeys tells us that architectural evidence suggests that in the
repair or reconstruction of monasteries in the fifteenth century the space

allotted to the living quarters was reduced. Moreover, in most of the remaining monasteries the west range of buildings which traditionally housed the lay brothers has disappeared. There are various explanations for this, one possible explanation being that since this range contained the living quarters of the conversi it was no longer needed and hence was pulled down. References in the papal registers to the dilapidated state of some monasteries, the buildings and offices of which are said to be in danger of falling down, suggest that with the disappearance of the conversi the buildings were allowed to fall into disuse and gradually deteriorated. On the other hand it is clear that in a few monasteries (Dr Leask instances Dunbrody and Inch) there never was a west range at all. At Holy Cross the west range was rebuilt in the fifteenth century but the dormitory of the *conversi* was divided into rooms during the rebuilding. In many of the reconstructed monasteries the chapter house is of small dimensions and there is at least one case (Bective) in which part of the church buildings was converted into dwelling apartments. All this goes to show that the size of the community in the Cistercian monastery had decreased by the fifteenth century and the picture presented to us is, as Dr Leask has well remarked, one of 'small numbers of monks living in greater comfort but occupying only parts of the extensive buildings'.

An interesting innovation in the reconstructed monasteries of the fifteenth century is the bell-tower. Although a very few monasteries seem to have had small towers from the beginning, the great majority had not, and all the towers now existing date from the fifteenth century. These towers were not always added simply to make churches more imposing. No doubt in some cases they were; but in an Ireland ravaged by war They served not only as belfries but also as strongholds to which the abbot and convent could repair if the monastery was attacked, and we know from Abbot Troy's report that they were sometimes used as vantage points from which to rain showers of missiles on unwelcome visitators and reformators. They were also sometimes used by outsiders as we learn from the records of the abbey of Duiske in which we read that a certain Richard O'Nolan was besieged in the bell-tower and was eventually overcome and compelled to surrender his son as a hostage.

Set somewhat apart from the main monastic buildings and in close proximity to the gate-house would have been the guest-house of the monastery. In later years, when the abbot had become an important personage in public life and was to a great extent separated from the community he had his own separate quarters near the guest-house where he dwelt with his servants. What is thought by some to have been the guesthouse at Holy Cross lies to the south-east of the main block of buildings, close to the river Suir. It is connected with the main buildings by a narrow wing attached to which is a small two-storey building which Dr Leask thinks may have been the abbot's quarters. This residence, though small, is well supplied with fireplaces and must, when roofed, have been a rather cosy dwelling place. It was the Cistercian tradition, following the Rule of St Benedict, that hospitality should be shown to all, without distinction, for Christ was to be received in the guest and especially in the poor. The Irish Cistercian monastery contained a special hospital for the sick poor to which reference is made more than once in the Register of Stephen of Lexington. Stephen evidently attached great importance to the care of the sick poor and threatened with severe penalties, the cellarer and subcellarer if they neglected to see that this hospital was well supplied with clean linen and whatever was needed for the care of the sick. There are interesting references in the Irish annals to people of distinction who 'went on pilgrimage' to Cistercian houses and ended their days there. Two of the most notable were women, the most well-known, perhaps 'notorious' would be a better word, being Derbhorgaill, daughter of Maelseachlainn, king of Meath, and wife of Tighearnan Ó Ruairc, king of Breifne. We are told that she went on pilgrimage to Droicheat Atha (meaning Mellifont) in 1186 and died 'on pilgrimage in the monastery of Droicheat Atha' in 1193. This implies that she lived at Mellifont for seven years until her death in 1193. Tradition has it that she was buried in the monastery and there is no reason for rejecting this tradition. Was there, them, a house for women pilgrims at Mellifont in the early years? From a certain reference in the Register of Stephen of Lexington, Fr Aubrey Gwynn SJ infers that there was a house of nuns attached to the abbey of Mellifont in 1228. I do not myself think tha the reference in the register to the abbot's house in the court of the nuns necessarily bears the meaning attributed to it by Fr Gwynn. However, we have definite evidence in the same register that grave scandals had arisen from the custom of receiving nuns into the Irish houses and that in at least two cases the nuns were not merely lodged near the monastery but formed part of the community living under the same roof as the monks but, no doubt, in a different part of the building separated from the monks, the whole complex of buildings forming in effect what might be considered a 'double-monastery' of men and women more or less modelled on the arrangement favoured by the Gilbertines, or on the older Irish tradition deriving from the famous Brigidine foundation at Kildare. The whole question of the relations of monks and nuns in these Cistercian houses deserves to be looked into and it is to be hoped that someone will tackle the problem some day.

There are many other matters one would like to consider. Where was the abbot's prison situated, for instance? Where did the monks have their recreation? We know that in Duiske there was a special place set aside within the precinct for the pastime of archery and that on one occasion a four-year-old boy was killed by one of the monks when he ran into the place where the monks were shooting their arrows at the target. It might also be asked what a four year old boy was doing in the monastery and who he was? What other games (if any) were played by the monks? Did the monks of Duiske play marbles, for instance? There is evidence that some of the Benedictines in England indulged in that game. Almost certainly the monks did not play hurling, for while the practice of archery is not only permitted but recommended to the king's faithful subjects in the houses of the Pale there was a stern prohibition against what is described as 'hurling with great sticks' and other Irish games for playing which one might be imprisoned, forfeit all his lands (if he had any lands to forfeit) and even incur excommunication!

ARCHBISHOPS OF CASHEL (PRE-REFORMATION)

Mael Isa Ua hAinmire fl. 1111.
Mael Iosa Ua Fogluda d. 1131.
Domnall Ua Conaing d. 1137.
Domnall Ua Lonngargain d. 1158.
Domnall Ua hUallachain d. 1182.
Muirges Ua hEnna d. 1206.
Donnchad Ua Lonngargain I d. 1216
Donnchad Ua Lonngargain II d. 1232.
Mariin Ó Briain d. 1238.
David mac Cellaig O Gilla Patraic d. 1253.
David Mac Cerbaill d. 1289.
Stiamna Ó Bracain d. 1302.
Mauricius Mac Cerbaill d. 1316.
William Fitzjohn d. 1326.
Seoan Mac Cerbaill d. 1329.
Walter le Rede d. 1331.
Eoin Ó Grada d. 1345.
Radulphus Ó Ceallaigh d. 1361.
George Roche d. 1362.
Tomas Mac Cearbhaill d. 1372.
Philip of Torrington d. 1380.
Peter Hackett d. 1406.
Risdeard Ó hEidigheain d. 1440.
John Cantwell I d. 1451/2.
John Cantwell II d. 1482
David Creagh d. 1503.
Maurice Fitzgerald d. 1524.
Edmund Butler d. 1551.

PART TWO

The Abbey of Inislounaght

5. FOUNDATION AND EARLY YEARS

It is not easy to determine chronological precedence among the early daughters of Mellifont. Different writers give different dates for the foundation of certain of those monasteries so that it is not always easy to determine which date is the correct one. Indeed, a regular succession of dates has been assigned to Suir abbey, as the Cistercians called the monastery of Inishlounaght; and most of these dates, it may be added, are altogether irreconcilable with St Bernard's definite statement that the monastery existed during St Malachy's lifetime. The situation is further complicated by the fact that although most historians make Suir a daughter of Maigue and a grand-daughter of Mellifont it seems more probable from a study of the facts that it was originally a daughter of Mellifont.

The foundation of the monastery of Suir (de Surio or Suriense of St Bernard) has been variously placed at 1142, 1151, 1158. 1159 and even as late as 1184 and 1187. The erudite Cistercian writer, Leopold Janauschek, in his indispensable and thoroughly-documented list of Cistercian houses,[1] gives a number of conflicting dates for this foundation, accepting 1157 as the most probable one. Yet St Bernard himself, whose testimony in this matter would appear to me to outweigh all others, states quite definitely that in his own lifetime there were already in existence five daughters of Mellifont, and he expressly names Suir abbey (Suriense) as receiving its first lay brother from St Malachy himself. As Malachy died in the early winter of 1148, on 2 November to be precise, and had probably made his last visit to Munster in the preceeding year or, at the very latest, in the early part of 1148, we must conclude that the monastery of Inishlounaght had been founded early in 1148, or more probably in 1147 at the latest. The exact date we do not know. It follows from what we have said that there are very strong reasons for doubting the generally received tradition which makes the abbey of Suir a daughter of Maigue, an abbey which was itself founded in 1148. The exact date we do not know. If Suir itself was founded in the early part of the year 1148 (if not in the year 1147) we should have to admit that Maigue founded a daughter-house in the very year of its own foundation, a most unlikely occurence. St Bernard not only refers to the existence of this abbey before the death of St Malachy, but seems to imply that it was a daughter of Mellifont. The abbot, Congan, was in all probability, one of the disciples of St Malachy, who was left behind by that holy bishop at Clairvaux, in 1140, to be trained in the Cistercian way of life with Gillacrist O Conairche, later abbot of Mellifont. If this was the case, Abbot Congan was personally known to St Bernard, having been brought into

1 Janauschek, vol. 1.

105

intimate contact with him at Clairvaux. We know that they corresponded, for Bernard tells us that it was at the request of Abbot Congan and his monks of Suir, that he wrote the *Life of St Malachy* and much of the materials for that life were supplied to him by the abbot and monks of Inishlounaght. Bernard, who, if this view be accepted, was the father abbot of Inishlounaght's mother-house, would surely not be mistaken as to the foundation date of a monastery with which he had such close relations. Nor is it reasonable to suspect that he could have been mistaken in placing it among Mellifont's early daughters. How, then, are we to explain the various dates which have been assigned this abbey? It may well be that the convent moved from place to place along the Suir before settling down permanently on the site near Clonmel known as Inis Leamhnachta (the holm or river-meadow of new milk). The historian of Clonmel[2] is of opinion that the later dates assigned to the foundation of this abbey are presumably the dates of the endowments settled on the monastery by its great benefactors, Domhnall Mór Ó Briain, king of Thomond, and Maelsheachlainn Ó Faolain, king of the Déise. The date 1187 is accepted by Janauschek as probably the date of the endowment (or perhaps the translation of the abbey to a new site) by Domhnall Mór Ó Brien. The date 1159, given by some authors as the date of foundation is in all probability the date on which Maelsheachlainn Ó Faolain endowed the community; for Maelsheachlainn ceased to be king soon after the Norman invasion. He was captured by the invaders after the fall of Waterford, together with Reginald, the king of the Norse-Irish of that city, in whose tower, still known as Reginald's tower, the two kings were taken prisoners. With them, at the time, were two other Norse-Irish leaders called by Giraldus Cambrensis, the two Sitrics, both of whom were slaughtered by the Normans. One of those Sitrics was a brother of Reginald or Ragnall, and it is probable that both Reginald and Ó Faolain would have shared the fate of the Sitrics had not Diarmaid MacMurchadha intervened and prevailed on their captors to spare their lives.[3] We hear so much that is bad and so little that is good of Diarmaid na nGall (who was, by the way, a great friend of the Cistercians and founder of the abbey of Baltinglass) that it is pleasant to be able to record this act of mercy to his credit. We next hear of Ó Faolain, in 1172, when he was among the kings who came to do homage to Henry II of England, and was sent back into his own country 'with honour and liberal gifts'.[4] Shortly afterwards, his power passed away for ever and the Anglo-Norman family of Le Poer, now better known as Power, came into possession of the greater part of his territory. Notwithstanding

2 Canon W.P. Burke, *The History of Clonmel* (Waterford, 1907). The chapter of this history concerned with the story of Inishlounaght appeared originally as a paper in the *Journal of the Waterford and South East of Ireland Archaeological Society* (1st series) vol. 1, no. 2, pp 85-93.   3 Giraldus Cambrenis, *Expugnatio Hibernica*, I, xvi.   4 Ibid., I, xxxii.

tha fact that Henry II granted Robert le Poer the whole of the present Co. Waterford as far as Lismore, the two Deise chiefs, Domhnall O Faolain, 'paramount chief of the two Deise', and Bric, chief of the Southern Deise, were still holding on to the remnants of their former greatness in the early years of the thirteenth century; they were fighting a losing battle, however, and though King John treated them with clemency they ceased to be independent chiefs. In 1204 Ó Faolain 'quit-claimed, to the king of the province of Dungarvan' as it was called.[5] He held two more cantreds but one of them was only for life, the other was his inheritence. He died in the following year[6] and with him passed away the ancient Feise principality.

The second great name associated with the endowment of Inishlounaght is that of Domhnall Mór Ó Briain, who reigned as king of Thomond from 1168 to 1194. His grants to the monastery probably belong to the years 1184 and 1187, which years are sometimes given as the foundation date of the abbey. Domhnall Mór was a very great benefactor to the Cistercians and besides endowing Inishlounaght, was the founder of the three important monasteries of Holy Cross, Corcumroe, and Kilcooly, to which list may probably be added Kilshanny. Domhnall Mór Ó Briain was one of the greatest men of his time, well known as a founder of churches and monasteries. He was also a great soldier. During his reign of twenty-six years he maintained himself as king of Thomond (or Limerick) against all opposition, and, with his principal seat in the former capital of the Norsemen of Limerick, he held sway over a kingdom that included the whole of the present counties Clare and Limerick and all north Tipperary. He was one of the kings who aided the Ard-Ri Ruaidhri Ó Conchobhair in the siege of Dublin in 1171, though he later made his submission to Henry II, king of England. The king was at that time on his way to Lismore to meet the Cistercian bishop Gillacrist, who held the office of papal legate in Ireland and who had been the first abbot of Mellifont. Cambrensis tell us[7] that Domhnall Mór came to meet Henry II 'at the water of Suir', and it is probable that both kings would have been entertained by the monks of Inishlounaght.

In the year 1185, Prince John came to Ireland, and in May of that year granted the abbot and convent of Suir a meadow in Glennewaydan on the south coast of Waterford. This was probably granted in return for the hospitality afforded him by the monks and the land thus granted formed the nucleus of a new Cistercian monastery which was founded from the abbey of Suir about the year 1200. When John became king, the grant was confirmed by him on the occasion of his visit to Ireland in 1210, when he is said to have been again entertained by the monks on his way to Dublin.

5 Orpen, *Ireland under the Normans*, ii, p. 327 gives the grant; cf. Curtis, *A history of medieval Ireland from 1110 to 1513* (Dublin 1923), pp 102-3.   6 *Annals of the Four Masters*, ad annum 1205.   7 Cambrensis, *Expugnatio Hibernica*, I, xxxi.

The abbey of Glenragh had by that time become a fact for there is reference to the absence of the abbot from the general chapter of the Order in the statutes of 1208, when he was subjected to the penalties laid down in the statutes for not attending the chapter in due course.[8] Canon Power has shown that the monastery of Glenragh (Gleann Gradha, in Latin *de Valle Caritate*) was the parish of Monksland, near Bonmahon in Co. Waterford, the very name Monksland (Fearann na Manach) remaining to show that this was once a monastic parish.[9] Glenragh was not, indeed, the only daughter of Inishlounaght which was, in fact, the mother of no less than three monasteries, namely, the one just mentioned in Co. Waterford, the abbey of Fermoy in Co. Cork, and the abbey Corcumroe in Co. Clare. The first Cistercian monastery to be founded in Ireland after the Norman invasion was that of Fermoy, known in Latin as *Castrum Dei*, which was colonised from Inishlounaght in the year 1170. Though the abbey is sometimes said to have been founded and endowed by the Anglo-Norman family de Rupe, better known to us under the form Roche, it does not appear that this family had, in fact, settled in the area as early as 1170. Indeed, the Roches do not appear to have settled in Co. Cork until the first quarter of the thirteenth century and it was not until 1300 that they became barons of Fermoy. It is thus likely that the abbey of Fermoy was originally a native Irish foundation as indeed, its parentage suggests. With the enfeoffment of Munster by the Normans, the influence of the invaders began to make itself felt in Fermoy, as in other Irish abbeys and it gradually became Normanised. It did not yield without a struggle, even a hard one in the course of which it joined in the rebellion raised by its mother house at the end of the visitation of 1228, and the Norman abbot, who had been forced on the community, was slain by the Irish.

The foundation of Corcumroe, Suir's second daughter, is ascribed to Domhnall Mór Ó Briain, king of Thomond, and, if this be correct, it must have been the last monastery to be founded by that great king, who was also the founder of Holy Cross. Though the official Cistercian tabulae give the date of foundation as 1195, while Domhnall Mór died in 1194, the discrepancy may be explained by supposing that all arrangements for the new foundation had been made before the death of the king and that consequently he, and not his son Donnchadh Cairbreach, should be given credit of founding this abbey. This abbey, with its sister house (Fermoy), was removed from the jurisdiction of Inishlounaght as a result of the rebellion of 1228, and the same year saw the complete suppression of Glenragh

8 Canivez, 1208:27.   9 For the site and identication of this monastery see Canon Power's paper 'The Cistercian Abbeys of Munster' in the *Journal of the Cork Historical and Archaeological Society*, 43 (1938) 99. See also *The Place-Names of Decies* (London, 1907), p. 164 and *Waterford and Lismore. A Compendious History of the United Dioceses* (Cork, 1937), p. 194, by the same author.

as an independent abbey, its possessions being transferred to the Anglo-Norman abbey of Dunbrody. Thus was the abbey of Suir deprived of all her daughter houses as a punishment for her rebellion against the authority of the Order.

The early history of Inishlounaght was uneventful, and it is not until the first half of the thirteenth century that it attains to any prominence in the annals of the Order or of the country. When it did come under notice at length, it achieved a very unenviable notoriety in connection with the general breakdown of monastic discipline which occured in the Irish Cistercian houses, especially those of Munster, and it played a leading part in what came to be known in the Order as the Mellifont Conspiracy. But before we come to speak of these events, let us record the little that has come to our notice of the abbey of Inishlounaght between the year 1210 and 1228, when the visitation made by Abbot Stephen Lexington brought matters to a head and produced a crisis, not only in this house, but in the whole Order in Ireland.

Whatever may have been the origins of Suir, and, as we have seen, it was probably a daughter of Mellifont, it was transferred in the course of time to the jurisdiction of Maigue, or, perhaps, the abbey grew so weak that a new community had to be sent in from that monastery, so that it, and not Mellifont, became the mother-house. By the thirteenth century, Suir was certainly universally recognised as a daughter of Maigue, and this is made clear by an incident which occurred some time before 1221 and caused the general chapter to take drastic action against the abbot of Inishlounaght. Contrary to the usages and tradition of the Order, the then abbot of Suir had been translated from Chore abbey (Midleton) to the sister abbey of Inishlounaght.

Chore abbey was a daughter of Maigue, and this decree of the general chapter, directed against the abbot of Inishlounaght on the grounds noted above, shows that at this period the latter abbey, too, was a daughter of Maigue. The punishment inflicted on the abbot of Suir for this violation of the Cistercian tradition was drastic; the chapter ordered his instant deposition from office and the abbot of Glandy (Co. Kilkenny) was commissioned to announce this sentence to the deposed abbot who, apparently, was not present at the general chapter.[10]

A new abbot was elected soon after, and this abbot attended the general chapter of 1222. He was one of the two abbots commissioned by the chapter to proceed in person to the place selected as the site for a new Cistercian foundation by one of the Anglo-Norman lords, Odo de Barry. They were asked to make a thorough inspection of the place and furnish a report to the next general chapter.[11] The abbot who joined with him in

10 Canivez, 1221:57. 11 Ibid., 1222:34.

this commission was his father-abbot (the abbot of Maigue). These abbots seem to have been remiss in their duty. When the next general chapter assembled it was discovered that the commission given to the abbots of Suir and Maigue had not been discharged by them, and so the chapter was compelled to entrust the affair to the abbot of Clairvaux in France, and the abbot of Whitland in Wales.[12] It is of some significance that two foreign abbots should have been entrusted with looking after this business of a new Irish foundation. Odo de Barry, one of the Norman invaders, would hardly have been *persona grata* to the Irish abbots of Suir and Maigue, who were probably having trouble at this time owing to effects of the Norman invasion on the Irish Cistercians in general.

In Munster, particularly, the struggle between Norman and Gael was very bitter, and the native race was gradually pushed back into the mountains. Swarms of colonists followed in the wake of the conquerors and penetrated even into the heart of Kerry and into the south-west country of Cork. The Cistercian monasteries of Munster were in the thick of the fray, and, peopled as they were by Irish monks, and owing their foundation and endowment to Irish kings and princes, their sympathies naturally lay with their own people against the invaders. Seeing their kinsmen violently dispossessed of their lands, and now confronted with the spectacle of one of the conquering barons founding and endowing a new Cistercian monastery with lands plundered from the Irish, they were naturally not very keen on carrying out their commission. The abbots of Clairvaux and Whitland took the matter in hand, however, and in the following year the new foundation was made in the territory of Cinel Aedha, the patrimony of O'Mahony's, which had now passes into the hands of the Anglo-Norman de Barrys.[13]

Inishlounaght, with the other Cistercian abbeys of Munster, and indeed, of all Ireland, was now on the eve of what was to be the great crisis in the affairs of the Irish Cistercians, and in order to understand the events which took place between 1227 and 1230, we draw attention to the troubles which were distracting the Irish Church at this period. John Comyn, the first Anglo-Norman archbishop of Dublin, had died in 1212. Though one of the invading race, he had shown himself not only an able administrator of his diocese, but a man who was anxious to do justice to the Irish. At the same time, he was a steadfast upholder of the independence of the Church and not the mere timeserver too many of his successors were. The man who succeeded Comyn as archbishop was of a very different character.

Henry de Loundres, who became archbishop of Dublin in succession to John Comyn, has been said to typify, more than any other of his generation,

---

12 Ibid., 1223:35. 13 Janauschek, i, gives the date of foundation as 22 February 1225.

the statecraft of those Anglo-Norman rulers in Ireland who had been trained in the harsh and often brutal school of king John's administration. As archbishop of Dublin (1213-28), as justiciar (1213-15), as papal legate (1217-20), and again as justiciar (1221-24), Henry of London left a permanent mark on the history of the Irish Church. The man who was remembered in Dublin as the builder of Dublin Castle and as 'Scorchvillein' ('Flayer of Serfs') by his tenants was also the man who first claimed, the title of Primate for the archbishops of Dublin; and there was a moment in his career when it seemed probable that he might make a radical change in the whole character of the Irish hierarchy, substituting English for Irish bishops in every diocese of the four provinces.

Such is Fr Aubrey Gwynn's summing up of the career and policy of this famous individual.[14] As justiciar, this archbishop wielded the secular power in the name of the king and was the chief justice of Ireland, whose business it was to go through the country trying, and hanging when necessary, the wretches who were convicted at his courts. Thus the Irish, who saw combined in the one man the offices of pastor and king's deputy, and who saw at the head of the invader's armies the man who professed to be a follower of the Prince of Peace were not thereby made more amenable to the efforts of these strange warrior-prelates to reform the Church of their ancestors and reduce the natives to obedience. The archbishop of Armagh, dying in Rome at the Lateran Council in 1216, was succeeded by an Anglo-Norman, Luke Netterville, the first of his race to occupy the chair of Patrick. The Anglo-Normans had now two of the four archbishops in their hands, bu they hoped to obtain Cashel also for the Cistercian Domhnall Ó Lonngargain had died in Rome during the Council. The hopes of the Anglo-Norman party were disappointed in this instance, for Domhnall was succeeded in the archbishopric by another. The new archbishop, who later became a Cistercian, was one of the strongest opponents of the efforts of the Anglo-Norman party to gain control of the Irish church. His successor, also a Cistercian, followed in the same tradition, and thus the Cistercians of Munster, as well as the archbishops of the province, became identified with the policy of national resistance.

The whole policy of the Anglo-Normans in Ireland regarding the Irish Church may be found summed up in the mandate of Henry III to the justiciar, Geoffrey de Marisco, on 14 January 1216-17, commanding him not to allow Irishmen to be elected or appointed to any cathedral church in Ireland. Three days later a second mandate ordered the justiciar to take

14 Aubrey Gwynn, SJ, 'Henry of London, archbishop of Dublin', *Studies*, September 1949, p. 295.

counsel with the archbishop of Dublin to procure by all means the election of the clerks of the archbishop of Dublin and other Englishmen to
sees and dignities, according as vacancies arose.[15] Thus was initiated as
part of the official governmental programme, the policy of filling the Irish
sees with Englishmen to the exclusion of the natives, a policy whoseheart-
edly adopted and pushed vigorously on by Archbishop Henry of London.
All the religious enactments in the various Anglo-Irish parliaments in
medieval times which had as their aim the exclusion of the Irish from
benefices and monasteries, are to be considered as but the logical development of this official policy. Though the popes later condemned that
policy the decision to issue the mandates referred to above must have had
the approval of the papal legate in England.[16]

   In 1217, the archbishop of Dublin was appointed papal legate for
Ireland, a position he held until 1220. This appointment was a great asset to
the archbishop in promoting the new policy. At this juncture, the archbishop of Cashel, Donnchad Ó Lonngargain, upset all the legate's well-laid
plans. The archbishop's predecessor had been carrying on a hard struggle
to defend the rights of his see against the pretensions of the Anglo-
Normans. Donnchadh now found himself in much the same position. A
mandate from the king of England in 1218 ordered the justiciar, Geoffrey
de Marisco, to take the archbishop's possessions into the king's hands.
Cashel had at this time what was known as a 'new town' and an 'old town'.
The old town had been in the possession of the church since the year 1101,
when Muircheartach O Briain, then king of Ireland, 'had made over Cashel
to God and St Patrick'. This town, or at least the greater part of it, the justiciar now seized. The archbishop appealed to the king, who later revoked his
mandate and ordered the justiciar to make restitution. This the justiciar did
not do. The archbishop thereupon excommunicated the justiciar. Things
now became so difficult for the archbishop that he had to fly to France
whence he made his way to Rome to appeal to the pope in person. In laying
his grievances before the pope, the archbishop took up not only his own
particular cause but that of the Irish people in general. A letter addressed
by the pope to James, legate of the Holy See in Scotland, on 6 August 1220,
makes this evident. As a result of the archbishop's representations the pope
dismissed the archbishop of Dublin from the office of legate. Commenting
on the pope's action, Aubrey Gwynn says: 'The withdrawal of legatine jurisdiction from the archbishop of Dublin would seem to be the first victory
won by the archbishop of Cashel in this battle of ecclesiastical diplomacy.'[17]

   A series of letters from Pope Honorius makes clear beyond all doubt
what were the 'intolerable customs' existing in Ireland against which the

---

15 CDI, i, nos. 736 and 739.   16 Aubrey Gwynn, op. cit., p. 302.   17 Ibid., p. 392. For the
papal letter see VM, p. 15.

archbishop of Cashel and his suffragans complained. The letter written by the pope to his legate, James, in Scotland, whom he now appointed legate for Ireland in succession to Henry of London, contains a scathing denunciation of some of the iniquitous customs introduced by the Anglo-Normans in Ireland.[18]

> It has come to our knowledge that certain Englishmen have, with unheard of audacity, decreed that no Irish clerk, no matter how honest or learned he may be, is to be admitted to an ecclesiastical dignity. We are unwilling to let so bold and wicked an abuse pass unheeded, and we order you by authority of these presents publicly to denounce this statute as null and void, inhibiting all Englishmen from enforcing it or from attempting anything of the kind in future. You are also to announce that Irish clerks whose merit is attested by their conduct and learning are to be freely admitted to ecclesiastical dignities, provided they have been canonically elected to the same.

Two days later, the pope, in another letter to the same legate, condemned other customs introduced by the English into Ireland, commanding the legate to make it his care that these customs were completely abolished, and to compel the English by ecclesiastical censures to allow the Irish to enjoy equal rights with themselves.[19]

> Our venerable brother the archbishop of Cashel has made known to us that in his province there has grown up through the insolence of the English the vice of a detestable custom, namely, that if an Englishman loses any of his property and swears on his oath that it has been stolen from him by an Irishman, six English witnesses are considered sufficient to confirm his statement on oath; but thirty Irish witnesses are not found sufficient to swear to the innocence of the Irish party who, in spite of their sworn testimony is compelled to make restitution as a thief. But if an Irishman loses his property and knows for certain that an Englishman has taken it and is prepared to affirm it on oath, the English refuse to accept his sworn statement.

On 19 March 1221, Pope Honorius III wrote once more to his legate James in answer to various other complaints made by the archbishop of Cashel and to condemn another evil custom then in vogue in Ireland. In fact, he condemned several such customs but in this letter he mentions

18 VM, no. 36, p. 16.   19 Ibid., no. 38.

especially that by which the verdict of twelve Englishmen on oath was taken as final against the word of prelates who came into court to protect their rights and possessions. This, of course, was nothing else than the custom of trial by jury, and in the event, the king seems to have had little or no difficulty in defending himself as far as this charge was concerned. But the letter contained an admonition to the legate to examine carefully into the truth of the charges brought by the archbishop against the English. It is clear that the pope was not going to be content with an *ex parte* presentation of the facts and wished to hear the other side as well. It is also evident that the king of England had written to the pope rebutting the charges made against him by the archbishop and accusing him in turn of bringing false charges.[20]

In answering the charge that an Irishman's word was not accepted in court, the king, or whoever drafted the reply to the charges brough by the archbishop, replied that the reason the English would not accept the sworn statement of any Irishman was the long experience they had of Irish savagery, and that this fact had been maliciously concealed by the archbishop of Cashel in presenting his case to Rome. At the time that letter was written the archbishop had been long back in his own country. In the interval between his leaving Ireland and arrriving at the papal court, he had become a Cistercian monk. It appears that on his way to Rome he passed through Citeaux and, while staying there, became so gravely ill that, thinking he was going to die, he took the Cistercian habit. He may have feared that his enemies at home would make difficulties for him on that score, refusing obedience on the ground that he was a monk; in writing later to the people of Cashel, the pope took cognizance of this, for he told them to be obedient to their archbishop and pointed out to them that the fact that he had become a monk did not absolve them from the duty of obeying him since, as he wrote, 'the habit of a monk and the dignity of a pontiff are not repugnant'.

The dispute between the archbishop and the Crown dragged on until at last the archbishop, his patience worn out, placed the whole province of Cashel under an interdict. By this time, Archbishop Henry of London had been appointed justiciar for the second time (1221) and was now more powerful than ever. Moreover, he was once more in favour with the pope who had, more or less, come round to the English side on the ground that the English king was a ward of the Holy See whose rights the pope must protect. The king's answers to the charges made by the archbishop had evidently impressed the pope. He now complained to the pope of the interdict laid by the archbishop on the province, asking that it should be removed. The pope commanded the archbishop to remove the interdict

20 Ibid., no. 46, p. 18.

within fifteen days. This the archbishop did and immediately afterwards hastened to Rome there to plead his cause once more. This time he got no hearing, for the pope had already empowered the bishops of Meath, Ossory and Kildare to try the case themselves without right of appeal. Worn out by his labours and suffering from ill-health, the poor archbishop returned to Ireland a disappointed man. Resigning his see soon afterwards, he retired into one of the monasteries of his Order, possibly Holy Cross, where he died in 1232. For the time being, victory was with his opponents.[21]

Following the resignation of Archbishop Donnchadh Ó Lonngargain, the chapter was divided, but the majority elected the Cistercian bishop of Cork, Maelmuire O Briain, said to have been a member of the community of Inishlounaght. This election, which did not please the English party, was set aside by the pope because of some undisclosed fault which occured during the election itself. The pope, having disappointed the pro-Irish party, went on to disappoint the pro-English party too. He appointed Michael Scott, the famous astrologer, to the archbishopric of Cashel. Scott renounced his provision on the ground that he did not understand the Irish language, a ground, be it noted, which never seems to have troubled the Anglo-Norman bishops at all.

Things now began to take a more favourable turn for the Irish party. On 28 April 1224, shortly before the appointment of Michael Scott to the archbishopric of Cashel, the pope had addressed a letter to his 'beloved sons and clergy of Ireland' in which he renewed his condemnation of the English statutes decreeing that no Irishman was to be promoted to ecclesiastical dignities, and this was followed by another letter on 9 May, embodying a final condemnation of the iniquitous decree.[22] Even before that, he had ordered the king of England to restore certain lands to the Church, among them the lands which had been seized unjustly from the abbey of Jerpoint. He had also addressed a bull to the chapter of Cashel granting a request made by them that the numbers of canons should not exceed twelve. It was the practice of the Anglo-Normans to increase the number of canons in various diocese so that they might be in a position to get men of their own party into the chapter and so secure a favourable decision when it came to electing a bishop. The chapter of Cashel was determined that his would not happen in the archdiocese if they could help it.

On 20 June 1224, the pope at last appointed Maelmuire O Briain to the see of Cashel. This reversal of the papal policy was a triumph for the

21 Annals of Innisfallen, ad annum 1232. The name of the monastery to which the archbishop retired is not stated. It might have been Inishlounaght or Holy Cross which were the two nearest to Cashel.   **22** VM, no. 55, p. 23.

Irish, for, as Fr Gwynn has pointed out, it meant that the pope had 'swung round from a position of careful neutrality in this dispute to open support of the Irish cause.'[23] Maelmuire, as a former monk of Inishlounaght, must have had the interests of the community at heart, and now as archbishop of Cashel he was placed in charge of the neighbouring diocese while his cathedral city was situated only a few miles away from the monastery. The time was coming when the monks might feel glad to have the support of the archbishop in the struggle which almost rent the Order in Ireland; but though the archbishop's sympathies must have been with the Irish monks, he could hardly have sympathised with the actions of the extreme element among them who, by their misconduct and open insubordination brought about a crisis in the affairs of their monastery which was not resolved until much harm had been done to religion and grave injury inflicted on the community to which they belonged. But the events that took place at Inishlounaght four years after the promotion of Maelmuire to the see of Cashel had their origin in the social and political upheaval which was convulsing Ireland at the time and cannot be either discussed or understood without taking this upheaval into consideration.

What was the position of affairs in Ireland at this time regarding the extension of Norman power? Meath had been almost entirely enfeoffed. The plains of Leinster had fallen into the hands of the Norman. North-East Ulster, too, had fallen, and Munster was being rapidly gobbled up. The forests and bogs of the midlands, Leix and Offaly, as well as the mountainous parts of Leinster and Munster, still held out, and, in fact, were destined to be the impregnable fortress from which the Irish counter-attack was later to be launched, which would result in the winning back of most of the conquered territories. But in the years with which we are now concerned, the first half of the thirteenth century, the Anglo-Normans held most of the eastern part of Ireland, practically the whole of Meath, including what is now called Westmeath, all Ulster east of the Bann and Loch Neagh, and the great plain of Munster. In Munster especially, the fight was savage and bitter. Indeed, all Ireland was a land of war and of the Cistercian monasteries then existing in the country, not more than four of five could be said to be situated in districts removed from the tumult of battle, The majority of the Cistercian houses were in what was known as the Marches between the opposing armies. The large group of houses in Munster was in a particularly difficult position. Owing to the disturbed conditions then prevailing, they had not security and were plundered again and again, now by one side, now by the other. They had eventually to call on the king of England for protection – presumably from his own barons, for he was hardly in a position to afford them protection from the

23 Aubrey Gwynn in *Studies*, December 1949, p. 401.

Irish. Nor is it likely that they needed protection from the latter, for future events were to prove very definitely on what side their sympathies lay. Having appealed to the king for protection a mandate was accordingly issued on 23 July 1227, ordering the justiciar to afford protection to the abbots of Mellifont, Baltinglass, Suir, Holy Cross and Maigue, together with their tenants, chattels and possessions. He was also to give them aid in recovering the rights of their churches which were, it was said, dispersed.[24]

One can easily imagine that under such conditions monastic observance was not likely to reach a high level. On the contrary, the ebb and flow of war around the monasteries must have had a most disturbing effect on the communities; and when to that is added the attempts which soon followed on the part of the invaders of trying to get a foothold in the monasteries themselves, either by ousting men of the old race from the abbacy and replacing them by men of Anglo-Norman stock, or by putting numbers of the latter into the same monasteries with Irsh monks. It is quite evident that there was bound to be trouble on a large scale. In houses which were either Norman or Irish, there would not be such danger of a breakdown of discipline and monastic observance; but in houses in which these two mutually opposed elements were brought together, differing as they did in language, culture and traditions, with racial animosities enkindled owing to the war then raging,all the elements for an explosion were present, and it needed but a spark to set them off.

We have seen how the king's protection had been sought for and obtained by certain Cistercian abbeys, including the houses of Maigue and Suir already mentioned and the abbey of Holy Cross. It is possible that some of the difficulties which beset these abbeys arose from grants of lands belonging to neighbouring dispossessed families being made by the conquerors to the monasteries. Alienation of monastic lands seems to have been going on at this time also, and the whole country round about these monasteries was being parcelled out between the barons and knights of the new race. While the Anglo-Normans had their castles and manors, and their towns were inhabited by the merchant class of Norman and Ostman stock, the native Irish had become the serf population. the hewers of wood and drawers of water for their Anglo-Norman overlords. And in the midst of this alien population, differing from them in race, language and tradition, dwelt the Irish Cistercian monks, most of them being the kith and kin of the dispossed Irish. These monks, drawn mostly from the local population, traced their descent back to men whose families had lived in these territories from time immemorial. Human nature being what it is, they could hardly be expected to welcome the newcomers with open arms. When war raged outside, between their own kinsmen and their Norman

24 CDI, i, no. 1533.

enemies, there can be little doubt as to where the sympathies of the Irish monks lay. With the coming of the Normans and the plantation of the area, a new element would have begun to infiltrate into the Cistercian communities. Where the Norman grew to any size, the house invariably became divided and internal dissension soon led to greater evils, each party seeking to secure the aid of their own adherents from without. In some cases, owing to the breakdown in discipline, the general chapter took steps to restore order by bringing in a new colony of monks from England. This only made matters worse, as we shall see.

The Irish Cistercians realised their danger. They saw bishoprics and abbeys passing into the hands of the newcomers and, convinced that their own turn must soon come, became deeply concerned. The turn of events, following on the accession of Henry of London to the see of Dublin, and the newly promulgated policy of Henry III regarding the Irish church, made it plain for all to see that the Anglo-Normans were determined to control that Church and, in view of this policy, already far advanced, there could be little doubt, that sooner or later, unless steps were taken to prevent it, the Irish monks would be in the minority in their own monasteries and the abbeys would pass into the hands of strangers. Perhaps it was this fear that gave rise to the movement resulting in what has come to be known in history as the Mellifont Conspiracy, and which was, possibly, or even probably, motivated by what would be called in modern times a spirit of nationalism, a spirit, let us say, of opposition to what was felt to be an alien tradition and to a state of affairs which aimed, at bringing the Irish houses founded from Mellifont under the control of the newly-arrived Anglo-Normans.

It is unlikely that this movement within the Order was due to a deliberate rebellion against monastic discipline. Had the Order in Ireland been allowed to develop normally without undue interference from outside; had the visitators sent to reform the Irish houses and restore a relaxed observance contented themselves with seeing that the Rule was observed, and tried to understand Irish ways and traditions; and above all, had they refrained from subjecting the native monks to foreign superiors, who had clearly no understanding of, and still less sympathy for such traditions, it is unlikely that the abuses which reached such a pitch in the second and third decades of the thirteenth century, would ever have attained such serious dimensions.

It was in Munster especially that an almost complete breakdown of monastic discipline occurred, and it is but right that we should bear in mind the position in Munster at that time. Not only were the Normans waging a war of aggression against the Irish, but the Irish themselves were at war with one another. The O'Briens were at war with the MacCarthys, and rival branches of the O'Briens and the MacCarthys were warring on one another with the aid of Anglo-Norman allies. Already a mixed race was being formed among the higher classes, and Richard, son of the William Burke, or de Burgo, from the baronies of Clanwilliam in Limerick and Tipperary,[25] was himself the grandson of king Domhnall Mór Ó Briain on his mother's side. Nowhere else in Ireland did the Norman's impress their character on a people as they did on the Irish of Munster. Everywhere throughout the province, the great Norman families were settled except in the more remote parts where the Irish still held their ground. A modern historian of the highest reputation has declared that Munster may be considered as one of the most French counties recorded outside France.[26] Even the character of the Irish language underwent some transformation in Munster, and had impressed on it the record of the former Anglo-Norman supremacy in the province.[27]

Here then is a fact which cannot be ignored in any attempt to assess fairly the widespread breakdown in monastic discipline in Irish Cistercian houses in the thirteenth century, and in particular the rebellions against the decisions of the official visitator which broke out in Munster just as the visiting abbot was about to take his departure from Ireland. To attempt to judge these occurances without taking account of the foregoing circumstances would be to run the risk of arriving at a conclusion not warranted by the facts.

6. REFORM

For a period of roughly seventy years from the introduction of the Cistercian Order into Ireland, the monasteries of white monks increased and multiplied, and during this period the Order seems to have been in a very flourishing condition. Indeed, until supplanted in the affections of the people by the sons of St Francis, the Cistercians were by far the most popular Order in Ireland with Irish and Anglo-Irish alike. Their monasteries became favourite places of pilgrimage and were even chosen by kings and nobles as their last resting places after death.

---

25 The Burkes of Limerick and Tipperary trace their descent from Edmund de Burgo, son of the Red Earl of Ulster (Richard de Burgo). Edmund died in 1338, but the de Burgo lands in Tipperary and Limerick came into the possession of the family long before the time of Edmund. His great-grandfather was Richard (I), lord of Connacht and son of William de Burgo, who first received a grant of those lands. This William de Burgo was the progenitor of the entire race of Burkes in Ireland and from him has come the designation Clann William.   26 Curtis, op. cit., p. 98.   27 The tonic accent in certain classes of words and the peculiar sound of certain vowels in Munster are stated by some authorities to be due to the influence of the French-Speaking Normans who later adopted the Irish language, becoming as the saying goes, 'more Irish than the Irish themselves' (*Hibernis Ipsis Hiberniores*).

Many were the instances of Cistercian monks and abbots promoted to the episcopate in those days, and a goodly number of these Cistercian bishops merited great praise from their contemporaries. Various entries in the *Annals of Ulster*, the *Annals of Loch Cé*, the *Annals of the Four Masters*, and the *Anglo-Irish Latin Annals*, show that these bishops were held in high esteem. No less than four archbishops who occupied the see of Cashel in succession (between 1182 and 1236) were Cistercians. Two at least of these archbishops were Cistercians before they were elevated to the episcopacy, while one became a Cistercian when actually archbishop and the fourth (Domhnall Ó Lonngargain)[1] was probably a Cistercian before he became a bishop. All these Cistercian bishops were ornaments of the Irish Church, men of piety, integrity of character and steadfastness of purpose; men, moreover, who lacked neither physical nor moral courage when it became necessary to oppose tyrannical kings and princes in defence of the rights and liberties of the Church.

It can be readily understood that an order which produced such men and had such a universal appeal as had the Cistercian Order in those days, must have exerted an enormous influence throughout the country. Before the coming of the Normans, the Cistercian Order had made immense strides and had attained a high degree of material prosperity without, however, declining from its primitive fervour and the rigour of its observance. With the advent of the invaders, a change soon made itself felt. The disturbed state of the country due to continual warfare, which was essentially a struggle between two opposed and very different civilisations and cultures, profoundly affected the Cistercian monasteries and brought about a disasterous decline, not only in monastic observance, but even in moral standards. The early years of the thirteenth century produced the first great crisis of the Cistercian Order in Ireland. In the year 1201, at the very opening of the new century, an echo of the Irish wars is heard in the decision of the general chapter, then in session at Citeaux, to write to the lord cardinal and to John de Courcy regarding the molestation and oppression to which the Irish were then being subjected. At this very time, John de Courcy was engaged in his triumphant campaign in Ulster, where he was founding a strong Anglo-Norman colony, and his relations with the Cistercians were particularly close, since he was helping to found and endow new houses of the Order in those parts. The enfoeffment of Munster was also in progress at this time, and it was in this very year that King John renewed to William de Braose the grant of the kingdom of Thomond.

The statutes of the general chapters from 1216 to 1228 are eloquent testimony to the fact that there was something radically wrong in the Irish Cistercian houses, especially in the *Filiatio Mellifontis*, at this period. That

1 He was the second in order of time.

grave abuses were prevalent in many houses is clear from the wording of the statutes themselves, but as to the precise nature of these abuses and the causes of the widespread collapse of monastic observance, the statutes are silent. Further information is available, however, in the reports sent to the abbots of Citeaux and Clairvaux, as well as to the general chapter of Stephen of Lexington, abbot of Stanley, in 1228. This very able abbot had been delegated by the abbot of Clairvaux, acting with the authority of the abbot of Citeaux and the general chapter, to make an extraordinary visitation of the Irish houses for the purpose of undertaking a thorough reformation 'in head and members' and was endowed with plenary powers by the supreme authority of the Order. Though we are concerned in this section only with the abbey of Inishlounaght it will be necessary to give a general outline of the events leading to the visitation of 1228.

The commission issued to Abbot Stephen of Lexington for the visitation and reformation of the Cistercian Order in Ireland was the culmination of a series of efforts to correct abuses in the Irish houses of the Order which the general chapter had attempted vainly to eradicate. Matters had reached such a critical state in 1227 that the Holy See had been requested, by the Cistercian bishops of Cloyne and Dromore, to appoint a Commission of Inquiry into the state of the Order in Ireland. The bishop of Cloyne, Patrick by name, had been a former prior of Fermoy, the senior daughter house of Inishlounaght, while Gerald, bishop of Dromore, had been at one time cellarer of Mellifont. These two Cistercian bishops were evidently not disinterested parties. Indeed, the bishop of Dromore was said to have been (when cellarer of Mellifont) the author of the whole conspiracy which was organised in that house against the abbot of Furness. The abbey of Fermoy, from which Bishop Patrick came, was also in the black books, the abbot having been deposed in 1227 by the official visitor. The commission sought for was actually issued by the pope, the three bishops who were thus appointed, being the said bishops of Cloyne and Dromore, and the archbishop of Armagh, Donatur Ó Fidhabhra. This commission seems to have been issued shortly before the general chapter of 1227, and may have forced the chapter to take immediate action. At any rate, the next occurrence of importance was the writing of a letter to Pope Gregory IX, in the name of the general chapter. This letter, written by the abbot of Citeaux, sought the revocation of the commission to the three Irish bishops. From certain references in the letter itself it is clear that complaints had been made to the Holy See by members of the Order who had written letters in which, it is alleged by the abbot of Citeaux, the true state of affairs was concealed while things which were simply not true were stated to be facts (*tacitas veritates et falsitates expressas*).[2]

2 Registrum.

In requesting the pope to revoke the commission already granted to the three bishops, the abbot of Citeaux notified the Holy Father, in the name of the general chapter, of the measures proposed for the reformation of the Order in Ireland by the same chapter. This letter was probably written immediately after the general chapter of 1227, at which a number of decisions relating to the reformation of the Irish houses had been taken. It seems clear that the Cistercians wished to keep future investigations in their own hands and did not wish the Irish bishops to interfere in what they felt was, after all, a domestic question. Even at the time the bishops had requested the appointment of the papal commission, the superiors of the Order had been engaged in a determined attempt to get at the root of the trouble in Ireland. All the disturbances seem to have centred at Mellifont and its filiations, and were probably, to a certain extent, bound up with the racial and political struggle then being waged in Ireland between Gael and Gall. Of the many irregularities then said to be prevalent in the houses of the Mellifont line, we have ample mention in the statutes of the general chapters though, unfortunately, few details are given as to the exact nature of these abuses. The first serious complaint may be dated from 1192, when it is alleged that the abbot of Mellifont[3] had refused to receive the visitator sent by the abbot of Clairvaux to make the regular visitation, and had even maltreated him. It was also alleged against him that he had deposed the abbot of a house which had which had been founded from one of his own daughter houses and had done this without the consent or knowledge of its father-abbot, substituting another abbot in place of the one so deposed. For these and other unnamed excesses of which he was accused, he was compelled to do penance.[4]

In 1216, the statutes of the general chapter disclose the growth in Mellifont of many 'enormities' which required to be corrected both 'in the head and in the members', and in the chapter of the following year it was found necessary to depose the abbot. If we may believe the Annals of Loch Cé,[5] the former abbot had been expelled 'through envy and jealousy' by his own monks and had died in exile, in either England or France, in 1216. His successor in the abbacy had refused to receive the official visitators and had suffered many glaring irregularities to continue in his house for a long period without making any attempt to correct them. He had also encouraged, or perhaps commanded, the lay brethren to close the doors against the official visitators at the time of the regular visitation, so that they were unable to get into the monastery. He was accused too, of allowing the abbot of one of his filiations who had been guilty of many excesses to go uncorrected, and for all these faults he was deprived of his office by the general chapter of 1217.[6] He had a companion in misfortune,

3 Canivez.   4 Ibid.   5 *Annals of Loch Cé*, i, p. 255.   6 Canivez, 1217:78.

for the abbot of Jerpoint was deposed by the same chapter on somewhat similar grounds. The visitation of this monastery, like that of Mellifont, seems to have been the occasion of startling occurences. Not only the abbot of Jerpoint himself, but four other abbots also, were implicated in the disturbances which took place on this occasion. These abbots had come, evidently by arrangement, to be present during the visitation, and on the third day had aided and abetted the abbot of Jerpoint in resisting the visitator. The general chapter, after an investigation, found that the abbot of Jerpoint had been guilty of contumacy, disobedience and disorderly conduct, and had incited the entire community (*totum conventum*) against the visitator.[7]

In the year 1219, the abbots of La Trappe (France), and Cwmhir (Wales) were commanded by the general chapter to make a visitation in person of those parts of Ireland where many abuses and irregularities had occured, and were commissioned to correct what needed corrrection and to lay down the regulations that seemed to them to be required. They were told to report the results of their visitation to the following general chapter.[8] The report of the two abbots must have been adverse, for the general chapter of 1220 commissioned the abbot of Clairvaux to correct Mellifont and other houses of the Order in Ireland concerning which there had been very grave complaints.[9] Once again we are left in the dark as to the nature of these complaints. If it should happen that the abbot of Clairvaux could not make a personal visitation, he was authorised to send delegates who should be zealous and jealous of the good name of the Order (*ferventes et aemulatores ordinis*) to correct excesses, and these were to be empowered to employ the aid of the secular arm should it be found necessary. The decrees of the year 1221 give us a hint that at some of the difficulties were of an economic kind at least and had resulted in the depletion of the ranks of the communities, for it was enacted that the Irish abbeys which had no communities, were to be reduced to the status of granges or else completely suppressed by the following general chapter.[10] From the evidence contained in Stephen of Lexington's Register, to be mentioned later on, it appears that Inishlounaght's third and last daughter house (Glenragh in Co. Waterford), was among the abbeys which had failed owing to economic difficulties.[11] It may be mentioned here that an earlier decree of the general chapter (in 1206) shows that even then the Irish houses were in financial straits, and that some of the Irish abbots had pledged the abbey lands.[12] The question of the correction of Mellifont came before the general chapter again in 1221, the abbot of Clairvaux being authorised to take it in hand and – a significant item this – it was fur-

---

7 Ibid., 1217: 25; 1217: 79. **8** Ibid., 1219: 33. **9** Ibid., 1220: 12. **10** Ibid., 1221: 21. **11** For Glengragh, see chap. 5 above and chap 8 below. **12** Canivez, 1206: 56.

ther decreed that he might introduce into Mellifont and other Irish houses, which were deemed to stand in need of reform, religious by whom the reform of the Order could be promoted in those parts.[13]

The measures taken by the general chapter seem to have produced at least a temporary improvement. From 1222 to 1226, we hear no more complaints of the Irish houses, but in the latter year the general chapter was once more forced to take the reformation of Mellifont abbey in hands. This time again, it was entrusted to the abbot of Clairvaux,[14] the father-abbot of Mellifont and the abbot directly responsible for all the *filiatio Mellifontis* in Ireland. The reform to be undertaken was evidently to embrace all the houses of the Mellifont line, and it is evident that the disorder was widespread. The abbot of Clairvaux did not make a personal visitation of the Irish houses, but he appointed as his delegates the abbots of Trois Fontaines and Froidmont. These two abbots carried out a series of visitations in Ireland, travelling extensively through the island, and appointing some new English abbots over Irish houses. The abbot of Froidmont, indeed, remained in the country after his co-visitor had left. Amongst the houses visited by these abbots were those of Mellifont, Bective, Baltinglass, Jerpoint, Duiske, Killenny, and apparently Boyle, Assaroe, Odorney, Newry and Fermoy. As a result of his report, the abbots of the five abbeys last named were deposed by the general chapter of the year 1227.[15] As the abbey of Maigue was, by this same chapter, taken away from Mellifont and given to Margam in Wales, while that of Suir was taken from Maigue and given to Furness in Lancashire, it seems likely that these two abbeys were among those visited. It would indeed be unlikely that the visitors would have made a visitation of Fermoy, a daughter house of Suir, without also visiting the latter abbey. All the deposed abbots were stated to have been concerned in the 'Mellifont Conspiracy' and no doubt the abbey of Inishlounaght was also involved. Later occurences would go to show that it was, but it is reasonable to assume that there was not at the time of the visitation of 1227 sufficient evidence available to connect the abbot of that house directly with the 'conspiracy.' The fact that the house was removed from the jurisdiction of Maigue would go to prove that it was considered to be in some way involved. The abbot at that time was a certain Brother D., as we learn from a charter preserved in Dijon, a charter granted to Citeaux by Donnchadh Cairbreach Ó Briain, then king of Thomond, and witnessed, among others, by the abbot of Inishlounaght (de Surio), whose initial only appears theron.[16] It is a fact to which some significance may attach that when Stephen of Lexington appeared at Suir

---

13 Ibid., 1221: 22.   14 Ibid., 1226: 15.   15 Ibid., 1227: 29.   16 Charter preserved in Departmental Library of Cote d'Or at Dijon, where it came from the archives of Citeaux after the dissolution of the French monasteries at the Revolution. There is a microfilm copy among the Fonds de Citeaux in the National Library of Ireland.

in the following year to carry out the visitation of that house there was no longer an abbot in control, his place being taken by the prior who, curiously enough, is also described in Stephen's correspondence as Brother D. What may have happened to the abbot we can only guess. Possibly he resigned before the storm broke.

The visitation of 1227 was not without opposition on the part of the Irish monks. We learn from the letters of Stephen of Lexington that there was quite a determined resistence in some cases. The abbot of Froidmont being compelled to leave Ireland before he had completed his visitation of all the houses, he delegated the abbot of Owney (another Anglo-Norman) to act in his place, In some instances, when the abbot arrived at a monastery for the purpose of commencing his visitation, he was driven away by the monks, who not only ill-treated him themselves but instigated other men to steal his horses, spoil his cattle, and kill his servants.[17] Amongst the new abbots created by the abbot of Froidmont was one at Baltinglass, apparently an Anglo-Norman. When this abbot arrived at the gates of his new abbey, he was met by the entire community, lay brothers and monks who rushing at him with one accord, seized his horse, threw him to the ground, and, having torn his seal violently from his girdle, drove him away amidst the greatest disorder; nor was he ever able to reenter his abbey except with the aid of an armed multitude.[18]

The general chapter of 1227 received the report of the abbots of Trois Fontaines and Froidmont, and took drastic action. Five abbots were deposed for their part in the conspiracy. In addition to the five thus deposed the abbots of Baltinglass and Bective seem to have been deposed by the visitators during the progress of the visitation itself. Mellifont was deprived of all jurisdiction over Maigue and Baltinglass, while Baltinglass itself was deprived of Jerpoint, and the latter abbey of Glandy (or Killenny), which now ceased to exist as a separate house, and was united to Duiske. Maigue was likewise, deprived of its daughter Inishlounaght, and a recommendation was made the Holy Cross should be suppressed entirely as a separate monastery and united to Owney. The general chapter, however, decided to take no action with regard to Holy Cross until a new report should have been made to the next chapter.[19] A promising beginning had thus been made of the work of reform, and the chapter therefore commissioned the abbot of Clairvaux to continue the good work so well begun.[20] The visitator appointed to carry out the visitation of 1228 was endowed with plenary powers to punish and even depose abbots and other officials; transfer monks and laybrothers from one house to another, even to houses outside Ireland; transfer abbeys from the jurisdiction of their mother houses to a new jurisdiction; amalgamate houses where nec-

---

17 Registrum xxxviii. 18 Ibid. 19 Canivez, 1227: 28, 29, 36. 20 Ibid., 1227: 28.

essary, reduce them to the status of granges or even suppress them alto-gether. He could also, if he found it necessary, transfer an entire commu-nity to another part of Ireland or even England, selling or otherwise disposing of all lands and acquiring new lands in their stead in the place to which it was proposed to remove the commmunity.[21] He could inflict censures, excommunications and interdicts not being excepted, and could likewise absolve from censures incurred and reconcile fugitives and apos-tates to the Order. He was, moreover, empowered to call upon the aid of the secular arm if he found it necessary to do so in carrying out the man-dates of the general chapter.

This visitator was Stephen of Lexington, abbot of Stanley (1223-9) and subsequently abbot of Savigny (1229-43), and abbot of Clairvaux (1243-56). Stephen was the youngest of four sons from Lexington (now Lexton) in Nottinghamshire, England. He was a Bachelor of Arts from Paris and also studied theology in Oxford. He entered the Cistercian abbey of Quarr in the Isle of Wright in 1221. In 1223 he was made abbot of Stanley in Wiltshire, a daughter-house of Quarr and a member of the filiation of Savigny, as was St Mary's, Dublin. Stanley was the mother-house of Duiske, founded in 1204.

It does not enter into the scope of this chapter to deal with the story of Stephen of Lexington's visitation of the other Irish monasteries except insofar as this is necessary to explain the situation which arose in Inishlounaght itself. Stephen came to Ireland in the spring of 1228 deter-mined to restore the authority of the general chapter over the Irish houses of the Order. We have detailed information regarding the visitation under-taken by Abbot Stephen by reason of the fact that his Register of Letters still exists[22] and contains among other documents a mass of letters and off-ical records relating to this very important visitation. Before leaving England, Abbot Stephen received letters of protection from Henry III, as we know from a letter written by the king to the justiciar of Ireland on 27 January 1228.[23] He appears to have landed at Wexford, and his first letter written in Ireland was penned either at Dunbrody or Tintern in March.[24] This letter was addressed to the community of Glenragh (de Valle Caritatis) the latest filiation of Inishlounaght. Glenragh was in financial straits at this time and was soon to be suppressed by the visitator and its lands transferred to Dunbrody, an Anglo-Norman house. This must natu-rally have irritated the community of the mother house at Inishlounaght,

21 Registrum, xxxviii.   22 This Register is preserved in the National Library of Turin, but there is a microfilm copy in the National Library of Ireland, Dublin (Neg. 2989). See also Cistercian Fathers Series, 28, Cistercian Publications (Kalamazoo, 1982), p. 13. Griesser, who first edited the letters suggested that the book of letters found its way to Italy when Stephen was marked in the castastrophe which overtook the General Council of 1241.   23 Hen. III ad justiciarium Hiberniae.   24 This is the opinion of Aubrey Gwynn.

and was not calculated to win them over to the policy of this their latest visitator.

We have no certain indication as to whether Stephen actually visited Glenragh himself, either now or at some later date. The register is silent as to any such visitation, but terms of this first letter would suggest that he hoped to visit them at some favourable opportunity. A later report on the state of the houses in Ireland[25] shows, by its reference to this community, that he had first hand knowledge of the situation in that house, either as a result of a personal visitation or from some other trustworthy source. It is likely enough that he visited the house himself, as he declared his intention of doing in the letter written by him to the community on his arrival in Ireland. As there is no mention in the Register of any such visit, nor does his itinerary allow us to think he could have made it between the time he arrived in Tracton in April 1228 and the time the council of abbots met in Dublin in June (by which time the state of the house was already well-known to Stephen), it would seem that this visit to Glenragh must have taken place while Stephen was still in Wexford, possibly while he was using Dunbrody abbey as his headquarters. It would have been quite an easy matter to make the journey from Dunbrody to Glenragh and back before he set out on his long and arduous visitation of the other Irish Houses.

Stephen's first letter to Glenragh,[26] a relatively unimportant commmunity, would go to show that he intended to visit that house at the earliest opportunity, as indeed his letter itself suggests. For he tells the monks that he has come to Ireland by the authority of the general chapter and with plenary powers to arrange and provide for the reform of the Order throughout the country. He summarises the complaints that have been made to him regarding the administration of the monastic possessions of Glenragh, and warns them against future neglect or dilapidation of the property of the house. In conclusion, he expresses the hope that he may at some favourable opportunity be able to take counsel with them and with other good counsellors concerning the future of their house. It may be added that the fact that this letter is addressed to the convent, and not to the abbot, suggests that there was at this time no abbot in charge of the house. Like that abbot of Inishlounaght, the father-abbot of the house, he seems to have disappeared before the visitation – a fact not without some significance.

Stephen's next letter was written to the abbot of Whitland, in Wales, informing him that the abbot visitator intended to make the visitation of his daughter house[27] (Tracton) and hence that there was no need for the abbot of Whitland to journey to Ireland that year. Stephen must have vis-

---

25 Registrum, xxxii.   26 Ibid., xi.   27 Ibid., xii.

ited Tracton about the end of March or early April, and it is probable that
he made the journey by sea from Wexford. From Tracton he wrote to the
community of Midleton (*de Choro*), then without an sbbot. He arranged
that the abbot of Tracton should make the visitation of that house and
then set out for Holy Cross abbey to which he had already addressed a
letter. He probably journeyed to Maigue and Owney through country,
which, though in Norman hands (for the most part), was in a very unsettled state at that period. A reference in a letter written about June to the
abbot of Citeaux[28] shows that he travelled in frequent danger of his life
from robbers and other malefactors, and among the 'many places' in
which he encountered such dangers was the abbey of Maigue. Indeed,
from the words of the letter it would seem that the danger in the latter
case threatened him inside the abbey itself and not merely in its vicinity,[29]
and though this may seem at first sight most unlikely, yet, when we consider what afterwards took place in that very house towards the end of the
same year, we shall hardly be surprised to hear that Stephen's life was in
danger during his visit to that turbulent community. Stephen's delay in the
abbey of Maigue cannot have been a long one. This abbey had been subjected to Margam in Wales by the general chapter of 1227 and seems to
have been provided with an Anglo-Norman abbot sometime previous to
Stephen's visitation. From a letter, written by Stephen when in Holy Cross
(about May), it appears that Patrick, the former subprior of Maigue, had
asked pardon and mercy for certain 'excesses' committed by him and had
been absolved by Stephen. The latter then sent him to the new mother
house (Margam) and asked the abbot of that house to subject him to the
penalties incurred by conspirators until such time as the general chapter
should have ratified the absolution granted by Stephen.[30] It is likely
enough that it was on the occasion of this short visit to Maigue, during the
course of his journey to Holy Cross, that Stephen was approached by the
former subprior for the absolution. From Maigue he would have gone on
to Owney, on the borders of Limerick and Tipperary. This was an Anglo-
Norman foundation, and it had already been suggested by the visitators of
the previous years that the Irish abbey of Holy Cross, which seems to have
reached the verge of extinction, should be suppressed as an autonomous
house and joined to the abbey of Owney. As the purpose of Stephen's visit
to Holy Cross was to determine whether this union with Owney should
take place or not, it is most probable that he visited the abbey of Owney on
the way and discussed the whole question with the abbot of that house.
There was, indeed, another reason why he should call upon the abbot of

---

28 Ibid., xxxi.   **29** In speaking of the attacks made on him at Kilcooly he makes it clear that
it was not in the monastery itself that he was attacked but in a wood near-by: *in nemore iuxta
Arvicampum,* but in speaking of the danger which threatened him at Maigue he says quite definitely *In abbatia de Magio* (Reg., xxxi.)   **30** Registrum, xix.

Owney. When the abbot of Froidmont left Ireland in 1227, he delegated his powers as visitator to the abbot of Owney and the abbot of Furness seems to have done likewise. The abbot of Furness had become the new father-abbot of Inishlounaght as a result of the far-reaching decisions of the chapter of 1227 and, as his delegate, the abbot of Owney was charged with the visitation and correction of that monastery. Hence it is probable that during this short visit to Owney, Stephen discussed the affairs of Suir as well as the affairs of Holy Cross with the abbot, and this is confirmed by a reference in a letter which he wrote to the convent of Inishlounaght soon after his arrival at Holy Cross.[31]

Stephen's letter to the community of Inishlounaght was written probably in May and, as has been remarked already, the fact that it is addressed to the community (*conventus*) and not to the abbot, nor even to the abbot and community, would indicate that there was no abbot in charge of the house at this time. As a matter of fact, we know from later letters and from the account of what happened during the visit of Stephen to the monastery in the autumn of this year, that the prior of the house was then ruling the community. Stephen had already written to one of Suir's daughter houses and had probably visited the same. He must have had a fair knowledge of the situation in Inishlounaght, even at this early stage of the visitation. In his letter to the community, he informed them that the decree of the previous general chapter by which they had been removed from the jurisdiction of Maigue and transferred to that of Furness in Lancashire had taken effect. He, therefore, commanded them in virtue of holy obedience to submit themselves fully to the abbot of Furness as their new father, and to do so with all devotion and humility as beseems sons of the Church and of the Order. He ordered them, moreover, to receive with meekness and reverence the Brother R., a monk of Furness, who had been commissioned by the abbot of Furness to act in his place when he is unable to make the visitation of Inishlounaght in his own person. Finally, he announced to the community that by his present letter he placed the house under the jurisdiction of Furness, giving the latter abbey full rights over it as a mother-house over her daughter according to the consititutions of the Order.

The rights given to the abbey of Furness over Inishlounaght included, as may be learned from another letter, that of putting new monks into the abbey, probably Anglo-Normans. Not only the abbey of Suir but its two daughter houses – Fermoy and Corcumroe – had been given to Furness (its third daughter house being suppressed), and the abbot of Furness had evidently been remiss in his obligations towards these new daughters. Certainly Stephen of Lexington seemed to think so, for he addressed no

31 Ibid., xvi.

less than four letters on the subject to the abbot, the last only of which has survived. This letter, written in June, 1228, informs the abbot of the means and measures by which it is hoped to restore discipline among the Irish monks and upbraids him with negligence towards his Irish daughters. In the course of the letter, Stephen remarks that this is his fourth letter on the subject. In this fourth letter, he complains of the abbot's neglect of Inishlounaght to which, apparently, he had previously promised aid both of men and money. He seems to have fulfilled neither promise. Up to the time of writing, Stephen had seen no sign of the proffered aid.[32] Whether, in fact, the monks from Furness came to Inishlounaght before Stephen's own visit in the autumn of the same year is not clear. In view of the violent opposition offered by the Irish monks to the abbot visitator on that occasion, and of the election almost immediately afterwards of a monk of the abbey of Furness to be abbot, we may conclude that a contingent of foreign monks had actually arrived at the monastery before this and that this influx may have been in part responsible for the extreme violence of the prior and his associates in opposition to the policy of the visitators.

For the moment Stephen Lexington took no further steps regarding the visitation of Inishlounaght and the appointment of a new abbot. As soon as he left Holy Cross after settling the affairs of that house, he seems to have directed his steps to Kilcooly where, as we learn from a letter written to the abbot of Citeaux and general chapter of the Order,[33] he was in danger of death from robbers in a wood near the monastery. From Kilcooly, he journeyed to Jerpoint and thence to Duiske and possibly visited Killenny (Glandy) also. He seems to have delayed some time at Duiske before proceeding to Dublin, where he held a council of abbots at which certain measures were taken for the reform of the Order in Ireland. But before proceeding to Dublin to attend this meeting, he addressed a letter[34] to Maelmuire (Marianus) O Briain, archbishop of Cashel, a former monk of Inishlounaght, in which he informed him of the projected council in Dublin, and asked him to receive kindly, and help in an effective manner, a certain Brother Vincent who had come to Ireland on business connected with the Order. He also complained that the former abbot of Baltinglass, Brother Malachy, who had been deeply implicated in the conspiracy and had, nevertheless, been treated with much favour because of a petition made by the archbishop on his behalf, had failed to carry out any of the promises he had made. There seems to be a rebuke contained in Stephen's words of reproach to the archbishop, and there is, perhaps, a hint that the archbishop's attitude in the matter is not all that might be expected from one desirous of the correction of abuses in the Cistercian

32 Ibid., xxv. 33 Ibid., xxxi. 34 Ibid., xxviii.

Order. This is not, of course, set down in so many words, but it is implied, and is borne out by a reference to Maelmuire in another letter[35] where Stephen states that the archbishop is 'an acceptor of nation, not of true religion; one who praises his own people rather than a well-ordered foreign mind.' Maelmuire, in fact, was looked upon with a none too favourable eye by the reformators of the Order in Ireland and was considered rather too pro-Irish in his leanings. We shall meet him again in the course of this chapter.

The council of abbots met in Dublin on 25 June, or, as the ancient record puts it, the morrow of the feast of St John the Baptist. The abbots there assembled drew up a report which was signed by the visitators and all the abbots present, and was later circulated to all the Irish houses. Among the measures of reform proposed by this council was the wholesale transference of Irish houses from their mother-houses to the jurisdiction of new mother-houses in England and Wales. We are concerned here only with the relations of the decree to Inishlounaght and its daughter houses. It removed Inishlounaght itself from the jurisdiction of Maigue, this being but a ratification of a change already made the previous year; but besides subjecting the abbey to the jurisdiction of Furness in Lancashire, it took from it its two daughters, Fermoy and Corcumroe, placing them also under Furness, while it decreed the complete suppression of Inishlounaght's third daughter house – that of Glenragh. This abbey was said to be too small and too poor and altogether insufficient in both movable and immovable goods to subsist as an autonomous house. Moreover, its community is stated to have been reduced at that time to only eight monks and nine laybrothers, while the monastic possessions had fallen to less than three carucates[36] of land and most of the goods were wasted or alienated. It was therefore decided to unite the abbey to the great Anglo-Norman house of Dunbrody which was accordingly done.[37]

The great principle which the reformators looked to as the surest guarantee of success was that the rebellious houses should be subjected to a foreign jurisdiction, but care was taken in carrying out this programme that each new mother house should have at least two daughters in Ireland. The reason given for this arrangement was that one at least of them might serve as a secure refuge for the mother in the event of the other (or others) 'withdrawing its neck from the yoke of the rule and of the Order by attempting to create detestable schisms or to institute contumacious and malicious conspiracies'.[38] Among the houses heavily pun-

---

35 Ibid., xxxiv. 36 A carucate, that is a ploughland. Originally a carucate signified as much land as a team could plough in a year, but the size of a carucate depended on the quality of the soil and on the practice of husbandry in various localities. 37 Registrum, xxxii. 38 'Ut si quando aliqua illarum collum de sub iugo regule et ordinis contumacibus et maliosis conspirationibus attemptet excutere aut detestanda scismata procreare, in reliqua filias altim

ished was that of Mellifont, the mother house of almost all the Irish houses. From the correspondence of Stephen of Lexington, it would appear that the situation in this house was so serious that sixty-eight out of a total of one hundred and ten religious revolted and actually left the house, carrying with them the charters, chalices and books as well as the processional cross.[39]

None of the Anglo-Norman houses were involved in these troubles, and that in itself is a fact of no little significance which gives colour to the theory that, apart altogether from a decay of monastic discipline, there was a life and death struggle going on at the time between the Irish and English monks for the control of the Order in this country. Unfortunately, it seems fairly certain that in the troubled times through which the country was then passing, the cause of reform came to be confused with the cause of Anglo-Norman aggression, with disastrous consequences to religion. To be a rebel came to mean something laudable instead of something which should be condemned as unworthy of a religious. Men who, in ordinary circumstances, would never dream of disobeying their legitimate superiors or of being guilty of any kind of insubordination, now found themselves at one with the mere malcontents and mischief-makers in defying the reforming ordinances. It was a deplorable situation, and one that could have been avoided. The policy of replacing Irish by English or Anglo-Norman abbots or monks only led to worse evils. It resulted in universal rebellion in Munster and the midst of which the foreign monks were forcibly ejected from the monasteries by their Irish colleagues. This, of course, was a glorious opportunity for those malcontents who are always ready to create trouble, a certain number of which may be said to have existed in all orders at all times. Had conditions been normal, such men would have been able to do very little, but in the abnormal conditions then prevailing they took the lead in scenes of violence and disorder, to the great detriment of religion and the scandal of souls.

The council of abbots held in Dublin on 25 June had decreed the union of Glenragh with Dunbrody, but there is some evidence that this union did not find favour with all the monks. A letter[40] written by Stephen Lexington to the Anglo-Norman abbot of Maigue about July of this year, informs him that he has commissioned him, in virtue of the authority invested in him by the general chapter, to put into execution the union of these two abbeys, and he authorises him, moreover, to take any action he may judge expedient against all rebels and resisters. The reference here to rebels and resisters seems to mean rebels and resisters to the decree of

refugium reperire possit mater unumque receptaculum, dum alterius insolentie intendit reprimende sicque commodius et espeditius pro causarum varietate aut temporis alterius per alteram oppressionem sublevet aut domet elationem' (Registrum, xxxii). 39 Registrum, lxii. 40 Ibid., lviii.

union and implies that this decree was not welcome in certain quarters. We shall hardly be mistaken if we conclude that the rebels and resisters in question were to be found for the most part in the two houses of Glenragh and Inishlounaght. The decree was, of course, put into execution despite any protests that may have been made to the contrary, but the monks of Inishlounaght were by no means satisfied, and both they and their daughter houses were to show a very much greater spirit of opposition before the year had come to a close.

Stephen returned to the south of Ireland about August, and it was probably during this period that he made his visitation of Jerpoint abbey. He had already visited Jerpoint on his way from Holy Cross to Duiske and had presided at the election and installation of an Anglo-Norman abbot in that house. The visitation of Jerpoint must have been a somewhat prolonged affair judging by the series of regulations which the visitor drew up afterwards and which finds a place in his register. It is likely, therefore, that this visitation was made during his second visit to Jerpoint when he was able to remain for a longer period. It was probably while at Jerpoint on this second occasion that he wrote his second letter to the community of Inishlounaght. He was now about to undertake a journey into Munster,[41] and the next group of letters in the register is concerned with that stage of the visitation. In his letter to the community of Inishlounaght he laments the ruin of discipline in that house. This letter gives us insight into the sad state of indiscipline into which the community had fallen.

From the whole tone of this letter, as well as from various references made by Stephen, it is evident that the community of Inishlounaght had been deeply involved in the rebellion against the authority of the Order, and the visitor now pleads with the monks to return to their obedience. He expresses his heartfelt sorrow and great grief that the plantation, most devoutly made by their holy fathers for the extension of divine worship and the salvation of souls, has, he is sorry to say, become a source of derision to seculars, a cause of shame to clerics, a by-word to the world and a source of ruin to the Order. He bewails not only the aridity but even the sterility of this vineyard of saints which had once flourished and brought forth plentiful fruits of virtue. He beseeches them, as most loving brethern and children of God, to return and learn that true wisdom consists in the fear of God and holy obedience. He warns them of the perilous state of those who, putting away from them the fear of God, are not afraid to give themselves up to rebellion. He exhorts them, in short, to return to their obedience, following the example of Mellifont and the other houses of the Order, and he firmly believes that they will be obedient to the Order in the future. He asks them to reply to his letter and to send to him two of their

41 Ibid., lxvi and lxviii.

seniors that he may treat with them more at length and more diligently concerning the affairs of their house.[42]

The monks of Inishlounaght replied to Stephen's letter and asked him to defer his proposed visit to their monastery until the justiciar should be present. As the letter summarised above does not mention any such visitation, it may be surmised that the notification of the visitation referred to by the monks was either given by word of mouth or was contained in another letter of which no copy has been preserved. As the existing register is by no means complete, the latter supposition may well be the correct one. That Stephen had notified the monks of his intention to visit their abbey may be gathered from the next letter in the register.[43] Before passing on to that letter, however, a word may be said regarding the monks expressed desire that the proposed visit should not take place until the return of the justiciar. The justiciar at this time was Richard de Burgo, who held office from 1228 till 1232. This noble, as son of William de Burgo, inherited the great tracts of land granted to his father in Limerick and Tipperary-territories later to be known as those of the Clanwilliam Burkes. William de Burgo had married·a daughter of Domhnall Mór Ó Briain, king of Thomond, so that his son, Richard was, in fact, half Gaelic, half Norman, one of the first representatives of the new mixed race which was then coming into being. His royal grandfather was, moreover, one of the principal benefactors of Inishlounaght. The abbey of Maigue, with which that of Suir was closely connected, was also an O Brien foundation, and the head of the rebel party there at this period was a grandson of the then king of Thomond, Donnchadh Cairbreach Ó Briain, and consequently a younger cousin of the justiciar. There is just a possibility that this blood relationship of the justiciar with the old Gaelic stock of the O'Briens of Munster, who were, in a special manner, patrons and benefactors of a whole group of Cistercian houses including Suir, Maigue, Corcumroe, Holy Cross and Kilcooly, was one of the reasons inspiring the monks of Suir to plead with Stephen for the postponing of the visitation until the justiciar should be present. Possibly, they hoped to find in him a friend and protector who would at least intercede for them with the abbot visitator.

Another reason may have been the close connection of Richard de Burgo with the town of Clonmel. The de Burgos received, at an early date, a grant of the entire district from Clonmel to Carrick, as well as considerable tracts of land in other parts of Limerick and Tipperary. At a later date, the Butlers replaced the Burkes in the Clonmel area, but at the date of Stephen of Lexington's visit to Ireland, the Burkes were still the important family in this district. William de Burgo had conferred the liberties of

42 Ibid., lxxi.   43 Ibid., lxxii.

Kilkenny on Clonmel, and in 1225 Richard de Burgo was granted a yearly fair at Clonmel on the Vigil of All Saints and the seven days following.[44] It has been said, with good reason, that the creation of the borough of Clonmel is probably due to Richard de Burgo[45] on whose death the town passed into the king's hands. In coming to Clonmel, them, the justiciar was coming to a town which was peculiarly his own. This town was built on a site adjoining the monastic lands of Inishlounaght, and as an immediate neighbour of the monks, the justiciar might be expected to be particularly interested in their community and would, in the normal course of events, be brought into close contact with them. But the justiciar was at this time in Connacht, whither he had gone to subjugate the vast territories granted to him in May, 1227, and it was by no means certain when he would return.

Stephen of Lexington had no intention of waiting until Richard de Burgo returned from Connacht before visiting the abbey of Suir, and he intimated as much to the monks in his next letter. Addressing himself once again to the community,[46] he explains first of all why it is he cannot postpone his visit until the return of the justiciar. He would, he says, agree to their petition if there were any reasons for doing so; but he had, in fact, before receiving their letter, summoned a number of abbots to meet him at the abbey of Inishlounaght so that by their counsel, as well as that of the monks of Suir themselves, he might undertake the duty imposed upon him of reforming their house. He gives another reason for not delaying the visitation until the return of the justiciar, namely, that it was uncertain when the justiciar would return, whereas the business on which Stephen himself was engaged admitted of no delay. He proposed to visit the abbey, therefore, in the course of the following week, some day after the feast of St Bartholomew (24 August).

Before concluding his letter Stephen gave the monks of Inishlounaght some salutary advice. He pleaded with them to direct their minds towards God alone and towards the patrons of their Order, Benedict and Bernard, contemplating not the things which are seen but those which are not seen; for those things which are visible are but temporal, while those which are invisible are eternal, namely, the pain of hell and the glory of heaven. To the prior, especially, he addressed himself and prays the Almighty that in his mercy he may illuminate the prior's heart and so lead him to a perfect knowledge of himself and to true and humble repentence. Although, like the prodigal son, he has gone away into a far country, yet, if he only returns to his father he will be received with all affection, will get the benefit of absolution and will be restored to the favour of the Order. God

44 *Close Roll,* 9 Henry III, part 2.   **45** So James F. Morrissey in a paper on Clonmel in the *Journal of the Royal Society of Antiquaries of Ireland,* 39, pt. 3 (September 1909) 244.   **46** Registrum, lxxii.

forbid that a christian, and above all a religious and a monk of the Cistercian Order – an order so acceptable in the sight of God and the angels and enjoying so great and resplendent a fame in the eyes of men, should neglect God and the Order and fly to the secular power like an apostate or an infidel. For it is much better to confide in God than in men, and to place one's trust in the spiritual weapons of prayer than in corruptible and worldly weapons.

Reading between the lines of this letter, we get a picture of a religious house in a state of disorder. The monks have rebelled against the lawful authority of their Order. The house is without an abbot and the prior, who should be an example to the rest and an upholder of authority, has placed himself at the head of the rebels and even called in the aid of the secular power to support him in his rebellion. Apart from the mention of rebellion, which is stressed in all the correspondence dealing with this monastery, we have no details concerning the abuses then reigning in Inishlounaght. Probably there were the usual disorders and 'excesses' of which we hear so much during the course of this Irish visitation. The reports to the abbots of Citeaux and Clairvaux and to the general chapter, copies of which are contained in the register, give us an idea of the general complaints. The most serious were the widespread violation of the law of enclosure, the wasting, squandering and alienation of the lands, substance and goods of the monastery, the exercise of proprietorship by the monks in utter disregard of the law and in violation of their vow of poverty, and the custom of admitting nuns into the monasteries of the Order in Ireland, which seems to have been almost universal, and is denounced by the visitator as leading to the gravest abuses and scandals throughout the land. Inishlounaght, indeed, is one of the houses of which there is specific mention of a monastery of nuns situated beside the monastery of monks, from which it was separated only by a small hedge.[47]

Stephen now takes up his pen to write to the abbot of Owney.[48] He tells him of the disquieting news he has received from Inishlounaght (probably from the monks who brought the answer to his earlier letter) and of how the prior of that house, with his accomplices, was in every way promoting rebellion against the Order, shrinking from no iniquity, and thinking all things lawful which were according to his will. Stephen informed the abbot that, with the help of God, he would be in Clonmel on the Saturday following the feast of St Bernard, that is on 26 August. His business there is in connection with the abbey of Suir and the election of an abbot. This he wishes to do in consultation with the abbot of Owney. He, therefore, requests, or rather commands, him to come to Suir abbey on that day. He has communicated more of his business by the bearer of the letter who will

47 Ibid., iii.   48 Ibid., lxxiii.

deliver, by word of mouth, certain matters which are to be kept secret, and hence not to be mentioned in the letter. Following on this letter to the abbot of Owney came another to the archbishop of Cashel.[49] In his letter to the archbishop, Stephen informs him that he has desired the monk who brings him the letter to communicate certain matters to him by word of mouth. He asks the archbishop to continue to show in the future the same diligence and devotion he has hitherto shown in promoting the cause of the Order. It may be taken as certain that the oral communication which the archbishop was to receive from the bearer of the letter concerned the affairs of Inishlounaght abbey and the rebellious prior and monks.

Stephen, as we have seen, had arranged to be in Clonmel on Saturday, 26 August. The next letter in the register must have been written after the visitation and is addressed to the newly-elected abbot of Inishlounaght,[50] being followed by yet another letter to the archbishop of Cashel[51] in which Stephen calls on the archbishop to fulfil his duty and to support the visitator in his efforts to reform a monastery situated, as he wrote, in the archbishop's own diocese (sic), and wholly in his power, being near his city and cathedral. In this letter he describes the scenes of rebellion which met him on his arrival at Inishlounaght. These two letters, then, were written after the rebellion which broke out on the occasion of Stephen's visit in August The account of the rebellion itelf, which is missing from this part of the register, is preserved, fortunately elsewhere in the same book. It is found in the beginning of the register and is numbered Epistle III in the published edition of the register. There is, however, not the slightest doubt that its proper place in immediately before the letter written by Abbot Stephen to the newly-elected abbot of Suir. It is indeed a report drawn up by the visitator in conjunction with four other abbots. The abbot of Owney's name does not appear among the signatures to this report, and it may be asked was he himself present at these proceedings at all? Though mention is made in the report of 'certain abbots' who accompanied Stephen on this occasion, none of the abbots are named. Unfortunately, the report is incomplete, part of the document being missing from the register, so that it begins abruptly in the middle of the narrative and all the events leading up to the actual visitation have been thus lost The report is signed by the abbots of Mellifont, Bective, Grey abbey and Tracton as well as by the visitator himself, and one is inclined to wonder if the abbots here named were themselves present at the events they so graphically describe. Probably they were, and it is possible that the abbot of Owney was also there, though he is not named in this document.

The abbot visitator arrived in Clonmel in due course and on a certain day, possibly 27 August, the Sunday after his arrival, preached in the parish

49 Ibid., lxxiv.   50 Ibid., lxxiv.   51 Ibid., lxxvii.

church (the present St Mary's Church of Ireland), to a congregation which included the four abbots and not a few of the Anglo-Norman nobility. The first attempt to make contact with the community of Inishlounaght was made on this same day. Among Stephen's followers was a lay brother from Dunbrody, who had been his companion and guide on all his journeys through Ireland. This brother appears to have set off in advance with some of the horseboys, and may have been sent by Stephen to notify the community of his approaching visit. Unfortunately, the incomplete state of the document makes it impossible to give any more details regarding this first expedition. The prior must have had word of the coming of the abbot visitator to Clonmel, for he had already made his preparations for the reception of the visitators. He seems to have had his spies out to signal the approach of the newcomers, and he had taken care to hide a number of armed ruffians in the nunnery which adjoined the monastery for, as Stephen had mentioned in a letter already quoted, he relied more on material than on spiritual weapons.

When the brother with his attendant horseboys hove in sight, the prior of Inishlounaght, with certain others, approached and began to use the most insulting language towards him and to threaten him. Perhaps it will be best to let our document speak for itself or rather to give a summarised translation for a complete translation would take up too much space:

> The prior leaped over the small hedge which separated the abbey from the adjoining nunnery and going in, he ordered certain evil men whom he had hidden there to rush upon the brother and the serving lads and to ill-use them as they well knew how. So it was done. Throwing themselves on the brother, they cast him from his horse and dashed him to the ground. Then, stripping him of his garments, all except the lay brothers little hood, they struck and buffeted him with their fists and knees and beat him with cudgels until he was almost at the last gasp ... One of the attendants succeeded in making his escape, and, running into the town, raised the alarm by his shouts; the other serving-lad was gravely ill-treated by the prior's accomplices.
>
> Meanwhile, there was great commotion in the town when news of this outrage was brought by the lad who had made his escape. The prior, therefore, and his accomplices, allowed the terrified attendant to go free and, setting the wretched laybrother on a horse, sent him back to the town, though he could scarcely hold himself in position of the animal. On reaching the town, he had to take to his bed for he was neither able to walk nor to ride. The abbots, therefore, hired a boat, and caused him to be carried by water to a certain monastery twenty leagues distant, being con-

vinced that he would never fully recover from the effects of his ill-
usage.

The visitator now held a consultation with other prudent men
to decide what was best to be done. It was decided to send certain
obedient men of the Irish nation to remonstrate with the prior and
the convent, and try to persuade them to return to the obedience
of the Order, and to move them to humble repentance. All was in
vain. Returning therefore from the abbey and meeting the visitator,
the said monks and certain abbots who were with them, told the visitator that the prior had thrown off his cowl and appeared in his
scapular holding a lance in one hand and a sword in the other,
while a scabbard hung round his neck. All the other monks and
laybrothers, except the aged and infirm, were armed in similar
fashion, as were also their secular accomplices. The prior now
swore an oath that if any of the monks or laybrothers should desert
him and go over to the visitator he would hurl his lance at him, and
he added that if the visitator came he would avenge upon him in
the most grievous manner the corrections made by him in the
other houses throughout Ireland, just as he had done on the lay
brother.

When the visitator prepared to go to the abbey himself he was
held back against his will by the other abbots who declared that they
though they were willing to risk their lives, neither they nor their
companions were yet prepared for death. When not a few nobles
and others had gathered in the parish church to hear a sermon
preached by the visitator, according to a promise made by him
when requested to do so on the preceding Saturday, word was
brought to them that his enemies were preparing to slay the visitator at the very gates. When the abbots were approaching the abbey
the monks came rushing on them from all sides, but the nobles
interposed themselves between the two parties and succeeded, after
a long time, in persuading the prior – whose men were drawn up in
order of battle – to allow the visitator to speak to him.

The visitator entreated the prior, humbly and kindly, striving to
bring him to a better frame of mind. He reminded him that he was
a Christian, a monk, a priest, and a Cistercian. He got only abusive
and insulting answers for his pains; but his threatening language
lost him the support of his own followers who now took the side of
the visitator. Moved to sorrow, the convent ceased to oppose the visitator and, humbly repenting of their crime, sought and obtained
absolution from the same. The visitator was then received into the
abbey, and having preached a devout sermon to the assembly, a
body of electors was nominated, and being assembled in the

church, unanimously elected their new abbot, a suitable man, learned and obedient, and a monk of the mother house.[52]

Following on the events just recorded, the prior of Inishlounaght was deposed, as he well deserved to be, and the visitator spent three days in the house doing what was possible during that period to restore order and discipline for the glory and honour of God. The newly-elected abbot was a monk of Furness, the new mother house of Suir, and it is to be noted that his election was unanimous. It must be remembered, however, that the election of the new abbot was carried out not by the community of Inishlounaght, who certainly would not have been unanimous in their choice of an Englishman, but by a body of electors nominated for the purpose.[53] Stephen was taking no risks and most of the elections carried out at this period in various houses through Ireland were so arranged that a dependable man would be chosen. In some cases, a list of names was supplied to the voters, who were not allowed to vote for anyone whose name did not appear on the list. Needless to say, no obnoxious person ever got on such a list, and the general policy was to exclude men of Irish race. The reason for this is given in the concluding words of the report containing the graphic pictures of the Inishlounaght rebellion reproduced above:

> All prudent and God-fearing men were agreed that no monk from any of the rebellious Irish houses, for whose sake the Order had toiled so much and exposed its own to danger of death for the past fifteen years and more, should be appointed abbot until a certain definite period of time had elapsed that they might thus prove their devotion and obedience to the Order for a certain space of time, and that they might learn, according to the tradition of the Order, first to be disciples before they become prelates, even as Joseph was first a good and faithful servant and later a lord.[54]

Stephen had seen the new abbot installed in Inishlounaght before he left that house to continue his work in other parts. He could not have had time to make a regular visitation of the house at this stage, for he had been only three days in the abbey after the surrender of the rebels. Urgent business called him to Dublin, and it is probably from there that he wrote his next letter to the new abbot of Suir. This letter was written in September and announces the forthcoming visitation of the monastery by Stephen. He hopes to be with them about the feast of St Michael (29 September) when the justiciar shall have returned from Connacht.

52 Ibid., iii.   53 Ibid., iii.   54 Ibid., iii.

He gives the new abbot some very good and practical advice in this letter, telling him to keep God ever before his eyes, to do nothing with precipitation, but to decide all things with the counsel of prudent and Godfearing men. He should seek as far as possible to be loved by his community. He is on no account to receive the former prior Brother D. into the house ever again. He should follow the advice of the Lord P. of Clonmel and strive not to antagonise either the justiciar or the Irish by speaking ill of or detracting them.[55]

Following this letter comes one to the archbishop of Cashel, Maelmuire O Briain. His displeasure with the archbishop is apparent in almost every line of this letter. He begins by complaining of the unprecedented state of affairs which met his gaze when he arrived at the abbey of Inishlounaght to hold a visitation according to the traditions of the Order and the duty incumbent on him by the tenor of the mandate he had received. He found himself in the midst of conspiracies and rebellions in which the monks were drawn up in battle array as it were against God and the Order. He says it would be impossible to give all the details in a letter, but he will hear from the bearer all that he needs to know about the outbreak. He calls on the archbishop to see that those responsible for this state of affairs are reprimanded and gravely punished, and he reminds him of his own responsibility in the matter:

> Beloved Father remember that his house of Suir is situated in your diocese and wholly in your power, near your city and cathedral see. Let the zeal of the Lord inflame you! Gird yourself with the sword of Peter and the dagger of Phineas! Show yourself a shepherd in your duty, a father in your love, a monk in your zeal for the Order! Let not Dagon raise himself up against the worship of God so close to the ark, that is, your cathedral church! Yea, cast him down and shatter him with such fervour, zeal and diligence that the enemy may be afraid ever again to dwell near you or to come nigh to the shadow of your wings! Prostrate at the feet of your holy Paternity in all humility and devotion, we beseech and exhort you in Christ Jesus our Lord, that you use your utmost endeavour for the sake of God and your own honour to punish as gravely as possible by your seneschal and bailiffs as well as by your officials, and deans, such a great offence against the Church of God and the Order![56]

In his letters to his own community of Stanley in England, Stephen refers at this period to the great dangers and difficulties of the Irish visitation. He does not forget to describe his experiences near Clonmel where

---

55 Ibid., lxxvi. 56 Ibid., lxxvii.

the lay brother who had been his companion in all his travels 'was beaten almost to death with lances'. Notwithstanding this, he tells his monks, he himself and his other companions have been so far preserved from harm, thanks to the divine goodness.[57] Writing to the abbot of Citeaux he speaks in a similar strain concerning the great tribulations, afflictions, and persecutions he has had to undergo in Ireland before his mission is completed. With the story of Suir still fresh in his memory, he makes a passing reference to the attack on the unfortunate lay brother, and then goes on to relate how certain ill-disposed persons (probably some of the disaffected monks of Inishlounaght) stirred up certain robbers to waylay Stephen's party, attacking them from the rear whenever they got the opportunity, and harrassing them daily. Most of these plunderers were following them on foot, but there were with them also about twenty horsemen.

The rebellion at Inishlounaght was followed by an even more serious outbreak in the monastery of Maigue in Co. Limerick, where the monks turned the abbey into an armed citadel and defended it by force of arms till an attempt to take it by storm had been repulsed with the loss of some lives. This monastery, as we have already noted, was bound by special ties to that of Inishlounaght having been its mother house before the changes made at the visitation of 1227. It was also under the protection of the O'Briens and the leader of the rebels was himself a grandson of the king. The visitator had been on the point of leaving the country when this last rebellion broke out and he had to postpone his departure to deal with the affair.[58]

Though details are given in the register concerning the treatment meted out to the rebel monks in many of the monasteries, nothing is said regarding the fate of the rebels at Inishlounaght beyond the fact that the prior was deposed and sent away never to be received back again. It is likely that the less guilty among the rebels were allowed to remain after they had been reconciled to the order and received absolution, and they would, no doubt, be subjected to a long and heavy course of penance. The ringleaders and the greater part of the more active rebels would, if we may judge by what occured in other houses, have been sent away to houses of the Order in England or France, never to return to their old home without a very special permission from the abbot of Clairvaux, a permission they were not likely to receive. The loss of so many monks would greatly reduce the numbers of the community had not the general chapter thoughfully provided for the eventuality by empowering Abbot Stephen to introduce monks of foreign race and tongue into the Irish monasteries whenever he deemed such a proceeding necessary for the maintenance of discipline or the reformation of the house. In this way a strong Anglo-

57 Ibid., lxxviii.   58 Ibid., iv.

Norman element was introduced into Mellifont, Maigue, and many other of the Irish houses, including, we may suppose, Inishlounaght. This, unfortunately, was to lead to further complications in the case of Inishlounaght and her daughter houses.

The great visitation of 1228 came to an end in November of that year, when fourteen abbots (most if not all of them English or Anglo-Norman) assembled at Tintern, in Co. Wexford, for the formal closing. They issued two documents embodying the decisions made by the visitator. Some of these decisons involved far-reaching changes and innovations in the Order, as the first of these documents plainly confesses, but these changes and innovations are defended on the grounds that they are necessitated by a state of emergency. The changes referred to are the transference of various houses from their old to new mother houses and the introduction of new monks into various houses. But there was more to come. Stephen of Lexington returned to England and there commenced to draw up a series of regulations to be observed throughout Ireland. These regulations were framed as a result of the experience gained by Stephen during his visitation of the Irish houses and were intended to remedy certain disorders which he had found to be prevalent. We can gain a good idea of what the general abuses in the Irish houses of the order must have been by studying the articles. They were probably sent to Ireland about May 1229, when Stephen wrote to the abbots of Dublin and Duiske delegating them to carry out the visitation for that year and into the procedure to be followed.

We have few references to the abbey of Inislounaght following the tumults of the Lexington visitation. Trouble spread to the abbey of *Castrum Dei*, Fermoy, in 1229-30, when Fermoy became the centre of violent rebellion against the authority of the general chapter. The abbey of Fermoy refused to recognise the new filiation to Furness. The abbot of Fermoy and a monk of Inislounaght, and some other monks were killed in 1230. The general chapter of that year excommunicated the murderers.

Around this time there were about thirty six monks and fifty lay brothers in the Inislounaght community. In 1238 , the archbishop of Cashel, Maolmuire O Briain, retired to the abbey of Inislounaght, where he died.

Tensions between Inislounaght and Furness continued and in 1449 Furness sent over a further party of monks. In 1273, the abbot of Abbeydorney, pretending to act with the abbots of Holy Cross and Tintern, deposed the abbot of Inislounaght, but the abbot managed to recover his position. In 1277, the abbot made complains to the general chapter against the abbots of Dunbrody, Abbeydorney and Holy Cross. The following year, in 1478, Inislounaght's affiliation to Monasteranenagh was restored.

7. POST-REFORMATION

The last half of the fifteenth century witnessed much unseemly struggles for the position of abbot of Inislounaght. In 1462 or 1463, following the death of Abbot Patrick O Donoghue, it was proposed that an Augustinian friar, Florentius Ó Maoilmhichil, be appointed abbot. However, his term of office did not last long. Within the year, a Richard Loundres had unlawfully detained the abbey. He, in turn, was removed from office in favour of a monk from Holy Cross, Diarmuid Ó hIfearnain. Then this incumbent abbot was himself accused by one of the monks, William Ydonhyn (O Dineen), of serious crimes. The abbot appealed his case but ultimately withdrew. It is not clear whether William was named abbot. We do know that Thomas O Cahill became abbot in 1492.

Abbot Thomas O'Cahill is said to have died in 1505.[1] Fr Flannan Hogan OSCO states that Abbot O'Cahill was succeeded by Walter Butler.[2] Fr Flannan suggests that Walter Butler was not a Cistercian as he is referred to as 'abbot and commendatory'.[3] This view is confirmed in the Calendar of Papal Letters, vol. xvii. Two papal mandates,[4] dated 20 April 1502, addressed to the abbot of the monastery of Motalea, diocese of Lismore and to James Scyortal and John Tobin, canons of the diocese of Ossory, were made in favour of Walter Buttiler, cleric of the diocese of Lismore. In the first, provision was made of the perpetual vicarages of the parish churches of Hylsylhayn (Kilsheelan) and Lonayn (Newtown Lennan) alias Balenoe in the diocese of Lismore. The mandate states that a Cistercian monk, one Thomas Ochayll detained the first and a priest, Maurice Ochayll, the second, with no title and no support of law. The mandate asks the three mandators to create a canonry for the petitioner, Walter Buttlyer, who had aserted that he was of noble, even comital and baronial birth, and to collate and assign the canonry and vicarage to him. The second mandate stated that a William Odonchu, a Cistercian priest and monk had unlawfully, claimed, to be abbot of de Surio and asks that the mandators appoint Walter Buttiller as abbot. In the following year a mandate[5] was issued on 24 April 1503 in favour of a Thady Oflyijd, cleric of the diocese of Lismore. The mandate was addressed 'to the abbot of the monastery of Suir (de Surio), diocese of Lismore, and the chancellor and Waaiter Buttiller, canon of the church of Lismore.' It is not clear whether Walter is recognised as abbot in this mandate. He was still abbot in June 1509, when

1 Grattan Flood, *The Mountaineer*, 1925-6, p. 22. (Mount Melleray abbey); no sources quoted. 2 F. Hogan, OSCO, 'Cistercians and Cistercian Abbeys in sixteenth and seventeenth century Ireland', unpublished thesis, NUI. 3 Exchequer Inquisitions, Co. Tipperary, Henry VIII in National Archives, Dublin: la4885 Inq.13. 4 CPR, xvii, pt. 1, nos. 785 and 789. 5 Ibid., no. 949.

he made a grant of a weir to John Burron and John Brahynnoke.[6] He was succeeded by James Butler, who was related to the Butler of Dunboyne and to the house of Ormond. Even before the dissolution James Butler gave extensive grants of monastic property.[7] One of the largest leases of three thousand acres was to Lady Joan Fitzgerald, wife of James Butler, the ninth earl of Ormond and to their son Edmund, of all the lands of the monastery in the county of Waterford lying between the Castle of Kilmanahan and the town of Clonmel.[8]

As well as being abbot, James Butler also held the post of Dean of Lismore, Fr Flannan thinks this may indicate that he was abbot *in commendam*.[9] In any event, he seemed to have been a rather disedifying character, as portrayed by Waterford and Clonmel juries.[10] James Butler surrendered the monastery on 6 April 1540.[11] There were only four monks left, three of them named Cahill and the fourth, Maurice Kenny. Only the latter is listed as receiving a pension.[12] It was for twenty shillings. The abbot, James Butler, was granted a pension of £5. 6s. 8d. 'payable out of the possessions of the abbey'.[13] He still remained dean of Lismore and was also appointed prior of the Church of St Patrick.

James Butler died in 1549 and was succeeded by Thady Conway. A nominal successor of titular abbots was maintained for some time after. Nicholas Fagan (1545-1617), a Waterford man, and said to have been nominated to the see of Waterford,[14] having being educated in Salamanca and Rome, was appointed by the pope about 1602 as abbot of Inishlounaght, which title he held until his death in 1617. Laurence Fitzharris, a native of New Ross,[15] was consecrated abbot in Waterford on Trinity Sunday, 1625, by Archbishop Fleming of Dublin. Abbot Fitzharris was a very distinguished member of his Order. A letter written by him[16] to Abbot Gerard Purcell of Abbeyleix, dated 20 September 1633, shows that Abbot Fitzharris, besides being abbot of Inishlounaght, was also the commissary and vicar general of the Cistercian Order throughout all the territories and kingdoms of England, Scotland, Ireland and adjacent islands and provinces, an office which he appears to have held from the abbot of Clairvaux. During the Confederate period, 1641-9, when the Cistercians were enabled to return for a time to Inishlounaght, he presided over the community there and was present at the historic synod of Waterford in 1646. He laboured in the parish until the coming of Cromwell to Clonmel in 1650. Fr Flannan Hogan suggests that there is evidence to suggest that Laurence Fitzharris became abbot of Tintern before 18 October, 1648.[17] It is recorded that he was imprisoned and exiled in 1650, but that he con-

6 Ibid. 7 Ibid., pp 38-9. 8 IMED, pp 254-6. 9 Op. cit. 10 Howe and Graves (eds), *The Social State of the Southern and Eastern Counties of Ireland in the Sixteenth Century* (Dublin, 1870), p. 202. 11 Extents, p. 339. 12 Ibid. 13 Fiants, Henry VIII, no.140. 14 Hartry, p. 267. 15 Ibid., p. 107. 16 Mss *Barberini Latini* no. 8642 f.77rv. 17 Hogan, op. cit.

trived to escape and returned to his parish a few years later. Imprisoned a second time it was ordered, in 1655, that 'he be shipped in the first vessel that sets sail for France or Spain'. His subsequent fate is uncertain, but it appears that he died in exile. Fr Thomas Laffan was Fitzharris's successor as abbot of Inishlounaght, appointed in 1648.

Abbot James Butler, as we have seen, had been presented to the vicarage of St Patrick's Church, which was a dependency of the abbey. Both Nicholas Fagan and Laurence Fitzharris served St Patrick's as parish priest. It is most likely that through the latter's influence at Clairvaux and Rome, during the earlier years of his priesthood, that St Patrick's church was privileged by the Bull of Pope Paul v in 1619:

> Paul the Fifth to every one of Christ's faithful who shall see the present letter, greeting and apostolic benediction. For the increase of religion and the good of souls, we grant through our pious charity, out of the heavenly treasures of the Church, mercifully in the lord, full indulgence and remission of the temporal punishment of sin, to all the faithful or either sex who truly penitent, having gone to Confession and Holy Communion, visit the Church of St Patrick *Abbatiae de Surio*), belonging to the Cistercian Order in the diocese of Lismore, Ireland, Such visit to be devoutly made on the feast of Pentecost or on the feast of St Patrick, any time from First Vespers to sunset on the feast day, the person so visiting to pray for peace among Christian rulers, for the uprooting of heresies, and the exaltation of Holy Mother Church. The present grant is to be valid for thirty years. We will also that the present grant be null and void in the case of persons to whom already a plenary or partial indulgence has been granted for visiting the said church. Given at Rome in the church of St Mary Major under the ring of the Fisherman on the sixth day of March in the year one thousand six hundred and nineteen, being the fourteenth of our Pontificate.

Dr Philip O'Connell, in his booklet on St Patrick's Well, describes the final chapter of the parish of Inislaunaght:

> In 1704, a Fr James Daniel, of a well-known Clonmel family, was parish priest of Inishlounaght and resided there; he appears to have been a secular. The Irish House of Lords in March 1766 resolved that the several archbishops and bishops of the Protestant Church should be directed to ask their parish clergy to return a list of the several families in their parishes, distinguishing which are Protestants and which are Catholics. A report for the parish of Inishlounaght was forwarded later in the same year by the Revd Joseph

Moore, Protestant rector of Clonmel. It states that in the parish there are 218 families, 202 Catholic and 16 Protestant, and adds that there is one Catholic priest 'who lives in and has the parish of Clonmel, and one Friar'. About this time the parish of Inishlounaght ceased to exist as a distinct ecclesiastical unit and was merged in the Catholic parish of St Mary's, Clonmel.

8. DISPOSAL OF MONASTIC ESTATES

The abbey of Suir, as it was known to the Cistercians, stood about three hundred yards north of the river where the present Church of Ireland probably marks the site of the ancient abbey church which lay to the north of the monastery proper. The memory of the monks is preserved by the name given to the point where the river makes a sharp turn to the north which is still known as the Turn of abbey. The Irish name, *Inis Leamhnachta*, meaning the island or 'inch' of the new milk, needs no comment. The monastery possessed extensive lands in the counties of Waterford and Tipperary. The 'extent' made at Clonmel in 1541 shows that the monastic possessions amounted to 1,256 acres in the two counties[1] and included in Co. Tipperary the lands of Inishlounaght proper, Grange, Ballyorcley, Kilmolash, Loughkoragh, Grangerwey and Kilmaveigh; and in Cos. Waterford the manor of Kilnamack and the lands of Greenane. Two days after the surrender[2] of the abbey by the then abbot, James Butler, leases were given of the abbey lands, Lord Deputy Grey securing the Tipperary portion, and the treasurer, Lord James Butler, kinsman of the abbot, the lands in Co. Waterford. The latter are described in the 'extent' of 1541 as the manor of Kilmack, but in the lease made out to James Butler the estate is described as extending from 'the bounds of Kilmanagh Castle on the west to the bounds of the Clonmel burgagery lands on the east'.[3] It was co-extensive, therefore, with that portion of the present parish of Inishlounaght which lies in Co. Waterford and has an area of 2,970 acres – more than twice the acreage given for the entire monastic possessions in the 'extent' of 1541.

Two years after the survey made in 1541, we find a grant to Sir Thomas Butler of Cahir, of the dignity and title of baron of Cahir ('Chaeir, otherwise Chaier downeyske') with an annuity of £15, issuing out of the lands of Inyslawnaghe, Ballyyortche, Kylmolaghe, Granghirwyr, Loghekyraghe,

1 *Extents*, pp 337-9. 2 The abbey was 'surrendered' on 6 April 1540. 3 Canon Burke in the *Journal of the Waterford & S.E.I. Archaeological Society*.

Kylmaweaghe and Clonmel in the county of Tipperary ... parcel of the possessions of the late monastery of Inyslawnag ...'[4] In May 1551, a lease for 31 years in reversion was directed to be made to William Crofton, of the possessions of the abbey of Inneslennaughe, in the county of Tipperary, being of the yearly value of £16 sterling.[5] In 1582, however, the lands were in the possession of Mary, the wife of John Aylward, who wrote to Elizabeth to be released from the rents 'as she had received nothing out of the lands of late because they remained waste above three years in consequence of the troubles there by undutiful subjects'.[6] How did these lands come to be in this lady's possession? She had them on lease from Cormac mac Tadhg MacCarthy who, on 6 October 1578, had received a fee-farm grant of the abbey and lands from Queen Elizabeth as a reward for his services against the Desmonds. The Queen heard the petition of Mary Aylward and, writing to the lords justices on 15 November 1582, directed them to release her from payment of rent 'in consideration of her offering to build and re-edify the castles, houses and churches upon those lands which the rebels had lately burned and other ways spoiled'. She took care, however to enjoin on her officers to 'have a special and careful eye' that she should not lose her rents longer than necessity required. In 1592 the lands were granted to Edward Feogh, Mary his wife, and their heirs, at the annual rent of £24 Irish money. Edward Gough's grandson was in possession in 1641, and he, being an Irish Papist, lost the lands in the Cromwellian confiscation.

The Civil Survey gives the meares and bounds of the parish of Inishlounaght as they them were (1654-5) both in Tipperary and Waterford, and the first item of significance which we note in the description of the parish as set forth in the Tipperary volume of the survey is the reference to the tithes. These tithes, great and small of the said parish 'lying and being in the Baronyes of Iffay and Offay and Glaunniheiry', are said to be impropriated to 'Patrick Geogh of Killmaniheen' in the county of Waterford, by patent from the Crown. This in itself would be sufficient to indicate the monastic status of the parish. Patrick Gough is said to have held the land in fee 'by descent from his ancestors'. The first of the Goughs to hold these lands was, as we have already seen, Edward Gough of Clonmel. Edward was succeeded in the ownership of the lands by his son James who was succeeded in turn by his brother Thomas, the father of the Patrick Gough who held them at the time of the Cromwellian confiscation. We discover from the Civil Survey that Patrick Gough held the lands of the entire parish with the exception of those of Killballynamona, Moorstown-Keating, Blackcastle and Ballycureen. These were held by James Keating, Robert Cox, Thomas Donoghue and Henry Mockler

4 Morrin, i, p. 94 and COD, where the original Latin grant is printed in full (iv, pp 238-41). 5 Morrin, i, p. 253. 6 Ibid., ii, p. 48.

respectively. The lands of Kilmolash, indeed, were held, not by Patrick
Gough but by William Gough, which he had by gift from his father Edward
and the aforesaid Patrick, proprietor of the reversion in fee. The lands of
Kilmolash then, formed part of the original monastic lands received by
Edward Gough. In Co. Waterford, Patrick Gough held the castle, town and
lands of Greenane and Kilmacomma as well as the town and lands of
Kilnamack. All those lands in Tipperary and Waterford formed part of the
original monastic lands of Inishlounaght. Though the lands of
Killballynamona, Moorstown-Keating, Blackcastle and Ballycureen (represented today by the town lands of Moorstown, Blackcastle, Currenstown
and part of the lands of Woodroffe) were not held by the Goughs, the
tithes of those lands were, and there is little doubt that they, too, formed
part of the monastic lands of Inishlounaght.

In the course of the centuries which have elapsed since the making of
the Civil Survey and the plotting of the Down Survey (1655-8), many
changes have been made in parish, barony, and townland boundaries, so
that it is not always possible to find, at first sight on a modern ordnance
map, the townlands and other denominations shown on the Down Survey
maps or listed and described in the Civil Survey. In some cases, new
parishes have been created, old parishes have been divided or united, old
names have been anglicised or new names invented, so that the older
denominations are sometimes found under a variety of disguises and are
often hard to identify. It is gratifying to learn therefore, that a suggestion
made by Dr Simington in the final volume of his monumental edition of
the Civil Survey (vol. ix, County of Wexford) is now being carried into
effect and will result eventually in bringing to light by means of a series of
maps the revolutionary changes which have occured in parish, baronial
and townland boundaries as well as in the rendering of place-names since
the taking of the Civil and Down Surveys in the period of 1654-1658. The
project envisaged by Dr Simington, and now officially approved, is nothing less than the superimposition and reproduction of the Down Survey
on the six-inch Ordnance Survey maps. 'By this process the revolution
which has taken place in the rendering of place-names, the changes
effected in parish and barony boundaries or by the creation of new
parishes, the re-emergence of old parishes united from time immemorial
are brought to light, it may be said, at a glance.'[7] Through the courtesy of
Dr Simington I have been enabled to inspect a specimen of this superimposition of the old on the new geography of Ireland in the case of the
parish of Inishlounaght, and it is possible to see almost 'at a glance' the
relation of the new to the old and to identify under their modern anglicised and, sometimes, unrecognisable forms old townlands or place-names

7 CS, ix, County of Wexford, Introduction.

which we meet in the Civil Survey, or in the monastic *Extents* of 1541 and which have since disappeared. From an examination of the superimposition of the Down Survey, on the six-inch Ordnance may, it can be said with confidence, that the so-called civil parish of Inishlounaght as shown on the modern county index maps of Tipperary and Waterford is substantially identical with the parish of Inishlonaghty as set out and described in the Civil Survey and as delineated in the maps of the Down Survey.

In 1541, according to the extent than made, the abbey church was still in existence and all the other monastic buildings were still standing as at the date of dissolution. Not a vestige now remains of this once famed church except a romanesque doorway, which has been built into the modern Protestant parish church, and possibly, the east window of the same church. Yet this abbey must have been, before its dissolution both extensive and beautiful for the very ruins were still objects of admiration in the early seventeenth century as we learn from Sir James Ware, 'whether you consider their beauty or their antiquity,'[8] *sive vetustatem sive venustatem spectes.* The lands of the abbey, as listed in the extent of 1541, consisted of the vills of Innyslawnaghte (which included the site of the abbey, the demesne lands and certain mountain-land in Co. Waterford), Baylyorcley, Kylmalasske, Loghkoragh, Grangerwey (?), Kilmaveighe (?), and the Grange of Innyslanaghter in Co. Tipperary, as well as the manor of Kylmack and the vill of Glanwydan in Co. Waterford. The demesne lands, with the site and precints of the abbey, are met with in the Civil Survey of 1654, under the denomination of *Abyneslewnaght* and the three weirs and two mills noted in the extent of 1541 as being then on these lands are again noticed more than a century later in the Survey: 'There are three weares on the River of Sewer between the lands of Abymeslewnaght aforesd and the lands of Gryenane and Kilnamacke aforementioned ye Barony of Glaunyhiry in the county of Waterford.' The mills had probably fallen into disuse, for they are described in the Civil Survey as being lately rebuilt. 'Upon the said colpe [states the Survey] stands the walls of an old Aby, one grist mill and one tuckinge mill both lately rebuilt by Thomas Batty of Clonmel Esqr and some cabbynns.' An additional piece of information, not given in the Extent of 1541, but found in the Civil Survey is the fact that a court leete and a court baron were usually held in the town (of Inishlounaght) 'as belonging to the Scite or Precinct of the sd. Aby.'[9]

The many changes since the taking of the Civil Survey in 1654 and the making of the Down Survey maps some time later, have led to the replacement of the name Abynesleqnaght or Abbey Inishlounaght by the simpler

8 Sir James Ware, *Coenobia Cisterciensia Hiberniae* (1626), printed by Gilbert in his *Chartularies of St Mary's Abbey, Dublin.* The reference to Inishlounaght occurs in vol. ii, p. 224.   9 CS, i, p. 307.

designation of Inishlounaght on the modern six-inch ordnance map. But
the Inishlounaght of the modern map is quite a distinctive townland from
the Abyineslewnaght of the ancient one. The latter included the greater
part of the present townlands of Loughtally (or Glenbane) and Marfield
as well as of the modern Inishlounaght. Marlfield, of course, is a purely
modern name. Loughtally is found in the Civil Survey under the form
Logh Itallen, but the ancient Logh Itallen was much more restricted in
area then the modern townland known as Loughtally, consisting only of
the more westerly part of the latter. The name Glenbane, by which Loughtally is otherwise known, is of ancient date and is referred to in the old
leases. Dr Newport White, in his *Irish Monastic Extents*, identifies the *Loghkoragh* of the Inishlounaght extent with the Loughtally of modern times,[10]
but does not think that the modern Loughtally does, in fact, represent the
ancient Loghkoragh. Loghkoragh is not, indeed, the only form under
which this name is found in authentic documents. In the grant of the dignity of Baron of Cahir made to Thomas Butler by Henry VIII, in 1542, it
appears under the form *Loghkyraghe* and is found under a similar form
(Loughkyrraghe) in a lease granted in 1519 by the abbot and convent of
Suir to Thomas Butler, a layman,[11] who may have been the same Thomas
Butler, later made baron of Cahir. From this lease, it appears to have been
a grange of Inishlounaght. Though the name Lougnkyrraght, as well as
that of Loghkoragh, has long since disappearedd from the place-names of
this parish, it still existed in a slightly changed form in 1654, and has been
incorporated into the long list of place-names preserved for us by the Civil
Survey. Turning once more to that most useful and informative work, Dr
Simington's edition of the *Civil Survey for Tipperary* (vol. 1, p. 307) we find
the meares and bounds of Shanballyard in the parish of Inishlounaght
described thus:

> The meares and bounds of Shanballyard another pt of the sd parish
> distant from the rest lying and being in the Barony of Iffay and
> Offay are as followeth. And first beginning at a bush called Scagh-
> nerinnie from thence in the North East by a heighway to the East
> end of a hollocke called Knockychireene bounded with the lands of
> Ballynatten and Mageonstowne in the parish of Moorestownekircke
> and Bary of Middlethird, from thence to the South East by a ditch
> and the *lake of Loghtykearagh* to a place called Beallbohyr ...[12]

Here, I think, is the Loghkyraghe of the Butler grant and the
Loghkoragh of the Extent. The townlands of Clashavaddra are cut off com-

10 Extents, p. 437.   11 Quoted by Canon Burke from the Record Office, Dublin, i D., Inquis.
Tip. Chief Rem., Hen. VIII, no. 14.   12 CS, i, p. 307. The modern townland of Decoy contains a drained bog. Might this represent the site of the lake?

pletely from the rest of the parish of Inishlounaght, and, together with the parish of Mora, form an 'island' of Lismore diocese surrounded on all sides by the archdiocese of Cashel. This isolated fragment of the parish probably represents the grange of Loghkoragh or Loghkyraghe, and the name 'Shanballyard' (Sean-Bhaile Ard) may contain in one of its constituent parts the 'vill' of the Extent, for the Irish 'baile' is frequently employed in the same sense as the latin 'villa' of the Extents. The original Loghkyrraghe is sometimes described as a vill, sometimes as a grange, In Shanballyard we have all the essentials for a grange in the strictest sense of the word, situated as it was, at the very extremity of the monastic estate and cut off from all the rest of the monastic lands.

Among the other lands mentioned in the extent of 1541 are those of Ballyorcley or, as the name is spelt in the Extent, Baylyorcley. This is evidently the Ballyorly of the Civil Survey, the Baliortlea of the Down Survey and the Ballyorthche of the patent rolls of Henry VIII. Though the name no longer appears on modern maps, there can be no doubt that it represents the townland of Barne. The name Barne is derived from the New Barne created by the planter Moore in the townland of Chancellorstoen adjoining Ballyorly. The whole of Ballyorley came into the possession of the Moore family and the name 'Barne' replanted that of Ballyorly. 'Barne Ó bhFatha' is pinpointed in the Civil Survey as located in the Woodroffe Demense.

The next place mentioned in the Extent is Kylmalasskem which is to be equated with the Killmolashy of the Civil Survey and the Kilmolash of modern times. The ancient Kilmolash was of somewhat great extent since it included part of what is now known as Woodroff. We have already spoken of Loghkoragh, which is next on the list, so we will pass to the following entry which appears to be the vill of Grangerwey. As some of the writing on the folio is obliterated, it is not really clear as to whether this and the following place-name are correctly interpreted in the printed Extent. The editor, indeed, prints them with a question mark in each case. The names Grangerwey and Kilmaveighe, which appear in the printed Extent, can both be supplied from alternative sources for they occur in the patent rolls of Henry VIII under the forms Grangehorwey, Granghirwyr, and Kilmaweaghe.[13] Neither of these two names is now known, nor does it seem possible to identify them. They had already disappeared at the time of the Civil Survey was made unless, the Grangerobbeene or Grangerobin of the Survey representes the Grangerwey of earlier days.

The identification of the vill or grange of Kilmaveigh, also called Kilmaveighe, Kilmavee, Kilmovey, and in some seventeenth century grants, Kilmurvey, and even Kilmurry, has been difficult. From the royal visitation of Cashel and Emly we know that Kilmaveighe was impropriate to Inis-

13 Morrin, i, p. 94.

lounaght. From other sources we learn that it was close to, if not within the limits of Asmayn, the old name for the parish of Boytonrath, and that it was leased in perpetuity by Abbot Walter Butler in 1503 to Thady Ó Heffernan, 'perpetual vicar of Asmayn in the diocese of Cashel'. From an inquisition taken in the reign of Queen Elizabeth,[14] we find that the lands, still held by an Ó Heffernan, were then known as the lands of Kilmavey and Ballynamaddaree, which by 1641 had become Dogstown. At that time, the lands were said to have been held by O Heffernan 'by descent from his ancestors'. There can be no doubt that the grange of Kilmaveigh is represented today by the townland of Dogstown.

If the townland of Patrickswell finds no mention in the Extent of 1541, neither do those of Gortmore and Cleynnodie which are mentioned in the Civil Survey, and the greater part of which is now incorporated in Patrickswell. In later days the church of St Patrick's Well was a rectory appropriate to the abbey and served by the Cistercians. It was to this church that the last abbot, James Butler, was collated on the suppression of the monastery and there he seems to have remained until his death in 1549, being succeeded in the vicarage by Thady Conway. The modern Gortmore, then, represents but a small fraction of the ancient townland of that name just as the modern Garryshane by no means as extensive as the ancient Garryshane, At the time of the Civil Survey, Garryshane reached to the river Suir and was bounded on the south by the lands of Greenane; it must, therefore, have included the present townland of Tobberaheena on the outskirts of Clonmel, where the well may still be seen. A lease, granted to Lady Joan Fitzgerald in 1539, mentions the mill of Tyberhony, which may possibly be Toberaheena though it seems at first sight to refer to some place in the county of Waterford.[15]

The last townland which we intend to mention in connection with the Co. Tipperary possessions of the abbey is that of Monksgrange, generally known to-day as Grange. It sometimes appears under the form Monksgrange, at other times it goes in the records by the name of the grange of Inishlounaght. We have already noted that two granges were mentioned in the Extent of 1541. First, we have the grange of Inishlounaght, called in the Civil Survey simply Grange, which appears in the Down Survey as Monksgrange, a name which it retains on the modern ordnance maps. This grange included all the present lands of Grange with the addition of Garrntemple, Coole, and the eastern portion of Carrickconeen. The western portion the latter townland formed the lands of Grangerobbin or Grangerobbeen of the Civil Survey and the Down Survey. The second grange appearing in the Extent is the mysterious Grangerwey which we have already mentioned.

14 Inquisition September 4 xxxvi.   15 This lease is printed in full in Latin in IMED, pp 254-6.

It is now necessary to refer to the lands in Co. Waterford. All the possessions of the abbey of Inishlounaght in the latter county are summed up in the Extent under three headings: the Manor of Kylmack, the Vill of Glanwydan and the Rectory of Glannewydan. The manor of Kilnamack, to give it its modern name, is said in the Extent, to contain sixty acres arable and pasture and eight acres of wood. The actual possessions held by the abbey in Kilnamack were much greater than would appear from the words of the Extent. The exact area of the manor of Kilnamack may be ascertained by having recourse to the records. For instance, the lease made out to James Butler, treasurer of Ireland, of the Co. Waterford portion of the monastic lands, describes them as extending from the bounds of Kilmanahan Castle on the west to the bounds of the Clonmel burgagery lands on the east. A more detailed description of those lands is to be found in the lease made by the abbot and convent of Inishlounaght in 1539 to Lady Joan Fitzgerald, wife of James Butler, ninth earl of Ormond, and this lease names a whole series of places of which there is not the slightest mention in the Extent of 1541. They are mostly in Co. Waterford, and include Kyervan, the weir of Glenbane (*gurgitem de Glyanbane*) the land of Murisculi, Coragh ne Monagh, Grynane, Insemor, Kilmoghone, Moyke, Dromcurrye, Kenayn, Knoke ne Cahirragh, ' the grange or vill commonly called Kyell ne make ...' and 'all other lands and dominions' between Kilmanahan and Clonmel.[16]

Many of the above names can be identified. Kyell ne make is undoubtedly the modern Kilnamack (Cill na Mac); Kyervan represents the Irish Cathair Bhan, now turned into Caherbaun, the name of a townland in the barony of Glenahiery and parish of Inishlounaght, Co. Waterford. Glyanbane is, of course, Glenbane (Gleann Ban), the name of a townland in Co. Tipperary bounded on the south by the river Suir; here it is used not for the townland but for the weir, which the monks had built on the river. Coragh na monagh represents the Irish Currach na Manach, a name which has now disappeared unless it is disguised under the place name Corragform (Currach Gorm) in Kilmacomma or, perhaps, the Cnoc na Manach which forms a subdivision of Mount Neill Wood. Another subdivision of the same Mount Neill Wood is Monkhill. The two forms would point to Cnoc na Manach as being the earlier designation of the hill, now known as Mount Neill. Grynane is the modern Greenane (Grianan) and on part of which lands the Presentation Convent now stands. It is tempting to try to identify Insemor with the modern 'Moores Island' of the ordnance map. It is unlikely, however, that the Insemor of the lease represents that island, which has been conjectured by the historian of Clonmel to be the Ilean Tybraghevyne mentioned in some of the old leases. Kenayn can

16 Ibid.

only be an attempt to represent the Irish Ceannain which is still preserved in the name Coill na Ceannainne, now anglicised Cannon Wood or Cannon Hill. Knocke ne Cahirragh evidently stands for the Irish Cnoc na Cathrach, the hill of the Caher, or stone fort, and may have reference to the same Cathair which gave its name to the townland of Caherbaun. Dromcurrye probably stands for Drom a Churraigh, but the name is not known. I am unable even to conjecture what places are represented by the names Muirisculi and Moyk. Moyk is evidently the hill on which stood the so-called 'Wood Castle' known to English speakers as 'Bagwell's Folly' and to Irish speakers as 'Caislean na Muice'. Finally, the Kilmoghone of the lease may safely be said to stand for the Irish Cill Mochoma (Mochoma's Church) from which the modern townland of Kilmacomma takes its name.

Besides the principal townlands mentioned in the lease some interesting sub-denominations are given. These appear to have been various fields belonging to the abbey, some, if not most of which were in the neighbourhood of Clonmel. Among the fields thise named we find the mill field (*campus molendini*), the dean's field (*campus decani*), the high field (*campus altus*), the Clonmel field (*campus Clonmell*). The mill of Tyburhony, which is also mentioned in the lease, suggests that the mill field of the same lease refers to it, and the name Tyburhony itself suggests the modern Tobberaheena. The objection to identifying Tyburhony with Tobberaheena is that the places named in the lease seem to lie in the Waterford portion of the parish. Immediately after Tyburhony is mentioned a place called Lemlismorlerane, which is now unknown.

The lease appears to refer to places in Co. Waterford, and this would seem to be the case from the terms in which it is made out. Nevertheless, there is a possibility that some of the names refer to places situated in Co. Tipperary. This might not appear probable from an examination of the lease itself, but it is suggested by an examination of other documents. The grant made to Cormac mac Tadgh MacCarthy in 1578, having named the lands and possessions in Co. Waterford and then adds 'the mill field, the dean field, the high field and the field of Clonmel and the mill of Tiphune and Lemlessmollerane with their appurtenances.' An Inquisition of 14 September, enumerates among the abbey possessions 'the four fields called Ivellen, Gortedegunny, Gortearde Gorteclomrally and Kilmerenane'. Here, undoubtedly, we have in Irish dress the place-names already noted, first in Latin in the lease of 1539, and later in the literal English rendering given above; and now, in the Irish forms, rendered, it is true, in English spelling. The 'Ivellen' mentioned in the inquisition is evidently the latter portion of the Irish form of the '*campus molendini*' or 'mill field' of the earlier documents, the full form of which should be Gortivellen, that is Gort a Mhuilinn, Gortedegunny represents Gort a degani, a half Irish, half Latin form of the 'dean field' while Gortearde represents the Irish Gort Ard, the 'high field' of the English and the 'campus altus' of the Latin documents – the campus Clomell or Clonmel field being disguished under the form Gorteclomrally, which is evidently intended to represent the Irish Gort Chluain Meala. Finally, the Lemlismollerane of the Latin document has become Kilmerenane in the inquisition of Charles I. An inquisition of 21 October, gives the same names under a slightly changed form – Gortwilliam, Gortedeganie, Gortarde, Gortclonemally, the mill of Tipperhenny, Lemnish and Molleran alias Kilmereran, all the said townlands being stated to be in the Co. Tipperary. The Tipperhenny of this inquisition is undoubtedly the Tyburhony of the lease of 1539 and, if the statement of the inquisition that all these lands were in Co. Tipperary be accepted as accurate, we may conclude that the Tyburhony of the lease is identical with the modern Tobberaheena, which was, as we know, in the parish of Inishlounaght and is not to be confused with the townland of the same name in the parish of Kiltegan. The Civil Survey makes no mention of a distinct townland of Tobberaheena in the parish of Inishlounaght, but gives the bounds of Garrychane as extending to the river Suir, thus embracing the modern Tobberaheena. It is worthy of note that in 1654 a grist mill stood on these lands said to have been lately built by Thomas Batty of Clonmel, and one is tempted to wonder if this was built on the site of the older 'mill of Tyburhony'.

Among the lands belonging to the monastery in Co. Waterford, the Extent of 1541 mentions Glannewydan. Here the monks are stated to have held a watermill and 260 acres of land, valued at 100 shillings. Moreover, the rectory of Glannewydan was impropriate in the abbey. Glannewydan also appears in the State Papers in the form of Glannewaydan and Glancwedan, while in Pope Nichola's Taxation (1292) it appears under the guise of Glyncfaydan.[17] All these forms may be resolved into the modern Ballyvaden, representing the Irish Baile Bhaidin, which Professor Power interprets as 'Wadding's Town',[18] and which is situated near Bonmahon in the parish of Monksland. The entire parish of Monksland, known in Irish as Fearann na Manach, takes its name from a Cistercian establishment founded from Inishlounaght at the beginnning of the thirteenth century. This was the abbey of Glenragh, which was later united to Dunbrody. To Professor Power belongs the credit of identifying the site of this monastery which had long been a puzzle to historians. After the suppression of the house as an independent monastery in 1228, the community of Inishlounaght lost all these lands, but as a result of various disputes with Dunbrody they finally seem to have had a moiety of the possessions

17 Printed by Power in his *History of Waterford and Lismore*. Glyncfayden is found on p. 343.
18 Power, *The Place-Names of Decies*, p. 164.

restored to them: namely, the townland and rectory of Glannewydan, otherwise Ballyvaden, the area of which is given as 576 statute acres.

The total area of the parish of Inishlounaght is given in the county index maps as 9,378 statute acres, of which 6,408 acres are in the county of Tipperary. If we add to this the acreage of Ballyvaden we have a total of 9,954 acres. Though it is quite likely that this acreage represents substantially the acreage of the dissolved monastery of Inishlounaght, there is just a possibility that the lands which, though forming part of the parish in 1641, were not held by the Goughs, did not form part of the monastic estate. It is only a possibility, and the fact that the tithes of all these lands, too, are stated in the Civil Survey to be impropriated to Patrick Gough by patent from the Crown would suggest that they were, in fact monastic lands. However, as there may be some reason, even if it be only a slight one, for not accepting these lands as part of the monastic estate, I prefer not to include them here. Deducting the acreage of the parish, we have something more than 8,500 acres left, and this would, I think, be the minimum figure for the extent of the lands possessed by the abbey at the time of the dissolution – a figure, be it noted, more than six and three-quarter times the amount given in the Extent of 1541. The monastic estate was, then, a very extensive one, and the historian of Clonmel has justly pointed out that the Clonmel citizen, taking a circle of a mile in radius, could hardly step outside those lands. Included in that area were, either in whole or in part, the modern townlands of Inishlounaght, Tobberaheena, Garryshane, Ballingarrane, Monkstown, Gortmore, Patrickswell, Marlfield, Glenbane (Loughtally), Barne, Coole, Deerpark (at Knocklofty), Grange, Garrintemple, Carrickconeen, Kilmolash, Woodrooff, Clonmore, Decoy, Shanballyard, Clashavaddra and possibly Currenstown, Blackcastle and Moorestown, all the foregoing townlands being situated in Co. Tipperary; and Greenane, Kilmacomma, Caherbaun. Glenabbey, Kilnamack, and Ballyvaden in Co. Waterford, the last townland alone not forming part of the parish of Inishlounaght from which, indeed, it is separated by the whole width of the county.

William Brabazan, 'under-treasurer of the lord of the king's [that is Henry VIII] land of Ireland', gives an account of sums realised by the sale of chattels following the suppression of the Irish monasteries by Henry VIII. The sum mentioned for Inishlounaght was liij*s.* iiij*d.* The account states that one bell in the abbey of Inishlounaght was unsold and unappraised. It also states that 'James Whyte of Clonmel ought to answer to the king for a bell weighing a hundred pounds weight pertaining to the late abbey of Inishlounaght at the time of its dissolution'. Brabazon records a sum of lxzij*s.* vj.*d.* 'for the price of two silver crosses called 'holye Crossys', one, to '… in the late abbey of Kilcowley [sic], and the other in the late abbey of Inneslonaghe [sic].'

APPENDICES

ABBOTS OF INISLOUNAGHT

Congan, first abbot.
Gilbert fl. 1283.[1]
Richard fl. 1310/1.[2]
John fl. 1324/5.[3]
John fl. 1409.[4]
Patrick fl. 1439-46/8.[5]
Richard (Oduelly) retired 1462.[6]
Patrick O'Donoghue elected 1462, died before 1464.[7]
Florentius O Maoilmhichil elected 1464, retired same year.[8]
Dermot O'Heffernan elected 1464.[9]
William O'Donoghue elected 1472, ? deposed 1476.[10]
Maurice O'Heffernan ? elected 1476.[11]
Thomas O'Cahill elected 1492, *vivens* 1495.[12]
William O'Donochu 1502.[13]
Walter Butler
James Butler last pre-reformation abbot,[14] 1510-40.
Thady Conway appointed 1549.
Nicholas Fagan 1609-17.
Laurence Fitzharris fl. 1633-55.

1 CDI 1284-95, p. 482.   2 Public Record Office (I), National Archives, 1a/49/12/ 131.   3 Rot. Pat. 32b (no. 123).   4 Ibid., 189 (no. 11).   5 AH 12 (1946) 16-7; CPR ix, p. 272; COD iii, pp 163-4; CPR x, p. 186.   6 AH 12 1946) 19.   7 Ibid., CPR, xii, p. 186.   8 CPR, xii, pp 186, 509-10.   9 CPR, xii, pp 509-10.   10 CPR, xiii, pp 13, 531.   11 CPR, xiii, p. 531.   12 Brady, ii, pp 246-7; IMED, pp 168 ff.   13 CPR, xvii, pt 1, p. 477.   14 Fiant (Hen.) 140.

TABLE OF THE LANDS OF INISHLOUNAGHT (TOTAL ACREAGE 12,387 ACRES)

County and barony	Townland	Acreage	Parish and diocese
Co. Tipperary, barony of Iffa and Offa east	Ballingarrane (part)	25-0-00	Inislounaght
	Ballingarane north	291-2-23	Lismore
	Blackcastle	531-2-09	
	Barne (part)	612-3-15	
	Clashvadra	42-1-00	
	Carrickconeen	337-1-36	
	Clonmore	93-2-28	
	Coole	147-3-00	
	Currenstown	210-2-39	
	Decoy	71-0-19	
	Deerpark	54-3-24	
	Garryntemple	294-2-20	
	Garryshane	48-3-08	
	Gortmore	33-1-21	
	Greenane (part)	51-0-18	
	Inishlounaght	360-1-19	
	Kilmolash Lower	293-3-10	
	Kilmolash Upper	88-0-00	
	Loughtally/Glenbaun	49-2-32	
	Marlfield/Abbey	29-0-00	
	Monksgrange	414-1-28	
	Monkstown	106-3-08	
	Moorstown	640-2-27	
	Patrickswell	326-2-22	
	Toberahenna	162-3-13	
	Shanballyard	309-1-20	
	Woodroffe (part)	780-0-00	
Co. Waterford, barony of Glenaheiry	Caherbaun	162-3-13	
	Greenane (part)	192-3-31	
	Glenabbey	084-0-20	
	Kilmacomma	1381-2-39	
	Kilnamack East	714-1-09	
	Kilnamack West	328-0-36	
		10,172-2-27	
	Russelstown (part)	140-0-00	Kilronan/ Lismore
Co. Tipperary, barony of Middlethird	Dogstown (Kilmavee)	406-1-30	Dogstown/Cashel
Co. Waterford, barony of Decies-without Drum	Ballynagigla Ballynasisila Bristeen Ballyvaden Carrickaready Kildwan	2118-1-15	Monkstown/Lismore (These formed the lands of the abbey Vallis Caritatis before before its suppression in 1228.)

LANDS OF INISLOUNAGHT

The Miscellanea of the Chancery in the PRO, London (Bundle 10, no. 14, 10 Edw. I) contain a writ and inquisition regarding suit of court at Kilsheelan for the land of Tachkerach which was claimed, both by Oto de Grandison and the abbot and convent of Suir. The king's writ, commanding an inquisition to be taken, is dated 17 February 1582 (calendared in CDI, ii, no. 1898). Theiner has printed the full text of two papal letter dated 30 July 1464 and 21 January 1468/9, respectively, while some light is thrown on the state of the monastery in 1537 by the findings of juries in the city of Waterford and the town of Clonmel printed from the originals in the PRO, London, by Herbert J. Hore and Revd James Graves 'The Social State of the Southern and Eastern Counties of Ireland in the Sixteenth Century' in the *Annuary of the Royal Historical and Archaeological Association of Ireland* for the years 1868 and 1869.

Sources

St Bernard's biography of St Malachy, *De Vita Sancti Malachiae, Episcopi Hiberniae* names the abbey of Suir as one of the Cistercian houses in existence at the time he wrote (*c.*1149/1150). CDI, ii, no. 1898 (original documents are preserved in the Miscellanea of the Chancery, London, in Bundle 10 (No. 14, 10 Edward I). Ibid., no. 2081. CDI, iii, no. 1187. IMED, 337-9; Exchq. Inq. (Tipp.) Hen. VIII (PRO Dublin); Fiants: Henry VIII Nos. 111, 140, 150, 166, 172, 338; Edward VI, No. 1142; Elizabeth, Nos. 2578, 2845, 3121, 4141, 5580, 5591; CPR, 34 Hen. VIII (Morrin, i, p. 94), 25 Eliza. (ibid., ii, p. 56), 16 Jas. I (CPR,. Jas. I, pp 410f), Charles I (Morrin, iii, pp 141-4, 286-8); DWIIPM (Deeds & Wills & Instruments appearing upon Inquisition Post Mortem the Rolls Office), vol. 22, Co. Tipp. Part 1, pp 59-78; RDC (Repentary to the Deeds of the Chancery 19/49/63), vol. i, pp 132 & 139; IMED, 254-6; COD, iv, 238-40; OSL (Tipp.) I, 39-50; DS. maps: barony Iffa & Offa, Co. Tipp., barony of Glenaheiry, Co. Waterford, parish of Inishlounaght called Inisleonaghty (in Tipp. map) and Abby Slunagh (in Waterford map); and cf. Co. Tipp. Composite Map, Sheets 76, 77, 82, 83 and for Co. Waterford, O.S. six inch survey Sheet 1; BSD, parish of Inishleonaghty. For identification of Dogstown with the Cistercian grange of Kilmaveigh (Kilmovee) see Exchq. Ing. (Tipp.) Henry VIII (Ing. 13) and Elizabeth (Ing. 21 & Ing. 47) PRO Dublin (1a 48 85). For identification of Glannewydan with Monksland (alias Farrenamanagh), Co. Waterford, see Fiant Henry VIII No. 150 and Fiant Elizabeth No. 2578. The four fields near Clonmel mentioned in a lease of 1539 and in other later documents were Gotard, Gortadegany, Gortavillen and Gortclonmally or Clonmel Field and appear to have been in that part of the abbey lands bordering on Clonmel. Gortard and Gortavillen can be identified from documents in PRO, Dublin (1A 56 1) (No. 2481: Miscellaneous Deeds Box 1 no. 107; 2482: ibid., no. 108; 2483:

ibid., no. 109; 2487: ibid., no 113; 2506: no. 12, Miscellaneous Deeds Box 2; 2510: ibid., no. 16; 2520: ibid., no. 6; 2521: ibid., no. 27. See also 2522 for two indentures relating to half of the Gortard lands, and cf. the Rental of Property of Revd Hugh Edward Prior (Deed 2538, no. 44 Misc. Box 2). Gortard lay in the present townland of Garryshane, Gortavillen in that of Tubberheena. The other two fields remain to be identified.

A lease dated 30 June 1539 survives among the Ormond Papers in the National Library of Ireland. It is made in favour of Lady Joan Fitzgerald, wife of James Butler (9th earl of Ormond) and their son Edmund, by the abbot (James Butler) and convent, and grants for a term of sixty years practically all the lands belonging to the abbey lying between Kilmanahan and Clonmel in Co. Waterford. The various lands are named in the document. Although the wording of the lease seems to refer to lands in Co. Waterford only, a certain number of the denominations named can be identified as lands located on the Tipperary side of the river Suir.

The Miscellanea of the Chancery in the PRO, London (Bundle 10, no. 14 10 Edw. I) contain a writ and inquisition regarding suit of court at Kilsheelan for the land of Tachkerach which was claimed, both by Oto de Grandison and the abbot and convent of Suir. The king's writ commanding an inquisition to be taken is dated 17 February 1282. (calendared by Sweetman, CDI, ii, no. 1898). Theiner has printed the full text of two papal letters dated 30 July 1464 and 21 January 1468/9 respectively (VM), while some light is thrown on the state of the monastery in 1537 by the findings of juries in the city of Waterford and the town of Clonmel printed from the originals in the PRO, London, by Herbert J. Hore & Revd James Graves, 'The Social State of the Southern and Eastern Counties of Ireland in the Sixteenth Century' in the *Annuary of the Royal Historical and Archaeological Association Association of Ireland* for the years 1868 and 1869. Other sources: CDI; CPR; FC 11 H 67; Exchequer Ing. Hen. VIII (Co. Tipp.); HC xiii; ICD; Registrum; Rot. Pat; Tax.I.Cist; Theiner; VM; Brady.

ARCHITECTURE OF INISLOUNAGHT ABBEY

Inishlounaght abbey is the only one of the four Tipperary abbeys to have been totally dismantled. The Royal Commissioners in 1541 gave permission to 'throw down' the church. Sir James Ware, writing in 1626, speaks of the monastic buildings as being remarkable for the beauty and design. The Civil Survey of 1654 refers to the walls as still standing and ruins were still visible in 1746, according to Smith in his *History of Waterford.* According to Lewis' *Topographical Dictionary* (1846), it was restored in 1818. He was referring to the small Protestant church.

In 1799 a Service was read among the ruins which then covered half an acre. In 1800 a small Protestant church was built there. This church was reconstructed in 1818 and included the present bell tower. The church incorporates some architectural features of an earlier building which were probably Cistercian. These include an elaborately sculptured east window as well as a fine Romanesque doorway of four receding aisles. This doorway is not the entrance to the present church but has been inserted in the west wall directly between the tower and the church proper and above the present entrance to the church.

There are a number of slabs in and around the church. One of them built into the boundary wall of the adjoining cemetery, south of the church, has a florated cross and some inscription. John O'Donovan in his Ordnance Survey Letters of County Tipperary, 1840, vol. 1, states that many of the ornamental stones of the abbey were to be 'seen at the head of the graves but no building at present graces the spot but a small, mean Protestant church about the size of a sentry box. A great honour to the Bagnalls!' O'Donovan goes on to lament the destination of the abbey by quoting an old Croppy Song:

> Da bhfuighmís cead chum marbhta.
> 's iad an ched bhert iad do leagfaimís
> 'sis deimhin gur binn do ghreadfimís-ne.
> Bagnall agus Maud

PART THREE

The abbey of Holy Cross

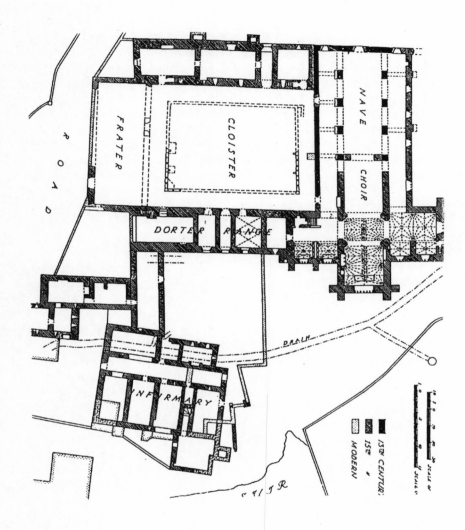

Plan of Holy Cross abbey, from H.G. Leask, *Irish Church and Monastic Buildings*, iii (Dundealgan Press, Dundalk, 1985).
Courtesy of Dundealgan Press.

9. FOUNDATION AND EARLY YEARS

Among the earliest daughters of Mellifont was the abbey of Monaster-anenagh known to Cistercians as *Monasterium de Magio,* founded in what is now Co. Limerick. From this abbey a very important foundation was made about the year 1182 by Donall Ó Briain, king of Limerick. This was the abbey of the Holy Cross of *Uachtar Lamhann,* near Thurles. There is some reason to believe that this abbey had begun as a Black Benedictine foundation, but had later adopted the Cistercian reform. If that belief is well-founded, the year 1182 must be reckoned not as the foundation date of the monastery of Holy Cross, but rather as the year in which it became Cistercian. This Benedictine foundation may itself have been preceded by a more primitive settlement of the native type; and indeed the Irish name of the site, *Cell Uachtair Lamhann,* does suggest that this was the case.[1]

The abbey of the Holy Cross is believed to have derived its name from a remarkable relic of the True Cross which the community possessed and which, in the course of time, became the object of great veneration, attracting throngs of pilgrims. Two very different accounts exist concerning the manner in which this relic came into the hands of the community, neither of which unfortunately can be substantiated. The first is from the pen of Fr Malachy Hartry, a monk of the community in the first half of the seventeenth century, who claimed, to have taken it from an old manuscript written in the Irish tongue.[2] This account claims that the relic was presented to the monastery by an unidentified queen of England, whose son had been slain nearby. The story abounds in marvels, is full of improbabilities and poses serious problems in chronology. It is not impossible, however, that a lady of noble rank, whether actual queen of England, as Hartry thought, or the widow of former king, as others would have it, did present a relic of the True Cross to the monastery. The date of the presentation depends on the identity of the supposed queen, and may have been in the thirteenth, the fourteenth, or even the fifteenth century. Since we know from the charter granted by Donall Ó Briain that the abbey was dedicated to the Holy Cross as early as 1182, if not earlier, we must conclude that even if the tradition we have been discussing be well founded, Holy Cross abbey derived its name, not from that relic, but from a relic it already possessed at the time the charter was granted. We may ask how this earlier relic was obtained.

In his Introduction to the *Study of the History and Antiquities of Ireland,* which appeared in 1803, Sylvester O'Halloran states positively that Murtough O'Brien, a former king of Ireland and granduncle of Donall

---

1 CDI, no. 2062; IMED, p. 349. **2** Hartry, p. 35.

Mór Ó Briain, received a relic of the True Cross from Pope Paschal II, in 1110. The relic, O'Halloran affirms, O'Brien later bestowed on the abbey of the Holy Cross. Although O'Halloran produces no evidence to support his assertion, the story in itself is not improbable if we suppose the gift was made, not by Muircheartach, who died long before the foundation of the monastery, but by his grandson, Donall Mór, whose charter is preserved among the collection of Ormond Deeds in the National Library of Ireland. Since Donall became king of Limerick (otherwise Thomond) in 1167, it is quite possible that he presented the relic to the Benedictine monks in 1169, the year in which, according to Sir James Ware, the monastery of Holy Cross was founded, though he gives as an alternative date 1182. Fr Malachy Hartry, in his *Triumphalia Chronologica Monasterii Sanctae Crucis in Hibernia*, strives to reconcile the two dates, and succeeds in doing so to his own satisfaction. According to this author, 'the first foundation or colonizing of this monastery was made by the Black monks, commonly called Benedictines. This was in the year 1169, and they lived here in a very beautiful place up to the year 1182.' The manuscript is defective at this point, but from what remains decipherable it appears that the author is arguing that the Cistercian monks succeeded the Benedictines in 1182. To sum up, then; we have a difference of opinion among authorities concerning the foundation date of Holy Cross. Some favour the year 1169, others the year 1182. In fact, the most probable year for the Cistercian foundation is 1181. It is indeed quite certain that the Cistercians did not make a foundation at Holy Cross as early as 1169. It is also certain that there was a tradition in the seventeenth century of the existence on the site, of a colony of monks, probably Benedictines, prior to the arrival of the Cistercians. We may conclude, therefore, that Donall Mór Ó Briain bestowed the relic of the True Cross on the community either in 1169 or 1181/2.

There is ample evidence that the monks of Holy Cross, at a later period, had in their custody at least two and perhaps more than two relics of the Holy Rood. We may take it for granted that one of these was the relic presented to the convent by Donall Ó Briain, and this was probably that which gave the abbey the name it has retained to the present day. The second relic may have derived from an English source, as indicated in the legend already noted, or it may have come to Holy Cross from the Ormond family, under whose protection the abbey had been taken after the establishment of the Angle-Norman hegemony in the region. There is some reason to suppose that there may have been three distinct relics of the True Cross in the possession of the monks at one time; and if the traditions attached to the different relics be well founded, the earliest one came from Rome to Holy Cross through the medium of the O'Briain family, while another came either from France or Jerusalem via England, and the third belonged originally to the earls of Ormond.

The charter granted by Donall Ó Briain to the monks of Holy Cross is still extant.[3] We give hereunder an English translation of the Latin Text:

> D. by the grace of God, king of Limerick, to all kings, dukes, earls, barons, knights, and other Christians, in whatever rank they may be throughout Ireland, everlasting salvation in Christ
>
> Know ye, all good Christians, that I have given, and by this my charter, have confirmed for ever, Cealluachtair Lamudni, Bali idubain, Bali iduibgin, Bali igerridir, Bali Imoeluchain, Cualu helach, Scirdach, Bali Icheallaich, Bali icorcrain, Iconligain, Cul Etti with their appurtenances in honour of Almighty God, and of the holy Virgin Mary, and St, Benedict and the Holy Cross, for the welfare of my soul and the souls of my parents, in fields, in woods, in pastures, in meadows, in waters, in fisheries and in mills, wholly and entirely, freely and peacefully to the monks of Holy Cross in the presence of Gregory, the lord abbot. Witnesses: Christian, bishop of Lismore and legate of the apostolic see in Ireland. M., archbishop of Cashel, B. bishop of Limerick, Donall mc Meiceochach, Ruadri uagradi, Gillapatrick ua Foelain, Diarmait ua Neill, Ragnall m meicconmara, Scanlan m. meicgormain.

It will be noted that the site of the monastery is *Celluactairlamudni* which indicates that there had been at one time a 'cell' in that place. From this we may deduce the existence of an earlier community of the native Irish type in this area before the arrival of either the Benedictines or Cistercians. The name *Cell Uachtair Lamphand,* the upper cell (or church) of Lamhand, implies the existence elsewhere in the area of a *Cell Iochtair Lamhand* and this in turn suggests that at one time the territory later occupied by the lands of Holy Cross abbey was divided into an 'upper' and a 'lower', and there are some indications in early Irish literature that this indeed, was the case.

Most of the denominations listed in the charter were evidently named from families settled on the land before the coming of the monks. Because none of the names occuring in the townland denominations are found among the names of the witnesses to the charter, we may surmise that these families had even then disappeared from the locality or had sunk into insignificance. Since the primitive statutes of the Cistercian Order required that monasteries should be constructed in places far removed from the haunts of men it became the custom when the monks received grants of land on which a population already existed to remove the population and to reduce villages and hamlets to the status of a Cistercian grange.

3 COD, no. 5.

In many cases this led to large-scale evictions such as happened in Yorkshire in England where whole villages, including parish churches, were levelled to the ground. We have no evidence to show that a similar state of affairs prevailed in Ireland. However, by the time Holy Cross came into being as a Cistercian house a change was coming over the policy of the Order and there are indications that the custom of leasing monastic land to tenants had crept in by the beginning of the thirteenth century. It is probable therefore, that the coming of the Cistercian into the area did not entail the removal of the population then dwelling on the land: but since the Anglo-Norman invaders were soon to swarm all over the area it is very probable that the mass of the native population had sunk to the level of serfs by the third decade of the thirteenth century. A possible reason for the absence from the locality of the family names borne by most of the denominations listed in the charter may be due to the rise of the O'Brien dynasty and the establishment of their supremacy over the whole of North Munster, including the area later to become known as Co. Tipperary, leading to the displacing of many of the aboriginal families by followers of the Dal gCais and the list of witnesses to the charter clearly reflects the O'Brien hegemony at this period.

Only three of the eleven denominations listed in the charter of king Donall can now be identified with certainty and only one retains its ancient designation, that, namely of *Bali Icheallaich* which in its modernised (and anglicised) form of Ballykelly is the name of a townland in the barony of Middlethird. The *Cul Etti* of the charter appears in later documents under various forms such as Culetty, Couletty, etc., and though the name has long since disappeared, the description given of the situation of Culetty in more than one medieval document enables us to identify it as the area now contained in the townlands of Lisbook and Ballycamus. It is a strange fact that the majority of the designations recorded in the original charter had already disappeared a century later. We may however, regard it as extremely probable, if not certain, that the lands of Holy Cross as detailed in the charter are represented today more or less substantially by the combined civil parishes of Holy Cross and Rathkennan, together with the townland of Ballykelly in the parish of Ballysheehan which, in the seventeenth century, formed a detached portion of Holy Cross parish, as is clear from the Civil Survey and the Down Survey. It appears certain, on the other hand, that, the lands of Beakstown, which now forms part of the parish of Holy Cross, were among the lands granted by Donall Ó Briain and listed in the charter. The rectory and vicarage of Beakstown became impropriate to the abbey of Holy Cross only in the fifteenth century and the lands, which had then been in the possession of the Purcell family for at least two centuries, continued to be held by them until the seventeenth century. They probably never at any time formed part of the monastic possessions. We may conclude, then, that the original endowment of Holy Cross abbey by king Donall Ó Briain amounted to approximately 8,000 statute acres. This large estate was centered in the lands of *Cill Uachtair Lamhann*, the name by which the place was known down to the middle of the seventeenth century. This name, the derivation of which is obscure, appears under various forms in medieval documents, the earliest being the form given in the charter of Donall Ó Briain (*Ceall Uachtair Lamuidnai*). In a confirmation of this charter it takes the form Celluacturlaumun, and in the medieval documents appears under such varied guises as Woctarlamand, Ochterlawyne, which suggests that the probable Irish form was Uachtar Lamhann.

Our knowledge of the early history of the abbey is very scant indeed. Beyond the fact that its first Cistercian abbot was named Gregory, that John, lord of Ireland and earl of Mortain, later to be king of England, confirmed the charter of Donall Mór Ó Briain, and that Muirgheas O hEinni, archbishop of Cashel and papal legate in Ireland died there in 1206, we know nothing of its history in the period 1182-1227.

It is possible that the Cistercian legate, Archbishop O'hEinni, had been a monk of Holy Cross before his elevation to the episcopacy and that for this reason he chose the abbey of Holy Cross as the place of his resurrection. At this period of its existence the monastery was just one of the many houses of Cistercian monks which had spread so rapidly through the country. Like many another Cistercian house in Ireland, but to a greater degree than most, Holy Cross abbey suffered from the vicissitudes of the times. The disturbed state of the country due to the constant wars waged by Irish and Anglo-Normans against each other as well as the internecine wars between the native Irish themselves played its part in impoverishing the house, which fell into dire poverty in the first quarter of the thirteenth century and by 1227 had reached such a sorry pass that it seemed to be on the verge of complete ruin. The general chapter, alarmed at the state of the Irish houses concerning which numerous complaints had been made, ordered a visitation of all the houses of the *generatio Mellifontis* to be carried out in 1227 with a view to the reform of those houses in head and members. The visitation was undertaken by the French abbots of Froidmont and Trois Fontaines. The economic situation in the abbey was found to be desperate and the general chapter of 1227 decreed that if the abbey was judged by the visitators to be incapable of subsisting by itself it was to be united to the abbey of Owney. This rather severe ordinance was part of the reforming decrees of that year which envisaged the transfer of four Irish houses to new mother houses in England and Wales and the suppression of the Irish monasteries of Killenny and Holy Cross whose lands and goods were to be united to those of Duiske and Owney respectively. This decree, however, was provisional, since it was subject to the approval of the visitators to be appointed by the general chapter for the following year. The mother house of Holy Cross (Monasteranenagh) was, transferred from the jurisdiction of its own proper mother, Mellifont, to that of Margam in Wales, and the annals of Margam state that in the year 1227 a number of brethren from that house, both monks and lay brothers, were sent to Ireland to reform the order. Most of the brethren sent from Margam probably found their way to Monasteranenagh, the mother house of Holy Cross, where they helped to precipitate the crisis in the following year which resulted in the sensational rebellion which occured in that house.

Holy Cross abbey was among the monasteries whose abbots and convents sought protection from the king of England in 1227 for their tenants, chattels and possessions as well as for themselves. The justiciary of Ireland was commanded by the king to afford them the required protection as well as to aid them in recovering the rights of their churches which were said to be dispersed. From a charter granted to the abbey of Citeaux, Donnchadhh Cairbreach O'Briain, king of Thomond, which though undated, was probably drawn up in the period 1224-26, we learn that the abbot who then ruled the abbey was Isaac. The circumstances under which the charter granted to Citeaux was drawn up deserve mention here. The general chapter had found it necessary to complain more than once of the non-attendance of many of the Irish abbots at the annual assembly of the heads of the order, and complaints in this connection are recorded in the proceedings of the chapters of 1203, 1208, 1212, 1215, 1216, and 1218. The reasons for failing to attend the general chapter were many and varied but the weak financial condition of many of the Irish houses meant that few could afford to travel to Citeaux. A partial solution was found in an appeal for aid to the Irish kings who generously came to the assistance of the abbots by binding themselves and their successors to defray part of the abbots' travelling expenses. Donnchadh Cairbreach, by his charter, granted two silver marks to be paid yearly 'in pure and perpetual alms' to the abbey of Citeaux and the brethern therein serving God, the payment to be made through the hands of the abbot of Maigue. Abbot Isaac of Holy Cross witnessed this grant in company with his fellow abbots of Maigue, Suir and Corcomroe. Sometime after this charter had been granted to Citeaux, Isaac ceased to be abbot of Holy Cross. The records unfortunately do not enlighten us on the circumstances of Isaac's resignation. What is certain is that by the summer of 1228, certainly before the 25 June of that year, Isaac was no longer abbot of Holy Cross, having been replaced by a certain R. whose name has not been preserved. This Abbot R. who appears to have been appointed by Abbot Stephen of Lexington during the great visitation of 1228 appended his seal to the decisions of the visitators in a charter drawn up at Dublin after a meeting of the abbots in St Mary's abbey on 25 June. Taking into consideration the policy of Stephen of

Lexington of filling abbatial vacancies with men of Anglo-Norman race we may assume that Isaac's successor was an Anglo-Norman. One of the earliest documents in the Register of Stephen of Lexington contains a reference to a monk of Holy Cross named Isaac and it is tempting to think that the Isaac here named, may in fact been the former abbot. The document is a licence issued to two monks and a *conversus* (lay brother) of Holy Cross to leave their monastery for the purpose of leading the eremitical life. The three brethren named in the document are the monks Isaac and Jacob and the lay brother Flann. The letter lays down the conditions under which the brethren concerned are permitted to lead the solitary life and is of sufficient interest to merit reproduction here.[4]

> To all the faithful of Christ, health in the Lord. Although our beloved brothers Isaac and Jacob, heretofore monks in Holy Cross, and Flann, a conversus of the same house, have for a long time ardently desired to give themselves up to the solitary and eremitical life, yet they have never dared to put this desire into effect, since they hold it for certain that it is not permitted to Cistercians monks to carry out such a resolution except with the counsel of the general chapter.
>
> Hearing therefore, that we had received from the said general chapter plenary powers to be used throughout Ireland, they have humbly besought us with all the earnestness of which they are capable, both in their own persons and through other reliable and God-fearing men, to allow them to fulfill their resolution. We therefore, having taken counsel with devout and prudent men and having considered diligently the resolution of the aforesaid monks and lay brother freely grant their petition and absolve them from obedience to the Order. Yet so as they strive for the future to lead the eremitical life utmost religious devotion moreover, we make the three men aforesaid fully subject to the jurisdiction of the archbishops and bishops in whose dioceses they shall dwell, so that if they, perchance, perceive them to have fallen away from their holy resolution to the scandal of religion, they may deprive them of our habit and chastise them in other way according as they may deem most expedient for the salvation of their souls and the honour of the church and the order.

Stephen of Lexington, the writer of the above letter arrived in Ireland in the spring of 1228 armed with plenary powers from the general chapter and commissioned by the said chapter, or rather by the abbot of Clairvaux,

4 Registrum, xx.

acting in the name of the chapter, to visit and correct and reform in head and members the houses of the *generatio Mellifontis* which were represented to the general chapter as being in a state of great disorder and in which many 'enormities' were said to have long existed. As the fate of Holy Cross abbey hung in the balance at the time in consequence of the report of the abbots of Froidmont and Trois Fontaines who had made a general visitation the preceeding year, it was to be expected that the abbot of Stanley would sooner or later pay an official visit to Holy Cross. His first letter to the abbot of that house was written sometime in April or early May and informed the abbot of his forthcoming visit. One of the purpose of this visit was to determine, according to the decision of the previous general chapter, whether Holy Cross abbey should continue to exist as an abbey *sui juris* or should be amalgamated with the abbey of Owney. The abbot of Holy Cross was commanded to prepare for the reception of the visitator and his companions and to have an inventory made of all the goods of the monastery moveable and immoveable. The letter reads as follows:[5]

> To the abbot and convent of Holy Cross. Greetings. With the help of God we shall come to your house on the Tuesday next following Ascension so that on the following day we may diligently inspect your lands and possessions and taking counsel with prudent men, may decide according to the decree of the general chapter whether your house should continue to exist as a separate abbey or should be unified to the abbey of Owney. Wherefore we command your abbot in virtue of the obedience he owes to the general chapter and under pain of deposition, to be present and to provide a decent place and all other necessary things for ourselves and the other abbots who are to come there as well as for our horses. Let him also take care that a list of all the goods of the house be written down clearly and distinctly on a special roll-chalices, vestments, cows, oxen, sheep, books and all other property, and let him have besides, men, that is monks and *conversi* or even scholars who are acquainted with the land and tenements of the house who may furnish a more complete and true account respecting these; so that when we have first considered the matter attentively we can then proceed more carefully and deliberately to settle the question and to decide what should be done regarding your house. Keep these letters until our arrival and then return them to us so that we may know how you have obeyed our instructions in this matter. Farewell.

Abbot Stephen of Lexington and his companions arrived at Holy Cross abbey in due course. He found that the abbey possessed land variously esti-

5 Ibid., xv.

mated as containing thirty or forty plowlands, or even more. Having made this visitation he came to the conclusion that by taking proper measures the abbey could be restored and put on a sound basis once more. In order to restore the temporalities, however, he felt it necessary to enlist the aid of the abbot of Dunbrody.[6] This abbot, like Stephen, was of Anglo-Norman stock and Dunbrody was a strong outpost of Anglo-Norman culture in the south east corner of Ireland. Stephen wrote to the abbot and commanded him to send to Holy Cross, for the space of one year a certain Brother D. whose services were to be enlisted in helping the abbot of Holy Cross to put the affairs of the monastery in order. The real cause of the collapse, however, was spiritual, and for that reason Stephen felt it necessary to take other and more drastic steps. Though he was prepared to recommend to the general chapter that Holy Cross should retain its separate existence, he felt that his could be permitted only on such conditions that would remove all danger of a re-occurrence of its former troubles and disorders. It was essential that it be removed from the authority of its former mother house and transferred to the jurisdiction of some other house in England or Wales. Stephen finally decided in favour of Margam, an abbey situated in Welsh territory and Anglo-Norman to the core.

Writing to the abbot of Margam after his departure from Holy Cross. Stephen informed him that although the general chapter had approved provisionally the union of Holy Cross with Owney, a daughter house of Furness, the decision had later been changed, following a meeting of abbots, and Holy Cross abbey was to retain its separate status. It would however, be subjected to Margam in future. The reference in this letter to a meeting of abbots suggests that it was written after a council of abbots, convened by the abbot of Stanley in his capacity of visitator of the Irish houses, with plenary powers from the general chapter, had met in Dublin in June 1228. It is possible, on the other hand, that the meeting here referred to is not the council of abbots that was held in Dublin but an informal confrontation between Stephen and the abbots who accompanied him to Holy Cross, and that the decision arrived at in consequence of that consultaiton was subject to revision by the Dublin council. In the event the council held in Dublin ratified the decision to maintain the separate existence of Holy Cross abbey while subjecting it to the jurisdiction of Margam as its new mother house.

The decision as to the future of Holy Cross abbey was approved and ratified by the general chapter of 1228. Following this it is probable that a contingent of monks from Margam was drafted into the Irish house to reinforce and reform (and incidentally to anglicise) the community there, The extant letters of Stephen of Lexington do not however, give the

6 Ibid., xxi.

impression that there had been a bad breakdown in regular discipline in Holy Cross abbey as had been the case in some of the other houses. The community as a whole, however, must have been basically sound for we find no charges brought against the monks of Holy Cross nor do they seem to have shared in the rebellion of the mother house against the disciplinary reforms of the abbot visitator. Stephen's very silence suggests that there was no serious complaint against the community as does his indirect testimony in nominating as one of the candidates for the abbacy of Boyle, Constantinus who, although then a monk of Maigue, had formerly been abbot of Holy Cross.

In 1234 a charter was issued by Henry III confirming earlier grants to the abbey and taking the convent under the royal protection. The original of this chapter has disappeared but its terms are preserved in an inspeximus, by Pierce Butler, earl of Ormond and Ossory, made at the request of the former abbot of Holy Cross, Philip Purcell, on 8 February 1538/9.

> Henry, by the grace of God king of England, lord of Ireland, duke of Normandy and Aquitaine, and count of Andegavia, to his justiciar of Ireland, and to all his bailiffs and faithful subjects throughout Ireland greetings. Know ye that we have received under our protection and defence the men, lands, goods, revenues and all the possessions of the aforesaid abbot, neither inflicting nor permitting to be inflicted on them any damage, injury, loss or oppression. And if any of their goods have been forfeited cause this to be corrected without delay. In testimony whereof we have caused these our letters patent to be made. Witnessed by myself at Hereford, on the second day of November in the eighteenth year of our reign.

10. THE GROWTH OF FEUDALISM

For some forty years, following the issue of the charter of confirmation by Henry III in 1234, the annals are silent concerning the fortunes of Holy Cross abbey except to record the punishment of an abbot on two different occasions for failure to attend the general chapter of the Order without any legitimate excuse. This occured in 1239 and again in 1246. The very silence of the annalists may be taken as an indirect testimony to the normality of community life during this period; for if anything abnormal had occured that would bring the abbey or its community into undue or unpleasant prominence it would scarcely have escaped the attention of the annalist.

The complaint made against the abbot in the matter of non-attendance at the general chapter was not an unusual one in those days. The difficulties of the journey, the dangers of the times and the great expense involved in this excursion overseas would in themselves be sufficient to account for the abbot's absence on the two occasions noted. A more serious indiscretion occurred, however, in 1272 or 1273 when the abbot of Holy Cross was found to have taken part with some other abbots in the unlawful deposition of the abbot of Inishlounaght, or if not in his actual formal deposition at least in a successful attempt to force him to resign. The abbot principally involved in this affair was the abbot of Odorney in Kerry, but, when the affair was investigated by the general chapter, the accusations brought against him were found to have no substance and the abbot was acquitted of the charges in the chapter of 1274. It is probable that the abbot of Holy Cross was equally innocent for nothing further is recorded in connection with this case in the proceedings of the general chapter, and indeed the fact that he received an important commission from the chapter in 1274 itself indicates his good standing with the Order at that time.

The commission entrusted to the abbot of Holy Cross, which was shared by the abbot of Tintern, concerned the action of a certain Brother John, a former abbot of Jerpoint, who had instituted a law suit against his abbey in the civil courts. Two years earlier the general chapter had found it necessary to commission the abbot of Mellifont to take action against the same Brother John of Jerpoint not only be means of ecclesiastical censures but even by having him imprisoned provided he could be apprehended. The abbot of Mellifont had evidently been unable to lay hands on the delinquent, and the use of ecclesiastical censures against him proved unavailing for he heeded them not at all. Now, two years later, John was seeking to recover a certain sum of money from the abbey of Jerpoint by means of a civil process. Such an action was contrary to the constitutions of the Cistercian Order and the general chapter felt itself bound to take action in the civil courts. If it so happened that he refused to obey the admonitions of the two abbots they were to declare him excommunicated by authority of the general chapter, and they were to cause sentence of excommunication to be pronounced against him in all the abbeys of the Order in the dioceses of Cashel and Dublin, where he then resided. In 1276 the abbot of Holy Cross received another commission, being selected with the abbot of Odorney as one of the arbitrators in the dispute between the archbishop of Cashel on the one part and the abbots of Maigue and Owney on the other. Unfortunately the proceedings of the general chapter as reported in the *Statua* give us no indication of what the dispute was all about. In the following year the abbots of Holy Cross and Odorney were again entrusted with a commission and received plenary power from general chapter to settle the complaint brought by the abbot of Inishlounaght against the abbot of Dunbrody. Though the statutes of the general chapter are silent concerning the precise nature of this complaint it may not be rash to assume that it was connected with the retention by Dunbrody of the property of the suppressed abbey of Vallis Caritatis (Glenawydan in Co. Waterford). This was a subject which kept cropping up again and again between Suir and Dunbrody until it was finally settled by the return to Inislounaght of the lands in dispute.

Half a century had now passed since the decree of 1226 which took Holy Cross abbey from its proper mother house and handed it over to the jurisdiction of Margam in Wales. During those fifty years no serious complaints had been made to the general chapter concerning the observance of the rule of the Holy Cross. The general chapter at the instance of David MacCearbhaill, archbishop of Cashel, who had himself taken the Cistercian habit in 1269, reversed the decree of 1228 and restored the houses of the Mellifont line to their former paternity, thus undoing at one stroke the work accomplished by Stephen of Lexington who, with not a little arrogance, had insisted in his report to the general chapter that the settlement imposed by him on the Irish monks was to be final and irrevocable. The decree of 1274 had, indeed, restored to the abbot of Maigue all his former rights over his daughter houses whose *Pater Abbas* he had now once more become. At all events it was not until the year 1278 that jurisdiction over the abbeys of Suir, Odorney and Holy Cross was finally relinquished by the abbots of Furness and Stanley in England and the abbot of Margam in Wales following on a new decree of the general chapter in that year. Technically the matter was now settled and the right to make the regular visitation of the abbey of Holy Cross was vested once more in the abbot of Maigue. However, this was a right which he was never to exercise again, because a private agreement was made between the abbots of Mellifont and Maigue by which the abbey of Holy Cross was to become in future the daughter of Mellifont. This agreement was, of course, subject to approval by the general chapter. It was brought before the chapter in September 1279 and was there duly approved and formally ratified.

The dismay and displeasure caused to the abbots of Furness, Stanley and Margam by the decree of 1274 restoring to the abbey of Mellifont her former daughter houses was shared by the king's officials in Ireland, and these did not hesitate to accuse the archbishop of Cashel of harbouring the design of subjecting to Mellifont all the abbeys of the English tongue in Ireland. This charge was actually made by the then justiciar, Robert de Uffard in a letter written apparently in 1277; and coupled with it was the further charge that the archbishop had lately made an Irish boy of twenty-two years bishop of Cork, for no other reason it would seem than to shame the English. Thirty years later it was charged against the abbot of Maigue that the reason he had alienated certain of the monastic lands was out of hatred of the English tongue so that English monks could not dwell there as had hitherto been the custom. Holy Cross abbey had always been an Irish house in personnel and in sentiment, even when subjected to the jurisdiction of Margam, despite the infusion of the Anglo-Norman or Welsh element into the community in consequence of the visitation of 1228. Unlike the abbey of Jerpoint in Ossory and the abbey of Maigue in Limerick, both of which had been founded by Irish kings but which later became so anglicised that they were among the houses whose abbots sat in parliament as peers of the realm, Holy Cross abbey remained essentially Irish; and despite the allegation of Archdall and others that the abbot of Holy Cross was an earl and sat in the Anglo-Irish parliament his name does not appear among those Cistercian abbots who were vested with the dignity of barons and received writs of parliamentary summons, a dignity which was denied the purely Irish houses.

The abbot of Holy Cross in 1275 was one Peter Ó Conaing who had succeeded another Irishman, David O Cussey, who had become bishop of Emly in that year. Peter O Conaing was still alive in 1281 and may have held office for some years longer. The abbot in 1297 also appears to have been Irish though his name has not been preserved; and the two abbots who ruled between Peter O Conaig's death and the accession of the nameless abbot of 1297 were also Irish, Maurice Mac Amrech and Richard Ó Finnore respectively. With the formal restoration of the house to the Mellifont line, however, and the breaking of the connection between Holy Cross and Margam, the abbey began to slip once more into financial difficulties. This may have been due in great part to the deep involvement of the Irish Cistercians in the wool trade, and particularly to the practice of the forward sale whereby the community contracted for a certain term of years ahead to deliver a specified amount of wool to the merchants with whom they traded, usually Italian bankers such as the firms of Ricardi of Lucca and Friscobaldi of Florence. Although this was a convenient way of raising ready money it was fraught with danger, since a bad winter or spring could mean the death of numbers of sheep and lambs with the consequence that the monks would be unable to fulfil their contract and would run into debt. This in fact, is what happened in many instances, and in Munster and south Leinster especially, heavy debts were incurred by the monks. The spring of 1281 was a bad one so that many sheep and lambs were lost, and matters were worsened by the fact that the following winter (1281-2) was also severe, leading to further and heavier losses. Among the monasteries which suffered as a result of the practice of forward selling was that of Holy Cross; and when to the debts thus accumulated was added the debt incurred by the grave mismanagement of the abbey's financial affairs by more than one abbot, and by worse than mismanagement by another, things were in such a bad way that in 1297 the civil authorities had to intervene. The immediate cause of the intervention was the alienation, without the king's licence, of much of the monastic land into the hands of a motley group which included Italian moneylenders, Anglo-Norman colonists and officials and at least one Irishman. The legal proceedings which followed afforded a welcome opportunity to secular power to interfere in the affairs of the monastery and to introduce a new colony of English monks into the house after the example of Stephen of Lexington more than half a century previously. The financial difficulties which beset Holy Cross abbey and resulted in this new crisis had their origin in a very simple way.

Abbot Peter Ó Conaing went to England on business and while there came to the assistance of two Irish bishops who found themselves in financial straits. The bishops were David Ó Cussey of Emly, himself a former abbot of Holy Cross and Matthew, bishop of Killaloe. Driven by necessity, as the records state, the bishop borrowed 100 marks from the Lombardi, a group of Italian bankers, or moneylenders who were active in Ireland at that period, and Abbot Peter became their security. The bishops died, leaving the debt unpaid, and the Lombardi family swooped on the unfortunate Abbot Peter who, being unable to pay, gave them the manor of Collety and Grangecorkeran to hold for fifty years. Since the manor thus alienated was worth fifty marks a year; this was equivalent ot handing over to his Italian creditors the sum of 2,500 marks in lieu of the 100 marks he actually owed them. Later on the moneylenders sold the said lands to the archbishop of Cashel for 300 marks and then caused the abbot to be distrained by the sheriff although the debt incurred by the abbot had already been paid by the fifty year grant of the land to the Lombardi. Incidently, when the latter sold the land to the archbishop they released the small debt in which the abbot was bound to them. The stock seized by the sheriff on their instuctions amounted to 41 oxen, 32 bullocks and 300 sheep as well as seven horses. Among the other facts brought to light by the inquisition taken in 1297 was the fact that a number of persons therein named had succeeded in obtaining possession of parts of the monastic lands by means which were, to say the least, doubtful, and some cases openly dishonest. Not all of those involved were persons of low estate for among such names as Master Philip M. Bathly, Adam Sampson, James le Mazyner, John Lawless and William Hackett, we find that of Walter de la Haye, escheator of Ireland. In a commentary on the facts revealed by the inquisition one modern writer states clearly and unambiguously that 'it was by flagrant sharp practice, by chicanery and guile, that these men had managed to lay hands on the broad acres' of the abbey but it must be confessed that one of Abbot Peter Ó Conaig's successor in the abbacy, by name Richard O'Finnore, does not come unscathed out of the inquisition.

This abbot was expecting soon to be remove from office. We are not told why; but evidently he had an uneasy conscience and felt or knew that, whether by reason of his actions or his negligence he had failed in his obligations as abbot and was now about to face the inevitable consequence, deprivation of office by the father abbot or the general chapter.

His action in allowing a blank parchment sealed with his official seal to come into the hands of another layman without the consent of his chapter gives us the measure of the man. The jury evidently considered that the blank parchment bearing the abbot's seal could only have come into the possession of the layman, James le Mazyner, with the consent of the abbot himself, and besides leaving the said James in a position to use the parchment for an unlawful purpose it also left him in a position to blackmail the abbot. Indeed the abbot's successor in order to recover the same parchment had to pay James a goodly sum of money. For these reasons, and for various other reasons not stated in the inquisition, James le Mazyner held of the abbot three carucates and eighty acres in Grangecor as well as the 360 acres of heath and besides the church of Ballycahill and nevertheless the abbot was bound to James in eighty marks. Although the justiciar recognised that the entry of the tenants named in the inquisition into the various parcels of monastic lands named 'wabsd', that is, was unlawful, the judgement finally given was not flattering to the Irish monks of Holy Cross. In fact the whole case was made the pretext for ordering the introduction into the monastery of English monks 'to the extent of half the convent'. The reasons given for this course of action are strangely reminiscent of those given by Stephen of Lexington for similar measures introduced by that redoubtable abbot seventy years earlier and deserve quoting here:

> And because of the taking away of the lands of the abbey chantries and alms which ought to be there for the souls of the king's progenitors and for the king himself, in whose protection the abbey is, have ceased. And the monks of the house, who are all Irishmen, are dispersed in diverse places. Nor can any of the tenants say that they have entry by assent or licence of the king. Judgement that said tenements with the abbey, and all goods, as well in the abbey as in the tenements, be taken into the king's hand and immediately delivered to the abbot of Dowysky to keep, to whom the justiciar has committed the custody until otherwise ordained.
>
> Likewise it is commanded to the abbot of Mellifonte, chief visitator of each house, that he cause to be placed in the said abbey monks of English race, to the extent of half the convent, as often monks of the abbey monks of English race, elsewhere. Because said dispersion and loss was made by said Irish monks, as commonly happens in every place where houses are placed under their rule.

This judgement is by no means flattering to the Irish monks. Not merely does it indict the monks of Holy Cross but condemns in one sweeping statement all the Irish monks of the order. While admitting that the English tenants who had entered into occupation of the monastic land had done so in violation of the law it laid the blame for all that had happened on the Irish monks themselves and went on to state emphatically that such occurences were commonplace wherever the Irish gained control of a monastery. This judgement fully agrees with the earlier one passed by Stephen of Lexington and causes us to ask ourselves if, after all, there was not something lacking to the Irish character which made Irishmen unsuited to the task of ruling religious houses. The historian of the Irish Dominicans resolves this doubt in his own fashion. In a critical commentary on the above judgement he remarks that it is a beautiful amalgam of justice and injustice, rapacity and hypocrisy.

> He (the justiciar) recognises that grave injustice has been done to the abbey, but calmly ignores the fact that it had been done mainly, if not wholly, by English colonists and Italian unsurers; and that it has been done undercover of English Law and by the aid of English officials. He throws the whole blame on the Irish monks and orders that steps be taken to ensure that one half of the community shall be English in future. He decides that the intruders have no right to the monks' lands; and then, with a peculiarly English sense of justice, he decrees that the whole of the monks possessions be forthwith seized and their revenues confiscated to the king.

In truth the English were glad of any pretext to get their countrymen into the Irish Cistercian abbeys and so bring those abbeys under their own control. This was not, however, so easy a task as might be imagined. It had been tried in 1228 with apparent success. The success was only apparent, for here in the year 1297 the Irish were still so firmly in control that a new influx of English monks was deemed necessary to remedy the situation. Though the English were only too glad to get their monks into the Irish abbeys, the better to control them and make them subservient to the English interest, it must at the same time be admitted that in this particular case the Irish monks themselves afforded them a perfectly plausible excuse for thus acting. One can scarcely blame Abbot Peter Ó Conaing for his disinterested, if indiscreet charity in coming to the aid of his two episcopal friends; but the same excuse cannot be made for Abbot Richard Ó Finnore, whose actions were such to embarass seriously the financial position of the community and who if the facts were as stated must be considered to have been guilty of very serious misdemeanours and of grave dereliction of duty.

Walter de la Haye, escheator of Ireland, was, as we have seen, one of those who obtained some of the land that had been alienated by the abbot of Holy Cross. He seems to have aided the monastery in other ways and, perhaps it was for this reason he obtained some of the monastic lands. Certainly it appears from the proceedings before the justiciar at Cashel in 1297 that he was accustomed to acquit the monks every year in the Exchequer of a great sum of money, and it was further stated that he had given them beforehand another sum of money by which the house could have been relieved 'if its custodians were wise'. It is not recorded if the abbot of Mellifont carried out the command of the court by putting English monks into the abbey. If he did, the policy cannot have been very successful for the abbey continued to retain close relationships with the Irish in the neighbouring territories. It remained on good terms with the English and Irish alike and continued to enjoy the royal favour. In the thirteenth year of the reign of Edward II (1320) it is recorded that Abbot Thomas, abbot of the church of the Blessed Mary of the Holy Cross, near Cashel, came into the king's chancery of Ireland the day next after the feast of Michael the Archangel and exhibited in the said chancery a certain charter not cancelled nor in any respect violated, under the seal of John, formerly lord of Ireland, and count of Mortain. This information is given in the preamble to a new charter given by Edward II which goes on to recite in full the charter granted by John sometime between 1195 and 1199 when he was earl of Mortain as well as lord of Ireland. John's charter was important to the community of Holy Cross since it granted that they should be free of all mulcts in the king's courts as well as from all toll on whatever they should buy or sell for their own use throughout Normandy, England, Wales and Ireland. For this reason it was that Abbot Thomas sought a renewal and confirmation of King John's charter, and his example was followed by later abbots who sought and received similar confirmations from both the king of England and the earl of Ormond and even from the Ó Briain of Thomond, successors of the king Domhnall, who founded the abbey. The scant information we have on the monastery during the fourteenth century suggests that the regular life went on to rule. The early Cistercians did not allow tenants on their farms nor serfs on their farms, but these rules had fallen in abeyance by the early decades of the thirteenth century. Tenants had already appeared on the monastic estates by then and the monks were extensive landlords a century later. Sheep farming and the wool trade had replaced the earlier emphasis on cattle breeding. The wool trade continued to be the main stay of the Cistercian economy for the best part of a century until the heavy losses and accumulated debts engendered in particular by their reliance on the practice of forward sales lead to the abandonment of the wool trade and its replacement of the rentier system.

After 1325 we hear no more of the wool trade and by 1400 manual labour had practically been abandoned and the Cistercian lay brotherhood was well on the way to extinction. Few leases have survived from this period of fundamental change; among these is a covenant made betwwen the abbot and convent of Holy Cross of the one part and two Irish chiefs, Malachy and Donal Ó Molrian by name, of the other part. It reads in translation as follows:

> On Monday next after the feast of St Peter in Chains it was agreed between the abbot and convent of Holy Cross on the one part and Malachy and Donal Ó Molrian of the other part that the said abbot and convent by common consent granted and to farm let to the said Malachy and Donal all the lands of Athsannoythit as long as it shall please us, from the first term beginning at Easter in the year MCCCLII. Paying yearly to the abbot and their successors viz, in the first year following from the making of these present 10s, viz. one moiety at Easter and the other at Michaelmas, and in each following year one mark, viz. one mark moiety at Easter and the other at Michaelmas, and so from year to year while they remain faithful to the abbot and convent,the peace and the abbey tenants. And that said Malachy and Donal pay all tithes and altarages to the abbot and convent and their successors. And that they shall answer at the courts of the said abbot and convent and their successors as often as they shall be required in the said land. And if it happens that the goods of said abbot and convent and all diligence for the restoration of the goods at their power. And if they are taken by the said Malachy and Donal they shall be held to the said abbot and convent in 100s sterling. Nor shall it be lawful for Malachy and Donal to give, sell, bequeath, assign or in any way alienate the said land convent sought and had. And if they do otherwise their farm shall cease and this writing shall have no effect. And to this writing both parties have alternately set their seals. Given they day, year and place aforesaid (August 5, 1352).

From this document it is clear that the feudal system had now been accepted by the Cistercians of Holy Cross. The abbot and convent have their tenants, their altarages, and we may suppose their other feudal revenues. (In Holy Cross two fairs were held every, one on 1 May and the other on 14 September, the feast of the Exaltation of the Holy Cross.) As Holy Cross abbey was a manor and possessed all the rights of a manor we may suppose that the various types of courts were held. The tenants and vassals were bound to come to plead and receive judgement in the manorial court. The court-merchant was used for settling of trade disputes, and also for trying strangers.

11. THE INVADERS TAKE OVER

Although the greater part of the monastic estate lay in the barony of Eile Ui Fhogartaigh part of the lands lay in the adjoining barony of Middlethird to the south and in the territory of Coill na Manach (now incorporated into the barony of Kilnamanagh) in the west This latter territory was the patrimony of the O'Duibhir (O'Dwyer) sept from time immemorial who, though they acknowledged the overlord of the earls of Ormond after the Norman invasion, retained their independence and continued to rule their own territory after the Irish usage.

Following the Bruce invasion in the early fourteenth century there was a remarkable Irish resurgence and the Anglo-Norman colonists were driven out of North Tipperary. Although they all held their ground in the territory of east and south of Holy Cross as well as in the Holy Cross area itself the Irish septs of O'Dwyer and O'Mulryan, the latter intruders from Owneybeg in Co. Limerick, grew in strength and influence and occupied all the territory to the west and north-west of the monastic lands. Both of these families were to furnish abbots to Holy Cross in the fifteenth and sixteenth centuries. Moreover, the Anglo-Normans themselves had become to a great extent Gaelicised, adopting the Irish language and culture, Irish customs and dress, and even evolving a system of local law based on a mixture of Irish (Brehon) and feudal law. The Butlers, Purcells, Cantwells, Burkes and other Norman families became in many respects indistinguishable from the native Irish with whom they freely intermarried, and we find many references to these 'degenerate English' who were divided into septs after the Irish fashion and had their chieftains even as had the Irish, called by the English 'captains of their nations'.

Tipperary or the county of Ormond, being a palatinate, was ruled by the earl of Ormond with practically regal rights, only the four pleas of the Crown (rape, arson, forestalling and treasure-trove) being reserved to the king. The lands of Holy Cross itself formed part, not of the palatinate, but of the cross of Tipperary, as did the other ecclesiastical and Crown lands.[1] Tipperary was not, as is commonly considered, unique in having a county of the Cross. The writs of parliamentary summons list also the Crosses of Meath, Kerry, Kilkenny, Wexford and Ulster (Ultonia). In the county of Cross of Tipperary the king's writ ran, while the writ of the earl of Ormond (with the exception of the four pleas already noted) ran in the palatinate or liberty of Tipperary. In practice, however, the earl of Ormond could not be ignored by the monks of Holy Cross, for here was the effective wielder of power in the area while the king of England was a remote figure whose

1 CS, Co. Tipperary, ii (1934).

power, at least in local matters, was far more shadowy. The Irish chiefs in the Ormond territories recognised (at least in theory) the suzerainty of both king and earl; but the practical independence of these same chieftains is evidenced by the fact that the earl entered into treaties with them as with independent rulers. In view of all this we are not surprised to find monks of Holy Cross seeking and obtaining grants of Liberties, exemptions and protection from the earl of Ormond. A typical grant of this kind is that given at Cashel by James Butler, earl of Ormond, lord of the liberty of Tipperary on 12 December 1364. By this letter of protection the earl exempts the abbot and convent of Holy Cross from all amercements in his courts and places in all his lordship, and from all secular service. He grants them and their successors freedom from toll in all their buying for their own use in markets throughout his lordship. He takes them and their successors, their goods, chattels, tenants, lands rents and all their possessions and those of their tenants under his special protection and defence. His officers are not to inflict any loss, damage, injury, impediment on the said abbot and convent, and nothing of their corn, hay, cows, pigs, sheep, horses, carts, carriages and other animals of the abbot and convent or of their tenants are to be taken against their will for his use or that of any of his ministers. The protection thus granted is to continue as long as they shall well and faithfully keep the king's peace. The original is in Latin, and as it is a typical document of its king we give here a full translation:

> James de Botiller, earl of Ormond, Lord of the Liberty of Tipperary, to all seneschals, sheriffs, provosts, bailiffs, servants and other lieges of the lord king, whosoever shall read these presents greetings.
>
> Know ye, that for the love of God, and for the salvation of our own soul and the souls of our predecessors and successors, we, have given and granted to Brother David, abbot of the church of the Blessed Mary of the Holy Cross near Cashel and to the convent of the same place and their successors, that they shall be free and quit for us and our heirs of all amercements in all our courts and places in all our lordship for whatever cause they may be emerced, and shall be exempt in so far as in us lies and as regards our lordship, from all secular service. Provided that the abbot and his successors appear before our Seneschal of the said Liberty, who is for the time being, on the first day of the assizes. We have granted also to them and their successors that they be free and quit of toll on all their goods and merchandise in all their buying and selling for their own use throughout our aforesaid liberty and lordship. And furthermore, we take under our special protection and defence the aforesaid abbot and convent with their successors, their goods, tenants, chattels, lands, rents and all their possessions and those of

their tenants. Being unwilling that anything of the corn, hay, cows,
pigs, sheep, horses, carts, carriages, or other animals of the aforesaid abbot and convent or of their tenants should be taken for our
own use or that of any of our ministers against their will, we command all our officers and all others who it may concern, not to
inflict any loss, damage, injury, burden or impediment of any kind
on the said abbot and convent or on their tenants, but to permit
them to enjoy and use the said liberties in all things. In testimony
of which we have caused these our letters patent to be made and
signed with our seal. Witnesses: Thomas le Botiller, Chancellor of
our aforesaid liberty; Sir John Lercedekn, Knight; Roger de Sancta
Brigida, sheriff of the said county; Thomas Brikyn, clerk and many
others. To continue as long as they shall well and faithfully keep
the king's peace and ours. Given at Cashel, the twelfth day of
December in the thirty-eight year of Edward III *post conquestum
Angliae.*

The above charter, like many of its kind, bears indirect witness to the
commercial activities of the medieval Cistercians. Unlike the English
Cistercians, the monks of Ireland have left no record of their commercial
activities, but references in this and other charters show that these activities were widespread. Not only did the Cistercians sell or purchase goods
at the markets nearest their monasteries but they not infrequently secured
the privilege of having markets of their own in their own towns or villages.
The document we have given above shows how the monks of Holy Cross
were granted freedom from toll in all they bought or sold for their own
use throughout the lordship of the earl of Ormond. A charter granted by
king John to the abbot and convent of Holy Cross almost two hundred
years earlier had exempted them from toll on all they bought or sold for
their own use throughout all the king's lands of Normandy, England,
France and Ireland. This exemption from tolls was very important at a
time when the collection of tolls was almost universal. The income from
tolls was intended to provide for the upkeep of roads and bridges, and the
many references to stallage, pontage, passage and lastage as well as tolls in
various charters granted to Cistercian houses in Ireland shows that quite
an amount of transport was involved in the commercial activities of the
monks.

The transport required for all this was provided by the 'horses, carts,
wagons and cars' mentioned in an agreement to be quoted, between the
monks of Holy Cross and a neighbouring lord concerning the right of way
granted by him through his land to those of the monks who had to go turf
cutting in the abbot's bog. But such transport was not necessarily confined
to land. Although we have no documentary evidence to suggest that the

monks of Holy Cross used the river Suir as a highway for this purpose the possibility cannot be dismissed out of hand. It is true that the monks of Holy Cross had obstructed the free passage of boats to some extent by the construction of weirs in connection with their fisheries; but they were obliged by law to leave a sufficient space between the weir and the opposite bank of the river to allow boats to pass freely and there are not wanting instances of the indictment of certain Cistercian abbots (not abbots of Holy Cross, be it said) for failure to observe that law.

One of the most pressing needs of the community of monks is a plentiful supply of water and of fuel and that was as true in the middle ages as it is today. Sited as it was by the river and blessed in addition by the presence of its lands of numerous wells of pure spring water, Holy Cross abbey was assured of a never failing water supply. For fuel, however, the monks depended principally on a good turf bog which lay in their lands, though at some little distance from the abbey and separated from the main bloc of monastic lands by the estate of one of the neighbouring lords. The shortest and easiest means of access to the monks' bog was through the lands of Thomas Stapleton, son of Sir John Stapleton, lord of Fertiana, whose lands bordered those of Holy Cross on the east and gave its name to a neighbouring parish. The spirit of 'good neighbourliness' that existed between the monks and the lords of Fertiana is evidenced by the agreement entered into on 30 September 1361, a summarised version of which had been printed in the *Calendar of Ormond Deeds*:

> Thomas, son of Sir John Stapleton, Lord of Fertiana, gives and grants to the abbot and convent of the B.V.M. of Holy Cross and their successors in all the lands and tenements of the same the right to go and return through all his lands of Ferten with their horses, carts, carriages and cars (*bigis quadrigis et carhis*), to carry and take away sods, turf (*focalia*) and all other necessaries from the bog (*mora*) of the said abbot, etc, to their monastery and to all their townlands and granges as often as they wish, rendering nothing therefore to him or his heirs for ever. Witnesses: G. son of John Stapelton, Walter (??) Sal, John Blonchard and Henry Mauderer. Given at Ferten on the morrow after Michaelmas in the 35th year of Edward III.

A glance at the Ordnance map makes it clear that the bog must have lain north of Fertiana in what is now the townland of Lidnagonogue. The patent issued to Thomas Butler, earl of Ormond, by Queen Elizabeth names Lisnagonogue as part of the monastic lands of Holy Cross. But the ancient Lisnagonogue was not identical with the modern townland of that name. A reference to the Down Survey map makes it abundantly clear that the ancient Lisnagonogue included within its bound a considerable part of what is now the townland of Commons, all the southern part of the said townland in fact. Here, then lay the bog of the abbot and convent of Holy Cross which supplied Holy Cross abbey with turf. Carville notes that on a fort in this townland (possible the Lios which gave the townland its name) may be seen the rectangular foundation of a church measuring thiry-eight feet from east to west and about twelve feet from south to north, and not far from the said foundation is another about fifteen feet square which, she thinks, may have provided summer accomodation for the turf cutters. That the Lios on which the building once stood was an important one may be gauged from the fact that it was ringed round with a triple rampart.

Toward the end of the century came Richard II king of England's two expeditions to Ireland. It seems that soon after his first arrival in this country he was approached by the abbot of Holy Cross or some of his monks with the request that he should inspect and confirm anew the charter granted to Holy Cross by his ancestor, John, formerly lord of Ireland and earl of Mortain.[2] This the king graciously did at Waterford, on 29 April 1395 in the following words:-

> Richard, by the grace of God, king of England and France and Lord of Ireland, to all to whom these presents shall come greetings. We have inspected a charter granted by our progenitor John, formerly lord of Ireland and earl of Mortain, to the church of the Blessed Mary of Holy Cross and the Cistercian monks herein, in the following words: (Here follows the charter of John already quoted earlier). We, moreover, ratifying and approving the aforesaid donations, grants and confirmations, liberties, customs and quittances all and singly contained in the said charter approve them for ourselves and for our heirs in so far as in us lies, by the tenor of these presents, and we grant and confirm them to the said church and to the monks now serving God therein, as the aforesaid charter reasonably testifies, and as they and their predecessors have hitherto been accustomed reasonably to use and enjoy the aforesaid liberties, customs and quittances from the time of their concession. In witness wherof we have caused these our Letters Patent to be made. Witnessed by myself at Waterford on the twenty-ninth day of April in the eighteenth year of our reign.[3]

During this century the terrible plague known as the Black Death swept through Europe, leaving a great death toll in its wake. The Cistercian Order suffered severely from the ravages of this pestilence and in many

2 COD, no. 15. 3 CPI.

monasteries the numbers fell. There is no reason to think that Holy Cross abbey escaped this dread visitation, but we have no contemporary record of the effect of the Black Death on the community. Towards the end of this century too, after the Black Death had passed away, the partial reconstruction of the monastery seems to have commenced and this was to continue for many years, culminating in the beautiful cloister arcade, part of which still survives and bears the name of Dionysius Ó Congail, an abbot who flourished about the middle of the fifteenth century. The financial condition of the abbey had been critical on at least two occasions. In the early thirteenth century as we have seen it had been brought to the verge of ruin, and in great part to the alienation of lands and the accumulation of debts as a result of abbatial mismanagement. This seems to have been remedied for no further complaints are heard on this score.

12. MONASTIC REVENUES, HOLY CROSS ESTATES, CHURCH GRANTS

HOLY CROSS ESTATES

In sharp contrast to the general run of medieval monks the first Cistercians did not possess a number of scattered manors, farms, fields and tenements in various parts of the country, but each community held a single block of land in the midst of which stood the abbey. These early estates of the Cistercian Order were generally of great extent when reckoned by modern standards and often included expanses of forest as well as moor and waste land.

The extent of an estate might vary from two or three thousand acres in the case of the small abbeys to forty or fifty thousand in the case of the larger ones. The possessions of Holy Cross, amounting to about eight thousand acres in their original extent would, therefore be considered quite a modest estate for a community of medieval Cistercians. The greater part of these eight thousand acres would have formed a single block of land surrounding the abbey on all sides, and probably corresponded to what later came to be called the parish of Holy Cross. Some detached areas were probably included in the monastic lands from the beginning. Once such area was certainly included for it is named in the charter[1] granted by Donal Ó Briain to the abbot and convent. This was the denomination known as Bali Ichealliach which is represented today by the

---

1 COD, v; Hartry, p. xlviii.

modern Ballykelly and part of Marshallstown. Other detached areas such as Kilcommon and the adjoining lands in the parish of Templebeg and the townland of Ballycahill in the parish of that name are known not to have formed part of the original endowement of Holy Cross abbey but to have come into the possession of the abbot and convent at a later date, the Kilcommon group of lands being the gift of the earl of Ormond. Other detached areas there were, concerning which we have no evidence as to how or when they came into the hands of the monks, if they did not indeed, form part of the abbey possessions from the beginning; in this category may be placed the townland of Lisnagonogue in the parish of Thurles and the townland of Garrane in the parish of Borrisleagh

Due to the absence of documentary sources it is impossible to identify the granges belonging to Holy Cross. Because Holy Cross was allowed to continue as a provostry after the dissolution of the monasteries in 1539 no survey was made of its possessions. Furthermore, the modern townland nomenclature which often preserves names incorporating the word grange and thereby helps to locate these monastic farms is disappointing in the context of Holy Cross. Out of a total of forty-two townlands within the former monastic estate only one contains the element grange. There is also the townland of Graignoe which could mean either New Grange or New Village and must therefore be classed as doubtful. The townland of Grange is in the parish of Holy Cross but it is not now possible to say which of the medieval granges it represents.

In the charter of Domhnall Ó Briain none of the eleven denominations named was called a grange. It may have been that the monks had not by them divided the monastic lands into granges: they may also have retained the existing denominations. In medieval sources we find mention made of five granges by name, the grange of Culetti or Coiletty, the Great Grange near Bridgetown, the grange of Belenather, Grangecor and Grangecorkeran. The grange of Culetti can be equated with the area comprised in the modern townlands of Lisbook and Ballycamusk. The 'Great Grange near Bridgetown' has been tentatively identified by Carville[2] with the modern townlands of Glenbane Lower and Upper and the townland of Graignoe, on the assumption that the bridge was one of the 'Twoford Bridges' across the Suir, linking Newtown on the right bank of the river with Glenbane Lower on the left. No attempt has been made to identify the granges of Belenather (Béal an Átha?), Grangecor or Grangecorkeran.

The Cistercian constitution forbade the monks to receive any revenues deriving from rents or services from tenants and they were also forbidden to have serfs; it also forbade them to use their mills and bakehouses for any purpose other than the provisioning of their own houses. Revenues

2 Carville, *The Heritage of Holy Cross* (Belfast 1973), chap. 7.

from ecclesiastical sources such as churches and chapels and advowsons of the same, altarages, obligations, mortuaries and tithes were likewise prohibited. Since these were precisely the gifts most frequently bestowed on monastic communities by pious benefactors it is not surprising that the Cistercians gradually succumbed to the temptation of accepting such forbidden fruit. We find it already established in a number of houses in the early years of Anglo-Norman rule and it is possible that it existed before the invasion.

We have no evidence of when the abbey of Holy Cross first acquired possession of churches and chapels but a protection issued by Henry III in 1227 for the abbeys of Mellifont, Baltinglass, Suir, Maigue and Holy Cross mentions the tenants and churches of their houses. A charter issued by the same king in 1233 speaks of the abbot's men (*homines*) meaning thereby either the tenants or more probably the serfs or betaghs. By the time Peter Ó Conaig became abbot the abbey was receiving rents from tenants on the monastic estates[3] and at this period also we have the first definite evidence of the possession of private churches by Holy Cross. The acceptance of such sources of revenue meant that the monks were no longer depending solely on manual labour as a source of livelihood. It did not mean that manual labour was abandoned as we know that the monks continued to work the granges all through the thirteenth century and into the first quarter of the following century. A departure had been made, however, from a fundamental rule and eventually manual labour was superseded completely by the adoption of the rentier system.

The monastic revenues were designated as either 'spiritualities' or 'temporalities'. The term 'spiritualities' had no spiritual connotation but was simply used to designate earnings from patronage, appropriated churches, chapels, rectories, vicarages, tithes, obligations, altarages and obventions, including offerings at the shrines and on the altars of the church. The temporalities referred to the revenues derived from manors, farms, rents, services and other unspecified items-such as fairs, markets and courts. The custom of celebrating mass on the granges, which had been authorised by Pope Alexander IV in 1255, had become necessary with the letting of land to tenants and the gradual adoption of feudalism by the monks. Many of the abbey churches became parish churches and it is significant how one finds repeated again and again in the surveys taken after the dissolution of the monasteries in the sixteenth century the phrase 'The abbey church has been from time immemorial the parish church'. Owing to the fact that no survey was made at Holy Cross we cannot now produce contemporary evidence to show that the abbey church at Holy

---

3 G. Mills (ed.), *Calendar of Justiciary Rolls Ireland, 1295-1303 (etc.)*, 2 vols, (Dublin, 1905 and 1914), p. 134.

Cross was, in fact, used as a parish church. It has been stated that the present Church of Ireland building (or an earlier one on the same site) was in use as a parish church in pre-reformation days. It is clear that if this were the case the abbey church could not have been the parish church. On the other hand we have the condition, inserted in a lease by the earl of Ormond and Ossory to John Cantwell FitzPeres of Byalachomiske, that the lessee should keep in repair 'the parish church of the said abbey'. This stipulation, taken in conjunction with the terms of an earlier lease by the same earl to James Purcell Fitzwilliam, dated 15 May 1572, makes it quite clear that, by the term 'parish church' in the Cantwell lease, the abbey church is meant. Cantwell's obligation to keep the parish church in repair is distincively stated not to extend to that part of the chancel then held by James Purcell Fitzwilliam. Now the lease to the latter shows that the rooms held by Purcell included the chapter house, the room over the chancel of the choir, the room over 'cross church of the Holy Cross ... *with a little way entering in the great stairs* of the said church to the upper rooms'.[4] The context here clearly shows that we are concerned with the abbey itself and with the abbey church. The words in italics (italics mine) refer undoubtedly to the small flight of stairs connecting the upper rooms with the night stairs leading from the monks dormitory to the abbey church. There cannot be the slightest doubt, therefore, that in 1572 the abbey church was the parish church and we may infer that it had been probably in use as a parish church before the dissolution fo the monastery.

In the medieval period grants of churches to monasteries were not uncommon. When a layman made a grant of lands to an abbey he sometimes included in the grant the church of which he was a 'patron' or which had been endowed by him and had come to be looked upon as 'his' church. Sometimes he made over to the monks merely the advowson of the church, that is, the right to appoint the incumbent on whom the bishop would confer jurisdiction. It could also happen, and frequently did happen, that the church itself was made over to the monastery so that the community became owners, and in such a case they also became either collectively or in the person of the abbot or some member of the community appointed by the abbot, rector of the church, being in fact the parish priest. He was also known as the 'parson' and this was the title by which the priest at Mellifont, who had charge of the parish church there, was known. Whenever the abbot and convent acquired a church in this way it became their absolute property and was said to be impropriate. When the church was within the precinct of the abbey itself it was usually ruled by a parson drawn from the community, but if it lay outside the abbey precinct a vicar was usually appointed from the ranks of the secular clergy being presented

4 COD, v, p. 226.

by the abbot and instituted by the bishop. The vicar, who did the actual work received a salary which generally amounted to one-third of the total revenues of the parish, the abbot and convent receiving the other two-thirds. Although the possession of impropriate churches was absolutely forbidden to Cistercians, the prohibition became a dead letter at a fairly early date and by the fourteenth century grants of impropriate churches became more and more common. Over such churches, the abbeys held all financial rights as well as right of patronage but they did not normally exercise spiritual jurisdiction over them. However, by a decree of 28 September 1487, Pope Innocent VIII granted to all Cistercian abbots quasi-episcopal jurisdiction, not only over their own monks but also over their tenants, vassals, subjects and servants, all of whom were thereby freed and exempted from 'all jurisdiction, superiority, correction, visitation, subjection and power of archbishops, bishops, and their vicars, etc.' and were subjected immediately to the Holy See. In this way the impropriate churches of Cistercians, including those to which parochial rights belonged, came under the jurisdiction, not of the bishop, but of the abbot, so that to the latter it pertained to visit such churches and to correct abuses.

Manorialism developed among the Irish Cistercians and their estates became in many instances gradually enlarged with the passing of the centuries. The number of impropriate churches likewise increased until in the end a very large number of parishes and other benefices was held by the Order in various parts of Ireland, many of these parishes being far removed from the monastery which drew their revenues. We will confine ourselves here to observing the growth of Holy Cross abbey in temporalites and spiritualities from the date of its foundation to the year 1539 when the decree for the supression of the religious houses in Ireland went forth. We shall not attempt to enter into minute details, but we shall note in chronological order the more important acquisitions, whether of lands or churches, made by the abbot and convent during the period under review. The earliest record of a grant of land to the abbot and convent of Holy Cross (apart from the original grant made by Domhnall Ó Briain) is that made during the reign of Henry II by Robert Travers, bishop of Killaloe, a grant which must be dated between 1216 and 1231. The denominations named in the original deed are those of Lestiakardin, Killcomyn and Balmacroy which are described as 'extending to the west to the river called Tirkynysy, and ascending by the mountain on the south to the stones called Firbragy and from that place by the mountains running up the height to Belanayn, and from that to Comyrytybryen'. Although most of the names mentioned in the grant are now obsolete there is no doubt whatever that the 'Killcomyn' of this deed is the modern Kilcommon in the barony of Kilnamanagh Upper, Co. Tipperary. The *History of the Diocese of Killaloe* states quite positively that 'Coum near Portroe is called 'Comryn-

tybryen' in a grant made by Robert Travers as bishop of Killaloe', I do not
know on what grounds the author locates Comryntybryen in the Portroe
area nor what reasons he had for identifying it with Coum near Portroe.
There is nothing in the grant itself to suggest that Comryntybryen was any-
where near Portroe and there is no evidence known to me to connect
Coum in any way with Holy Cross abbey. On the other hand there is evidence of Patent granted by Queen Elizabeth to Thomas Butler, earl of
Ormond, to show that Kilcommon formed part of the Holy Cross possessions at the time the abbey was dissolved, and there is evidence of the Civil
Survey (Tipperary, vol. 2) that the parish of Templebeg (of which Kilcommon and the neighbouring townlands formed part) was wholly impropriate to the abbey of Holy Cross. It is true that the names Lestiakardin
and Ballmacroy are now obsolete but the Down Survey map shows that the
latter name was still known in 1654 under the slightly altered form of
Garran Ballymacrow, while Kilcommon appears on the same map as
Killcomyn. Moreover, the modern Ordnance Survey maps show in this
area the townlands of Cummermore and Commerbeg which may represent the Comryntybryen of the Ormond Deeds and it is no coincidence
that further south in the neighbouring parish of Aghcrew is the townland
of Knockantybrien. The superimposition of the Down Survey on the ordnance survey shows clearly that the lands of Killcomyn and Ballymacroy
are represented today by the townlands of Knocknakill, Church Quarter,
Kilcommon and Loughbrack in the detached part of the parish of
Templebeg in Cashel archdiocese. These were the lands granted to Holy
Cross abbey by Robert Travers in the thirteenth century.

It is probable that the letting of land to tenants had commenced at
Holy Cross before the coming of Stephen of Lexington to Ireland in 1228.
The first specific reference to the abbot's men is found in a charter of
1233 and this may either refer to tenants or serfs. Almost a generation
later we have recorded an agreement between Thomas, abbot of Holy
Cross, and Theobald Walter, butler of Ireland, by which the abbot with the
consent of the convent and of his lord, the abbot of Margam, leased to the
said Walter half a carucate of land in Culletti. The conditions were that
Theobald should have the lease for life but that at his death the land with
all its appurtenances were to revert to the abbey. Although the deed is
undated it seems to have been drawn up between 1273 and 1278. This
deed identifies for us the situation of Culletti, one of the denominations
listed in the original foundation charter of Domhnall Ó Briain. The half
carucate of land in Culletti is said to have lain between the little river (rivu-
lum) of Cullettti and the said Theobald's lordship of Ardmail. This area
now forms the modern townlands of Ballycamusk and Lisbook, and since
the deed suggests that only part of Culletti was included in the lease it is
probable that the area leased corresponded to Lisbook only.

CHURCH GRANTS

The first grant of a parsonage to the abbey of Holy Cross of which we have evidence is that made by Geoffrey le Bryt, knight, of the parsonage of the church of Dounnemonet (Donamona or Donamonad), which Curtis dates approximately between the years 1270 and 1284. There seems to have been some doubt as to the location of this church. That it was in the diocese of Killaloe is certain, but it was certainly not in the barony of Tulla, Co. Clare, as stated by Professor Curtis, for in the royal visitation of 1615 it is noted as being in the deanery of Ormond, and this is confirmed by the visitation of 1622. The church of Donamona, had become merged in the parish of Kilmore after the reformation and the dissolution of the monasteries. The lands of Donamona are noted in the Civil Survey of Tipperary, 1654 (vol. ii, p. 242) where it is shown to be in the barony of Upper Ormond. About a century and a half after the grant of the parsonage of Donamona by Geoffrey le Bryt, we have a record of the appropriation to Holy Cross abbey by James (O Lonergan), bishop of Killaloe, and his dean and chapter, of the vicarage of the parish church of Dunnamonad with mandate to Thatheus Maccomnan, archdeacon of Killaloe, to induct.

Another instance of the process by which 'private' churches came into the hands of the Cistercians is afforded by the grant[5] made in 1364 by William, son and heir of Robert Hacket, to the abbot and convent of Holy Cross and their successors 'for the good of his soul and that of Ana Ynymcgylpatrick his wife, and the souls of his ancestors and successors' of the rectory of the church of Burgagenefarne (borrisnafarney) 'as freely as he and his heirs can give it in perpetual frankolmoign'. Though this grant was given at Clonmel on 9 March 1364, there seems to have been a delay of thirty-five years in carrying out the provisions, for as late as 1399, we find Matthew, bishop of Killaloe, commanding his archdeacon Cornelius O'Dea to induct Philip, lord abbot of Holy Cross, into the rectory of Buryesnafearna, the said abbot and convent having been presented to the rectory by William Haket, its patron.

The landed possessions of Holy Cross received an increase in 1429 by the grant[6] of the vill of Balagh Cathyll (now Ballycahill) made to the abbot and convent by James le Bottiller, earl of Ormond. By this charter the earl granted and confirmed to the abbot and convent the vill of Balagh Cathyll with all its rights and appurtenances as well as the homages and services of all the free tenants pertaining in anyway to the said vill or land. The abbey of Holy Cross thus acquired not only an augmentation of its landed property but an increase in the number of its tenants and consequently in the revenues accruing to the abbey by reason of rents and services due from

5 Ibid., ii, no.396, p. 84. 6 IMED, 26, p. 19.

those tenants. The abbot and convent agreed on their part that they and their successors should maintain for ever a lighted candle of wax before the high altar of the abbey church for the praise and honour of God and his Immaculate Mother, the Virgin Mary, on the vigils and feast days of Christmas, the Epiphany, Easter and the Finding and the Exaltation of the Holy Cross, the Ascension, Pentecost, the feast of the Holy Trinity, the feast of Corpus Christi, the feasts of the Assumption and Nativity of the Blessed Virgin Mary and the feast of all Saints. This wax candle was to burn before the high altar on the aforesaid vigils and feast days from the first vespers of the feast until after the second vespers, in default of which the abbot and convent bound themselves and their successors to pay to Sir James le Botiller and heirs forty silver *denarii* as often as they might fail to maintain the said candle according to the conditions laid down in the indenture. It was agreed moreover that Sir James and his heirs should have the right to distrain in all the lands and tenements of the abbot and convent and their successors for the forty denarii for any day on which the abbot and convent and their successors should have failed to maintain the light burning before the altar according to the conditions already noted. The conditions laid down in this indenture and the means taken to ensure that those conditions were carried out indicate, perhaps, that the earl was not unaware of the danger that the monks might neglect to fulfill the term of the grant. This was a period during which a growing number of abbots owed their appointment not to the free vote of the community as required by the Cistercian constitutions but to the papal provision; and many, if not the majority of these 'provisors' aspired to the abbatial office simply and solely for the sake of the substantial revenues they might hope to receive, or, in some cases, for the sake of the power they might hope to wield, the influence they might hope to exercise and the social status they might emjoy in the public life of the period. The occupation of the abbatial office by such men led to the impoverishment of the communities they were supposed to rule, the neglect of divine service, hospitality, almsgiving and other works of charity, and the earl may well have felt that men who were prepared to neglect the graver duties of their office would have little scruple in neglecting such a minor obligation in keeping a candle burning before the altar in the abbey church. This is not to say that the earl necessarily mistrusted the good faith of the abbot and community of Holy Cross when he made the grant in question. If the abbey had not had a good reputation at the time it is scarcely conceivable that the earl would have made the grant at all; but knowing the conditions of the time and realising the possibility of the abbey falling into the hands of a 'provisor' of the kind we have sketched above, it would only be ordinary prudence on the part of the earl to make provisions as far as in him lay for any eventuality. He may have had a premonition of what was to come. Less than twenty years later, the illegitimate son of the abbot who ruled the convent at the time of the grant was made, became himself abbot of Holy Cross and was the first of a series of provisors whose abbatial careers were no credit to themselves and contributed not a little to the spiritual decay of the community.

The grant of the vill of Ballycahill was made at Clonmel on 9 August 1429 and was followed after a short interval by a grant of the vicarage.[7] This was made by Richard O Hedian, archbishop of Cashel, with the assent of his dean and chapter, and the bishop's mandate to the archdeacon for the induction of the abbot and convent 'or their procurator aeconomus or syndic' is dated 22 September of the same year. In the following year the advowson of the rectory of Beakstown which had belonged to Thomas Archer, 'lord of Corketen and Stourtwes', was, with the rectory itself, presented to the abbey of Holy Cross. By a second grant made on the same day (6 June 1430) the vicarage of Beakstown was made over to the monastery. This appropriation of the rectory and vicarage of Beakstown was made by the archbishop of Cashel following the grant by Thomas Archer of the advowson and the rectory and meant in effect that the rectory and vicarage of Beakstown were now wholly impropriate to the abbey of Holy Cross.

Earlier it was stated that the original lands granted to Holy Cross abbey are represented today more or less substantially by the combined parishes of Holy Cross and Rathkennan. On the 19 November 1431, Diarmaid Ó Duibhir, (Diarmicius Odubhyr) *sui nationis capitaneus*, made a grant of the lands of Rathkennan and Cillin Clonferad to Holy Cross. This would seem at first sight to show conclusively that Rathkennan could not have been included in the original grant made by Domhnall Ó Briain. However, among the lands enumerated as part of the monastic possessions in the latter half of the thirteenth century (*c.*1275-81) are the grange of Ballycorkeran, Tippergeel, Bridgetown, Rathkennan, and the great grange near Bridgetown. From this it is clear that Holy Cross abbey held the lands of Rathkennan at least 150 years before the grant made by Dermicius Odubyr, and since we have no record of any previous grant of these lands we may assume with some probability that they were part of the original possessions of the abbey. If that be the case they must be sought for under a different name among the lands enumerated in the charter granted by Domhnall Mór Ó Briain. The grant of 1431 therefore, should be understood rather as an act of restitution – the surrender of a claim to lands which had once belonged to Holy Cross but which in the course of time had come into the possession of the lords of Kilnamanagh. That the church as well as the lands of Rathkennan belonged originally to Holy Cross may be inferred from the fact that in the deed of appropriation of the vicarage of

7 Ibid., 29, p. 22.

the parish church of Rathkennan to the abbot and convent of Holy Cross (27 October 1452) it is stated that the said vicarage used to belong to the abbot and convent, *dicta vicaria ad dictum monasterium abbatem et conventum spectabat et pertinebat.* It appears therefore, that this appropriation was in reality a restitution to the monks of a church they had formerly held.

It would seem that Abbot Fergal O Heffernan, who ruled the abbey from 1423 to 1448, was vigorously pursuing a policy which had as its aim the recovery for the abbey of lands and churches which had become alienated in the course of time. This would seem to apply also to the church of Ballycahill which, more than 130 years earlier, had been held of the abbot by the layman James le Mazyner whom we have already met in these pages. The grant of the vill of Ballycahill to Holy Cross in 1429-30 was followed the same year by a quit claim made by John, son of Geoffrey Sall in *avour* of the abbot and convent of Holy Cross to all his rights in the messuages, etc., of Ballycally (now Ballykelly). In 1431 came, as we have seen the restitution of the lands of Rathkennan followed in 1432, by another grant of land in Ballycahill. The donor this time was Nicholas White of Thurles who, by a charter dated 30 March 1432, granted and confirmed to Abbot Fergal and the monks of Holy Cross 'one vacant messuage and one carucate of land with its appurtenances'. By this time the most marked feature of the political scene was the re-emergence of the native Irish and the waning power of the English sovereign even in the great Anglo-Irish lordships. In North and West Tipperary the O'Kennedys, the O'Briens and the O'Mulryans were now powers to be reckoned with and men with whom the earl of Ormond himself did not disdain to enter into treaties. The O'Dwyers too, though more closely connected with the Butlers, whose overlordship they recognised, were lords of Kilnamanagh in their own right and down to the seventeenth century the area controlled by them was known not as the 'barony' but the 'territory' of Kilnamanagh. It was but natural, in view of the Irish resurgence that the monks of Holy Cross should seek to have their rights and privileges confirmed to them by Irish as well as by English rulers, and in view of the fact that the abbey itself was a royal foundation of the Thomond dynasty it was appropriate that the confirmation of the charter granted by Domhnal Mór Ó Briain should not be sought from one of the family. There can be little doubt, I think, that the Inspeximus and Confirmation of the said charter by 'Tatheus O'brien, princeps Tuomonie' dated 29 July 1434, was made at the request of the abbot and convent of Holy Cross. Having quoted in its entirety the original charter granted by his ancestor, Donall's successor, now styling himself 'prince of Thomond' ratified and approved and confirmed to the said church and the monks then dwelling therein, the donations, concessions, confirmations and customs contained in the said charter for himself and his heirs as far as in him lay.

In 1450 Stephen Sampson of Tubberadory granted to Abbot William and the monks of Holy Cross all his lands and tenements with all their appurtenances in and of Tubberadory 'to have and to hold to the said abbot and convent and their successors in perpetuity' on condition that the abbot and convent paid the said Stephen, his heir or his executors forty *solidi* of silver 'of good and lawful money', viz. 13*s*. 4*d*. annually for three years, half to be paid at Easter and the other half on the feast of the Exaltation of the Holy Cross (14 September); and if Stephen should survive for more than the said three years the abbot and community were to pay him an annuity of six shillings and eight pence during his life. They also obliged themselves to pay him three measures of corn and five measures of oats every year as long as he lived. It was further agreed that if Stephen's son, William Rother Sampson, should plough in any of the lands or tenements of the abbot the convent within the county of Tipperary, he should not pay any rent to the said abbot and convent beyond one penny to be paid on the feast of the Holy Cross *pro recognitione dominii* only.

The parish of Glankeen, a parish practically coextensive with the ancient territory of Ui Luighdheach, was appropriated to the abbey of Holy Cross in 1485 by David Creagh, archbishop of Cashel.[8] In the deed of impropriation dated 10 July 1485, this annexation, appropriation and perpetual incorporation of the vicarage in Holy Cross and the transference to the abbot and convent of the cure and administration of the said church is stated to have been carried out with the consent and agreement of the dean and chapter of Cashel out of reverence for the Saving Wood of Holy Cross and in honour of him who hung upon it. In his mandate to the dean of Cashel (John O Hedian) for the induction of the abbot and convent it is laid down by the archbishop that the interests of the parishioners are not to be neglected by reason of this appropriation. The incorporation or impropriation was made in perpetuity, but with a clause which read 'saving to ourselves and successors our ordinary and extraordinary rights in the same vicarage', and the abbot and convent were expected to present to the bishop or his successors a chaplain to be admitted by him or his successors to the cure of the said vicarage. This meant that while the abbot and convent were to be the vicars of the church of Glankeen they were to present a chaplain to the bishop who would be admitted by him to the church to look after the souls of the parishioners. Since this chaplain was not himself a vicar he had no real security of tenure, nor, unless a particular arrangement or agreement was made between the abbot and convent on the one part and the bishop on the other or between the abbot and convent and the chaplain himself, could he be sure of getting a decent wage. In default

8 Ibid., 55, p. 48.

of such an agreement his wage like his tenure of office depended solely on the will of the abbot and convent, which in practice meant that of the abbot. This was the last endowment of the kind of which we have recorded. Later still, in 1527, a further grant of lands was made to the abbey by Walter Walsh, provisor of the Common Hall, Cashel and the college therof, presumably the house of Canons Choral, these lands being situated in what was known as Le Pryry or in Irish (*hibernice*) Tybyrhory. The lands thus granted would seem to have been situated in what is now the townland of Toberadora.

We see, then that from the early period the abbey of Holy Cross was endowed by the generosity of rich and powerful benefactors with abundance of lands and churches, and these lavish gifts of 'temporalities' and spiritualities' should in the ordinary course of events have caused the abbey to grow rich and flourishing. Strange to say, however, Holy Cross abbey seems to have remained a poor and even impoverished monastery for the greater part of its existence. In the early part of the thirteenth century it was, as we have seen, on the verge of ruin. It fell into poverty again towards the end of the same century by reason of various alienations, abbatial mismanagement, and the unlawful entry of outsiders into the possession of monastic lands and rents. At the beginning of the fourteenth century its value in the ecclesiastical taxation of Ireland appears as £17. 0s. 8d. in striking contrast to the £50 of its sister house of Inishlounaght, the £40 of Duiske, and the £60 of Maigue, its own mother house.

In 1424, the parish church of Ballynaclogh in Upper Ormond was appropriated to Holy Cross abbey on the grounds that the resources of the monastery were at that time 'insufficient for maintenance and hospitality'. The value of the monastery had by 1448 fallen to £13. 6s. 8d. despite the fact that in the interval between 1424, when the abbey was unable to maintain hospitality, and the year 1448, quite a number of grants, including both lands and churches, had been made to the house. From 1448 onwards, however, there was a steady improvement in the financial state of the monastery which was valued in 1455 at 40 marks sterling (£26. 13s. 4d.) by the year 1492 this had increased to 100 marks (£66. 13s. 4d.).

The causes of the impoverishment of the abbey in the thirteenth century have already been considered. In the fourteenth and fifteenth centuries much of the straitened circumstances of Holy Cross abbey was undoubtedly due to a spate of building activity which seems to have begun towards the end of the fourteenth century and continued well into the fifth decade of the fifteenth century. To the fifteenth century in particular we owe the beautiful arcade and the greater portion, if not the whole, of the eastern section of the church as well as the western doorway and window. The many appropriations of churches and the various acquisitions of lands and rents by the community during these two centuries should, in the ordinary course of events, have sufficed to make it a reasonably wealthy house. The extensive restoration undertaken during this same period, however, and the very elaborate style of workmanship in which it was carried out must have proved a great strain on the resources of the community. Notwithstanding the fact that this intense building activity must have been extended over a considerable period, we have, as far as can be ascertained, but one reference to it in any contemporary document. This solitary reference occurs in a letter of protection issued to the abbot, Fergal Ó Heffernan, by James le Botiller, earl of Ormond, on 15 March 1431/2. Among the various classes taken under the earl's protection in this document were the *clerici ad opera monastery mendicantes*, from what we may conclude that *clerici* were sent out collecting contributions for the building fund, and that monasteries of the middle ages like those of our own day are monuments to the piety of the faithful by whose generous assistance their construction became possible. The cloister arcade was completed during the abbacy of Dionysius Ó Congail some time before 1455 and this was probably the last stage of the work of restoration undertaken at Holy Cross abbey. Once the building operations had been completed the way was clear for succeding abbots to improve the financial condition of the house.

From this time forward the monastery began to flourish materially and to grow in wealth and a new source of revenue was derived from the throngs of pilgrims who now began to make their way to the abbey to pay homage to the relic of the Holy Cross exposed for public veneration. In only one contemporary document (as far as I am aware) is there any reference to the pilgrims who came to reverence the relic of the True Cross and this single reference occurs in a papal mandate addressed to the archbishop of Cashel, the chancellor of Killaloe and a canon of Cashel named Denis Ó Hogán. The mandate is dated on 7 January 1489/90. From it we learn that the faithful were accustomed to make offerings at the wood of the Holy Cross in the church of the monastery, which offerings were collected by collectors appointed for the purpose. In giving the yearly value of the monastery at that time 50 marks (from a later mandate we learn it should really have been given as 100 marks) it is stated that his did not take account of the offerings made by the faithful at the Wood of the Holy Cross. When these offerings are taken into account we may suppose that the yearly value was actually in excess of probably very much in excess of 100 marks. This will help to explain the keen competition there seems to have been among ambitious clerics from the middle of the fifteenth century until the ultimate dissolution of the monastery, to snatch the rich prize of this abbacy; and the story of intrigues and rivalries that centered round this tempting prize is by no means an edifying one. Naturally enough, men who were attracted to the abbey, not by reason of zeal for religion, but because they hoped to capture a rich benefice and 'live on the fat of the land' as well as to enjoy the power, pomp and prestige that went with the abbatial office in those days, were not likely to advance the true interests of religion; and the lives of some of those latter-day abbots were sadly wanting in the virtues one would expect to find in men dedicated to God in the monastic and priestly state.

A papal mandate[9] was issued on 14 May 1490 to the abbot of St Mary *de Ferma* (Ferns), the prior of St John the Evangelist, Inyscoriahy and the treasurer of the church of Leighlin. It asks them to enquire into a rather extraordinary petition of a Gerald Machduyll, cleric of the diocese of Leighlin who suggested that he should take over collections made in the dioceses of Leighlin and Ferns. These collections were made 'in consideration' of the relic of the true cross by a number of 'questors' or collectors. From the collection, a certain annual pension was paid to the abbot of Holy Cross. Gerard Machduyll accused the collectors of abusing their position by scandalous use of the funds collected. He claimed, he would clean up their act and at the same time increase the pension payable to the abbot!

13. SOME ABBOTS OF HOLY CROSS

ABBOT FERGAL O HEFFERNAN

We have not many details of the lives of the three of the leading abbots who ruled the abbey of Holy Cross during the period 1423-1534. We do, however, know a certain amount about them, and although the actual details are not many, they are sufficient to give us an overall picture of three forceful and outstanding personalities. This does not mean that they were model religious or that they in any way approached the ideal abbot depicted in the Rule of St Benedict. Far from it. The first of these abbots in order of time was Fergal O'Heffernan who was abbot from 1423 until 1447 or 1448. We have already seen that he was one of the abbots responsible for the restoration and rebuilding of a great part of the abbey church and domestic buildings and surely deserves the gratitude of succeeding generations by reason of that fact alone. He was not, however the originator of that great work, for there is evidence that it extended over a considerable period and was begun before the end of the fourteenth century. It is not indeed possible to name the abbot who was responsible for initiatingg the project. Apart altogether from the fact that our list of the abbots

9 CPR, xv, 594, p. 306.

of Holy Cross is incomplete, we have no contemporary references which might help us to fix a date with any certainty. Only two abbots are known to us in the period 1364-99, which is most likely the period during which the work commenced. These abbots were David, who was abbot in 1364, and Philip who ruled in 1399. If Philip suceeded immediately to David, the honour of commencing the undertaking must be assigned to one or other of these two abbots. It is quite possible, however, that one or even more abbots intervened between David and Philip, in which case any of these abbots might equally have been the person responsible for the initiation of the project. All we can say with certainty is that the work of rebuilding must have taken many years to complete and was carried out under a succession of abbots, among whom must be numbered Abbot Philip (and possibly Abbot David), Abbot Fergal O'Heffernan, Abbot Odo O Grady (if he was actually abbot for any length of time), Abbot Dyonisius O'Congail, and possibly his successor, Abbot William. To Abbot Denis O'Congail, we are indebted for the beautiful cloister arcades, the exquisite carved stones which lay scattered and hidden for centuries until their discovery in the third decade of the present century when they were assembled and re-erected in their original position by the Board of Works.

We first meet Fergal O'Heffernan's name in a document issued by James Butler, earl of Ormond, on 3 March 1429. This was a pardon issued to Fergal, abbot of Holy Cross and to the convent of that place. If the 'pardon' was really necessary and not a mere matter of form it would scarcely rebound to the credit of the abbot and monks of Holy Cross; for what would we think today of a community of Cistercian monks who had to receive a public pardon for such heavy grievous transgressions as 'all seditions, felonies, homicides, murders, conspiracies, extortions'? The full Latin text of which the following is a translation has been published by Dr Newport B. White.

> James Le Botiller, earl of Ormond, Lord of the Liberty of Tipperary, to all to whom these presents shall come Greeting. Know ye that of our special favour and because of the charity by which we are moved towards the monastery of Holy Cross we have pardoned Fergal O'Heffernan, abbot of the said monastery and the convent of the same place there serving God, the suit of our peace which pertains to us of all seditions, homicides, murders, conspiracies, confederations, extortions, false allegiances, adherence to enemies of our Lord the king and of ourselves, and likewise of escapes of robbers and felons and receiving of the same or of any other outlaws, and of every and all offences, oppressions, contempts and deceptions against the statutes and ordinances of our lord the king and of all transgressions and injustices of whatsoever kind perpetrated by the

said abbot and convent in whatsoever way within our said Liberty up to this day, arson, rape, forestalling and treasure trove alone excepted. We have also pardoned the said Abbot Fergal and his convent the outlawries and the forfeitures to us of their lands and tenements, goods and chattels which they may have incurred on the occasions aforesaid, and we have granted to them our enduring (*firmam*) peace which pertains to us. Provided that they stand to right in the Court of our Liberty aforesaid if any wish to appear against them there and act well and faithfully in future towards the lord king and ourselves and our faithful people. In testimony whereof we have caused these our Letters Patent to be made. Witnessed by myself at Clonmel, the third day of March in the seventh year of the reign of king Henry VI *post conquestum Angliae.*

A letter of protection issued by the same earl of Ormond some fourteen years earlier is of interest as showing that, when it was written, the Anglo-Normans of Kilkenny and Tipperary had already adopted Irish traditions and with them, the prerogatives enjoyed by Irish kings including such exactions as *coinmhe* and *buannacht.* From the tenor of the document, it is clear that the earl himself imposed such exactions and considered that he acted lawfully in so doing. In this he was at one with the majority of the Anglo-Irish lords who in such matters preferred the Irish custom 'because' as Professor Curtis says, 'they found the prerogatives of Irish kingship more lucrative and suited to native tradition than their feudal ones'.

Of Fergal O'Heffernan's early life we know practically nothing, and the little we do know is not altogether edifying. From certain references in the *Calendar of Papal Letters* it transpires that while still a simple cleric, and probably before he became a Cistercian, he became the father of an illegitimate child by a married woman. Notwithstanding his earlier failure in clerical celibacy there is no evidence that Fergal was guilty of any notable misconduct during his tenure of the abbacy of Holy Cross. We have no reason to suppose, therefore, that Fergal's life as a Cistercian was in any way irregular or that as abbot of Holy Cross he was in any way remiss in his abbatial duties or negligent in the obligations of the priestly state. Certainly the fact that he seems to have held office for more than twenty years and that during all that time there is no record of any charge or accusation being brought against him affords a strong presumption in his favour; for it must be remembered that this was a period in which ambitious clerics (and even laymen) who coveted abbatical benefices were accustomed to denounce the incumbents to the Roman Curia and did not scruple to use any means, fair or foul, including charges of gravest nature, charges which were, often as not, entirely baseless, in order to bring about the ruin of their rivals and have themselves appointed in their stead.

The work of restoring the monastic buildings must, as we have seen, been already in progress when Fergal O'Heffernan became abbot and a reference in the *Calendar of Papal Letters* shows that in 1424 the resources of the monastery were already 'insufficient for maintenance and hospitality'. Besides continuing to advance the re-building of the abbey church Fergal occupied himself in recovering lands and churches which had been alienated at one time or another and we find during his tenure of office, that the monastery received numerous grants under this heading. In 1429, a grant was made to the abbot and convent of the parish church of Ballynaclogh and in the same year the vill and vicarage of Ballycahill were added to the monastic possessions followed in 1430 by the rectory and vicarage of Beakstown, in 1431 by the lands of Rathkennan and in 1432 by more lands in Ballycahill. In 1445 the abbot of Morimond in France was appointed by the general chapter visitator and reformator-general of all the Cistercian houses in England, Ireland, Scotland, Wales and Denmark and some other provinces with a view to reforming those houses in head and members. Three years later we find Fergal O'Heffernan associated with Patrick O'Donoghue, abbot of Inishlounaght, in a visitation of the abbey of Dunbrody, acting as it would seem by virtue of the commission received from the abbot of Morimond in his capacity of reformator general. This is the last notice we have of Abbot Fergal O'Heffernan; it occurs in a papal document dealing with the election of a new abbot in Dunbrody and states that the resignation of the former abbot was made to Fergal O'Heffernan, abbot of Holy Cross and Patrick, abbot of Inishlounaght. The date of the abbot's resignation is not given, but another papal mandate making provision of Holy Cross abbey to Dermot O'Heffernan, son of the former abbot, shows that Fergal was already dead in April 1448.

Following the death of Abbot Fergal rival, claimants appeared on the scene in a struggle for the coveted abbacy and in the resulting confusion, the O'Dwyers and O'Mulryans succeeded in gaining unlawful possession of some of the monastic property. The struggle seems to have lasted for some eight or ten years and one of the two families named above may have been the one mentioned in a papal mandate as responsible for the intrusion of one of their members into the abbacy in opposition to the lawful abbot whom it was alleged, was compelled to make a 'voluntary' resignation of his office owing to the fact that he could not succeed in maintaining himself as abbot in face of the concerted opposition he encountered from his enemies. Not until all the controversies had died down and a new abbot was securely settled in the rule and administration of the monastery was it possible to take steps to restore to the abbey its plundered possessions. This was finally undertaken by Abbot Matthew O'Mulryan whose own family seems to have enjoined in the plundering of the abbey lands. The new abbot found himself compelled to appeal to the pope, whose mandate to the archbishop of Cashel, together with the archbishop's mandate, for the citation of the accused parties is preserved in the collection of Ormond Deeds in the National Library of Ireland.

From the somewhat confused account of these incidents contained in the *Calendar of Papal Letters* it would appear that Odo O'Grady, a monk of Holy Cross, was canonically elected abbot after the death of Fergal O'Heffernan. Odo obtained the rule and administration of the monastery but was not long in office before he found himself opposed by powerful interests who were endeavouring to install their own kinsman in the abbacy. Finding it impossible to continue his rule and administration, and having no hope of recovering it owing to the power of his adversaries, he is said to have resigned his office. Dermot O'Heffernan, the illegitimate son of the former abbot, thereupon sought to have provision made to him of the abbey and for this purpose had recourse to the Holy See, representing that the abbey was vacant by the resignation of Odo O'Grady, the former abbot. The charge brought at a later date by one of Dermot's rivals that he had immediately succeeded his father owing to the circumstance that Odo (as was alleged) had ruled the abbey only momentarily 'and not for a whole natural day' seems to have been unfounded. In a statement of the case set forth to Pope Nicholas v on behalf of Dermot it was stated that not only had Odo been canonically elected abbot 'followed by due confirmation ... and by possession' but that it had not been his fault that he had not continued in possession longer, perhaps even for his lifetime; that he had resigned the said rule and administration, and that it was believed that the monastery had really become void by the resignation made by him and lawfully admitted, and not by the death of the former Fergal.

Following these representations the pope issued a mandate that provision should be made to Dermot of the monastery but it does not appear that this mandate was ever made effective. At all events, notwithstanding the mandate in favour of Dermot which was issued on 27 April 1448, we find a certain Abbot William in possession in July, 1450 and we may reasonably conclude that this William is the individual who is stated in one of the documents already quoted to have been the kinsman of certain enemies of Odo O'Grady and who appears to have attained the abbatial office after the resignation of the latter, aided, as we must suppose, by powerful family interests. The references in the document to the enemies who were forcibly endeavouring to procure the election of their own kinsman make it reasonably certain that this is exactly what they succeeded in doing after their powerful opposition had brought about the resignation of Odo. Who were these 'enemies'? Evidently some powerful family in the neighbourhood of Holy Cross was involved, and of the three leading families whom we know to have been in a position to exercise such pressure in an abbatial contest, the O'Dwyers, the O'Mulryans and the De Burgos, one is inclined to suspect the O'Dwyers, in this instance. It is possible, then, that the Abbot William who held office in 1450 and who apparently obtained the abbacy for the first time in succession to Odo O'Grady and at no long interval after the death of Fergal O'Heffernan, was a kinsman and name-sake of Abbot William O'Dwyer who was later to figure as one of the 'refor-matores' of the Cistercian Order in Ireland.

We do not know how long Abbot William continued in office. He apparently retained the abbacy until his death and was succeeded by Dionysius O'Congail whose name may still be seen on the cloister arcade of Holy Cross abbey. Abbot O'Congail was succeeded in 1455 by Dermot O'Heffernan who for seven long years had been urging his claims at Rome. On 4 April 1454, Pope Nicholas V granted a mandate to certain judges on the petition of Dermot Heffernan to inquire into the facts alleged by Dermot and, if after inquiry, the facts were found to be as stated, the provision formerly made to Dermot was to hold good. It appears from the tenor of the papal mandate that when Dermot made his petition to Pope Nicholas in 1454 he had already been blessed abbot. Pope Nicholas died before his grant could be drawn up, but his successor, Pope Callistus III decreed that the said grant should hold good from the said date whether the abbey was void by the resignation of Odo O'Grady or by the successive deaths of William or Denis O'Connell, or in any other way.

The case of Dermot O'Heffernan thus seemed to have been finally and (as far as he was concerned) satisfactorily settled in April 1455. *Ach ni mar a siltear bítear.* Another Cistercian, this time a monk of Owney, was already contemplating the possibility of becoming himself abbot of Holy Cross and had recourse in the usual way to the Roman Curia, making a number of grave accusations against Abbot Dermot. And so we find a new mandate from Pope Callistus III concerning the case of Dermot O'Heffernan. From this mandate, dated 23 October 1455 it appears that Pope Nicholas V had already been informed before his death that Abbot Dermot had commit-ted homicide and dilapidated and alienated many of the monastic goods. He had been excommunicated and publicly declared so by the collector of dues of the papal camera in those parts for non-payment of fruits due from him. He was also charged with taking part in divine offices while under excommunication 'in contempt of the keys', thereby incurring irregularity. These charges and others were brought against Dermot by Matthew O'Mulryan, a monk of Owney, who also resurrected the old charge that Dermot succeeded his own father immediately in the abbacy since Odo O'Grady did not hold possession of the rule and administration for a whole natural day. The pope had ordered a judge to summon Dermot before him and to inquire into the truth of the allegations. If the charges were found to be true, Matthew was to be appointed abbot in his stead. The pope, however, had died before the letters could be drawn up.

Pope Callistus III now commanded the archbishop of Cashel to take action in the matter and to deprive Dermot of the abbacy if he should be found guilty. The outcome of the affair seems to have been the deprivation of Dermot. At least Dermot disappears from the narrative at this point and Matthew O'Mulryan appears as abbot of Holy Cross.

ABBOT O'MULRYAN – THE REFORMATOR

We have seen how the powerful families of O'Dwyer and O'Mulryan had availed of the opportunity afforded by the rivalry of various aspirants to the abbacy to enter into and seize part of the monastic lands. Although the new abbot's own kinsmen had shared in the spoliation, the abbot determined to recover for the convent what had been unjustly seized upon by Conor O'Dwyer, 'Captain of his nation', and his kinsmen and sons of Tadgh and Philip O'Dwyer, as well as by Tadgh mac Philip O'Mulryan and his followers. Armed with a papal mandate to the archbishop of Cashel he caused the offenders to be summoned before the archbishop, there to answer the charges brought against them by the abbot regarding the wrongful occupation of the abbacy lands and property. Not only laymen but even clerics were involved in these charges; for the *Custos* of Toomevara, a certain Brother Patrick O'Maythyr, was accused of having unlawfully alienated and seized the rents, fruits and crops of the church of Borrisnafarney which, as we have already seen, belonged to the monastery of Holy Cross. These proceedings took place in the year 1466 and ten years later the same abbot is found in the ecclesiastical court of Cashel in an action against the rector and vicar of Ballysheehan concerning the tithes of Ballycally (Ballykelly). Here again the abbot was successful, judgement being recorded in his favour by Thady O'Lauthnan (O'Louhnan), official of Cashel.

In the year 1468 the mantle of 'reformator' of the whole Cistercian order in Munster fell upon Abbot Matthew O'Mulryan. In that year he, with his associate, Roger Boley, a monk of Mellifont, who was later to become one of the most energetic abbots of that house, was commissioned by the general chapter to act as reformator, not only of the Cistercians in Munster but of those of Leinster as well. The two reformators were endowed with the most ample powers, including that of appointing and deposing abbots and made something like a general visitation of the provinces of Munster and Leinster during the course of which they entered with great zeal on the task of correcting and reforming the various houses of the Order in those parts.

While engaged on this visitation Abbot Matthew[1] held a public assembly, presumably of Cistercian abbots, in the parish of St Mary, in the city of

1 IMED, A 35(48), pp 41-2.

Kilkenny where the abbot of Tintern, one John Yoyng, made humble submission to the two visitators, begging and receiving at their hands absolution from the censures he had incurred for various faults and crimes. The
list of crime contained in this document is truly horrific including as it
does heresy, simony, dilapidation, alienation and squandering of the goods
of his monastery, theft, sacrilege, homicide, perjury, sorcery, conspiracy,
adultery, incest, fornication, crimes of violence against the person, forgery
of apostolic letters and other unspecified crimes and excesses. The prestige and standing of Holy Cross abbey at this period may be judged from
the fact that its abbot was accounted worthy of receiving such a special
commission from the general chapter and that not only he but his predecessor and his successor, exercised the important powers and occupied the
onerous position of reformator of the Irish Cistercians. But the fact that
the abbey's prestige stood high should not blind us to the fact that with the
death of Abbot Fergal O'Heffernan a marked deterioration set in and
Abbot Fergal's successors must be judged, not by the dignity of the office
they held nor yet by the importance of the functions they exercised on
behalf of the general chapter, but by their own actions and the quality of
their monastic life.

Abbot Matthew seems in the early part of his abbatial career to have
been a man of great determination, able and willing to restore his
monastery both in temporalities and in spiritualities. Whether he had the
same zeal for the spiritual life as he had for the 'spiritualities' of the
monastery is however, open to question. In his old age, we are told, he suffered from the gout and was unable to govern his abbey. Yet he would not
resign but clung obstinately to the dignity and office of abbot. Such is the
account given by the Cistercian writer Malachy Hartry who lived in the seventeenth century and was himself a member of the Holy Cross community.
According to Fr Malachy the community at last grew tired of Abbot
Matthew and elected William O'Dwyer to the abbacy in his stead; but the
new abbot was obliged to go to Rome three times before he at length
obtained possession of the abbacy by apostolic authority. Though the same
writer assures us that the new abbot ruled the abbey in a praiseworth and
religious manner there are grave reasons for doubting that the reason
Abbot Matthew O'Mulryan had to resign his abbacy in favour of William
O'Dwyer was because he suffered from gout which rendered him unable
to govern his abbey.

We have, indeed, a contemporary account of the circumstances in
which William O'Dwyer succeeded Matthew O'Mulryan as abbot of Holy
Cross and this account comes from no less a person than William O'Dwyer
himself. William was interested in bringing about the removal of Matthew
from office and for that reason the accusations brought against the latter
in the documents we are now about to summarise must be treated with

some reserve. Before dealing with the evidence contained in the *Calendar of Papal Letters*, let us see in the first place who this William O'Dwyer was and how he comes into the picture.

William O'Dwyer was the illegitimate son of a preceptor of the house of Clonoulty of the Hospital of St John of Jerusalem. Having received the usual dispensation, to be promoted to holy orders and to receive a benefice even with cure of souls he, without seeking or obtaining any other dispensation had provision made to him, by the ordinary, of the precentorship of Cashel, described as a non-major dignity, which happened to become vacant about that time. Under pretext of this provision he took possession of the precentorship and held it for some time, enjoying its emoluments. He had higher ambitions than a mere precentorship, however, and casting around for some likely dignity his eyes rested on the rich abbey of Holy Cross in the diocese of Cashel. There was a difficulty here, it is true. There was an abbot already ruling that house and before William could achieve his ambitions, that abbot would have to be removed. This difficulty was not, however, insurmountable. The removal of the incumbent could be accomplished without too much difficulty according to the method prevailing at the time, namely, the denunciation by William of the abbot, whose dignity and office he coveted, and the preferment of a number of charges against him. The usual procedure in a case of this kind to have a court of judges delegate set up to hear the cause in Ireland, and it was generally provided in the papal mandate setting up such a court that if the charges against the defendant should prove to be true he should be removed from office and his accuser appointed in his place. This practice was unfortunately but too common during the fifteenth century and led to great scandals in monastic houses. It was one of the abuses that Primate Octavian of Armagh had strenuously and successfully fought in his own diocese for thirty-four years.

William O'Dwyer, now ensconced as precentor of Cashel, had recourse to the Roman curia with the object of having Abbot Matthew removed from office. To achieve his purpose he made a series of accusations of the gravest character against Matthew whom he charged with having notoriously and continually violated his obligation of clerical celibacy, being, as was alleged, an open fornicator and adulterer who had offspring by several women, had engaged in trade and caused wine to be sold in taverns with which he was very often inebriated. He was also accused of having by his negligence permitted a certain fee belonging to the abbey to remain in the hands of laymen. What are we to think of these charges? Were they true or were they simply invented for the purpose of discrediting the abbot and supplying a motive for his deposition? That William O'Dwyer hoped to be made abbot in place of Matthew is, I think, scarcely to be doubted. In his petition, it is true, he had expressed the desire to serve God with the convent of Holy Cross under the regular habit, but he was quite well aware that if the abbot was deposed he himself, according to established custom, would be the most likely candidate for the office. That in order to secure this end he was prepared to have recourse to the most unscrupulous tactics will not surprise anyone who has any acquaintance with the state of affairs in fifteenth century Ireland, as revealed in the *Calendar of Papal Letters*. It is probable that the charges made by William were a mixture of truth and falsehood. One thing is certain, they served their purpose, and the outcome of the entire affair was the deprivation of Matthew and the appointment of William to the abbey of Holy Cross.

Two mandates in connection with this case are summarised in the *Calendar of Papal Letters*. The earlier of the two is dated 7 January 1489-90, while the second bears the date of 8 July 1492. From the earlier of the two mandates we learn that the pope, on receiving William's complaint, had caused inquiry to be made into his charge against Matthew. Thomas Michil, a canon of Cashel, was ordered by the pope to receive William, who had been rehabilitated, as a monk of Holy Cross abbey and was authorised to give him the regular habit and receive his profession. If William would accuse the said Matthew before him he was to summon the latter and, if he found the charges brought by William to be true, was to deprive and remove Matthew and in that event to make provision to William, if found fit, of the abbey of Holy Cross, and appoint him abbot thereof. The pope, at the same time, dispensed William to be so appointed and to rule the monastery for three months only, even without having made his profession. These papal injunctions completely ignored the fundamental laws and usages of the Cistercian Order, laws and usages which had been approved and confirmed by the Holy See itself, for under the Cistercian Constitution no abbot could be appointed to rule a house of the order unless he were himself a monk of the order having made his profession in due course after a regular novitiate, and he should be elected by the community of the house of which he was to be abbot. Neither was it lawful for any person not a Cistercian to receive a novice to the Cistercian habit, still less to admit him to profession in the Order. Unfortunately, the fifteenth century papacy, despite the vigorous protests of the general chapter and the superiors of the Order, had reserved practically all abbatial appointments to itself, and the constitutions of the Order were regularly and systematically ignored in making thses appointments and men were appointed only too often whose first care was to enrich themselves at the expense of the community they were supposed to govern.

The attempts by William O'Dwyer to gain possession of Holy Cross abbey were not immediately successful. The struggle continued from 1489 or perhaps earlier, until 1492, when it was at last crowned with success.

Thomas Michil, indeed received William O'Dwyer as a monk of Holy Cross according to the terms of the mandate; but, having made inquiry into the charges brought by William against Matthew, he promulgated what William considered an unjust judgement by deciding in favour of Matthew. The consequence of all this was that William now found himself a Cistercian, bound by the rule and obligations of a monk, but as far removed from the office and dignity of abbot as ever he had been in the past – not exactly what he bargained for. He now appealed to Rome against what he termed an unjust sentence and in the course of this appeal he restated his case and brought forward the selfsame charges, but added that although Matthew's fornication and adultery were so notorious as to be known to all, he was unable to produce witnesses to prove the alleged acts. Nevertheless he pointed out that in as much as Abbot Matthew had sons and daughters living, who had been christened and brought up as his sons and daughters and who were then reputed and held to be his children, the facts of his fornication and adultery could not by any means be concealed. In consequence of this appeal another papal mandate was issued addressed to the archbishop of Cashel, the chancellor of Killaloe and Denis O'Hogan, a canon of Cashel. These were commanded to summon Abbot Matthew and the others concerned and, having heard both sides, were to decide what was just Moreover they were to execute the former letters addressed to Thomas Michil as if they had been directed to themselves.

Following on this mandate a new trial was held. Matthew O'Mulryan was summoned before Denis O'Hogan, canon of Cashel, who having heard both sides, promulgated a definitive sentence by which he decreed that the judgement previously pronounced by Thomas Michil absolving Matthew O'Mulryan from blame was wrong. In consequence of this definitive sentence, Abbot Matthew O'Mulryan was deprived of his office and provision was made of the monastery to William O'Dwyer. However, even then there seems to have been snags. Though William was now the canonical abbot of Holy Cross, he had not yet obtained possession of the rule and administration. According to his own statement, made later in the course of a further appeal, he had almost obtained possession, but though he did not say so in so many words, it appears from his account that Matthew considered possession to be nine points of the law and was resolved not to be dispossessed. For some time there must have been a deadlock. This was finally resolved by what William terms 'a friendly agreement' made between Matthew and himself by virtue of which Matthew agreed to leave William in peaceful possession 'or almost', of the rule and administration of the monastery on condition that William should pay him a yearly pension from the fruits of the house. This 'friendly agreement' was nothing less than simony, and both parties to the simoniacal compact incurred ipso facto the papal sentence of excommunication promulgated against simoniacs.

Meanwhile Matthew himself had appealed against the decision in favour of William. In consequence of this new appeal the pope issued letters joining the abbot of the monastery of SS. Cuan and Brogan in Mothel, in the diocese of Lismore, to the archbishop of Cashel, the chancellor of Killaloe and Denis O'Hogan for the hearing of the cause. On receipt of these letters Matthew caused William to be summoned for judgement before the archdeacon of Cashel commissioned to act in his stead by the abbot of Mothel, and since William did not appear (being summoned as he himself complained to a place to which he dared not go in safety) the archdeacon promulgated a definitive sentence in favour of Matthew. William, declaring this sentence to be unjust, again appealed to the apostolic See. In the meantime, he entered into yet another 'arrangement' with Matthew concerning the pension he was prepared to pay the abbot, if the latter would leave him (William) in peaceful possession of the abbey of Holy Cross. Following on this second simoniacal bargain William again had recourse to the Holy See, confessing this time that he had entered into two such agreements with Matthew by reason of which both of them had incurred the guilt of simony and consequently the penalties and censures attached to that crime, and alleging that since this was the case neither William himself nor Matthew had any right in or to the rule and administration of the monastery.

Following on William's appointment the pope issued a new mandate addressed this time to the bishop and chancellor of Lismore and to Robert Hedron, a canon of the same diocese. In this mandate, having related all the foregoing circumstances, he ordered the three above named to absolve William from the sin of simony and the censures he had incurred thereby, enjoining on him at the same time a salutary penance, William was to be fully rehabilitated, while Matthew and the others concerned were to be summoned and the whole case again investigated; the decision of the judges was to be without appeal and enforced by ecclesiastical censure. Moreover if it were found that neither William nor Matthew had any right to rule and administer the monastery by reason of the simony and censures therby incurred and if they found that William was a fit and suitable person, they were to make provision to him of the abbey of Holy Cross, whose yearly value, we learn from this mandate, did not exceed 100 marks. Notwithstanding the defect of William's birth the pope granted him special dispensation and indult to be blessed by a Catholic bishop in communion with the Holy See. This was the end for Matthew. He was replaced by William in the government of the abbey; and William having attained the object of his ambitions, continued to rule the abbey of Holy Cross until his resignation, following another simonical agreement with the incoming incumbent in 1534.

On 28 February 1506, a papal mandate[2] ordered the dean of the church of Cashel to absolve William, abbot of Holy Cross from the sentence of excommunication. William had petitioned the pope, accusing the late Donatus, bishop of Emly, of fabricating apostolic letters in order to appoint a certain Edmund Mares, canon of Cashel, as abbot of Holy Cross. William, the incumbent abbot, had been accused of violence against both Donatus and Mares and of imprisoning Donatus. In his petition William claimed, he had made his peace with Donatus before Donatus died from natural causes and that he also made peace with Mares.

We have seen that Abbot Matthew O'Mulryan had occupied at least for a time the office of reformator of the Cistercian Order in Ireland and had carried out a visitation of Munster and Leinster in association with Roger Boley, a monk of Mellifont. Roger Boley himself became abbot of Mellifont after the death or resignation of Abbot John Waring, and although we do not know the precise date on which he succeeded to the abbacy we learn from the *Statute Rolls of Ireland* that he was already in possession of the rule and administration of the monastery in the year 1471-2, at which time he was a newcomer to the abbatial chair. At the time of his association with the abbot of Holy Cross in the visitation of Munster and Leinster, in 1468, he was still a simple monk.

As abbot of Mellifont he bent his energies to the task of reforming his monastery which seems to have been in a miserable state at the time of his accession. From various references to this abbot in the *Statute Rolls of Ireland* it is evident that he was a man of great energy and of no mean ability. He successfully reformed his abbey and restored both its fame and its fortunes; but there is no evidence that he ever held as did his successor, the office of reformator of the Irish Cistercians.

The next abbot who appears in the role of reformator, of the Irish Cistercians was Walter Champfleur, abbot of St Mary's abbey, Dublin. Walter was already abbot of St Mary's at the time Abbot Matthew O'Mulryan held the office of reformator and became himself reformator of the Irish Houses in or about the year 1487, holding the office until the year 1492 when he was succeeded for a time by the new abbot of Holy Cross, William O'Dwyer.

Considering the circumstances in which William O'Dwyer was appointed abbot of Holy Cross it is, to say the least, somewhat surprising to find him invested with the office of reformator of the Irish Cistercians almost as soon as he had become abbot, and we are not surprised to discover that this appointment was deeply resented and indeed looked upon as something calamitous by Roger Boley's successor in the abbacy of Mellifont, Abbot John Troy. This able man who became abbot of Mellifont

2 CPR, xvii, 536, p. 390.

in 1486 was a lifelong worker in the cause of reform and almost from the first an uncompromising opponent of Abbot William O'Dwyer whom he openly denounced to the abbot of Citeaux as a subverter and destroyer of the order, a pretended reformator, more anxious to enrich himself than to reform the houses he visited. Abbot Walter of Dublin appears to have held the office of reformator from 1487 to 1492 approximately. From a letter preserved in Octavian's Register[3] in Armagh it is clear that the abbot of Holy Cross had already taken Abbot Walter's place as reformator of the order in Ireland by the year 1493. The appointment of William O'Dwyer to this office is all the more surprising when we consider that both the abbot of Mellifont and the abbot of Dublin were at that time protesting in the strongest manner to the abbot of Citeaux against the system of provisions. The O'Dwyer appointment exemplifies the evils of this system. Here was a man foisted into the abbey of Holy Cross and appointed to the abbatial office over the head of the convent which according to the rules and usages of the order should have had a voice in the election of its own abbot. At the time of his provision he was not even a Cistercian and the pope, while arranging that he should receive the Cistercian habit with a view to his assuming the abbacy, did not actually require him to make his profession before he became abbot but allowed him to rule the monastery for some three months before he made his profession. It is obvious therefore that William O'Dwyer was an abbot before he was canonically a monk. Moreover he did not receive the habit of the order from an abbot of the order as was required by Cistercian usage but from a secular priest who had no authority to perform such a function. To promote a man from a non-major dignity in the diocese of Cashel to the care of one of the most important houses in Ireland was bad enough in the eyes of his contemporary abbots. To make him abbot even before his monastic profession was worse but the crowning grievance was that a man appointed in such a manner should almost immediately be thrust into the responsible office of reformator of the Irish Cistercians.

The new reformator soon came into conflict with Abbot Troy of Mellifont.[4] Troy had punished a monk named Thomas Hervey for some misdemeanour by depriving him of whatever office he held in the community. Hervey then absconded from the cloister without the permission of his abbot, thus technically making him an apostate from the religious state and incurring in consequence certain ecclesiastical censures. This monk now brought a number of charges against Abbot Troy and appealed to the abbot of Holy Cross in his capacity as reformator, adducing the authority of the community of Mellifont, or certain members thereof, for

3 Fr Colmcille OCSO, 'The Irish Documents in Octavian's Register, Armagh', *Seanchas Ardmhacha* (1957), ii, 269-94.   4 Octavian's Register, 134.

statements contained in his accusation. The abbot of Holy Cross accepted the charges made against Abbot Troy without reservation and not only dispensed Hervey from the penalties incurred by him but even went so far as to command Troy to restore Hervey to his former status and offices in the community. He further exasperated the abbot of Mellifont by appointing the recalcitrant monk to the office and dignity of abbot of Comber.

When the monks of Mellifont learned of the charges brought by Thomas Hervey against their abbot, they drew up a formal statement exonerating Troy and declaring that the letters written by Hervey adducing their authority for the charges brought against his abbot were false. Following on this statement came the formal appeal of the abbot himself to the Holy See. In the course of this appeal, the abbot of Mellifont complained of the conduct of the abbot of Holy Cross in compelling the abbot of Mellifont to restore Thomas Hervey to his former status and offices in the monastery, without undergoing any correction or punishment for his faults, and actually appointing him abbot of Comber. Foreseeing the grave consequences that could arise in the order as a result of such conduct and fearing that this might lead in future to even greater evils, by giving cause to professed monks of the order to wander outside the cloister as apostates (Hervey, it will be recalled had left the cloister without the permission of his abbot), the abbot had appealed to the Holy See, subjecting himself and his monastery to its protection. John Troy's appeal was successful; but he did not forget the attitude taken by the abbot of Holy Cross in this matter, and his later correspondence with the abbots of Citeaux and Clairvaux shows that he had indeeed a very poor opinion of William O'Dwyer as a reformator of the order in Ireland. He declared that he was beginning to despair of ever obtaining a remedy for the same, observing as he did the daily subversion of the whole order by apostolic provisions, and seeing that enemies of the order were appointed to responsible offices even by the abbot of Citeaux. He deprecated that appointment of men of no learning who were raised aloft and made reformators or, to speak more truly, destroyers of the order, such as William O'Dwyer and others of his kind. From this and other letters it is clear that Abbot Troy was at the time urging the appointment of a suitable reformator for the Irish Cistercian houses. He did not mind who might be appointed provided that he should be good and useful for the reformation of the order. He complained vehemently however that such a person had not yet been appointed. Taken in conjunction with his references to the abbot of Holy Cross in his letter to the abbot of Citeaux[5] already quoted, this can only mean that William O'Dwyer was still acting as reformator of the Irish Cistercians when these letters were written and that John Troy was still working for his removal from that office.

5 Fonds de Citeaux Archives de la Cote d'Or, II H 20.

The numerous complaints made by the abbot of Mellifont against the abbot of Holy Cross at length bore fruit and an important document preserved in Octavian's Registrar shows that by the summer of 1496 William O'Dwyer had been replaced by Abbot Walter Champfleur of Dublin and Abbot John Troy of Mellifont, who now appear in the role of joint reformators. We may assume, in the absence of evidence to the contrary, that the removal of Abbot O'Dwyer took place during or following the general chapter of 1495. One of the first acts of the new reformators was to summon the abbots of Ireland to a council at Skreen in Co. Meath. Among the twenty-one monasteries represented at this council was the abbey of Holy Cross. The abbots of Dublin and Mellifont continued to be associated in the work of reform until January 1497-8, when the abbot of Dublin died leaving John Troy the sole reformator of the Order in Ireland. In a long and important report submitted by Troy to the abbot of Citeaux following the death of Abbot Walter, he details the various measures taken for the visitation and reformation of the Irish houses and speaks his mind quite frankly regarding the appointment of seculars to the rule and administration of Cistercian abbeys. He is not afraid to tax the abbot of Citeaux himself with a cerain responsibility in this matter, complaining that he has appointed men who from being seculars are promptly made into Cistercians and have scarcely received the habit of the order when they are invested with rank and dignity of abbots and even of reformators. He passes the most severe judgement on such men who, without any knowledge of the religious life or instruction in the regular observances of the order, are appointed not merely abbots but visitators and reformators of monasteries and who, when placed over monasteries and monks, have no care for the divine worship or for regular observances but, blinded by avarice and worldly pleasures, and given up to the vain display of superiority, drag down their subjects with themselves and plunge them into the same pit. There is little reason to doubt that in penning these words Abbot John Troy had in mind men of the type of William O'Dwyer, abbot of Holy Cross.

The difficulties and obstacles which beset the path of a reformator in those days, and the thankless nature of the task imposed on him, moved Abbot Troy to petition the abbot of Citeaux to relieve him of that office. His petition was not acceded to; instead he was given two companions to aid him in the work and these were to be associated with him as reformators. The two abbots thus designated were John Oram who had succeeded Abbot Walter in St Mary's abbey, Dublin and William O'Dwyer, abbot of Holy Cross. One can well imagine the feelings with which John Troy heard of the appointment of the abbot of Holy Cross as joint reformator with himself and the abbot of Dublin. We do not however, have to rely merely on our imagination. Writing once more to the abbot of Citeaux, John Troy

referred to the sad state of the Irish Cistercians but expressed his opinion
that a remedy might yet be found. He implored the abbot to select some
prudent and discreet religious, a well instructed man, for the purpose of
reforming the order. He was prepared to take on the task himself provided
he received the power to select and associate with himself one other abbot.
However, he made it clear in the letter that he did not wish to be associated any longer with either the abbot of Dublin or the abbot of Holy
Cross. The former he described as being languid and slow to labour, the
latter as more intent on enriching himself than on reforming the order,
oppressing rather than relieving the monasteries he visited. It does not
seem that the abbot of Holy Cross was again appointed reformator. This
was the last letter written by Abbot Troy which has survived to our own day.
He died some time afterwards and was succeeded both as abbot of
Mellifont and reformator of the Irish Cistercians by the same Thomas
Hervey who had formerly been such a thorn in his side.

William O'Dwyer continued to rule the abbey of Holy Cross for many
years after the death of Abbot John Troy and even for some years after that
of Thomas Hervey. He remained in office, in fact, almost till the eve of the
suppression of the Irish monasteries under Henry VIII. Among the references to our abbot in various documents of the period 1501-34, one of the
most curious as well as one of the most interesting is that found in the
British Museum MS. Add. 40674, relating to the battle of Knocktoe which
was fought on 19 August 1504, and has been described as 'the most spectacular battle that had been fought in Ireland since Strongbow'. From the
account of this battle in the manuscript mentioned above we learn that
while masses were being sung in St Patrick's cathedral, Dublin, for the success of the earl of Kildare and his army, the monks of Holy Cross were
singing masses for the success of his opponent, the earl of Clanrickard, the
particular mass selected by both parties being that of the Five Wounds. We
learn futhermore that the stipend for the singing of this mass amounted
to five shillings which, allowing for the depreciation of money since the
sixteenth century would be the equivalent of about £16 sterling today.
From the narrative in the British Museum manuscript it would appear that
it was not just one mass which was to be said but five masses successively.
Ellen Burke, daughter of the lord of MacWilliam and wife of John Butler
of Thurles besought the abbot of Holy Cross then called Duyr (goes the
story) that one of the monks selected by him should sing the mass of the
Five Wounds successively for her father's prosperity in the battle. The
monk, it is said, sang the first mass and had got as far as the *Agnus Dei* in
the second mass when an angel appeared to him and warned him to proceed no further in his petition for it was granted to another. On this the
monk gave her back the five shillings in the presence of the abbot and
others of his brethern.

Another document of no small interest, this time an official Cistercian document, is preserved among the Ormond Deeds and has come down to us from the days when William O'Dwyer ruled the abbey of Holy Cross. This document which is dated 9 August 1499, is a letter from William, abbot of Maigue, to William, abbot of Holy Cross, and relates to a third William, a monk of Maigue named Brother William O'Mananan, who desired to transfer to Holy Cross abbey and to settle permanently there as a professed monk of that house. From the terms of the letter it is evident that it was written in reply to a letter from the abbot of Holy Cross in which the latter had expressed himself willing to receive Brother William to profession if the said brother obtained letters of recommendation from his own abbot. The abbot of Maigue, in reply, informs the abbot of Holy Cross that, moved by the desire of saving his soul, Brother William has repeatedly sought permission to transfer to the abbey of Holy Cross; in view of which fact, and considering that it is incumbent on the abbot to provide for the salvation of the souls of his subjects, and considering moreover that in every place we serve one Lord and fight in the service of one king, Christ, he, the abbot of Maigue, with the consent of his convent has agreed that the said Brother William should be absolved from his obedience in that monastery and should be allowed to make his profession in the hands of the abbot of Holy Cross. He commends the said Brother William as one who lived a praiseworthy life while a monk of Maigue, and asks the abbot of Holy Cross that, when the said monk shall have made profession in that abbey, his former abbot may be informed of the fact by letters patent of the abbot of Holy Cross. The desire of the monk of Maigue to settle in Holy Cross for the good of his soul implies that Holy Cross was still a house which enjoyed a good reputation in the order at the time this letter was written. At the very least it shows that one monk thought he had a better hope of saving his soul there than in his own house. It shows also that at a time when religious discipline was dangerously lax and many of the monasteries were in a lamentable state, ruled, as they too often were, by abbots who led notoriously irregular lives, there were still holy devout men to be found in some of the Irish Cistercian houses.

ABBOT PHILIP PURCELL

We have a few notices of Abbot William O'Dwyer between 1501 and 1534 but none of any importance until we come to the latter year when he ended his career as abbot of Holy Cross in circumstances not unlike those in which he commenced it. He had been forty-two years in office when at last he decided to retire, but before retiring he drove what may be called a hard bargain with the man who was to succeed him, Philip Purcell, a cleric of the diocese of Cashel, who does not appear to have been a Cistercian at all before he was provided in 1534. It is doubtful if he was even a priest at the time he became abbot. This, of course was nothing new. In a report made by the abbot of Mellifont (John Troy) to the abbot of Citeaux, written not earlier than February 1498, the writer declared that many of the provisors were not even ordained.

If the measure of his success as a reformator is to be gauged from the state of his abbey as revealed by the visitation of 1536 we must conclude that he was a very indifferent reformator indeed, who, while devoting himself to the extremely difficult task of visiting, correcting and reforming all of the monasteries of the order in Ireland, unaccountably neglected to order the affairs of his own house. The contract entered into between himself and his successor needs to be considered here. Until the material contained in the papal registers for this period has been published, or at least calendared, we cannot hope to investigate all the circumstances concerning the resignation of Abbot William O'Dwyer and his replacement by Philip Purcell. Although the documentery evidence stresses that these conditions were made after William's resignation this would seem to be a subterfuge intended, perhaps, to evade the charge of simony. Nowhere in the document it is stated or implied that William was to be succeeded in the abbacy by Philip Purcell. The fact that Purcell did succeed William as abbot of Holy Cross and that his position as abbot was evidently recognised and accepted by the Cistercian order, strongly suggests that this document was drawn up following a private agreement based on the conditions laid down in the public document. Despite the fact that these conditions are said in that document to have been made after the abbot's resignation, it is to be noted that the compact is essentially one between an abbot *de regimine* and a diocesan cleric. The opening formula shows that this is the case, 'Brother William, by the patience of God, abbot of the monastery of the Holy Cross of Woghterlawe of the Cistercian Order ...' There is nothing in this phrase to indicate that William O'Dwyer, at the time this indenture was made, was the ex-abbot of Holy Cross. The plain meaning of the words is that at the time of writing he was actually the abbot holding the rule and administration, and this is confirmed by the fact that the seal affixed by him to that part of the indenture remaining in the possession of Philip Purcell was not his own private seal but the common seal of Holy Cross abbey. Only in his capacity of abbot could William have lawfully affixed that seal to the deed. It appears therefore that although this deed may have been drawn up after the abbot submitted his resignation into the hands of his superiors, that resignation had not yet been accepted at the time the agreement was signed. I would go so far as to suggest that the deed was possible drawn up before the abbot's resignation but not signed until after the resignation had been submitted to the competent authorities. Until the resignation had actually been accepted the abbot would still remain in office and could legitimately use the official seal of Holy Cross abbey.

It has been suggested that the document we are now considering was devised by the foresight of the monks themselves who, in order to avoid the total suppression of the monastery, mapped out a plan of campaign involving the alteration of the status of Holy Cross and the secularisation of the monastic chapter. In this view the monks aimed, at turning the monastery into a provostry and Philip Purcell into a provost This is a view I find hard to accept.

The bargain entered into between Abbot William O'Dwyer and Philip Purcell[6] was but one instance of numerous sordid bargains of the same type, details of which may be found on page after page of the *Calendar of Papal Letters*. Even had he been a layman, he could under the procedure in vogue at the time, have had provision made to him of the abbot. He was, in fact, in essentially the same position as Abbot O'Dwyer had been forty-two years previously, when he sought to replace Matthew O'Mulryan as Abbot William, as we have seen had to receive the Cistercian habit and ultimately had to make his profession in the Cistercian order as a condition of becoming abbot of Holy Cross, and it is most probable that Philip Purcell had to do likewise. That Philip was accepted as a regular abbot by the higher superiors of the order is clear from the visitation card drawn up by the abbot of Newry in 1536. Abbot Philip Purcell is not mentioned by name in this document, but it is quite certain from other sources that the abbot who ruled Holy Cross at this time was Philip Purcell. That he was a true abbot *de regimine* and not a mere commendatory abbot is clear from the visitation card itself which contains no less than seven references to the responsibility of the abbot for enforcing the regulations laid down by the visitator. The prior of the monastery shared this responsibility with the abbot, though in a subordinate capacity. The abbot in conjunction with the sacristan was to see that the abbey church was kept clean and in a decent condition; with the cellarer he was to take care to provide the community with all that was necessary and so avoid all occasion of murmuring. The abbot and convent were strictly and firmly commanded to lead chaste and regular lives; monks who had offended against poverty by keeping or storing money were to hand that money to the abbot to be used for the monastery. No monk was to absent himself from the house without seeking and obtaining special permission from the abbot, or should the abbot be absent, from the prior. We must conclude from all this that Philip Purcell was the lawful abbot of Holy Cross, recognised as such by the higher superiors of the order and so could not have been a married man

6 IMED, no. 97 (A55), pp 73-4.

with (or without) children unless, of course, he had separated from his wife and children to enter the monastic state. Finally, on the very eve of the general dissolution of the Irish monasteries, an inspeximus of the various charters granted to Holy Cross abbey was made by Piers Butler, earl of Ormond and Ossory, in which the earl expressly states that the inspeximus was made at the special request of Philip Purcell, now abbot of the said church of the Blessed Mary of Holy Cross. Thus we have unequivocal evidence from different sources to show that from 1534 to 1539 Philip Purcell was recognised both within and without the order as the true and undoubted abbot of Holy Cross.

The terms of the compact entered into between this man and William O'Dwyer may now be summarised: It was agreed that William should have a third part of all the obligations of the Holy Cross during his lifetime as well as a third part of all the crops of the monastery sown that year, and one half of all the sheep, pigs and grain then in the house. He was to obtain also a third part of all the horses and oxen or his choice of three ploughs (*carucae*); and though it was provided that all the utensils of the former abbot should remain the property of the house, he was to have the use of them when necessary as long as he lived. Moreover, he was to have all the utensils of his own chamber during his lifetime except 'the better basin', and he was to enjoy all the 'spiritualities' of the parish of Ballycahill for the rest of his life. He was, besides, to have a ploughland of free land in the monastery and the liberty of twenty-four cows with his sheep for himself, and six free cows for the providers of his caruca, and one baker to be chosen by himself. He had to bind himself, however, not to dilapidate or alienate any of the aforesaid goods which were to remain the property of the monastery and were to revert to the monastery after the death of Brother William. He was also to have his choice of all the rooms of the monastery for himself, the abbot's room alone excepted, and he was to have the dwelling place of Philip Reagh for himself and his serving man, and another dwelling place for his animals. In conclusion it was agreed by both parties to the indenture that the earl and countess of Ossory with their son James, and O'Dwyer, Captain of his nation, and the sons of the aforesaid abbot should be sureties.

Philip Purcell who succeeded William O'Dwyer as abbot was a scion of the Tipperary branch of the Purcell family and a cousin of the baron of Loghmoe, the head of that branch. He was related also to the earl of Ormond. He had been little more than two years in office when, in October 1536, the visitation of the monastery, was carried out by John, abbot of Newry, delegated for the purpose by Richard, abbot of Mellifont and father abbot of Holy Cross. The visitation card left by the visitor in accordance with Cistercian custom is now housed in the National Library of Ireland, and is the only document of its kind that has come down to us from the medieval period.[7] It is evident that many of the abuses noted by the abbot of Mellifont at the close of the fifteenth century were still prevalent though not, perhaps to the same extent. We find in the card evidence of the neglect of the divine service, the relinquishing of the religious habit, the wholesale violation of poverty, neglect of the psalmody, carelessness concerning the observance of enclosure and other practices opposed to the purity of the rule and inimical to regular observance. The visitator strictly enjoined on each priest of the monastery the celebration of mass at least four times a week unless he was legitimately impeded; and no priest was to presume to celebrate until he had first made a devout confession and received absolution. Those who offended in this matter twice to be punished by fasting twice a week on bread and water and undergoing the penalties prescribed by St Benedict for what he terms a 'light fault'. The abbot and prior were commanded to see that the three massess prescribed by Cistercian usage, namely, the mass of the day (the conventual mass), the mass of the Blessed Virgin and the mass for the dead were said daily, and that on all Sundays and the feasts of two masses the matutinal mass was not omitted.

The cantor was commanded to mark on a tablet each week the name of the priest who was to celebrate each of the said masses. In future the religious were to rise for the office of Vigils at the proper hour each day (the actual hour of rising is not specified in the card) and this was to be carried out by all without distinction, those only being excepted who were prevented by infirmity or burdened by heavy labour the day before. If a religious failed to conform to these prescriptions he was to receive the discipline in chapter that very day and was in addition to be deprived of his pittance of food for that day.

The abbot and prior were strictly commanded to see that the divine service in choir before the high altar was to be performed with greater service and this applied both to the psalmody and the other parts of the office. It was to be sung more slowly and distinctly. No religious was to enter the choir for divine service without his cowl; and the cellarer was ordered to supply candles or caused them to be supplied every day for vigils according as there was need. The abbot and sacristan were to see that the church was kept in a clean and decent condition, and this injunction applied particularly to the high altar with its ornaments and all its appurtenances. The Body of Christ was to be kept with the greatest security and reverence in a precious pyx on a corporal, and one lamp or candle was to be left burning continually before the most Holy Sacrament or the Body and Blood of Our Lord Jesus Christ, at least during divine service. The abbot and cellarer were to provide all that was necessary for the commu-

7 IMED, no. 103 (A60), pp 81-4.

nity according to the resources of the house so that each brother might receive what was needful and proper and no occasion might be given for murmuring.

It would appear from another regulation that acts of proprietorship involving violations of the vow of poverty were not infrequent, some of them being of a grave nature. The monks were reminded that poverty, as well as chastity, were so closely connected with the monastic rule that even the Sovereign Pontiff might not dispense therein, and the Benedictine constitutions are quoted on this point regarding the use of *peculium*. Mention is made of the possession of money by monks who buy animals and other goods with that money, sometimes in their own name, sometimes in the name of another, giving such animals to be reared by others, the increase or profit to be returned to themselves or to another (in whose name they trade) and thus, coveting filthy lucre, they hide the said *peculium* to the great danger of their own souls. *Peculium* of this kind was to be restored to the abbot to be applied by him to the uses of the community and for the utility of the monastery; and those guilty of holding such *peculium* or who did not return the money they had amassed were to be excommunicated.

The frequent references in the papal letters to the children of professed monks priests and abbots of the order and the overwhelming evidence from various sources that the obligations of celibacy were lightly regarded by clergymen of all degrees, secular as well as regular, force us to conclude that monastic enclosures must have been widely disregarded. In some cases the monastic buildings themselves were in such a dilapidated condition that the monks were compelled to abandon them and wander about in search of the means wherewith to live. Many of the monks, we are told in an official report had thrown off the religious habit and were living outside their monasteries, sometimes indeed among the nobility. Women, too, some of them of doubtful character, had access to the domestic buildings of the monasteries, and though we have no direct evidence of this, it is reasonable to assume that in Ireland as in England at this period much of the domestic work was perfomed by paid servants, including maidservants. The visitator deemed it necessary to make regulations with a view to preventing the religious wandering about or remaining at night on the granges or in public places. Hence all monks were commanded to sleep in their dormitory each night and to spend the entire night there; and no one was to absent himself from the monastery under pain of suspension without the special licence of the abbot or, in his absence, that of the prior. More significant still is the injunction that women were not to be allowed to enter the dormitory under any circumstances, while special care was to be taken that no woman of doubtful character should remain or tarry within the enclosure of the monastery or in the nearby village.

The abbot visitator would appear to have had a high sense of the duty imposed on him in acting as delegate of the abbot of Mellifont in this visitation and it is evident that he was determined as far as in him lay, to put an end once and for all to the abuses which still existed in Holy Cross abbey.

14. THE DISSOLUTION

Already the king of England was preparing to dissolve the religious houses in Ireland, and in 1537 an attempt was made to carry through parliament an act for the total suppression of the Irish monasteries. Owing to the strong opposition encountered, this ambitious project had to abandoned. Nevertheless thirteen houses were actually dissolved in October of that year and the houses thus suppressed included the five Cistercian abbeys of Baltinglass, Bective, Duiske, Dunbrody and Tintern, all of which were situated either in the 'pale' proper or in the English sphere of influence and were for the most part Anglo-Irish in personnel.[1]

The general suppression of the Irish monasteries took place in 1539 when all the remaining Cistercian houses, with the exception of Holy Cross, Owney and Newry, were nominally dissolved and had their property expropriated. I say 'nominally dissolved' because in fact most of the Cisterican houses outside the Pale continued to exist until a later period. The three of the Cistercian houses which were exempted from the dissolution were allowed to continue their corporate existence as monastic communities of secular priests, the existing abbot of the Cistercian community becoming in each case the provost. In this way the members of these three communities continued as heretofore to live in a religious life of some sort in common, conforming to the king's authority in spiritual matters and thus accepting the 'reformed' and schismatic church of Henry VIII. That the monasteries of Holy Cross and Owney were allowed to continue as colleges of secular priests was due almost certainly to the powerful influence of the earl of Ormond. What special circumstances led to the granting of the same exemption to the abbey of Newry, I cannot say. One might have thought that the loyal monasteries of the Pale should have been allowed to continue in the same fashion as the three monasteries named above; and indeed the lord deputy himself with his council did make an effort to have six monasteries spared, including the Cistercian houses of Jerpoint and Dublin.

1 R. Dudley Edwards, *Church and State in Tudor Ireland* (Dublin, 1935), p. 69.

Writing to Cromwell[2] the lord deputy and council declared that it would be

> for the common weal of the land and the kings honour and profit that six of the religious houses intended to be suppressed should be allowed to continue, changing their clothing and rule into such sort and order as the king's Grace shall give them ...

The first abbey named is that of St Mary's, 'adjoining to Dublin a house of White monks'.

The letter continues:

> In the said house of Saynt Marie abbey hath been the common resort of all such of reputation as hath repaired hither out of England ... For in their houses commonly and other such like, in default of common inns which are not in this land, the king's deputy and all other His Grace's Council and officers also Irishmen and others restoring to the king's Deputy in the quarter is and hath been most commonly lodged at the cost of the said houses. Also in der both gentlemen children and other, both of mankind and women kind be brought up in virtue, learning, and in the English tongue and behaviour and to the great charges of the said houses.

The lord deputy and council had made their representations in May 1539. In July of the same year the abbot and convent of St Mary's abbey wrote to Cromwell in similar terms,[3] reminding him of their loyalty and past services rendered and professing their readiness to do the king's pleasure in all things if only he would

> vouchsauf that this pore house might remayn without dissolving; chaunging our habite and rules, as it shall please the kinge's Highnes to devise and command, where unto we shal be obedient in all things ... and we shall continue His Grace's daily pore ora-tours, and pray to God for the long prosperous welfare of your hon-ourable Lordship as our especiall preservatoure ...

Beside this letter, which was addressed to Cromwell in his public and offi-cial capacity, the abbot and convent sent another and more private letter the same day enclosing therein a present, the nature and value of which we are not told, but which was evidently intended as a consideration with a view to securing his good offices with the king on their behalf. Despite

2 *Calendar of State Papers, Henry VIII* (London, 1860), vol. iii, pt. iii, pp 130-1. 3 Ibid., p. 49.

the obsequious tone of the letter and their abject professions of loyalty and obedience and their servile readiness to change their habit and rule and conform themselves to the king's religion if he will allow them to continue in existence, their petition was rejected and their monastery dissolved. Holy Cross was spared that fate. As there has been a general tendency on the part of historians to conclude that the survival of Holy Cross abbey for so many years after the general suppression was due to a policy of connivance on the part of the earl of Ormond; that the monks were, in fact, driven out in the first instance and then enabled to return more or less secretly in a furtive manner from time to time, it is perhaps advisable to discuss the matter in some detail here and to set forth the facts as clearly as possible. At the general dissolution of the monasteriess of Ireland, Holy Cross abbey ceased to exist legally as a Cistercian house and was converted into a provostry of secular priests, Philip Purcell, the last abbot, being granted the provostship for life. After Purcell's death the monastery was to pass to James Butler, earl of Ormond, a very close friend of Henry VIII. However James Butler died before the transfer was confirmed by Queen Elizabeth to his son Thomas, who had succeeded him as earl. The abbot and convent continued in existence, therefore, though Philip Purcell, now the legally constituted provost, appears to have betaken himself to Loughmoe, the seat of the Purcell family, returning to the abbey only when the business of the house made it necessary for him to do so. It is not clear whether or not he actually married, but the Cistercian writer, Malachy Hartry, states in evident sorrow that 'he gave way to worldy lust and so begat children illicitly'. That the community life continued without interruption, after the general dissolution of the monasteries, is clear from the available evidence. Malachy Hartry in his account of Holy Cross states that 'this monastery of ours was the last suppressed, at least in Munster and Leinster, as tradition and the letter of the last abbot prove', and he quotes a letter of the last abbot which makes this fact quite clear. Writing to a certain Walter Archer in Clonmel on 20 March 1559, Philip Purcell states inter alia that 'the abbey of Hollie Crosse was never suppressed under the late kinge ...'

Philip Purcell's testimony is confirmed by two leases now preserved among the Ormond Papers in the National Library of Ireland, and dated respectively 1558 and 1559. The first is the lease to John Purcell and Elicia his wife of certain lands belonging to the abbey. In this document[4] Philip Purcell styles himself provost or abbot of Holy Cross and states that the lease is granted with the consent of his community assembled in chapter. The second lease[5] is made out to Richard Wale, and here again Philip styles himself provost or abbot and states that the lease is granted with the

4 IMED, 94, 121.   5 Ibid., 96, 124.

consent of the community (*conventus*) after a special meeting had been called in the chapter house. These two deeds show that more than twenty years after the suppression of the Irish monasteries the monks of Holy Cross were still living in community and at least, as far as the leasing of lands was concerned, were observing the customary conventions laid down by the Cistercian usages for such transactions. The documents thus bear out the testimony of Malachy Hartry, who writes in his history of Holy Cross abbey that

> for twenty-four years at least, from the twenty-eight of the reign of Henry VIII, for six of the reign of Edward VI, and five of Queen Mary, up to the fifth of Elizabeth, he (Philip Purcell) presided over the monastery of the Holy Cross during the storm and confusion.[6]

This statement is fully borne out in the available evidence. It is hard indeed to understand how a Cistercian community could continue to exist under such circumstances; their abbot had adopted the religious changes inaugurated by Henry VIII, and the community seems to have acquiesced in this policy. He had turned the abbey into his own private possession at least for life. He drew the monastic revenues and acted in various capacities as head of the community, signing deeds, convoking the brethren in chapter when certain matters had to be decided, and consulting them regarding the steps he was about to take or wished to take. In a word he acted exactly as if he were still abbot of a fully organised and orthodox, Cistercian monastery.

It is impossible to conceive that Henry VIII would have allowed the community of Holy Cross to continue in existence even in the modified form of a provostry of secular priests unless the members of that community had acknowledged, at least through their superior, the king's spiritual supremacy and renounced thereby their allegiance to the pope. That the abbot did so, at least outwardly, admits of no doubt, but it is not clear what the position of the community as a whole was in this matter. It seems probable that, like their brethren of St Mary's abbey, Dublin, the monks of Holy Cross accepted the king as supreme head of the Church in Ireland, changing their habit and rule according to the king's pleasure and continuing their existence as a community or college of secular priests in Henry's national church. Nevertheless it seems probable that, while thus temporising, they remained Cistercians at heart and awaited the day which they hoped would seen dawn in which a reconciliation between king and pope would set everything right again. Perhaps they did as some of their brethren in England had done, accepted the king's supremacy 'in so far as

6 Hartry, p. 70.

it was permitted by the law of God'. Whatever the explanation may be, Fr Malachy Hartry does seem to imply in one passage of his work that both abbot and community accepted the changes in religion imposed by Henry VIII for he speaks of 'the aforesaid Philip who had submitted himself and his community to the new religion of Parliament ...' Moreover, since the community continued to maintain its corporate existence as provostry under Edward VI it would seem that the monks accepted the further changes imposed during the reign of the monarch. The question may then be asked: Did they actually conform to Protestantism, at least for a time? Had they done so it would not be unique in the history of the order, for we know that the abbot of Loccum (Hanover) in Germany with his community, did in fact embrace the new Protestant teaching and joined the Luthern Church; yet the community continued to live the Cistercian life even as Lutherans and the Protestant abbot actually delegated one of the neighbouting Catholic abbots to act as his representative at the general chapter.

It is very probable, we might say certain, that the Cistercians of Holy Cross had ceased to be schismatics during the reign of Queen Mary. Indeed, that queen would not have tolerated a schismatical community and the time servers who changes their religious opinions under Henry VIII changed back with equal alacrity under Mary Tudor, just as they had no difficulty in accepting the Protestant establishment under Edward VI and were to make another change about under Queen Elizabeth. The monks of Holy Cross were not however as fickle as all that. They do not seem to have fallen away again after the death of Mary Tudor but remained steadfast to the Church and to the order thence-forward until their final disappearance in the eighteenth century.

Philip Purcell granted his life interest in the property of Holy Cross abbey to Thomas Butler, earl of Ormond, in 1561.[7] This deed, signed by Purcell, was witnessed by John Riane, William Dowyed and John Walshe, all of whom were probably monks of Holy Cross. The John Riane who witnessed this deed was probably the individual known as Shane MacDonnell O'Mulryan otherwise called John, monk of Holy Cross, who appears in yet another deed under the guise of John Monk;[8] this John O'Mulryan may well have been the abbot of the community and if so, may even have ruled it until his death, notwithstanding the fact that the abbey passed into the hands of the earl of Ormond, who was then a Protestant (he returned to the faith of his fathers before his death). The connection of the monks with their old home was not broken even then.

It is true that they were now legally banished, and Hartry tells us that the ornaments of the church made of gold, silver and silk stuffs, including

---

7 IMED, p. 98, Deed 126. 8 COD, v, p. 220 (no. 199); IMED, p. 268.

fifteen silver-gilt chalices, were profaned by the spoiler's hands and were scattered 'not among the poor but among the rich' so that (to use his own words)[9] 'the whole monastery, formerly the scene of the holy life of the Cistercian monks, was nothing but a den of robbers, or a stall for horses, oxen and brute beasts'. But the earl of Ormond, despite his profession of the Protestant religion, continued to protect the monks and gave them a lease by means of which they were enabled to remain as tenants in the old abbey, though in ever diminishing numbers as the years went by. It is pleasing to be able to record here that the *quondam* abbot, Philip Purcell, returned to the faith of his fathers in his last days and strengthened with the sacraments of the Catholic Church, 'slept in the Lord' about the year 1564.

When the monastery of Holy Cross had been erected into a provostry at the dissolution of the Irish monasteries, Philip Purcell had been made provost for life with the stipulation that the abbey with all its possessions was to pass after his death to James Butler, earl of Ormond. As James died before Philip and was succeeded in the earldom by his son Thomas, King Philip and Queen Mary issued letters patent on 13 September 1558 by which the right of James to Holy Cross abbey and its possessions was confirmed to his son Thomas. We find among the Ormond Deeds a letter from Queen Elizabeth to the earl of Sussex confirming the letters patent of King Philip and Queen Mary and directing new letters patent to be made out for the grant of the lands of Holy Cross to the earl of Ormond. The letter is dated 20 November 1562. There is also in the Ormond deeds the grant made by Queen Elizbeth to Thomas Butler, earl of Ormond, of the site and lands of Holy Cross abbey. This grant bears in the great seal of Ireland and is dated 3 October 1563. Following the death of Philip Purcell and the grants made to the earl of Ormond by Philip and Mary and Elizabeth the position of the Holy Cross community underwent a radical transformation. From 1539 until 1561 the community maintained its corporate existence and this status was fully recognised by Henry VIII and the monarchs who succeeded him. After 1561 however all this was changed. The earl of Ormond now became the legal owner of Holy Cross abbey and its possessions, and the monks, or what remained of them, became his tenants. They were possible not disturbed at this time and may have been allowed to remain until 1571 when we read of the earl leasing a room in the abbey to a certain John Monk who should rather be called the monk John – his real name was O'Mulryan or Ryan – for he appears to have been not only a monk of Holy Cross but probably Purcell's successor as abbot.[10] From a deed of 1572 we learn that his full name was Shane Mac Donyll O'Mulryan otherwise called John Monk.

9 Hartry, p. 72. 10 COD, v, p. 226.

It is very probable that this Shane Mac Donyll O'Mulryan alias John Monk whose signature appears in another deed of 1572 (in Irish characters) as John Rian, is the same individual as the John Riane who was one of the three witnesses present at the sealing and delivery of the grant by Philip Purcell to Thomas Butler, earl of Ormond, of his life interest in the property of the dissolved monastery of Holy Cross. By an indenture[11] of 5 March 1571/2, the earl of Ormond granted to the said John Mac Donyll O Mulryan the town or village of the grange of the Holy Cross to have and to hold for a term of twenty-one years at the annual rent of £4 while by another indenture dated 16 May 1572, the same John was granted 'the chamber wherin he now dwells in the cloister of said Holy Cross abbey with the appurtances, to have and to hold to said John for a term of twenty-one years at the annual rent of 10s.' Under the terms of this indenture John was obliged to repair and uphold the chamber with slates skin, timber, lathes and pins. Two other deeds in the Ormond Collection, one of 1580, the other of 1581, show that John Rian also held portion of the tithes and oblations of the abbey besides the town or hamlet called the grange of the Holy Cross already mentioned. John Ryan had disappeared from Holy Cross abbey by 1580, for, by an indenture dated 14 April of that year, the earl of Ormond leased the hamlet called the grange of the Holy Cross which 'was of late set unto John Monk of the same' to a certain John Cantwell[12] on the grounds that the conditions under which John Monk received his lease had been broken by the said John. Another indenture dated 12 September 1581 granted to John Cantwell Fitzpiers 'the altarages of the late dissolved abbey of Holy Cross with all tithes, oblations, etc., belonging therto, in as large a manner as John O'Ryan lately held the same as tenant to the earl ...' From this it is clear that John Ryan had by then ceased to inhabit his room or cell in the abbey. There is no evidence that he had any community with him at this time; but if he was the successor of Philip Purcell in the abbacy, as seems probable, it is likely enough that he had the care of souls in the territory belonging to the dissolved abbey and acted in effect as parish priest of Holy Cross.

As far as exterior appearances are concerned, John Ryan was merely one of the tenants of the earl of Ormond of whom there was at this period at least one other domiciled in the abbey, namely, James Fitz William Purcell of Ballycormky, who by an indenture of 15 May 1572, was granted 'one cellar within the cloister called the chapter house, the room or loft over the chancel of the choir, and the room over the cross church of the Holy Cross ... with a little way entering in the great stairs of said church to the upper rooms for a term of twenty-one years at annual rent of 16s., with provision that said James shall not go about to spoil, rob, or misuse him-

11 Ibid., p. 220. 12 IMED, p. 272.

self towards the inhabitants of Holy Cross.' Yet, though John O'Mulryan or John Monk was but a tenant of the earl in part of the old abbey, it is stated expressly that he was a priest for he is designated chaplain in the indenture of 15 May 1572. Was he succeeded at Holy Cross by William O'Dwyer who, according to the Revd Denis Murphy sj, was abbot in 1579? It is tempting to speculate whether this William O'Dwyer of 1579 may not have been identical with the 'William Dowyed', who with John Riane already mentioned and John Walshe (the latter very probable another monk of the old abbey), was a witness to the deed by which Philip Purcell transferred his life interest in the abbey to the earl of Ormond. Despite the temptation to indulge in such speculation it appears to me that in this instance Fr Murphy has simply misinterpreted a statement found in Archdall's *Monasticon Hibernicum*. Archdall, in his article on Holy Cross abbey, states that Philip Purcell was abbot in 1538 and in the very next sentence tells us that 'William O'Dwyer was the last abbot'. He gives no date for William, but in a later paragraph records an inquisition taken on the Thursday next after the feast of All Saints, which found that the last Abbot William O'Dwyre was seized of two messauges in Francis Street, Cashel, which messuage was given by David Comyn to Fergal, formerly abbot of the house. By the 'last abbot' is almost certainly meant the abbot who preceded Philip Purcell and who was abbot until the very eve of the reformation. Purcell was abbot only five years when the house was turned into a provostry, of which he himself became provost for life. Though technically the last abbot he was, in Catholic eyes, a renegade. He went over to the new religion and judging him in this light, we might be inclined to call his predecessor, Abbot William O'Dwyer, the last Catholic abbot of Holy Cross. However, I do no mean to insinuate that Archdall looked on it in that light. In his list he places Purcell before O'Dwyer and this I think, was a genuine mistake on his part. He calls William O'Dwyer the last abbot, and by William O'Dwyer in this instance I take it he means the historical William O'Dwyer who was the last abbot but one before the dissolution, who was succeeded (not preceded) by Philip Purcell. He, I believe, was the William O'Dwyer referred to in the inquisition of 1579.

When in 1581 the earl of Ormond granted to John Cantwell the altarages of Holy Cross together with all the tithes oblations, etc., for twelve years, he laid down the conditions that John Cantwell was to keep in repair the parish church of the said abbey and the chancel and choir therof 'except such of the chancel as James Purcell fitzWilliam possesses'. He was also to find a sufficient and lawful curate to serve the cure to the parishioners there and to administer all the sacraments and sacramentals according to the Queen's Majesty's proceeedings, not permitting any service or ceremony contrary to her Highness' proceedings to be said or used in the church. When we consider that during all this time the relic of the Holy

Cross was held in the greatest veneration and was even exposed to the people who came in great numbers to reverence it, these last conditions in the above deed would seem to be no more than legal manouevres for the purpose of circumventing the law and making a pretence of complying with it while actually using it as a means of allowing the monks to remain in the abbey as tenants to the earl. The fact that one or more of the various tenants named in the leases made by or on behalf of the earl were in reality monks would not, of course, be apparent on the face of the document.

There is ample evidence that the relic of the Holy Cross was exposed for veneration at this period and that great crowds of pius catholics continued to come in pilgrmages to the abbey for that purpose. In 1567 we find no less a person than the lord deputy (Sydney) complaining to the Queen that 'there is no small confluence of people still resorting to the Holy Cross'.[13] In 1579 James Fitzmaurice Fitzgerald is said to have visited the abbey to venerate the relic a few weeks before his death[14] at the hands of the Burkes, while in 1583 Dermot O'Hurley,[15] archbishop of Cashel made a pilgrimage to the shrine shortly before his capture by the English. It is a fact of no small significance that the archbishop had actually found shelter at the earl of Ormond's castle in Carrick-on-Suir, where he fell into the hands of his enemies, having been betrayed by Fleming, Baron of Slane, one of his own co-religionists. The fact that the earl, knowing who and what the hunted man was, had given his shelter under his own roof indicates that in spite of his outward profession of the Protestant religion his sympathies were secretly with his Catholic countrymen, and certain it is that the veneration of the holy relic at the abbey could not take place without his knowledge and connivance. In 1586 Camden writes of the 'famous abbey' to which the people still come to do reverence to the relic of the Holy Cross. 'It is incredible' he states, 'what a concourse of people still throng hither out of devotion. For this nation obstinately adheres to the religion of superstition of their forefathers.'[16] Another testimony of the same period describes the relic as 'the idol of the Irish national more superstitiously reverenced than all the idolatries of Ireland'.

The foregoing testimonies go to show that the relic of the Holy Cross of Woghterlawn was being venerated publicly by the faithful during this entire period and that consequently there must have been some monks in Holy Cross abbey at the time. That the community as such existed there until 1561 has already been shown. That one or more monks continued in residence there during the period 1561-86 is deducible from what has

13 Sydney Papers in Grose's *Antiquities of Ireland*, i (London, 1791), quoted by D. Murphy in Hartry, p. lxiii, note 6.   14 M. Callanan, *The Abbey of Holy Cross* (Dublin, n.d.), p. 38 (no source indicated).   15 Rothe, *Analecta de Rebus Catholicorum in Hibernia*, ed. Patrick F. Moran (Dublin, 1884), p. 430.   16 Camden, *Britannia*, ii, p. 134 (London, 1722), quoted by Murphy in Hartry, p. lxiv.

been said in the preceding paragraphs. Moreover our supposition on this point is verified by the statements made in the annals of the kingdom of Ireland and in Lughaidh O'Clerigh's *Beatha Aodha Ruaidh Ui Dhomhnaill.* The annalist tells us that in 1600 Hugh O'Neill visited the abbey with his army, had the relic brought out to him and presented gifts to the monks,[17] while in O'Clerigh's life of Red Hugh O'Donnell[18] we read that in the year 1601 the latter visited the abbey and 'asked the prayers and blessings of the monks'. The writer adds that he also presented oblations, offerings and alms to the monks, for which they were grateful. It is evident, then, from the testimony of contemporary documents and writers that from 1539 to 1601 there was in the abbey of Holy Cross an unbroken line of Cistercian monks. Thanks to the connivance of the earl of Ormond that line was continued even though the monks were, in the words of Fr Malachy Hartry, 'forced by persecution to go away for a short time' notwithstanding which they returned again to their beloved abbey 'through zeal for their order and for the welfare of souls'.[19] We can trace the line of abbots down to the year 1579 or thereabouts after which there is a blank until 1603. Nevertheless, the fact that during the period 1567-1601 we hear of large crowds of pilgrims resorting to the monastery to venerate the relic of the Holy Cross, and the presence in the abbey of monks in whose care that relic remained, leads us to infer that there was during the interval between the death of John O'Mulryan in 1579 and the accession of Bernard of Foulow in 1603 one or more abbots who maintained intact the line of abbatial succession which commenced with Abbot Gregory in or about 1180. In our next chapter we shall endeavour to trace the line of abbots and the fortunes of the community of Holy Cross from the accession of Abbot Bernard in 1603 to what seemed to be the final extinction not only of the community of Holy Cross but of the Cistercian Order itself in Ireland by the death of the last Irish monk of the order in the abbey ruins sometime before the year 1752.

15. SEVENTEENTH-CENTURY REFORM

After the downfall of Hugh O'Neill and the defeat of the Irish and Catholic cause, the monks had once more to leave the abbey; but they only awaited and opportunity of returning and in 1602 or 1603 Richard Foulow, in religion Brother Bernard, was appointed abbot by apostolic

---

17 AFM ad annum 1600. **18** *Beatha Aodha Ruaidh Ui Dhomhnaill,* ed. D. Murphy SJ (Dublin, 1893), p. 303. **19** Hartry, pp 31 and 75.

authority.[1] Harty tells us that he was the first abbot to be appointed in this manner after the suppression of the abbey, by which is probably meant after the final dissolution of the community on the disappearance of Philip Purcell in 1561. I have suggested in the last chapter that John MacDonyll O Mulryan who dwelt in the abbey from 1572 (if not from 1561) to 1579 or thereabouts was in fact the successor of Philip Purcell in the abbacy. If this was actually the case (it is only an assumption on my part) and if Malachy Hartry is correct in stating that Richard Foulow was the first abbot to be appointed by apostolic authority after the suppression of the abbey, we must suppose that John O'Mulryan was elected in the ordinary way by the members of the community, which at the time of Purcell's final cession of power still maintained a corporate existence. If there was indeed, an election it probably took place before the sealing and delivery of the grant made by Purcell to Thomas Butler, earl of Ormond, of his life interest in the property, to which deed 'John Riane' himself was one of the witnesses. If the community, as we may suppose, had dwindled away into one or two monks at a later period it is probable that John O'Mulryan had no successor as abbot until the appointment of Richard Foulow in 1602 or 1603. On the other hand references already given from various sources to the presence of a community at Holy Cross during the latter half of the sixteenth century would suggest that there were then present sufficient abbatial succession by the normal process of election. It must remain a matter of doubt, then, as to whether there was any abbot *de regimine* in Holy Cross abbey between 1579 and 1602.

Though the newly appointed abbot was unable to take up his abode in the monastery in 1603 he seems to have gathered about him a little community, the members of which probably acted as missionary priests among the faithful of the parish and the dependent churches. He even received novices to profession, and on such occasions seems to have come to the abbey in person for the purpose of carrying out the ceremony of reception. Not only did the new abbot receive novices; he also maintained fairly close relations with the continental houses of the order, and especially with Clairvaux, the house from which the greater part of the Irish Cistercian abbeys had sprung. In 1606[2] he sent one of his subjects to Clairvaux to be trained in the discipline of the religious life under the reforming abbot, Denis L'Argentier, the founder of the Strict Observance. This is of interest as showing the tendency then manifesting itself among the disorganised Cistercians of Ireland to return to the more strict observance of the rule. The brother thus sent to Clairvaux was Thomas O' Leamy, called in religion Brother Bernard, who later became abbot of Kilcooly.

1 Hartry, p. 74. 2 Ibid., p. 74.

In 1603[3] the abbot of Holy Cross determined to bring his monks back to the monastery to celebrate the feast of St Bernard in a worthy manner. Malachy Hartry tells us that

> setting aside all fear, he summoned and invited great numbers to his monastery. The concourse of the faithful increasing day by day on account of the great feast and the strange novelty brought the secular clergy of whom but a few were to be found, from remote provinces and cities. He resolved to carry out the chanting of the office in choir, in which kind of duty he was well trained ...

The result expected was that the authorities got wind of the affair and a troop of cavalry was sent down to Holy Cross by the viceroy, Sir George Carew, with orders to seize the abbot and put him in chains. It is even stated that a reward was publicly offered for the cutting off of the abbot's head. However, the attempt failed and the abbot was able to keep his head; but he was forced to go into hiding. His subsequent adventures are briefly related by Hartry:[4]

> By day he lay hidden; during the whole night he journeyed on, taking no rest He got safe on board a ship at Wexford. Soon after he landed in France, and urged on by his affection went on a pilgrimage to the tombs of our holy fathers Malachy and Bernard at far-famed Clairvaux. He remained five months at the abbey of Clairvaux, wonderfully comforted. Having been summoned to the general chapter to be held in the month of May following at the famous mother-house of Citeaux, he was chosen, appointed and confirmed Vicar General of the Order of the Cistercians for Ireland, England, and Scotland, by the most reverand lord Brother Nicholas Boucherat, General, and by the vote of all the capitulars. From France, he went to Spain and Madrid. He stated to His Majesty his case in reference to past years when at one time, during the reign of Philip II he was chaplain to the royal fleet; and he made known his own condition to his majesty who readily granted his petition and sent him away satisfied. While in exile he passed two years at least in the town of Bilbao, living very piously. (He hired a house outside the city in the vineyards, and lived there as a monastery) ... No one of his countrymen was bold enough to take our exiled Abbot Bernard across in his ship, for this was a crime of high treason and declared to be such throughout Ireland. But with God's aid and by the help of a French vessel he returned safe to his

3 Ibid., p. 76. 4 Ibid., p. 78.

native country where he wrought a very great reformation among the Catholics and witnessed the constancy and firmness of many converted to the faith by him, with God's help, at Cashel, his native city ... He was attacked by a mortal disease on a journey passing by the monastery of Athassel, formerly of the order of Canons Regular of St Augustine. Fortified with the sacraments of the Church which he received with piety and religious sentiments he died at the said monastery. His body was brought to his own monastery of Holy Cross and laid reverently in the tomb of the abbots.

Because the manuscript of the *Triumphalia* is mutilated the date of Abbot Bernard Foulow's death has not been preserved. Allowing for his five months sojourn at the abbey of Clairvaux and his visit to the general chapter in May as well as for his more than two year's stay in Spain, we may assume that he returned to Ireland in 1606 or 1607; but we have no means of ascertaining how long he was labouring in his native diocese after his return before he was seized with the illness which brough his to the grave. We can, however, fix roughly the date of his death from data supplied by Fr Malachy Hartry. Malachy tells us that for the space of four years after the death of Abbot Bernard 'not a few secular prists worried their brains to obtain the honour of commendatory abbot of Holy Cross'.[5] They were disappointed in their expectations for, on 7 October 1611, Luke Archer, that very day professed as a monk of the Cistercian Order was, by apostolic authority, appointed abbot of Holy Cross in succession to Abbot Bernard.[6] This would place the latter's death some time in the year 1607 which would agree fairly closely with the time he is said to have spent in France and Spain before his return to Ireland. He cannot then have been labouring on the Irish mission for any considerable time after his return; certainly not more than a year.

The briefs appointing Abbot Bernard's successor were expedited from Rome 'for good and valid reasons' at the instance and request of Abbot Paul Ragget, at that time vicar general of the Cistercian Order in Ireland. This remarkable man, a native of Kilkenny, succeeded to the office of vicar general after the death of Bernard Foulow. Like most of the Irish Cistercians of that period he left Ireland for Spain where he joined the order, becoming a monk in the abbey of Our Lady of Nogales, in the diocese of Astorga. After his profession he completed the usual course of studies in philosophy and theology and was then sent on the Irish mission; he was later appointed abbot of St Mary's, Dublin, by apostolic authority, and was on his way to Rome in connection with the business of the order when he attended the general chapter at Citeaux where, we are told, his

5 Ibid., p. 80. 6 Ibid., p. 84.

amazing knowledge was shown at the public sessions. This chapter appointed him vicar general of the Cistercians in Ireland, England and Scotland. In his presence it was that Fr Luke Archer made his vows in 1611, having received the novice's habit the previous year. A native of Kilkenny, Luke Archer had served for some years in the ranks of the secular clergy, being appointed archdeacon of Ossory and parish priest of St Patrick's, Kilkenny.[7] He had been already sixteen years a priest when he decided to embrace the Cistercian life. Having made his profession, as related, he was appointed abbot of Holy Cross and blessed according to the usual ceremonies of the Ritual. Owing to the dangers and difficulties of those troubled times the new abbot was unable to take possession of his monastery at that time. This however, did not deter him from working for the salvation of souls and we soon find him appointed *custos* or guardian of the see of Leighlin by Bishop Creagh of Cork and Cloyne. On 7 March 1614, he was appointed by the Holy See vicar apostolic of Leighlin and later still he became vicar general of Ossory. In 1618 he succeeded Abbot Paul Ragget as vicar general of the Irish Cistercians, the then vicar general having been banished from the country by the English authorities. In fact of course Abbot Paul Ragget remained the official and *de jure* vicar general of the Irish Cistercians and was so recognised by the general chapter even after his banishment from Ireland; but since his exile lasted no less than fifteen years his duties as vicar general were *de facto* exercised by Abbot Luke Archer with the approval, no doubt, of the general chapter.

Five years after the abortive negotiations concerning the proposed invasion of Ireland had finally been abandoned Abbot Paul Ragget returned to Ireland. He was then far advanced in years but still full of zeal for the work of God and the advancement of the Cistercian Order in his native land. James I had by then been succeeded by his son, Charles, who had adopted a more tolerant policy towards the Irish Catholics. This changed attitude on the part of the Crown led the abbot to hope that the Cistercians might be restored to something of their former glory, and the bishop of Ferns in a letter to Propaganda (18 November 1633) stated that the abbot had intended to carry out the reformation of the Cisterians in Ireland had not death put an end to his plans. He died in the city of Kilkenny in October 1633, six months after his return from exile.

Abbot Archer not yet being able to return to his monastery of Holy Cross set himself the task of effecting a restoration of the order in Ireland as far as possible; and for this purpose he commenced a visitation of the various houses, visiting the very ruins of the former monasteries and appointing superiors *adnutum* where necessary. This he did, not in the capacity as abbot of Holy Cross but as vicar general of the Irish Cistercians,

7 Ibid., p. 86.

with which office he was now invested. It was clear from various sources, including the reports from bishops to Propaganda, that he encountered much opposition from certain secular priests who had been appointed by their bishops to the cure of souls in parishes belonging to the suppressed monasteries of the order. Such priests were considered to be holding these abbeys *in commendam* and much friction developed between the Cistercians and the parocial clergy – and in particular between the abbots and the bishops, in consequence of these appointments. The churches of the Cistercians including those to which parochial rights beonged came under the jurisdiction, not of the bishop of the diocese, but of the abbot so that it pertained to the latter to visit such churches and to correct any abuses that may have existed. So thought the Cistercians but the bishops soon showed that they were of a different opinion. The claims of the Cistercians eventually brought Abbot Luke Archer into conflict with the archbishops of Cashel and a very acrimonious dispute developed. These matters will be treated in a later chapter; here we shall content ourselves with an outline sketch of the work carried on by Abbot Archer on behalf of the order. The facts here recorded are to be found in Malachy Hartry's *Triumphalia.*

On the first day of September 1618, according to Fr Malachy, Abbot Luke Archer was made vicar of the Cistercian order throughout Ireland. However the records of the Cistercian general chapter show clearly that the vicar appointed in 1618 was not Abbot Luke Archer but the abbot of St Mary's abbey, Dublin, namely Abbot Paul Ragget. At that time the general chapter met every five years and the records show that the abbot of Dublin was re-appointed vicar in 1623 and again in 1628. There is no record available for the year 1633, but as Paul Ragget died that year his place must have been taken by someone else, probably by, Abbot Luke Archer who seems to have acted as the exiled vicars deputy during the latters long absence and would therefore be the person most likely to succeed him in practice. Abbot Archer had been carrying out the duties of vicar since 1618 and that this arrangement had been sanctioned by the general chapter appears certain. Hartry tells us that Abbot Luke

> employed the dignity conferred on him entirely for the general good and advancement of the order; and he seriously reflected how he might extend it for the salvation of souls and he anxiously considered, too, by what means could increase the number of his monks who, he saw, were too few, thought there were in the Catholic kingdoms many adorned with piety and learning who were soon to be seen to their native country as an ornament and honour to the order. Meanwhile some came to the Revd Lord Abbot humbly asking and petioning to obtain the monks habit. These after first enquiring both into their virtues and their manner of life and morals and find-

ing fit, the Reverend Lord Abbot, in virtue of the authority given him by the most reverend Lord Citeaux and General of the whole order to admit members in with their free and voluntary consent, admitted into the order, to the profession and vows of the order.

It must be understood however that Luke Archer was not the only abbot officiating in Ireland at this time nor was he the only abbot who admitted novices to the order in Ireland. Yet, though Abbot Luke and other Irish abbots received novices into the order from time to time, it is scarcely to be doubted that most of the Cistercians who were on the Irish mission prior to the year 1620 joined the order on the continent.

In 1623 the Irish Cistercians addressed a petition to Rome[8] asking permission in times of war and schism when it would be impossible for them to dwell in their monasteries according to rule to acquire secular houses and there to carry out the offices and other religious exercises to which they were obliged by their profession without having to obtain the licence of the local ordinaries. It was probably in virtue of a permission received as a result of this petition that Abbot Archer moved his little community to Kilkenny city, where he hired a house which he fitted up as a place of refuge. The Cistercian regular observance is said to have been religiously carried out in this house,[9] to which a novitiate was attached. Not only those aspirants who wished to become members of Abbot Luke's community of Holy Cross were admitted to this novitiate but those also who wished to make profession for other houses of the order in Ireland. Many of the monks had been secular priests before entering the order and these were usually sent on the mission as soon as they had made profession. These monks were always appointed to the cure of souls within dependencies of the ancient abbeys. This became the regular custom and gave rise to much friction with the bishops who claimed, such parishes as coming under their own jurisdiction. Numerous instances are on record of appointments of this kind made immediately or almost immediately after the profession of monks who had been recruited from the parochial clergy. Not all the newly professed monks were sent out on the mission in this fashion. Those not yet ordained or who had not yet completed their studies were usually sent ot the Continent to one or other of the colleges maintained by the Cistercians at the more famous universities, including the college of the Irish Cistercians at Douai. Thus we find references to Irish monks who, on making their profession, were sent to Louvain, Paris, Bordeaux, Douai and other such colleges to complete their theological studies. Some of those students died abroad but most of them returned home in due course to labour on the Irish mission.

8 *Wadding Papers*, ed. B. Jennings (Dublin, 1953), no. 25, pp 69-70.   9 Hartry, pp 105-7; 287.

During all this time the Irish Cistercians had been endeavouring to rebuild their shattered forces in the hope of restoring the order to its pristine vigour in Ireland. They might, perhaps, have succeeded had the time been more propitious; but in the circumstances of the time everything was against them. The difficulty of establishing monasteries on anything like a regular basis was almost insuperable. Occasionally there would be a lull in the persecution and the religious would emerge into the open; but a new persecution would sooner or later flare up compelling them to go into hiding once more. Novitiates were essential if the order was to take root again in Ireland, but regular novitiates could scarcely exist when the abbeys themselves had ceased to exist The setting up of a house of Cistercians with a novitiate attached in Kilkenny city was a big achievement for which Abbot Luke Archer deserves great credit; but it did not solve the problem. As long as there was a toleration of religious activities it served its purpose, but whenever persecution became rabid again the religious had once more to scatter. Perhaps the safest plan would have been to establish a central novitiate for a number of houses for the Irish Cistercians on the Continent from which regular relays of new monks could be sent to the Irish mission field. An attempt was indeed made but did not unfortunately succeed. According to Cistercian usage each community should have its own novitiate, but this proved impracticable in those days of persecution; hence, as the years went on Abbot Archer's novitiate, intended primarily for the monks of Holy Cross, came to be looked upon as a general novitiate for the whole of Ireland, the novices making profession for the various houses for which they were intended. In his all embracing charity and zeal the abbot did not stop at that, he attached to the novitiate, at least during the period in which it was situated in Kilkenny, a seminary for the education to secular priests.

When toleration increased during the reign of Charles I some of the scattered Cistercian communities attempted to regain possession of their old abbeys and this was especially the case during the short lived triumph of the Irish cause from 1641 to 1650. In many cases the abbeys were in ruins or in a very dilapidated state and the monks had to accommodate themselves as best they could within the tottering walls. We have no means of knowing how many convents were established, even on a small scale in their old homes during these eventful years. Some few references occur in the annals of the period which give us a glimpse of small bands of monks striving to set themselves up in the ruins of the abandoned abbeys; but even before the outbreak of the war attempts had been made to re-establish some of the old communities.

On Trinity Sunday, 1625,[10] three Cistercians received the solemn abbatial blessing in St John's Church in Waterford city. The ceremony was per-

10 Ibid., p. 106.

formed by archbishop Thomas Fleming of Dublin assisted by the abbots of
Holy Cross and Kilcooly, and four or five other monks of the order took
part in the rite. The newly blessed abbots were John Madan, abbot of
Graiguenamanagh, Patrick (Christian) Barnewall, abbot of Mellifont, and
Laurence Fitzharris, abbot of Inishlounaght. Two years prior to his blessing Patrick Barnewell had opened a little oratory at Drogheda where he
presided over a small community.[11] The importance of Holy Cross abbey
at this period may be gauged from the fact that the bulk of the Drogheda
community, which was intended as a restoration of the ancient Mellifont,
came from Holy Cross, including the master of novices who was no other
than Malachy Hartry himself. The priests of this community continued to
minister to the spiritual needs of the people of Drogheda and the surrounding districts, particularly those comprised in the ancient lands of
Mellifont, until they were forcibly dispersed after the outbreak of the war.

From 18 September 1618 to 21 April 1637, Abbot Luke Archer had
presided not only over his own community of Holy Cross but also over the
destinies of the Irish houses of the order. He had set up a central novitiate
in Kilkenny from which novices went out to all parts of the country and
from which came forth various alumni who as abbots were later destined
to play an important part in the work of the order in Ireland. Among the
novices received by him were some who later laid down their lives or suffered imprisonment or persecution for the faith. Finally, having reached
an advanced age and being bowed down more with infirmities than with
the weight of years, and having undergone much toil and labour in the
office of vicar general, he decided to resign therefrom and confine himself solely to the government of his own monastery of Holy Cross. He had,
indeeed, borne uncomplainingly and even joyfully the heat and burden of
the day and as Hartry stated:

> he never showed himself slow or inactive during those laborious
> years ... As often as there was need during vicariate he did not heed
> bodily hardships; he did not dread the extremes of summer or
> winter during his long journeys, rendered most difficult by the snow
> and floods, in order to promote in person the reform of the order,
> and of this fact we are all witnesses.

The novitiate was now removed from Kilkenny to Holy Cross abbey and
the monks entered once more into the possession of their old home. Here
they continued to live, and here the abbot's successor dwelt with his convent until the Cromwellian campaign drove them out again. By that time,
however, Abbot Luke had gone to receive his reward. Dying in 1644, he

11 Ibid., p. 283.

was buried with his predecessors in the abbey church and was succeeded as abbot by the man he had himself chosen some seven years earlier, Fr John Cantwell. Fr John, a native of Tipperary, had been unanimously elected abbot by the whole convent assembled in chapter in 1637, Fr Malachy Hartry acting as notary apostolic on that occasion. The venerable Abbot Luke was then an old man and foreseeing his approaching end, wished to appoint a coadjutor with right of succession in good time lest, as he informed his monks, the abbey should fall into the hands of ambitious persons after his death. It was an usual arrangement; the abbot did not resign to make way for his successor but continued to rule the community after his successor had been elected. He was in fact, an abbot with a coajutor abbot, something unique in the Cistercian order.

Shortly after the election of John Cantwell (whose name in religion was Louis) a momentous step was taken in the projected restoration of the Irish Cistercians.[12] This was the founding of the new Irish Congregation of St Malachy and Bernard. On 18 September 1638 all the Irish abbots met in a national chapter for the election of a superior general and unanimously chose Patrick Plunkett, abbot of St Mary's abbey, Dublin, as head of the new congregation. The capitular fathers then proceeded to the election of a procurator general and the choice this time fell on John (Louis) Cantwell,[13] coadjutor abbot of Holy Cross. His election was unanimous, and shortly afterwards he set out for Rome to conduct the business of the Irish abbots there and to seek from the Holy See certain favours in connection with the re-establishment of the regular observance of Citeaux in Ireland. A letter written[14] by Cardinal Richelieu (at that time claiming to be abbot general of the Cistercian Order) to Cardinal Antonio Barberini, dated 15 January 1639 informs the cardinal that the congregation of the Cistercian Order erected some time ago in Ireland by virtue of apostolic bulls had sent one of the religious, John Cantwell by name, to the Court of Rome with a view to the reestablishment of regular observance in the said order in Ireland. Richelieu asks Barberini to afford the Irish abbot all possible assistance in obtaining his requests while maintaining at the same time the authority of the abbot of Citeaux, head and Superior General of the whole order, over the Irish congregation without any dimunition. The abbot's mission was successful. In March 1639 the acts of the Irish chapter were approved and confirmed by the Holy See and new priviliges and favours were granted to the Irish Congregation.

Patrick Plunkett was now superior general of the Irish Congregation. Settling in St Mary's abbey he set up therein an oratory after the example of the oratory constructed in Drogheda by Abbot Barnewell. Here he

12 Ibid., p. 112.   13 Ibid., p. 218.   14 Mss *Barberini Latini* 7951 f. 1588 (edited by G. Mac Niocaill in *Galvia*, iii, p. 15.)

laboured with six monks until the outbreak of the war in 1641 caused him to withdraw from Dublin. The soldiery in fact rushed into the oratory, seized on all the monastic property and brought monks and novices to Dublin Castle by night. They were questioned about the part they played in the rising. Hartry gives a graphic picture of their expulsion from the city:

> Though innocent, they were accused of many crimes of which they had never thought; and when nothing could be proved against them they were thrust into a dark prison. The next night they were again examined, and being again found guiltless of anything suspicious they were driven out of the city almost naked by the soldiers about ten o'clock at night, in a great storm, in snow and rain; and they passed the rest of the night which had grown more wild, lying on the ground by a hedge.

Most of the abbeys were by this time in ruins or at the very least in an extremely dilapidated state. Even Holy Cross abbey which had been used intermittently by the Cistercians for a number of years was in a sad state of disrepair. When John Cantwell took charge of the community after the return of the monks from Kilkenny he had to build another dwelling to house the monks and he had also to 'cover in the whole church which, through the inclemency of the seasons and the cruelty of the heretics, had remained without a roof'. The abbey of Holy Cross was not the only abbey occupied or partly occupied by a Cistercian community in those years; the ancient abbey of Kilcooly was also occupied. This information is given quite incidentally by Fr Malachy Hartry when he mentions that the first who presented himself to the community of Holy Cross 'amid the ravages of war such as Ireland had never seen before' was Fr John Stapleton,[15] who received the habit of religion on 19 July 1645, and made his novitiate in the monastery of Kilcooly with another brother. This is the only contemporary evidence we have concerning the existence of a Cistercian community at Kilcooly during this period. It would seem from the reference that the professed members of the community of Holy Cross dwelt in their own abbey while the abbey of Kilcooly was used as a novitiate for the Holy Cross novices. Indeed it is possible that the central novitiate at Kilkenny had been set up at Kilcooly after the return of the monks to Holy Cross. After completing his novitiate in Kilcooly Fr John returned to Holy Cross where he made his vows and later proceeded to Paris to enter on his studies.

If we were considering here the Irish Cistercian as a whole instead of confining ourselves to the single monastery of Holy Cross many pages

15 Hartry, p. 114.

could be written on the story of the order during the years 1641-50. Leaving that story over for another occasion it suffices to say here that in those troubled times the Irish Cistercians, though their numbers were few and the dangers many, shared to the full the miseries and sufferings of their people and played their part nobly in the conflict; so much so that a contemporary writer, Archdeacon Lynch, as the editor of the *Triumphalia* remarks, 'bears the highest testimony to the zeal of the Fathers ... in ministering to the wants of the people during the most trying times'. When the Confederation of Kilkenny was formed the Cistercians gave it their whole-hearted support. Among the signatories to the declaration at Kilkenny were four Cistercian abbots;[16] and when the supreme council in 1646 made a peace with Ormond, which in the opinion of the papal nuncio and the vast majority of the clergy, violated the Confederate oath, the Cistercians joined with their brethren in the ecclesiastical congregation held at Waterford which condemned the peace. Among the abbots who signed this declaration were John Cantwell, abbot of Holy Cross, Patrick Plunkett, abbot of St Mary's, Dublin, Laurence Fitzharris, abbot of Inishlounaght, and James Tobin, abbot of Kilcooley. On the other hand when at a later period, the majority of the Confederates deserted the nuncio, some of the Cistercian abbots were to be found on the side of the temporising party. The number of those supporting the Ormond faction was, however, so small that the authors of the *Commentarius Rinuccinianus* take no account of them, with one supporting exception; and in discussing the conduct of the various religious orders they declare that the 'Bernardines' (as they call the Cistercians) all stood for the nuncio. The important exception was Patrick Plunkett, who, from being abbot of St Mary's abbey, Dublin, and superior general of the Irish congregation of St Malachy and Bernard, had become bishop of Ardagh in 1647. This man now became one of the most active of the Ormond faction in opposing the policy of the nuncio and the Old Irish under Eoghan Rua O Neill. The Irish Cistercians as a whole, however, stood staunchily by the nuncio in the crisis and proved themselves as true to the cause of Ireland as they did to the Faith.

16. STRUGGLE WITH PAROCHIAL CLERGY

We have already seen how Abbot Archer met with no little opposition from various diocesan priests in his efforts to restore the Cistercian Order in Holy Cross abbey and in other parts of Ireland. We intend in this chapter

16 Comment Rinucc, i, p. 326.

to give some more details regarding the struggle between the Cistercians and the parochial clergy during the period now under survey. It must be remembered that during the suppression of the monasteries in the sixteenth century the Cistercians enjoyed very extensive privileges among which were included certain rights which seemed to the bishops of the seventeenth century to be an infringement of their own rights. These rights and privileges were still being exercised by prelates of the order in the Catholic countries on the Continent, but in Ireland they had fallen into abeyance in the long interval that had elapsed since the destruction of the monasteries. The Cistercians coming from the Continent to restore the order in these parts clung tenaciously to the privileges and rights that were the common heritage of the order, and though many of the claims put forward by them seemed to the Irish bishops to be altogether outrageous, they were, in fact, based on privileges granted expressly to the order by the Holy See itself; and in their fight for the retention of these privileges against the resolute opposition of the bishops, the monks of the Irish congregation had the full support of their superiors in France. The confusion and bewilderment of the Irish bishops at the far-reaching claims put forward by the Cistercians is understandable. Nearly a century had passed since the order had ceased to be a power in the land, and, with the passing of the great monastic estates, the rights and privileges exercised by the monks had passed out of men's memories. As in Egypt of old, so in seventeenth-century Ireland a new generation had arisen 'which knew not Joseph'.

The greatest source of trouble and dissension arose from the claim of the Cistercians of the right to appoint to certain parish churches and the right to perform acts of jurisdiction in these churches without being subject to episcopal control, denying to the bishop even the right of visitation of such churches. The order claimed that all Cistercian abbots had quasi-episcopal jurisdiction, not only over all their own monks, but even over all their tenants, servants and secular subjects. Originally, indeed, the abbots of the order had jurisdiction only over their own monks. In 1487 they were granted quasi-episcopal jurisdiction over their 'tenants, vassals, subjects and servants' and all Cistercian monks and nuns, abbots and abbesses together with all their goods, vassals, subjects and servants were taken under the protection of the Holy See to which they were immediately subjected, being at the same time exempted and freed from all 'jurisdiction, superiority, correction, visitation, subjection and power of archbishops, bishops and their vicars, etc ...' Circumstances of course had changed completely between 1487 and 1603. The feudal order had come to an end and the great religious revolution of the sixteenth century had also intervened. The monastic estates had passed into the hands of laymen and, in most cases, the churches formerly served by monks or impropriate to the monasteries had come into the hands of the diocesan clergy. With the return of the monks came a renewal of ancient claims. The Cistercians, of course, were not the only religious who found themselves in conflict with the bishops and the parochial clergy on these issues; other religious orders were also involved and the contest may be seen to have been universal.

Abbot Luke Archer had not been long in charge of the abbey of Holy Cross before he found himself at issue with the archbishop of Cashel, David O Kearney,[1] regarding the right of appointment to the parish of Holy Cross. The priest in charge of the parish at the time was a member of the diocesan clergy and as such claimed to derive his jurisdiction, not from the abbot of Holy Cross, but from the archbishop of Cashel, and this notwithstanding the fact that he had been appointed by Abbot Archer's predecessor, Abbot Bernard Foulow. A long and acrimonious dispute resulted which was finally brought to a head by the drastic action of the abbot who

> after long and careful discussion of the controversy and many very friendly adminitions … at last employed extreme measures … using the censures of excommunication against the aforesaid priest in virtue of the authority which he possessed; and the sentence of anathema wass pronounced in a house within the crumbling walls of the monastery by Matthew Roche, then Vicar General Apostolic in the diocese of Leighlin.

The priest thus censured, the Revd David Hennessy, is said to have been appointed parish priest of Holy Cross in 1599 and to have fixed his residence amid the ruins of the abbey, arranging its choir as a parish church. The house within the crumbling walls of the monastery referred to above, may have been the priest's residence or possibly the structure which served at the time as parish church. More than a century later the parish church is described as 'a small thatched building with two deal doors and tow glass windows in the abbey ruins; in its interior was a badly constructed stone altar on which were placed two wooden candlesticks, and the walls were adorned with paper pictures.'

If David Hennessy was appointed parish priest in 1599 it is hard to see how it could be truthfully stated by Malachy Hartry that he owed his appointment to Abbot Archer who did not receive the Cistercian habit until 1610. Even Archer's predecessor in the abbatial office Abbot Bernard Foulow, did not himself become abbot until the year 1603 and so could not have appointed Fr David Hennessy to the office of parish priest in

---

1 Archbishop Kearney's report to Rome in 1609 complained about Cistercian abbots. See Moran, *History of the Catholic Archbishops of Dublin* (Dublin, 1864), Appendix xvii, p. 431 (original *Relatio* in Barberini Archives, Rome).

1599. The truth is that Fr David Hennessy was appointed in the first instance by Abbot Bernard Foulow and hence the appointment cannot have been earlier than 1603 when Bernard Foulow became abbot. The appointment was renewed by Fr Luke Archer when he in turn became abbot in 1610. That such was the case is clear from Fr Hennessy's own statement given below in which he declared that he had received and held the cure of souls in the monastery of Holy Cross and in the parish and territories of the same from Abbot Foulow, and that after the death of the said abbot he had received and held the same cure for some years from his successor Luke Archer. The trouble between Abbot Luke and the Revd David Hennessy came to a head about 1618 when Abbot Luke took the drastic action already noted. The sentence of excommunication pronounced by the abbot against Fr Hennessy did not however, deter the latter who was encouraged in his resistance by the vicar of Cashel, a friend of his, and 'continued to say mass and administer the sacraments'. The vicar himself assisted at mass said by the excommunicated priest and encouraged the laity of Holy Cross to follow his example, declaring that the power of the abbot to inflict the censures was null and void. The archbishop of Cashel himself, David O' Kearney, although deprecating the harsh treatment meted out by the abbot to the recalcitrant priest and deploring the scandal caused by the whole affair, did not support the claim of the Revd David Hennessy and Fr Malachy Hartry in rebutting the claims of the latter was able to bring forward proof of his assertion that the archbishop had given no jurisdiction to Fr Hennessy within the limits of the abbey. A letter written by the archbishop himself to Abbot Archer, published in Triumphalia, runs as follows:

> To his worthy respected friend Fr Like Archer give these etc., 'Worshipfull Sir, and because ... it had been a scandal to Sir David to be now removed from his function speciallie at this time when these false speeches are going about. You will do verie well not to remove him till you know further, and trulie in my opinion none can stand in better steede than himself for your purpose in that place as yet (in the abbey of Hollie crosse), and I know he will be directed by yourself may agree, etc. I take leave with the hartiest commendations this twelfth of April 1618. Your Worship's moste assured frend, John Harries D. Cassellensis.

The Mr Kearney of the above letter has been assumed by the editor of the *Triumphalia* to stand for the archbishop's brother, Fr Barnaby Kearney SJ but it is more probably stands for the archbishop himself. The name 'Harries' is an alias assumed by the archbishop to evade legal penalties attaching to the excercise of ecclesiastical jurisdiction. The foregoing letter makes it clear that while the archbishop thought that the abbot would be well advised not to remove the Revd David Hennessy from his parochial functions at least for the time being, he by no means supported his pretensions against the jurisdiction of the abbot. Perhaps this attitude of the archbishop influenced the Revd Mr. Hennessy in his final decision to submit to the abbot. Having maintained a stubborn resistance for about three years he at last submitted and humbly begged pardon and absolution which the abbot was most anxious and ready to grant. The instrument of submission to which the parish priest subsequently subscribed admitted in full the claim of the abbot to sole jurisdiction in the lands and territories of the abbey of Holy Cross. Present on the occasion of this solemn declaration of submission were three Cistercian abbots, the vicar general of the diocese of Ossory, a doctor of sacred theology and a Franciscan priest who was later to become provincial of his order. The instrument reads as follows:[2]

> I, Sir David Henesie of the Dioces of Cassell prieste do be thees presents acknowledge and make known that I am hartelie grieved and repentant for all and singular to offences I have committed either in word or deede against, or to the prejudice of the honor, credit and authoritie of the Right Reverend Fr Luke Archer, right and lawful Lord Abbott of the Holly Crosse in the dioces of Cassell, or any other dependinge of him, specially Sir Matthew Roch prieste, for which I have desearved to be censured by the said Fr Luke. And do therfore most humblie crave to be absolved of the excommunication and all other censures denounced against me for my disobedience and misbehaviour towards the said Lord Abbot and his authoritie, promising by God's grace to make sufficient amends both by recallinge what approbrious speeches my coller onelie suggested me against the aforenamed Lord Abbot and his adherents in such places as theu might have wrought anny sinister impression in the hearers, and speciallie in the verie Abbey of the Hollie Crosse the next S. Barnabas his day, and also by foregoing heerafter, as I do by thees presents forgoe, desist and resign any title, claime or chardge I did or cold claims in or belonginge to the lands, territories or jurisdiction of the said Abbey of the Hollie Crosse, meaninge and faithfullie promisinge not to intermedle or undergoe heerafter any cure, chardge, or any other excercise or function within precinct or territories of the said monasterie without the aforesaid Lord Abbot's allowance, warrant and direction. In withnes wherof I have heerunto subscribed my name the first of June 1621.
> Sir David Henesie.

2 Hartry, p. 92. Note: 1621 old style; i.e. 1622.

Being present : Mortaghe Dowlinge, sacerdos et Doctor Sacrae
Theologiae. Thomas Roth, sacerdos, Vicar, Gen. Dioc. Ossor, et
Pronot Apostolicus. Frater Nicholaus Shee, postea Provincialis
Ordinis Minorum. Frater Thomas (alias) Johannes Madan, dictus
Abbas de Mothalibus. Frater Stephen Shortall, electus Abbas de
Beatitudine. Frater Thomas Bernard O Lemy, electus Abbas de
Kilcooley.

Having thus made submission to the abbot and received absolution
from him, the parish priest both in his own person and by his friends
sought to be admitted anew to the cure of souls in the parish of Holy
Cross, acknowledging at the same time that such admission would be by
the authority of and during the good pleasure of the abbot to whom he
promised to pay due reverence and obedience in all things. He was thereupon reappointed parish priest though only provisionally and temporarily
until such time as one of the abbot's novices, Brother John O'Dea, should
have made his profession expressly for the monastery following which he
was to be appointed parish priest of Holy Cross. Before restoring David
Hennessy even in this provisional and purely temporary capacity, however,
the abbot required him to subscribe to another declaration in which the
abbot's full right to exclusive spiritual jurisdiction and the cure of souls in
the territories of the abbey was set forth and recognised. The second declaration ran as follows:[3]

I, David Henesy, priest, declare before these here present, the I
received, had, and held the cure of souls in the monastery of Holy
Cross and in the parishes and territories of the same from the Revd
Lord Richmond. Foulow of happy memory, deceased, abbot of the
aforesaid monastery of Holy Cross. I declare too that after his
decease I received, had, and held the same cure for some years
from his successor, the Reverend Lord Luke Archer, the present
abbot of the same monastery. Moreover I declare before these present here that I have now received the same care area as before, by
the authority and gift of the aforesaid Lord Luke Archer Abbot of
Holy Cross, of the Cistercian Order, and Vicar General of the same
Order throughout the kingdom of Ireland etc., to whom I promise
and yield submission and obedience in each and everything belonging to the said office laid on me by him and his successors, or by any
other peson appointed by him or them at his or their pleasure, at
any time without any appeal or resistance, and the aforesaid Lord
Luke, Abbot, and his successors or anyone named by them, can sub-

3 Ibid., p. 94.

stitute in my place whomsoever they please. Moreover I promise that I will not apply or show any relic or cross inside or outside of the aforesaid monastery without the special command and permission of the aforesaid Lord Luke, the abbot, or his successor, or the person appointed by him. In faith and proof of each and all of which I have put my hand and seal to this.

Dated the twelfth day of the month of February 1621.
Sir David Henesy.

Although the archbishop of Cashel had not suppported the Revd David Hennessy in his dispute with the abbot he had himself complained to Rome some nine years earlier regarding the claims of the Cistercians. In a report addressed by him to Rome in the year 1609 touching on the state of religion in Ireland he had complained that the abbots attempted to get for themselves all the emoluments (which were small) and left nothing for other labourers by which to make a living. It seemed only right, however, that those who bore the heat and burden should receive something by way of reward. He was of opinion therefore (*salvo superiori judicio*) that the emoluments of benefices, priories and monasteries in each province should accrue, at least as long as the heresy and schism lasted, to those who laboured de fact to in the province, and especially in the places where the monasteries were situated. He warned the Congregation that if the abbots continued as they had begun they would draw down upon themselves and the bishops the indignation both of the heretics and the catholics, and he waxed sarcastic at the thought that the abbots should have even the slightest hope of ever recovering the emoluments to which they pretended since, he declared, 'not even the sovereign pontiff himself nor the kings of France or Spain could accomplish that'. The archbishop in fact believed that even in the event of a reconciliation taking place between the church and England there would be very little likelihood that the dissolved abbeys and priories would ever again be restored to their former owners. Abbot Paul Ragget, who was vicar general of the Irish Cistercians when Archbishop O'Kearney made the above report was fully determined to guard most jealously the rights and privileges of the order he had the honour as well as the duty to represent. For some time the dispute between the abbot and the archbishop waxed hot, but at length, thanks to the good offices of Dr Rothe,[4] later to become bishop of Ossory, who was appointed to arbitrate between the two antagonists, the disputants were reconciled to the great satisfaction of the Holy See. We are told, indeed, that Dr Rothe's conduct on this occasion secured for him two pow-

4 Ibid., 88, note 1.

erful patrons at Rome, namely Maffeo Barberini and Cardinal Veralli, protector of Ireland, both of whom wrote to congratulate him on the result of his arbitration. Barberini later became pope under the title of Urban VIII.

Unfortuately the dispute between the archbishop of Cashel and the vicar general of the Cistercian Order in Ireland broke out again in 1631. The persons involved were different though the dignitaries were the same. Archbishop O'Kearney had been succeeded in the see of Cashel by Archbishop Walsh while Abbot Ragget had been banished from Ireland and Abbot Luke Archer had become for all practical purposes vicar general of the Cistercian Order in Ireland. The archbishop had rekindled the fires of controversy by appointing another secular priest to the charge of Holy Cross and the abbot had refused to recognise the right of the archbishop to make this appointment. The relations between them were not improved by the fact that the monks of Holy Cross frequently took the famous relic outside the diocese and province without seeking the permission of the archbishop, Dr Walsh, who wrote to Propaganda in 1632 complaining of this.[5]

> There is in our diocese a monastery under the title of Holy Cross which possesses a remarkable piece of the Cross of our Lord. This is exposed to the veneration of the faithful and great numbers of people frequently come there out of devotion. The Superior of this monastery is Bro. Luke Archer, an excellent and religious man, who accompanied by other monks of his order takes the relic at will outside the diocese and the province without getting or asking permission from me.

The archbishop then went on to complain of the claims made by the Cistercians, and his letter affords us a glimpse of the action taken by the clergy, in the province of Cashel to resist such claims and to defend the episcopal and parochial rights.

> Quarrels and contentions frequently occur between the brethren of this order and the local ordinaries with regards to the lands and jurisdiction of the monasteries. The ordinaries adverting to the fact that these questions are full of uncertainties and beset with difficulties, proposed on my initiative certain articles of mutual agreement with the aforesaid brethren by which all occasions of scandal and strife might be done away with. A private meeting was held recently by the bishops and vicars general of the province in the city of Limerick where certain regulations were drawn up and sanctioned,

5 *Spic. Ossoriense*, i, p. 177.

which are to be accepted and carried into effect by all for the defence of the episcopal and parochial rights, with that moderation, however, which was then judged opportune and necessary.

Though the archbishop complained of the carrying of the relic of the Holy Cross outside the diocese and province by the monks it is thought by some that this was no abuse which had crept in during the calamitous times following on the suppression of the abbey, but an old and well established custom which had existed for centuries. There is indeed evidence that such a custom existed prior to the dissolution of the monasteries in the sixteenth century, but we cannot say how far back it goes. The second cause of complaint concerned the jurisdiction claimed, by the abbots over the former parishes and territories belonging to the monasteries and had been, as we have already seen, a perpetual bone of contention between the monks and the bishops since the dissolution of the monasteries. This controversy, which dragged on for years, was not peculiar to the Cistercians; almost every order was involved and these unhappy dissensions were a source of considerable weakness as well as scandal to the Irish church.[6]

17. CROMWELL ENDS THE SECOND SPRING

What may be called the second spring of Holy Cross abbey came to an end with the coming to Ireland of Oliver Cromwell followed by the collapse of the Irish resistance in 1650. Then it was that the Cistercian Order in Ireland entered on what then seemed the final phase of its history. It had indeed been almost exterminated though some few monks, enjoying the now empty and in fact dangerous title of abbot, still wandered here and there in disguise, ministering as best they could to a war weary and ravaged flock. Others, like Abbot John Cantwell of Holy Cross and Abbot James Tobin of Kilcooley, languished in prison and were later banished from the kingdom. Details of the Irish Cistercians of the immediate post Cromwell period are lacking. The little community which had been set up at Drogheda had been swept away as early as 1641. The community of Holy Cross must have likewise disappeared following on the Cromwellian conquest Malachy Hartry apparently made his way back to the abbey where he seems to have written his last work, the *Synopsis*, which he completed on 18 April 1651. He probably died at Holy Cross and presumably was buried there, but the date of his death has not been recorded. Since

6 C. Ó Conbhuidhe, *Cîteaux* 18 (1967) 325-50.

to this man, more than to any other, we owe what little knowledge we have of the history of the Irish Cistercians during the first half of the seventeenth century and since to him also we are indebted for the fascinating account of the fortunes of the abbey of Holy Cross during the century that followed the suppression of the Irish houses of the order, it is only fitting that some account of his life and labours should be given here.

Malachy Hartry himself in his last work *De Cisterciensium Hibernorum Viris Illustribus* has left us a short account, not only of the most notable of his contemporaries in the Irish Congregation of the order, but also of himself, though he nowhere mentions himself by name in the manuscript. He does indeed at the conclusion of the work designate himself as Brother John *alias* Malachy Hartry, Cistercian, but he does not say that the certain Brother N., whose activities he summarises in his last page, was in fact himself. He was born in Waterford about 1579 and at an early age went to Spain where he studied for some time in the Irish college at Lisbon. He then entered the monastery of Paracuel in the diocese of Palencia in Spain where he made his profession, returning to Ireland in 1619. The seas at this time were infested by pirates, the Moorish or Algerian pirates being particularly active in the Mediterranean and even making forays out into the Atlantic. Only twelve years later the famous sack of Baltimore was to take place when the pirates guided by an Irishman (Hackett from Dungarvan) descended on the coast of Cork. The vessel carrying Fr Malachy and his companion, Fr Stephen Shorthall,[1] later abbot of Bective,[2] seems to have fallen in with a band of pirates. Unfortunately Fr Malachy gives no details of what occurred beyond the bare statement that Stephen Shorthall was taken captive during the voyage and after suffering much at the hands of the Moors was later set free by them. He visited Flanders where he spent some time in the Cistercian monastery of Les Dunes, but it is not clear from his narrative whether the visit to Flanders took place before his return to Ireland or at some date subsequent to his return. On his return to Ireland, Fr Malachy joined the community of Holy Cross where he seems to have remained until 1623 when the community transferred to Kilkenny. He tells us that on the day after the feast of Corpus Christi in the year 1623 the abbot exposed the relic of the Holy Cross on the altar of his public oratory in the city of Kilkenny and he continues: 'I venerated it with the rest of the crowd of catholics of every degree.' He did not remain long in Kilkenny, for he was sent soon afterwards to Drogheda with Patrick Barnewall, the newly appointed abbot of Mellifont. The two Cistercians built a modest oratory in the town of Drogheda, completing the work in the autumn of 1623. On 20 October of

1 Charles de Visch, *Bibliotheca Scriptorum Sacri Ordinis Cisterciensis*, p. 297. Quoted by D. Murphy in Hartry, p. 276, note 3. 2 Hartry, pp 277-9.

the same year he brought the first two novices for the new foundation from Kilkenny to Drogheda and continued to act as master of novices at Drogheda for some years. He was later transferred back to Munster where we find him holding the office of prior of Mothel (Co. Waterford) in 1626. He was one of the superiors who met at Jerpoint on 2 October of that year when an attestation was drawn up in favour of Thomas Fleming, archbishop of Dublin, which Malachy, in common with the other Cistercian superiors, signed. In 1628 he held the office of prior in the Cistercian church in Waterford city. It was there he laboured with Thomas Madan[3] during a period of persecution when they rented and underground dwelling and erected an altar there for the solace of the catholics. He gives a pen picture of this little oratory in his own book: 'There was no daylight in it but by means of candles lighted through the day he and I recited the divine office, celebrated mass preached and administered the sacraments to the very great joy and comfort of the faithful, and so cheered the hearts of the sorrowing catholics.'

Fr Malachy was back in the abbey of Holy Cross in 1640. After that year he disappears from our ken. That he was still alive in 1651 is clear from the Synopsis, the concluding words of which show that it was not completed until 18 April of that year. The fact that the manuscript was later preserved in Holy Cross abbey would seem to indicate that he returned there before his death or may, indeed, have lived there continually from 1640 until his death, which probably occurred soon after 1651. Fr Malachy seems to have devoted a good part of his time to literary labours and although only two of his works have come down to us we learn from his own account that he wrote many others. The two which have survived are preserved in the museum of St Patrick's College, Thurles, bound together in one volume. These are the *Triumphalia Chronologica Monasterii Sanctae Crucis in Hibernia*, being an account of the history of Holy Cross abbey and the *Synopsis Nonnullorum Sanctorum Illustrium Hibernorum Monachorum Cisterciensium*, which is an account of the more illustrious members of the Irish Houses of the Order, and the latter work is especially valuable for the light it throws on the labours of the Irish Cistercians of the seventeenth century and for the information it supplies relating to the abbots and monks who worked in the Irish mission fields in those days of persecution.

The connection of the Cistercian Order with Holy Cross abbey was maintained down to a comparatively late period, almost to the year 1752. Long before that, of course, the monastery had fallen into ruin. We have seen that even in the year 1618 a building had been fitted up inside the abbey to serve as a parish church, though at that time the abbey church itself could not have been completely in ruins. A John O'Dea was parish

3 Ibid., pp 286-9.

priest of Holy Cross in the 1620s. He was appointed abbot of Corcumroe around 1628.

The bells, or some of them, were still in existence as late as 1640 when on the occasion of the remarkable cure of a sick man the abbot ordered that the bells 'should ring merry peal as on a feast'. By the year 1654 all that had changed. The Down Survey of that year gives us some idea of the state to which the once splendid abbey of the Holy Cross of Uachtar Lamhainn was then reduced. The brief unsympathetic reference in the Survey expresses better, perhaps than could the pen of the historian or the tongue of the most eloquent orator, the sad fate that had overtaken the Cistercian Order in Ireland. 'Ye olde aby church of Hollycrosse in ruins and several cabbins inhabited', runs the entry; but there is very good reason to believe that in the vicinity of that old mouldering ruin, probably in one of the cabins mentioned in the Survey, a poor outcast monk of the once famous abbey hid himself away hoping for better days and guarding jealously that precious relic which had give its name to the abbey.

Following on the restoration of Charles II, the Cistercians began to appear again though in greatly diminished numbers. We have evidence that there was at least one Cistercian living in the neighbouring diocese of Ossory at this period. A petition presented to Propaganda, seeking the appointment of the Revd James Cleere as bishop of Ossory and seemingly written between the years 1661 and 1665 bears the signature, among others, of Frater Clemens Archer, ordinis Sancti *Bernardi*. We have no further details concerning this Cistercian priest, who may have been a relative of Abbot Luke Archer of Holy Cross and of another Fr Archer, pastor of St Mary's, Kilkenny, who also signed the petition. The Archer family was a well known, highly esteemed and ancient family in Kilkenny, which had given many sons to the church; among these were the abbot already mentioned and his, not less renowned, kinsman Fr James Archer of the Society of Jesus. Another kinsman, Walter Archer, who died in 1604, is mentioned by Bishop Rothe in his *Analecta* as one who had suffered a long and rigorous imprisonment for the faith. He is not to be confounded with another of the same name who lived at a later period and presented to the church of Holy Cross a silver chalice which is still in existence.

Though matters improved somewhat during the reign of Charles II, there were intermittent bursts of persecution and it was during this very reign that St Oliver Plunkett was martyred. The surviving Cistercians were dwindling away in numbers. They continues indeed to retain a feeble foothold in Munster long after they had disappeared from the other provinces, and in the case of Holy Cross that foothold was maintained for nearly eighty years more. Archbishop Brennan of Cashel presided over a provincial synod in 1685. At this synod there were present, besides the archbishop himself, one other bishop, seven vicars general, the procurator of Cloyne and two Cistercian abbots. Though the abbots are not named nor are the monasteries to which they were appointed mentioned, there is little if any doubt that one of them was the abbot of Holy Cross. In a report on the diocese of Cashel presented to Propaganda in 1667 and dated from Kilcash, archbishop Brennan stated that there were three Cistercian abbeys in the diocese. The abbeys, which he did not name, were Holy Cross, Kilcooly and Hore abbey (Cashel). He added an interesting detail: that there was then in one of the said abbeys one abbot and one monk. The abbey this singled out as the dwelling place of one of the smallest Cistercian communities that ever existed was undoubtedly Holy Cross abbey, where the regular succession of abbots was maintained even in the very ruins of the house down to the second half of the eighteenth century.

As we have seen, John (Louis) Cantwell had been abbot of Holy Cross when the lord lieutenant and general for the parliament of England, as Oliver Cromwell styled himself, landed in Ireland on 15 August 1649. With the surrender of Galway in 1652 the war came to an end and was followed by the Cromwellian plantation and settlement, which brought down the great Anglo-Irish families into the same common ruin as the men of the older race. At the end of the campaign Abbot John Cantwell of Holy Cross languished for a time in prison before being banished to the Continent where he breathed his last among the Spanish Cistercians. He was succeeded in the abbacy by Peter Thomas Cogan from Cork, who seems to have been appointed about the year 1665 and was abbot of Holy Cross until his death some thirty-five years later. This is the abbot of whom mention was made by Archbishop Brennan in his report to Rome already quoted; the abbot who lived alone in his monastery except for the companionship of one solitary monk who formed his entire community. In 1690 war swept over the land once more and the Williamite army arrived in due course in the neighbourhood of Holy Cross. The soldiers are said to have pillaged the village and the monks disappeared for the time being. When the tide of was receded, however, Abbot Cogan returned to the abbey where he died on tenth August 1700, and was buried in the abbey church. An entry in the *Triumphalia* in a different hand from the rest of the manuscript notes that 'the Reverend Lord Thomas Cogan, abbot of the monastery of Holy Cross, died in the same monastery, August tenth in the year of the Lord 1700. May he rest in peace. Amen.'

Abbot Cogan was succeeded by Bernard Lahey who according to one opinion, was the last abbot of Holy Cross. It has been stated on the other hand that Abbot Cogan was the last abbot, Bernard Lahey being just an ordinary monk who did not enjoy abbatial rank. This opinion is based on the fact that the community by this time became so reduced in numbers as to be insufficient to form a chapter. As a matter of fact Cistercian abbots were being appointed to various abbeys throughout the country for at least a century prior to the death of Abbot Cogan, and it is almost certain that John (Louis) Cantwell was the last abbot of Holy Cross to have been elected by the votes of the monks; and even he was an exception in that period of papal appointments. Abbot Cogan himself, the predecessor of Bernard Lahey had been appointed by apostolic authority; so there is no reason for holding that Bernard Lahey could not have been appointed abbot in like manner and every reason for thinking that he was. Canon Power accepts Bernard Lahey as an abbot without question. The fact that 'Edmund Lahey' is registered in 1704 as pretended popish priest of the parishes of Holy Cross and Templebeg (the latter being part of the ancient Holy Cross) tends to confirm the supposition that he was, in fact, abbot. On the other hand the record of his death preserved in the final pages of the *Triumphalia* and probably entered therin by the last monk of Holy Cross styles him simply Brother Bernard Lahey, and makes no mention of the abbatial office of dignity. It has been stated, indeed that Bernard Lahey was appointed parish priest of Holy Cross in 1675 by Abbot Cogan, but no authority has been adduced for that assertion. Out knowledge of this Cistercian is indeed, meagre. We learn from the particulars recorded at this registration in 1704 that he was then fifty-six years of age. He must have been born, therefore, about 1648 and an entry in the *Triumphalia* which was made by a hand of later date than Malachy Hartry's tells us that 'Bernard Lahey received the habit in the monastery of Holy Cross when the Reverend Lord Thomas Cogan was abbot in November 1671'. He was ordained the following year at Liseene by archbishop William Burgett of Cashel. The last recorded 'miracle' wrought by the relic of Holy Cross is stated to have occurred on 29 October in the year 1723, when Fr Bernard Lahey applied the relic to a certain Edmund Hackett of Kilrush who had been deaf and dumb for eighteen months and was cured by the application of the relic. It is to be noted that in this case Fr Bernard, who was then parish of Holy Cross, is not styled abbot, nor is there any hint in the few entries that relate to him in the manuscript that he ever at any time bore that title or held the abbatial office. His death is recorded in another entry which tells is that he passed away on 28 April 1724. Before he died he made a will in which he left 'all that he had got by Fr Thomas Cogan, his predecessor, to Fr Edmund Cormick'.

Fr Edmund Cormick, the last monk of Holy Cross and the man who had the melancholy distinction of being the last of the Irish Cistercians of the ancient regime, was overseas, probably in Spain, when Abbot Bernard Lahey died. Returning to Holy Cross he claimed, the office of parish priest by right of his succession, but this claim was not recognised by the archbishop who appointed one of his diocesan clergy, Fr John Dorroney, to the charge. Though Fr Cormick's claim was disallowed by the archbishop it is not impossible that he was titular abbot of Holy Cross. In the absence of any documentary evidence for or against it is impossible to give a decisive judgement; but it is known that he himself claimed, to be abbot and that he was generally regarded as abbot by the people of the neighbourhood It is of some significance that in the returned for the dioceses of Cashel and Emly in connection with the *Report on the State of Popery in Ireland* (1731) we find the following entry for Holy Cross and Ballycahill: 'Edmund Cormick, commonly called Ld. Abbot of Holy Cross'. How Edmund Cormick continued to live at Holy Cross we do not know. It is generally held that Fr Bernard Lahey was succeeded as parish priest of Holy Cross by Fr John Dorroney, who is supposed to have been already in possession when Fr Edmund Cormick appeared on the scene. We have the evidence of the *Report in the State of Popery in Ireland* in proof of fact that this was not the case. The priest in charge of Holy Cross, according to that report, was Edmund Cormick who also afficiated in Templebeg and Ballycahill, both members of the ancient parish of Holy Cross. There is no mention in the report of Fr John Dorroney. It would appear then that up to at least 1731 Fr Edmund Cormick acted as parish priest of Holy Cross and was commonly held by the people of the parish to be abbot of Holy Cross. The date of his death is unknown. He was certainly dead by 1752 when Archbishop James Butler who was coadjutor to his kinsman Archbishop Christopher Butler of Kilcash, made an episcopal visitation of the parish of Holy Cross on 21 June of that year. During the course of that visitation the parish priest exhibited certain effects which he said had been given him in the house of a Mr Thompson where he states, 'I found all the effects of the abbey that the last Cistercian there had left after his death.' Among the effects were a particle of the True Cross and 'one old book in parchment entitled *Triumphalia Cronologica de Cenobia Sanctae Crucis, etc.*' No mention is made in the Cashel Visitation book of the date of the death of Fr Edmund Cormick. That he was alive in 1731 is certain, and the report on the state of popery gives us to understand that he was then acting as parish priest of Holy Cross. Walter Harris, who edited the works of Sir James Ware, testifies that he had the manuscript of the *Triumphalia* in his possession for a time by courtesy of 'the officiating Romish priest of the parish of Holy Cross who did me the favour to lend them to me in the year 1733'. It is not clear from this account whether by the words 'officiating Romish priest' Harris meant Fr Dorney or the Cistercian Fr Edmund Cormick. If the latter, he may have died some time between 1733 when he was certainly officiating in the abbey and 1737 when, as the diocesan registers of Cashel and Emly show, he was administering the sacrament of Baptism in the parish of Holy Cross. On the other hand he may not have died then; he may merely have lived on for some years in the 'wretched cabin' in the west range of the abbey. With the death of Fr Edmund Cormick the last link with the Cistercian Order was broken and the

Mellifont line was brought to an end after more than five hundred and ninety years.

By the providence of God the Cistercians were to return to Ireland, but more than three quarters of a century were to elapse before this happy restoration was accomplished. With the foundation of Mount Melleray on the slopes of the Knockmealdown mountains in Co. Waterford a new chapter was opened in the history of the Irish Cistercians, but that was still in the unforeseeable future when the last monk of the order was laid to rest in Holy Cross abbey. In the course of time the ownership of the old abbey passed from Butlers to John Armstrong of Farney Castle. John's son William acquired by marriage the estate near Roscrea called Mount Heaton which in 1878 became the property of the Cistercians and is now known as the abbey of Mount St Joseph. Thus time brings its revenge. There was to be a second spring too for the old abbey of Holy Cross itself. In 1703, James the second duke of Ormond, granted to Lt. General Frederich Hamilton the land and abbey of Holy Cross. In 1730 Hamilton rented the land to William Armstrong. In 1834 William Henry Armstrong of Mount Heaton, Kings County and Lausanne Switzerland, granted to Revd Charles William Wall (1780-1862) of TCD and later vice-provost of TCD, Holy Cross abbey and lands. Dr Wall commenced the valuable restoration work. In 1869 the Church of Ireland Disestablishment rent Act was passed. This empowered the Commissioners of the Church of Ireland to transfer all important buildings into the care of the State upon trust for preservation as National Monuments and that they were not to be used again as places of public worship. This included Holy Cross. By 1967 the restoration of the abbey church as a parish church was gaining local support. This required amendment of the Irish Church Act of 1869 by Dáil Éireann.

On 21 January 1969, a Bill was introduced into Dáil Éireann making provision for the restoration and reconstruction of the abbey church as the parish church of Holy Cross. By 23 April of the same year, the Bill had passed through all its stages and a few days later was signed by the President of Ireland. This happy event cleared the way for the work of restoration and reconstruction which has been in progress ever since. The church was rededicated to the Holy Cross on 29 September 1975 and formally reopened the following Sunday, 5 October. And here we may fittingly bring as close our history of the Cistercian abbey of Holy Cross of *Uachtar Lamhainn*, described by an unknown medieval poet as that 'full house with many new clean storeys wherein can meet all the men of Eire'. '*Teach lán na leibheann nuaghlann dál fear nEireann san eanbhrugh; ainm De do mhór a mhiorbhaal, siodhbhrugh ógh a agus éarlumh.*'

APPENDICES

ABBOTS OF HOLY CROSS

Gregory
Adhamh d. 1206.[1]
Isaac
Constantinus
Daibhi (O Cathasaigh ?) bishop of Emly 1275.[2]
Peter O Conaing fl. 1280.[3]
Maurice Mac Amrech
Richard Ó Finnore
Thomas O Gorman fl. 1340.[4]
David fl. 1364-8.[5]
Phillip fl. 1399.[6]
Dionisius (O Conaill ?) fl. 1409.[7]
Fergal O' Heffernan elected 1423, vivens 1432, d. before 1448.[8]
Hugh O'Grady elected 1448, resigned after one day.[9]
Dermot O'Heffernan elected 1448, deprived shortly after, abbot *de facto* 1455?[10]
William (O Conaill ?) elected 1450, d. before 1455.[11]
Mathew O Mulryan elected 1455; *vivens* 1490.[12]
William O Dwyer elected before 1495, ?d. 1533.[13]
Phillip elected 1533, last pre-reformation abbot.[14]
John O'Mulryan
Bernard Foley 1603-7.
Luke Archer 1611-44.
John Cantwell 1645, died *c.*1665.
Thomas Cogan fl. 1671, d. 1700.
Bernard Lahey ? d. 1724.
Edmund Cormick ? 1725, d. before 1752.

LANDS OF HOLY CROSS

The remains of the archives of this abbey include the foundation charter granted by Dómhnall Ó Briain, king of Limerick, as well as an inspeximus of a confirmation of the same granted by John, lord of Ireland and count of Mortain. Dómhnall Ó Briain's charter is reproduced in facsimile in the second volume of Gilbert's *National Manuscripts of Ireland,* and in the Revd Denis Murphy's edition of *Triumphalia Sanctae Crucis.* Thirty-seven deeds

---

1 F. 4. 23, f. 127v. 2 CDI 1252-81, 199. 3 *Calendar of Justiciary Rolls Ireland,* ed. J. Mills (Dublin, 1905), I, p. 135. 4 F. 4. 23, f. 127v. 5 COD, ii, 84; F. 4. 23, f. 127v. 6 IMED, 12-3; COD, ii, 242. 7 Rot. Pat., 189 (no. 11). 8 Brady, ii, p. 127; Hoberg, p. 186; IMED, 26; CPR, 11, pp 2-4. 9 CPR, 10, p. 389; 11, p. 200. 10 CPR, 10, p. 389; 11, pp 2-4, 199-200. 11 IMED, 29-30; cf. CPR, 11, pp 2-4. 12 CPR, 11, pp 199-200; Brady, ii, p. 248. 13 IMED, pp 168 ff. 14 Ibid., pp 71, 95-6.

from the archives have been calendared or printed in full by Curtis and White in the COD and IMED. The texts printed in full number twenty-five exclusive of the charter. The text of John's charter of confirmation contained in an inspeximus made in 13/14 Edw. II is printed in full in CPI, p. 9. The archives of Holy Cross came to the earls of Ormond with the grant of the monastic property in 1563. The deeds include grants of lands, tithes, rectories and vicarages to the abbey, letters of protection to the abbot and monks from the earl of Ormond, agreements and indentures between the abbot and convent and others as well as leases of the monastic property. Included is the only specimen of a Cistercian visitation card to survive from pre-reformation times in Ireland. This document, which has been neglected by scholars, gives us a last glimpse of Irish Cistercian government in action just three years before the dissolution of the monasteries. Another unusual document is an agreement drawn up between an outgoing and an incoming abbot, the latter, not yet an Cistercian at the time, as to the terms of the former's resignation. Owing to the fact that the abbey was not formally dissolved but became a provostry with the abbot as provost the archives come down to the year 1561 when the provost or abbot, Philip Purcell, made over to Thomas Butler, earl of Ormond, the life interest in the property of the dissolved monastery which he himself had obtained in a royal grant. The Ormond Deeds contain a letter from Queen Elizabeth (paper copy) dated 20 November 1562 ordering letters patent to be prepared for the grant of the property to the earl, and the grant itself, dated 3 October 1563, is also extant. Ten abbots and four monks are named in the deeds that survive.

About the same time in which Kilcooly received its charter from Dómhnall Ó Briain, the same king issued a charter to Holy Cross abbey by which he gave and confirmed to the monks for ever the lands designated therein. Eleven places are named in the charter, but only three of the eleven can be identified with any degree of certainty. One of these, the first place named in the charter, was the site of the abbey and the name by which it was then known continued in use until the seventeenth century. It appears in the charter as *Cealluactairlamudni* while in King John's confirmation of king Dómhnall's charter it is called *Celluacturlaumun*, and in other medieval documents it appears under various forms such as Woctarlamand, Whoghtyrlawyn, Waterlanyn and Ochterlawyne, to mention but a few of the many which suggest that the Irish form was probably *Cell Uactair Leamhain*. The monastery became known as that of the Holy Cross of Weghtyrlayn, but by the seventeenth century the old name had been dropped from the title and the place is now called simply Holy Cross. Six or seven of the place-names set down in the charter were evidently based on the names of families settled on the lands or owning the various lands before the coming of the monks. All the names recorded in the charter have now become obsolete with the exception of Bali Icheallaich which still survives as Baile Ui Cheallaigh or in its anglicised version Bally-kelly the name of a townland in the barony of Middlethird. The Culletti of the charter appears in later documents under various forms such as Culetty, Couletty, etc., and though the name itself has long since disap-peared the lands can be identified from a description given of their situa-tion in a medieval document. They would seem to be represented today by the lands of Ballycamusk and Lisbook in the parish of Holy Cross and barony of Eliogarty. It is a strange fact that the majority of the designations recorded in the charter of King Dómhnall had already disappeared a cen-tury later. Although only three of the eleven denominations named in the charter can now be identified with any degree of certainly we may assume that the original lands are represented today more or less substantially by the parishes of Holy Cross and Rathkennan as depicted on the ordnance survey map and the townland of Ballykelly with part of Marshallstown in the parish of Ballysheehan. The townland of Beakstown, however, which at present forms part of the civil parish of Holy Cross was never part of the monastic lands. It was in the hands of the Purcell family in the thirteenth century and was still in their hands when the monastery was dissolved in the sixteenth century; but the rectory and vicarage of Beakstown had become impropriate to the abbey of Holy Cross in 1430 and it is in conse-quence of that impropriation that Beakstown appears as part of the civil parish of Holy Cross on the ordnance map.

Besides the lands in the immediate vicinity of Holy Cross abbey, now included in the parish of Holy Cross and the parish of Rathkennan and the townland of Ballycahill in the parish of that name, the monks of Holy Cross held a certain number of lands and granges elsewhere in the county. In the parish of Templebeg they held two separate groups of lands widely separated one from the other. The first of these two groups of lands was that of Kilcommon and Ballymacroy and Lestiakardin granted to the abbot and monks of Holy Cross by the bishop of Killaloe in the period 1216-31. These places are now in the diocese of Cashel. The names Lestiakardin and Ballymacroy have become obsolete but Kilcommon still survives. The other lands in this parish held by the abbot and convent of Holy Cross were those of Athsannoythit which they granted and to farm let to Malachy and Dónal Ó Molryan in 1353. These are probably to be equated with the lands of Synnathbothy (alias Symathbothy) which Robert Purcell held in capite of Edmund le Botiller in 1308. They must, therefore, have come to the monastery between 1308 and 1353. They are now represented by the two townlands of Athshanboe and a number of adjoining townlands in the parish of Templebeg, barony of Kilnamanagh Upper.

From a contemporary memorandum printed by Dr Newport White, we learn that in November 1431, Dermot O'Dwyer *sui nationis capitaneus* made a grant to Holy Cross of the lands of Rathkennan and Cillin

TABLE OF LANDS OF HOLY CROSS (TOTAL ACREAGE 12,596 ACRES, ALL IN CO. TIPPERARY)

Barony	Townland	Acreage	Parish
Eliogarty	Ballycamusk	590-2-27	Holy Cross, 6485-1-32
	Cloghane	266-2-34	
	Farneybridge	248-2-37	
	Glenreaghmore	3431-1-17	
	Glenreaghbeg	227-2-20	
	Grange	371-2-34	
	Holycross	641-2-01	
	Killeenyard	231-1-17	
	Lisbook	80-1-18	
	Lisnagrough	231-2-14	
	Monamoe	314-1-22	
	Newtown	303-0-05	
	Raheen	247-0-08	
	Whitefort	142-1-11	
Middlethird	Glenbane Lower	832-1-36	
	Glenbane Upper	395-1-06	
	Graignoe	588-1-31	
Eliogarty	Lisnagonogue	261-1-14	
	The Commons	180-0-00	Thurles, 180-0-00
	Garraun	564-0-26	Borrisleigh, 564-0-26
	Ballycahill	405-0-18	Ballycahill, 881-3-31
	Garranamona(part)	346-0-00	
	Moneydas	130-0-13	
Middlethird	Ballykelly(part)	200-0-00	Ballysheehan, 270-0-00
	Marshaltown(part)	70-0-00	
	Tobereadory	385-0-00	Geale, 385-0-00
Kilnamanagh Lower	Rathkennan	699-3-03	Rathkennan, 786-2-21
	Rathkennan Wood	86-3-18	
Kilnamanagh Upper	Athshanboe	152-0-10	Templebeg 1, 1380-3-26
	Athshanboe(Lau)	336-0-01	
	Cappaghclogh	66-1-13	
	Graceland	27-2-35	
	Gorteenadiha	30-2-03	
	Knocknalough Com	473-0-10	
	Knockmehill	213-1-13	
	Knockmehill East	17-3-05	
	Newtown	63-1-16	

Barony	Townland	Acreage	Parish
	Church Quarter	280-0-20	Templebeg 2, 1662-1-05
	Kilcommon	237-2-10	
	Knocknakill	276-0-16	
	Knocknabansha	500-3-04	
	Loughbrack	367-2-35	

Conferad. However, Rathkennan is enumerated among the lands held by Holy Cross in the latter half of the preceding century (c.1275-81) and may have formed part of the original endowment of the abbey. In that case, the memorandum of 1431 should be understood as referring not so much to an original grant on the part of Dermot O'Dwyer as to an act of restitution, a surrender of a claim to lands which had at one time belonged to the abbey but which in the course of time had come into the possession of the lords of Kilnamagh. In 1429 the vill of Ballycahill was granted to the abbey by the earl of Ormond and in 1432 Nicholas White of Thurles granted all his lands and tenements in Tubberadory to the monks who, in 1527 received another grant in the same area from Walter Walch, provisor of the Common Hall, Cashel. This is the last recorded grant of land made to the abbey of Holy Cross. One other parcel of land deserves to be mentioned – a place called in a deed of 1558 the villata of Garrane Rathenohan in Borrisleagh. This is better know today as the townland of Garraun near Two Mile Borris, Thurles.

The total lands enumerated here as belonging to the abbey of Holy Cross amount to a little more than 12,500 acres. From the medieval Register of Stephen of Lexington we learn that when that able administrator made his visitation of the abbey in 1228 he found that Holy Cross then possessed lands variously estimated as containing thiry or forty or even more plowlands. Bearing in mind that these figures probably relate only to arable land it is reasonable to assume that the sum total of lands held by Holy Cross at the period of the visitation might well amount to ten thousand acres or more. Taking into account the various grants of land made to the abbey between the period of Stephen's visitation and the suppression these figures would agree tolerably well with the estimated acreage of the monastic estates at the time of the dissolution of the abbey, about 12,600 statute acres. They suggest that over the centuries the lands of Holy Cross remained substantially as they were in the early days of the foundation.

Sources

Charter from Dómhnall Ó Briain *c.*1182-6. Facsimiles of this charter have been published in FNMI, ii, p. lxii and Hartry. Original grant of Holy Cross to Ormond is not in National Library. An English summary may be found in COD, i, pp 2f. A confirmation of this charter by John, Lord of Ireland made *c.*1195-9 has been printed in full in CPI, p. 9, and English summary appears in COD, i, p. 7. For the identification of the various lands and granges the following sources have also been used: COD, i, 22, 63; ii, 7, 50, 66; v. 204, 220, 222, 226, 304 (nos. 325-6), 311-12; vi, 42, 90, 169. IMED: xii (Postscript), 5, 19, 22, 23, 26, 29, 44, 67, 71, 86, 94, 96, 98, 269-70. Fiants Elizabeth: Nos. 563, 3414, 3514. CPR, 5 & 6, Philip & Mary (Morrin, i, p. 394 (no. 2) and 5 Elizabeth (ibid., p. 481, no. 84). No details are given but the queen's letter dated 20 November 1562 and the letters patent dated 2 October 1563 by which the grant of Holy Cross abbey with its lands, temporalities and spiritualities was made to Thomas Butler, earl of Ormond, are preserved in the collection of Ormond Deeds in the National Library of Ireland.

Thirty-seven deeds from the archives have been calendared or printed in full by Curtis and White in the COD and IMED. The texts printed in full number twenty-five exclusive of the charter. The text of John's charter of confirmation contained in an *inspeximus* made in 13/14 Edw. II is printed in full in CPI, p. 9. The archives of Holy Cross came to the earls of Ormond with the grant of the monastic property in 1563. The deeds include grants of lands, tithes, rectories and vicarages to the abbey, letters of protection to the abbot and monks from the earl of Ormond, agreements and indentures between the abbot and convent and others as well as leases of the monastic property. Included is the only specimen of a Cistercian visitation card to survive from prereformation times in Ireland. This document, which has been neglected by scholars, gives us a last glimpse of Irish Cistercian government in action just three years before the dissolution of the monasteries. Another unusual document is an agreement drawn up between an outgoing and an incoming abbot, the latter, incidentlally, not yet a Cistercian at the time, as to the terms of the former's resignation. Owing to the fact that the abbey was not formally dissolved but became a provostry with the abbot as provost the archives come down to the year 1561 when the provost or abbot, Philip Purcell, made over to Thomas Butler, earl of Ormond, the life interest in the property of the dissolved monastery which he himself had obtained by a royal grant. The Ormond Deeds contain a letter from Queen Elizabeth (paper copy) dated 20 November 1562 ordering letters patent to be prepared for the grant of the property to the earl, and the grant itself, dated 3 October 1563 is also extant. Ten abbots and four monks are named in the deeds that survive.

Other sources are the Civil Survey (Tipperary), vols. i and ii (parishes of Temploughter and Templebeg, Holy Cross, Rathkennan and Borrisleagh (now Two Mile Borris) and of the OS barony maps (Middlethird, Eliogarty, Kilnamanagh and Kilnalongurty) as well as of the Composite Map of Tipperary Sheets 33, 34, 39, 40, 41, 42, 46, 47, 52, 53.

Additional information concerning this abbey is contained in the Memoranda Rolls, transcripts (PRO Dublin [National Archives]), the Calendar of Justiciary Rolls, Ireland; the Register of Stephen of Lexington; the Harris Collectanea (vol. xiii); and TCD, MSS. F4. 23 including the names of some abbots not elsewhere recorded; Brady; CPR; Harl. Chart. 75 A 5; Hoberg; Rot. Pat; Tax.I.Cist; VM; Canivez.

NOTES ON THE ARCHITECTURE OF HOLY CROSS

Roger Stalley has stated that 'an unusually ornate church and a remarkable array of monastic buildings made Holy Cross the most distinguished monuments of fifteenth century Ireland.'[1]

In the first volume of his Ordnance Survey Letters of 1840 on the antiquities of the county of Tipperary John O'Donovan quotes from Gough's Camden.[2]

Holy Cross was a celebrated abbey founded on the river Suire two miles southwest of Thurles, by Donagh Carbragh O'Brien, king of Limerick. The remains are of beautiful Gothic and among them is a tomb of the person who brought hither a piece of the true cross, 1557. The architecture of this building is uncommonly fine.

In the centre is a high square tower and at the east end a small chapel twenty four feet by twenty one with an arched roof, and on the south side the tomb of the founder with a cross but no inscription; between the nave and steeple is a space of twenty one feet and a half broad and thirty long, divided from the nave by an arch and supposed to have made part of the Church. On its south side are two chapels about ten feet square, between which is a double row of Gothic arches, supported by twisted pillars about two feet four inches asunder. Here the ceremony of waking the monks was performed and the holy relique kept as observed by Mr. O'Halloran (and after him by Doctor Campbell). Mr. O'Halloran has engraved it in a plate, which by mistake is reversed. On the north side of the choir are two other chapels, each seven feet by eleven, like the

1 Stalley, *The Cistercian Monasteries of Ireland*, p. 245. 2 *Letters: Antiquities of County of Tipperary*, i (1840), Flanagan reproduction, 1930, p. 172.

former. Between these and the opposite side aisle the whole is
arched by opposite the south chapel is an open space with a staircase leading to the steeple in whose north angle are steps to the top.
The nave is fifty eight feet by forty nine, with aisles reaching to the
choir.

Nothing could have been more highly finished than the steeple
and chapels, which are built of marble and limestone, but the nave
with its aisles and the adjoining chapels are miserably mean.

O'Donovan then quotes Archdall:[3]

The architecture of this erection was uncommonly fine; the building consists of an high steeple nearly square, supported on each
side by a beautiful Gothic arch and in the centre by a great variety
of ogives passing diagonally from each angle etc; on the east side
thereof is a small chapel twenty one feet in breadth and twenty four
in length. The roof is arched and beautifully supported by a
number of ogives from the sides and angles. On the south side is a
gothic tomb which according to O'Halloran is that of the founder
with a cross thereon but inscription; the tradition of the place however informs us that this tomb was erected for the good woman who
brought the holy relique hither; between the nave and steeple is a
space of twenty one feet six inches in breadth and thirty in length.
Detached from the nave by an arch which we suppose made a part
of the choir, the nave is forty nine feet broad and fifty eight long; on
each side is an arcade of four arches with lateral aisles which pass on
either side of that part we conclude to have been the choir; the
entrance is by a door at the west end, under a large window. On the
south side of the choir are two chapels, each about ten feet square
and both of them arched and supported as the other parts of the
building; between these are a double row of gothic arches supported by twisted pillars, each distant about two feet four inches
from the other; here the ceremony of waking the Monks was perfomed and not where the holy relique was kept, as remarked by a
respectable writer, in a plate which by mistake is reversed; on the
north side of the choir are two other chapels, each of them seven
feet long and eleven broad with roofs supported in like manner as
the others, and between these and the opposite lateral aisle the
whole is arched but opposite the south chapel there is an open
space with a large flight of stairs leading to the steeple etc., in the
north angle of which are stairs which ascend to the top.

3 MH, ii, p. 658.

The difference in the work of this Monastery is very extraordinary; nothing could have been more highly finished than the steeple and chapels, which are built of marble and limestone, yet the nave, the aisles and adjoining ruins are miserably mean. On the south side the ruins cover a considerable space.

The river Suire which before it reaches the sea is so amazingly extensive flows near the ruins of this Monastery in a small stream. A parish church with a few wretched cabbins are the only remains of a once celebrated town.

John O'Donovan in his *Ordnance Survey Letters* gives us an idea of the architecture of the abbey of the Holy Cross, as he saw it in the middle of the nineteenth century:

This tower is supported by four arches, of which the eastern and western are of the same dimensions and characteristics and measure twenty feet in width and about twenty five feet in height. The northern and southern arches are of equal dimensions, being ten feet seven inches in width and about twenty one feet in height that is, four feet lower than the other two.

The choir of this abbey is forty five feet long and twenty two feet ten inches in breadth. The east window is pointed, remarkably small for such a building as this. It is only ten feet three and three-quarter inches in width and about sixteen feet in height!! It is constructed of chiselled limestone and divided into six days by stone mullions ramified above and forming twenty five compartments of different forms (figures).

I take this arch and the wall in which it is to be only a few centuries old. It looks quite modern and is very mean in its style of architecture. It was probably built since the Reformation. From the face of the western division of the choir arch to the west gable of the nave measures ninety five feet. The breadth of the nave is twenty three feet in breadth and extend all the length of the nave, that is from the choir arch to the west gable.

The west gable contains a pointed doorway constructed of cut limestone and over it a large pointed window divided into six bays by stone mullions ramified above and forming ten compartments.

On the north side of the choir is a tomb of the O'Fogartys, Chiefs of South Ely or Elyogarty, adopted by Mr Lanigan of Castle Fogarty, now the representative of that ancient family, as his own family tomb and he is justly entitled to it. The inscription on this tomb is in the Black Letter and now much effaced; it begins:*Hic jacent discreti homines St Donat O'Fogarta et Ellena Porsell Uxor ejus qui obiit A.D. MCCCCC.*

Opposite this is the beautiful tomb of the Good Woman who is supposed to have obtained the piece of the true cross which was preserved in this abbey.

Tradition says that the son of this good woman, while he was performing a Station at Tobernamnamaha in the Townland of Ballynahow in the Parish of Ballycahill, was murdered by O'Fogarty of Castle-Fogarty, and that when the Good Woman, his mother, came to hear of it she repaired to the abbey of Holy Cross and kneeling before the High Altar prayed that a *Braen Aillse* (cankerous) might fall on the tomb of O'Fogarty and continue to flow (*stillare*) until the family should become extinct; and she had no sooner finished her prayer than a drop commenced to fall from the ornamented roof over the High Altar on the family tomb of the murderer of her son; and behold! this drop continued to flow (fall) until about 50 years ago when the last heir of Castle-Fogarty was hanged in Clonmel for Ribbonism.

The last possessor of this ancient property was Dr Fogarty of Castle-Fogarty who died without issue; after his death the property would have devolved to this unfortunate youth already mentioned, who was his fraternal nephew, and when he was hanged it devolved to the father of the present Mr. Lanigan, the Doctor's nephew by his sister, who now enjoys it. His house speaks great wealth and magnificence.

In the south side aisle opposite the south Chapel is the tomb of O'Kearney inserted in the north wall with this inscription:

Monumentum hoc infra scripti fieri fecerunt 13, August 1646.

Hic jacet Barnabas O'Kearny filius Edmundi de Sancta Cruce et Joanna Ny Clery als. Kearny ejus uxor. Ille obiit die – mensis – .. vero dic mensis – A. Dni Quorum animabus propitietur Deus.

It was never finished because this family lost their property soon after.

To the south of the abbey Church was the cloister, a square area measuring ninety three feet from north to south and seventy four feet from east to west There were originally three ranges of cells, one at the west, another at the east and third at the south of this area, but the south one is now totally destroyed except the entrance gateway, which remains in tolerable preservation.

To the east of the eastern range of cells above mentioned are shewn the ruins of what is called the abbot's house and its appurtenances but it is not eas to know what it should be called.

The ruins of this abbey entirely disappointed my expectations; the architecture of the choir and side chapels is indeed truely beau-

tiful but they are not lofty nor magnificent but the nave and side
aisles are contemptible, but I am almost certain that this mean part
of the abbey is not more than four or five centuries old.

Canon Power's description of the remains in the 1920s is as follows:[4]

The surviving remains are of more than ordinary interest; some
unique features present themselves. Most important are the monastic church ruins. The cloister square is traceable but, except for the
church, there are no survivals of the surrounding buildings.
Outside the quadrangle – to the south-east and, between the main
block and the river, are extensive and confused remains of a mass of
buildings – the abbot's house, the guest chambers and the abbey
mill. The guest-house seems to have been unusually large; spacious
accomodation for visitators was, doubtless, a necessity owing to the
number of pilgrims drawn to the abbey by the fame of its relic.

The church is complete – with aisles and tower in addition to the
essential nave, chancel and transepts (each with two chapels). It has
a total internal length of one hundred and thirty feet minus a few
inches, with a width of twenty two feet across the nace, forty-three
feet six inches across the nave and aisles and seventy five feet two
inches across the transepts. Unlike Boyle and Dunbrody, Holy Cross
has retained little of its original architectural detail. Everything
points to an elaborate restoration of rebuilding in the fifteenth century. The Romanesque doorway in the south aisle has however survived from the earlier period. A spendid perpendicular window,
fifteen and a half feet high by ten feet six inches wide and divided
into six compartments by stone mullions, lights the nave from the
west There is a similar window, only of different design and somewhat more ornate, in the easter gable. Apart from the west window
the nave had no direct light; there were no clerestories, but there
was, an indirect light through the north aisle which had five good
sized windows. The south aisle had also one window on its west
gable. Across the nave, a greatway (thirty-one feet) to the west of the
transept crossing, extends a stone screen of the kind we have met
elsewhere. This is pierced by a pointed doorway. The tower of the
usual Cistercian type, has a groined ceiling with moulded ribs; in
plan, however, it is not square but oblong – the north-south sides
being the longer. There are various irregularities in the measure-
ments; it is probably that these are accidental and not intended as
architectural refinements: the north transept is longer and wider

4 Power, Mount Melleray manuscript.

than the south and even the width of the church varies. The north transept and its two chapels as well as the chapels of the south trasept have groined ceilings but the ceiling of the latter transept itself is ungroined. Separating the two south transept chapels is a delightful double arcade enclosing a space three or four feet in breadth; the purpose of this unique structure has been the subject of controversy. Its arches are supported by slender twisted columns of great beauty. As at Kilcooley and Corcomroe the high altar, of stone, remains still *in situ*; it measures ten feet in length, by three feet six inches broad and three feet in height. Somewhat similar in style to the singular arcade of the south transept just referred to is the monument in the chancel known as the tomb of the 'Good Woman's Son'. This, like the arcade, has occasioned a world of controversy for most of which the monk who wrote the *Triumphalia Chronologia* is indirectly responsible. Hartry, the monk in question, asserts that the object is a tomb but it is evident that it is really the *sedilia*. Identity of the 'Good Woman' to whose son the monument was stated to have been erected, is important, in connection with the further question: whence the famous relic came to the abbey. Opposite the *sedilia*, in the north side wall of the chancel is the alcove for the founder's tomb. At the south end of the south transept we have the night stairs leading up to the monks dormitories, two fine chambers extending the whole length of the easter range. Before we take leave of our church attention must be called to the mural paintings in the north transept. These are very remarkable but, covered as they are with a growth of algae, they are almost certain to escape the casual visitator's notice. They depict in colour a hunting scene, in which appear a crouching stag, two hunters with bows and arrows and a third individual blowing a horn and holding a hound in leash. Mural paintings in Irish church are exceedingly rare; we have them also in Knockmoy, Clare Island, St Audeon's in Dublin and the Franciscan Friary of Adare and this pretty well exhausts the examples.

The chapter-room is small, only eighteen feet by fifteen; it is evidently part of the original structure and the fact that it was never enlarged suggests that the community did not at any time much increase in numbers. The *Fratry*, or Day-room, is also of small size, but the cloisters are ample – about one hundred feet by seventy five, inclusive of the ambulatory. A very valuable survival is a small section of the cloister arcading which was found on the spot, and reerected. There are now no remains of buildings on the south side, but it is clear, from it foundations, that the refectory was parallel to the south cloister and not at right angles to the latter. Evidently, therefore, the original refectory was never enlarged in the west side of the quadrangle are cellars on the ground floor and the dormitory of the conversi overhead.

Attentive study of the ruin makes it clear that the church was practically rebuilt or extensively restored towards the end of the fourteenth century, and this though the domestic parts of the abbey were left untouched. As a matter of fact here and there can be traced outlines of some original lancet windows closed up at the restoration. Considering the abbey's association at a later with the House of Ormond it is likely enought that the restoration was carried out at the expense of the Butlers. This hypothesis would explain how the house in question came to take the place of the O'Briens as patrons of Holy Cross. The interior of the church has long been used as a public burial place – with pernicious results to buildings and sightliness. Of the many tombstones a few of the least modern bear inscriptions of some historical importance. In the niche for the founder's tomb ther is now inserted the grave monument, with sixteenth century blackletter inscription, of a Donal O' Fogarty and his wife Elena Purcell. Not far from the last, and in front of the high altar, is a slab inscribed in Roman capitals to the memory of Maurice O Kearney and his wife Elisia Purcell. These Kearneys were hereditary keeper of St Patrick's staff of Cashel. Another of them is commemorated in the seventeenth century mural tablet in the south aisle . He is Barnabas O Kearney, sone of Edmund keeper of the staff, and his wife was an O Cleary.

Apropos of inscription it is as well to note here that let into the south parapet of Holy Cross Bridge which spans the Suir just by the abbey, is a large slab with the arms of Butler and O Brien and bearing the following legend:

Ad Viatorem, Nicholaus Cowli me fabricavi(t)
Jacobus Butler Baro de Dunboyne et
D. Margareta Brien eius uxor Hunc
Pontem collapsum erexerunt suis
Insignibus adornarunt Anno Domini 1626.
[James Butler, baron of Dunboyne, and his wife Lady Margaret Brien rebuilt this fallen bridge (and) adorned it with their arms, 1626.]

The reader will notice that Richard Cowly, the stonecutter, knew his Irish better than to style a female, O Brien. By erection of the bridge the descendant of the sixteenth century granted of the abbey estate flattered himself, perhaps, that he expiated in part, or satisfied for, the treason of his ancestor.

The most recent authoritative observations on the Holy Cross Architecture are those of Roger Stalley in his monumental work *The Cistercian
Monasteries of Ireland.* He states:[5]

> The first impression of Holycross is of a compact, rugged building,
> lacking the finesse which one normally associates with Gothic.
> Modern battlemented parapets give the church a fortified air, a view
> enhanced by over-sized buttresses and a formidable crossing tower.
> But within this dour framework, there are individual features of
> interest and beauty. There is no need to quarrel with the opinion
> expressed by John Harden in 1797, when he described the abbey as
> 'an exquisite piece of antiquity' and 'a ruin the architecture of
> which is more than ordinarily elegant for this country and alone
> sufficient to reward a long ride.'

Stalley goes on to explain:[6]

> As a place of pilgrimage, Holycross was unique among the Cisterc-
> ian houses of Ireland and the rebuilding that began about 1430
> must, in some measure, be explained by a desire to provide a more
> worthy setting for its precious relics. The builders concentrated
> their activities on the eastern arm of the church and much of the
> original nave was left intact. The early work is recognisable through
> its rough rubble masonry, which contrasts with the well coursed
> blocks used for most of the reconstruction. A late twelfth-century
> doorway from the cloister survives at the east end of the south aisle
> and in the west wall there are vestiges of the lancets which prec-
> ceded the sixteenth-century reticulated window. The north arcade
> of the nave, with crude rubble piers unmoulded pointed arches,
> also remains from the original building. The late Gothic builders
> were, therefore, content to keep the structure of the old nave, while
> inserting new windows and two new doorways. It is strange that no
> clerestory was added at this time, for even with the huge west
> window, the nave is relatively dark.
>   At the east end, most of the late twelfth-century walls were dis-
> mantled, though some of the foundations may have been reused.
> The scale of the new work was not radically different from what
> went before and the height of the main vaults is only 28 feet (8.5
> metres). The chief change was the introduction of rib vaulting
> designed with various patterns of liernes and tiercerons. The ribs
> dies back into fine tapering springers, so that there is no need for

5 Stalley, op. cit., p. 113.   6 Ibid., pp 117-20.

responds against the wall. The interior is thus unencumbered by wall shafts and even the inner arches of the crossing rest on corbels rather than engaged columns. Although vaults were constructed over most of the eastern arm, for some unexplained reason a high vault was never erected over the south transept, one of many anomalies in the fifteenth-century building campaign.

Stalley also observes:[7]

> The style of Holycross reveals relatively little influence from contemporary English architecture. Indeed the general design is the very antithesis of English Perpendicular. There is no openess or clarity of space: the transepts seem cut off from the rest of the church and the solid walls at the east end of the nave inhibit diagonal vistas. The broad grid-like windows of Perpendicular are conspicuously absent and there is an overwhelming impression of thick inert masonry. The interest and beauty of the building lies not in any unified architectural impression but rather in a series of isolated features, particularly vaulting patterns and tracery forms. The inspiration for these stems from English architechture of the Decorated era, about a hundred years earlier. Even the corbels which support the arches of the tower and transept chapels have typically Decorated profiles. In the past it has been normal for architectural historians to accept this time lapse as an inevitable consequence of the abbey's provincial location, but it is hard to believe that after 1300 or 1350 it suddenly began to take a hundred years for English ideas to filter across the Irish Sea. The anachronistic style of Holycross, and of many other fifteenth-century Irish buildings, is better explained by historical factors.

He draws particular attention to the west range:[8]

> It is to Holycross that one must turn for the only complete west range, built as part of the remodelling of the abbey in the fifteenth century. It is a dour building in roughly coursed limestone, with relatively few windows. The ground floor was equipped with a barrel-vaulted passage, cutting through the range and serving as the main entrance to the cloister. Three barrel-vaulted cellars provided space for storage. All this is entirely characteristic of Cistercian practice, but the layout of the upper floor was less typical. It was planned as three private apartments and represents one of the most fascinating

7 Ibid., pp 120-1. 8 Ibid., p. 172.

pieces of domestic architecture in the country. Two straight mural staircases led up from the cloister and each chamber was furnished with its own garderobe, the latter neatly incorporated into a pair of turrets. Looking south was an attractive window with curved splays for window seats. Complete with fireplaces, these were spacious and confortable rooms. The basic concept of a hall of chamber with vaulted basement underneath had been a standard formula in domestic architecture since the twelfth century, but a suite of such rooms is far less common. It would be intriguing to know for whom the rooms were designed – whether as private flats for three of the brethren or for the more illustrious visitors to the shrine of the true cross?

Stalley is critical of recent restoration work:[9] 'In 1971-5 the abbey was restored as the local parish church, and since then many alterations have taken place in the claustral buildings. Some of the more recent work is of an unacceptably low standard for what is one of Ireland's outstanding national monuments.'

9 Ibid., p. 246.

PART FOUR

The abbey of Kilcooly

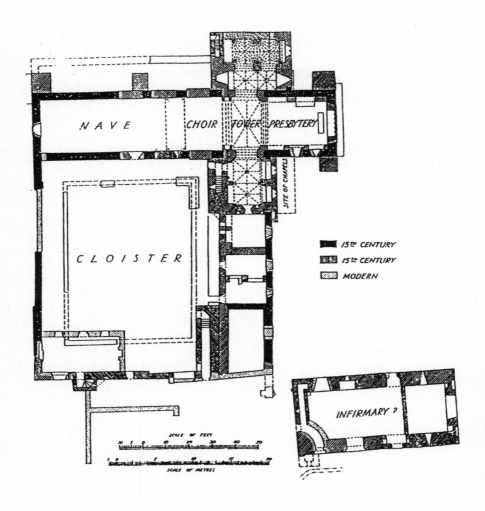

Plan of Kilcooly abbey, made by the Royal Archaeological Institute

18. FOUNDATION AND EARLY YEARS

The abbey at Baltinglass *(Vallis Salutis)* founded by Diarmuid Mac Murchadha, king of Leinster, in or about the year 1148, became the mother of four daughter houses, viz., Abbeymahon *(Fons Vivus)* in 1172, Jerpoint in 1180, Abbeyleix *(Lex Dei)* in 1184 and Rosglas or Monasterevin *(Rosea Vallis)* in 1189. Of the four daughter houses just named, one, at least would seem to have existed as a Benedictine monastery before it became affiliated to the Cistercian Order. This was the monastery of Jerpoint, one of whose daughter houses, Kilcooly *(de Arvicampo)* lay on the fringe of the great plain of Tipperary at the fool of the Slieveardagh plateau and has been described as 'probably the most beautiful Cistercian ruin in Ireland' although comparatively little known.[1] That it is so little known is due no doubt to the fact that, unlike the majority of our ruined abbeys, it stands in private grounds, and this also probably accounts for the fact that the abbey church is so singularly well preserved, in marked contrast to some of our better known abbeys.

The name Kilcooly, by which the monastery is popularly known derives according to the common opinion from the Irish *Cill Chuile*, meaning the church of the nook or angle. The name is supposed to refer to the fact that the site of the church lay in an angle formed at this point by the boundary line between the kingdoms (and dioceses) of Ossory and Cashel, now represented by the boundary between the counties of Kilkenny and Tipperary.[2] The name given by the Cistercians to the monastery and recorded both in the statutes of the general chapter and the official tabulae of the Order was *(monasterium) de Arvi Campo*, meaning the monastery situated in the plain of corn (a reference both to the fertility of the soil and to the Irish territorial name *Magh nAirbh*, on which the Latin name is undoubtedly based). From the charter[3] of Dómhnall Mór Ua Briain, king of Limerick (Thomond), it would appear that the abbey of Kilcooly was a rededication of an older monastic establishment founded originally by St Colman of Magh nAirbh, a decendent of Aenghus man Nathfraic, king of Cashel. In his charter the king states that the grant is made 'in reverence of Gregory Olanan, comharb of Magh Airbh' and that the lands granted, including the site of the monastery, were granted with the counsel of the said comharb as well as with the consent of the king's nobles.

The charter of Dómhnall Ua Briain, it should be noted, makes no mention of the Cistercian Order though it does make specific mention of the

1 Patrick Canon Power, 'The Cistercian Abbeys of Munster', *Journal of the Cork Historical and Archaelogical Society* 43, no. 158, p. 96. 2 An alternative explanation of the name has been proposed by Canon Power, viz., *Cill Cumhaill* (Coole's church or cell). 3 COD, i, p. 2.

Blessed Virgin and St Benedict. This suggests a Benedictine connection of some sort but not a Cistercian one. This reference to St Benedict and the absence of any allusion to the Cistercian Order is common to the charters granted to the abbeys of Killenny, Ossory, Kilcooly and Holy Cross. On the other hand the reference to the Coarb of St Colman in the Kilcooly charter implies a link up of some sort with pre-Norman Irish monasticism. Moreover, the terms of the charter show that the community of *B.M. de Arvicampo* was already in existence when the grant of land was made for the purpose, expressly stated, of constructing a monastery in honour of the said B.V.M. Since *Arvicampus* was a large area extending into Co. Kilkenny as well as Co. Tipperary, and since St Colman's original monastery of Daire Mór is thought to have been located in what is now the townland of Derryvella, in the said territory, about seven miles south west of what later became the abbey of Kilcooly, I would suggest that this pre-Norman community which had possibly adopted the Rule of St Benedict, was in all probability the twelfth century successor to the original community of St Colman of Magh nAirbh. The community seems to have been transferred to the new lands donated by Domhnall Mor Ua Briain at Kilcooly, the name of which place also indicates a pre-Norman monastic settlement. It is probable that Kilcooly was a monastic site which had been abandoned or had simply been left vacant by the extinction of the native Irish community which had occupied it at one time. This transference of land site (from Derryvella?) to Kilcooly was made with the assent of the then coarb of St Colman, Gregory Olanan, and the name Gregory again suggests that the coarb himself may have been a Benedictine monk and may, perhaps, have been the first abbot of Kilcooly.

In a paper published some years ago[4] I put forward the opinion that Jerpoint, the mother house of Kilcooly, was probably not originally a Cistercian foundation. Although Jerpoint was certainly in existence before the year 1170[5] the official *tabulae* of the Cistercian Order are practically unanimous in placing its foundation in the year 1180. If, then, we accept the testimony of the *tabulae* and admit at the same time that the abbey was already in existence before that date we must assume that Jerpoint was not originally a Cistercian house and consequently that the date 1180 given in the *tabulae* records, not its actual foundation, but rather of its affiliation to the Cistercian Order. Much the same may be argued concerning Kilcooly; not all the *tabulae* indicate the year 1184 as the date of that abbey's foundation and various other dates have been assigned some of which are manifestly too late. Sir James Ware assigns it to the year 1200, a date also given

---

4 C. O Conbhuidhe, ocso, 'The Origins of Jerpoint Abbey, Co. Kilkenny', *Citeaux* 14 (1963) 293-306.   5 Janauschek, no. cccclxix; Gearóid Mac Niocaill, *Na Manaigh Liatha in Eirinn* (Dublin, 1959), taibhle 1.

in the TCD MS. LS E.3.8, a seventeenth century compilation.[6] The Register of the Honour of Richmond, quoted by Ware.[7] gives the date 1209. Some authors attributed the foundation to Dómhnall Mór Ó Briain's son, Donnchadh Cairbreach.[8] and one Cistercian *tabula* places it as late as 1250.[9]

Since there are no witnesses to the copy of the charter preserved in the Ormond Deeds (National Library of Ireland) we have no means of fixing the actual date of the grant which the editor of the Ormond Deeds has tentatively ascribed to the year 1182; but in any case we may take the year 1184 to be the most probable date of the foundation of Kilcooly as a Cistercian house. All things considered, it seems best to accept the period 1180-4 as the period of Kilcooly's accession to the Cistercian Order whether by direct foundation from Jerpoint or otherwise, and to assume that the year 1200 marked the completion under Muircheartach Finn of the work begun by Dómhnall Mór Ua Briain. Donnchadh Cairbreach could not have been the founder of the abbey though he may have been a generous benefactor. He did not become king until 1210 and would not have been in a position to endow Kilcooly before that year. The most probable date of foundation, therefore, is the year accepted by Janauschek and backed by the authority of MS. *Dunensis*, namely 1184.

Comparatively few details have come down to us of the history of Kilcooly abbey. It had indeed, for the most part an uneventful history. Unlike many of its contemporaries, the abbot of Kilcooly was not a great temporal lord who sat among the peers in the Anglo-Irish parliaments and councils of the Pale. The monks seems to have been occupied exclusively with their monastic duties and rarely do we find mention of the abbey in the annals. Only once does there seem to have been anything like internal trouble of a serious nature, and that was during the so-called Mellifont Conspiracy[10] in the first quarter of the thirteenth century when a general breakdown of discipline occurred among the Irish communities of the *generatio Mellifontis.*

The first mention of the abbot of Kilcooly in the statutes of the general chapter is found under the year 1201. At that period William Marshall,

---

6 Sir James Ware, *Coenobia Cisterciensia Hibernia,* reproduced by Gilbert in his edition of the *Chartularies of St Mary's Abbey, Dublin,* ii. For the notice of Kilcooly, see p. 236.   7 Ware, op. cit., in Gilbert's *Chartularies,* ii, p. 236.   8 Such authors seem to labour under the impression the Domhnall Mor Ua Briain was succeeded immediately by his son Donnchadh Cairbreach. This is not the case. Domhnall was succeeded by Muircheartach Finn who reigned until 1210 when he was succeeded by Donnchadh Cairbreach. If the abbey were founded in 1200 or even in 1209 it would have been founded not by Donnchadh but by Muircheartach. However, the foundation by Domhnall Mor admits of no doubt, although it should be noted that the actual deed preserved in the National Library of Ireland has been deemed from a study of the handwriting to belong to a later period than the twelfth century and consequently cannot be the original document.   9 Kongelige Bibliothek, Kobenhaun, Cod. Thott. 138. This is a late fifteenth-century MS. from the monastery of Ijssellstein in Holland.   10 For the Mellifont Conspiracy, *Registrum.* A translation in English is available by Professor Barry W. O'Dwyer

earl of Pembroke, was anxious to found a Cistercian monastery in his territory and had petitioned the general chapter to that effect. The abbots of
Dublin and Mellifont were entrusted by the chapter with the task of
making inquiries into the matter and, as neither of these abbots was present at the chapter that year, the abbots of Jerpoint and Kilcooly were
directed to communicate the commission to the absent ones.[11] They
appear to have taken the direction of the chapter lightly, for at the next
year's session they were both punished for failing to communicate the
chapter's mandate to their fellow abbots of Dublin and Mellifont. As neither of them was present at the chapter of 1202 the abbot of Clairvaux was
directed to notify them that the general chapter had imposed a penance
on them for their neglect of its ruling. They were to perform for three
days the penance enjoined by the Rule for those *in levi culpa*, being commanded to fast on bread and water for one of the said days and forbidden
to enter the abbatial stall for forty days.[12]

Our next notice of Kilcooly is in connection with the Irish visitation of
Stephen of Lexington, abbot of Stanley (England), in 1228. Baltinglass
abbey, the mother house of Jerpoint, was one of the houses most deeply
involved in what came to be known as the Mellifont Conspiracy, and its
daughter house shared its guilt. In 1217, the abbot of Jerpoint as well as
the abbot of Mellifont had been deposed by the general chapter, and
although we hear nothing of Kilcooly and its community at that particular
time, it is hard to imagine that they can have been unaffected by what was
happening in their mother house and in many of the other houses of the
generatio Mellifontis. On 9 May 1228, Abbot Stephen of Lexington had completed a visitation of Holy Cross and was on his way to Kilcooly when he
had a narrow escape from death at the hands of a party of robbers in the
vicinity of the abbey.[13] It is unlikely that he made a regular visitation of
Kilcooly at this juncture; but in a letter written to the prior and convent of
the monastery which, though undated, appears to have been penned in
the autumn, Stephen announced that he had deposed their abbot because
of his neglect of his house and his disobedience. He gives some details in
the letter. For seven continuous years the abbot of Kilcooly had not made
an appearance at the general chapter. Moreover, by reason of his ill-health
he was almost always in the infirmary and unable either to rule the abbey
of to protect it from its enemies. Stephen indeed threatened him with
anathema unless he forthwith yielded to the decrees of the visitator: and
the community was warned that anyone who continued to recognise him
as abbot would incur the same anathema.[14]

under the title of *Letters from Ireland, 1228-1229* (Cistercian Publications, Kalamazoo,
Michigan, 1982); and an account in Irish of the whole proceedings of Abbot Stephen in 1228
under the title *Comhcheilg na Mainistreach Moire* (Baile Atha Cliath, 1968). 11 Canivez, 1201:
40. 12 Ibid., 1202: 32. 13 Registrum, no. xxxi. 14 Ibid., lxxxi.

On the occasion of his journey from Holy Cross to Duiske in May 1228, Stephen paid a visit to Kilcooly as well as to Jerpoint; but his letter to the prior and convent of Kilcooly written in the autumn shows that the visitation proper of that house had still to be made, for he states that he has commanded the abbot to return to his house in time to be present at this visitation. Stephen was in Munster in August and again in September. He spent some time in Clonmel and visited the abbey of Suir (Inishlounaght) on two distinct occasions, the last being towards the end of September when he made the regular visitation. He could, therefore, have made the visitation of Kilcooly either in August or September, and presumably did so.

After the deposition of the abbot, the abbey of Kilcooly seems to have remained vacant until the following summer, for Stephen, in a letter written on 21 May 1229,[15] in which he delegated his powers of visitation for that year to the abbots of Dublin and Duiske, expressly mentioned the fact that Kilcooly abbey was then vacant. His delegates were commanded to take counsel with the abbots and other prudent men concerning the state of that house, and after very careful deliberation were to act as they deemed most fitting, useful and advisable. Of the outcome of this latter visitation we know nothing. We may conclude, however, from analogy, that in due course an election took place and a dependable Anglo-Norman monk took over control of the destinies of the house, as had already happened in so many other abbeys during the course of Stephen's progress through Ireland. Despite the good intentions of Abbot Stephen and the attempted reformation of the house, and despite the fact that a new abbot had been appointed we find the general chapter of 1233 compelled to take cognizance of the fact that the new abbot, like his predecessor, was proving remiss in his duty of attending the general chapter. No less than eight of the Irish abbots were absent from the chapter that year so that the Capitular Fathes felt themselves obliged to punish the offenders by enjoining on them the penance prescribed by the *Usages* in such cases.[16] Six years later the abbot of Kilcooly was again an offender in this matter and was once again punished by the chapter,[17] while in 1246 he again received a penance for the same fault.[18]

The curtain now descends, and for twenty-seven years we catch not even one glimpse of the abbot or community of Kilcooly. In the year 1275 they appear once more in the records of the general chapter in consequence of a quarrel between the abbots of Kilcooly and Rosglas.[19] The cause of the quarrel is not stated nor is the outcome of the dispute known. It was referred by the chapter to the abbots of Maigue and 'Ysionay' (per-

15 Ibid., lxxxxiv. 16 Canivez, 1233: 47. 17 Ibid., 1239: 54. 18 Ibid., 1246: 55. 19 Ibid., 1273: 56.

haps Abbeyowney or Inislounaght), who were to act as arbitrators and who, it must be presumed, delivered a verdict in due course. Some years later (in 1279) the abbot of Kilcooly was himself commissioned by the general chapter to act in conjunction with the abbot of Tintern as referee in a dispute between the abbots of Suir and Dunbrody.[20] Here also the subject of Vallis Caritatis, a daughter house of Suir in the county of Waterford and parish of Fearann na Manach (Monksland), the lands of which, after its suppression by Stephen of Lexington in 1228, had been allotted to Dunbrody.[21] The abbot of Kilcooly received two more commissions in the same chapter being appointed in conjunction with the abbot of Odorney to act as referee between the abbots of Tintern and Owney,[22] and being associated with the abbot of Tintern as arbitrator in a quarrel between the abbots of Chore (Midleton) and Tracton.[23] The complainant seems to have been the abbot of Chore who, incidently, was a newcomer to the general chapter, his predecessor having been deposed by the chapter of the previous year in consequence of not having attended the general chapter for eight years.[24] This is the last notice of the abbot of Kilcooly contained in the statutes of the general chapter.

For a whole century (1279 to about 1380) only one recorded incident relieves the monotonous blank of the long years. This is noticed by Archdall in his *Monasticon Hibernicum* and is, indeed, the only incident recorded by that author in the history of our abbey. He informs us that, in 1341, Thomas O'Rourke was abbot and that he, by the assistance of Richard O'Brennan and Gerald Olycan, with William of Lisnamuck, chaplain, 'did seize by distress at Drumlonam, the chattels of James, son of Laurence Warner, to the amount and value of forty shillings'.[25] Judging by his name this abbot was a native of the district in which the abbey was located, for in the parish of Fennor, some at least of whose townlands formed part of the monastic possessions, there is a townland named Inchy-Rourke (Inse Ui Ruairc) in which can be seen in the middle of a bog the ruins of a castle said to have been built by a family of the O Rourkes who formerly dwelt in that area.[26] Thomas O Rourke in fact is the only abbot whose name has come down to us from a period preceding 1444. From a roll of amercements preserved in the Ormond Deeds, and of uncertain date but probably to be assigned to the period 1370-90, it appears that the abbot was fined a sum of two shillings for not supplying two armed horsemen as he was bound to do.[27]

The Ormond Deeds record that the abbot was summoned to the court of the Liberty of Tipperary to do suit in 1432.[28] The abbot thus summoned

---

20 Ibid., 1279: 80. **21** These lands were later restored to Suir which held them at the suppression of the monasteries in 1539-40. **22** Canivez, 1279: 79. **23** Ibid., 1279: 85. **24** Ibid., 1278: 19. **25** MH, p. 664. **26** OSL Tipperary, i, p. 160 (MS., p. 447). **27** IMED, p. 229. **28** Edmund Curtis, op. cit., iii, p. 91.

was possibly Thomas Bovil who was later succeeded by Philip O Mulbardayn alias O Brothe (O Brophy). Philip ruled he monastery for a number of years and was probably responsible for the rebuilding of the abbey after the disasterous fire of 1444. The fifteenth century was a century of wars and devastation in Ireland and this may help to account for the burning of the monastery by armed men. No record remains of the circumstances in which the abbey was destroyed, but the fact of the destruction is noted in a papal mandate for the year in question. The mandate, dated 14 February 1444,[29] is summarised thus:

> To David Ofoy, a Cistercian monk of the Blessed Virgin of Kilcooly (*de Arvicampo*), in the diocese of Cashel. Dispensation at his recent petition, containing that the said monastery had been almost completely destroyed and burned by armed men, that its abbot, Philip, has left it and betaken himself to England with two monks in search of food and clothing, and has given David, who is a priest, and on whose behalf James, earl of Ormond (ormonie), has also petitioned the pope, licence to serve any ecclesiastical benefices, to receive and hold any benefice in Ireland with or without cure, event won't to be governed by secular clerks.

How long the abbot remained in England we do not know, but he was certainly back in Ireland and established once more in his abbey by 1450.[30] It seems that in the meantime provision had been made of the abbey to Odo O Grady who, having resigned his charge of Holy Cross abbey into the hands of Patrick, abbot of Inislounaght, had been promoted to Kilcooly.[31] We later find him acting as abbot of Hore abbey in Cashel which he ruled at the time of his death.[32] It may be doubted if he was ever in possession of the rule and administration of Kilcooly; it is hard to see how he could have been in lawful possession since, as far as we know, Philip P Mulbardayn or O Mulwanayn alias O Brothe was the lawfully elected abbot in 1444 and continued to hold that office until his death in 1465. We have no evidence that he either resigned or was deposed. It is possible that following his departure to England after the burning of the abbey it was thought that the abbey had become vacant: and it may be assumed that on this supposition Odo O Grady had petitioned for and obtained provision of the abbey from the pope. If so, he must have relinquished his position on the facts of the case becoming known, and was then fortunate enough to have provision made to him of Hore abbey which may have been vacant at the time or may have become vacant soon afterward.

Perhaps the temporary intrusion of Odo O Grada into the abbacy of Kilcooly accounts for the fact that Abbot Philip began to feel his position

---

29 CPR, ix, p. 458. **30** Ibid., x, pp 511-12. **31** Ibid., ix, p. 389. **32** Ibid., xii, p. 12.

insecure and, in the year 1450, sought to fortify his tenure of the abbacy against all assault by seeking provision from the pope himself. It is true that he had been elected in accordance with the rule and constitutions of the Order, having obtained the votes of the community and having himself consented to the said election and been confirmed in the first place by the father abbot of the house and afterward by the abbot of Citeaux himself. He had been installed by their authority and had received from them full power to rule and administer the abbey. Nevertheless, instances are not wanting in the fifteenth century of the removal of abbots by papal mandate and the provision of their abbeys to others, sometimes indeed to men who were not even members of the order, even in cases where there was no doubt that according to the usage of the Cistercian Order they had been lawfully elected and had received the rule and administration in a legitimate manner. It was only natural that Abbot Philip should wish to assure himself that this should not happen in this case, and so we find in the papal registers a mandate dated 24 September 1450.[33]

> To the archdeacon of Cashel. Mandate at the recent petition of Philip Ymillbardan alias Ibrogaid, monk of the Cistercian monastery of Kilcooly (*de Arvicampo*) etc., containing that on the voidance of the said monastery by the death of Abbot Thomas Bovil the convent unanimously elected the said Philip who consented to the election and got it confirmed first by the father abbot of the said monastery and afterwards by the vicar general; in those parts of the abbot of Citeaux (the abbot of Dublin), by their ordinary authority, and in virtue of the said election and confirmation was induced into possession of the rule and administration and still exercises the care .therof; but now doubts whether the election and confirmation hold good – and if he finds Philip fit, to make provision to him of the said monastery, value not exceeding 16 marks sterling, still void as above; whether it be so void, or be void by the resignation of the said Thomas, or be void in any other way ...

For the next sixteen years Philip ruled the monastery and was the recipient of many papal mandates in 1454, 1455, 1458 and 1459. He distinguished himself by rebuilding the abbey church, although on a smaller scale. This restoration followed close upon the large scale rebuilding of the neighbouring abbey of Holy Cross with which, indeed, it has many affinities. We are fortunately able to identify the sculptor responsible for some, at least, of the beautiful carvings in Kilcooly abbey, for he has left his name on some of the monuments carved by him. The carving of the

---

33 Ibid., x, pp 511-12.

inscriptions on various monuments between 1526 and 1587 was the work of Rory O Tunny, son of Patrick, and it is more than likely that the earlier fifteenth century carvings were the work of his father. At one time the abbey church was furnished with aisles, but at the rebuilding the aisles were removed so that the present nave is aisleless. To this restoration, carried out under the direction of Abbot Philip we owe the beautiful west window in decorated style and the flamboyant east window as well as the sedilia in the choir, those of the abbot and the prior. These have been described by Professor Power in his article on Kilcooly abbey:[34]

> The abbot's seat ... and the prior's sedile opposite are beautiful pieces of stone carving; there is nothing like them in any other Irish abbey or church. The abbot's sedile on the epistle side, is the richer and more elaborate; its canopy (perpendicular) suggests that it is a comparatively late addition; the sides are deeply moulded and overhead stretch three splays of foliage ornament; overhead also, inset in the wall, are two slabs carrying coats of arms. Of the same period and style is the prior's sedile, on the gospel side, opposite, but here the decoration is less exuberant. These two lovely examples of late stone work corresponds to the two carved monuments of Holy Cross – the sedilia and the arcade. One can hardly help thinking that they are all from the same master hand and that the hand in question was an O Tunney's.
>
> The transepts are brimful of interest for the architect, with their graceful ribbed vaulting, their panelled reliefs, their elegant dado of undercut stonework and the handsome columns which separate the chapels, two in each transept ...

It is possible that the work of restoration begun under Abbot Philip was not completed until during the rule of his successor. Abbot Philip's own monument lies within the abbey, originally a floor-slab near the founder's niche in the presbytery. It has since been removed and inserted in a perpendicular position in the north wall of the presbytery.[35] It has been stated that the abbot's best monument is the abbey church itself, and with this judgement one cannot but agree. The inscription on the slab informs us that Philip O Mulwanayn (O Mulwardayn?), former abbot of the house, lies there together with his parents who performed many good works, spiritual as well as temporal. The date given is 1463. Despite the eulogy contained in the inscription Abbot Philip was by no means a model religious.

---

34 Power, op. cit., p. 97.   **35** It is to be regretted that the site of the tomb in which the abbot and his parents were interred has not been marked by some simple slab as was done in the case of tombs discovered during the excavation at Mellifont abbey, Co. Louth, during the 1950s.

If no worse he was certainly no better than more than a few of his contemporaries in those degenerate days. Dying in 1463, he was succceeded in the abbacy by his own son, and from thence almost to the eve of the suppression of the monastic orders in Ireland the abbey was to be ruled by members of the same family.

19. DECLINE AND DISSOLUTION

In 1458 William O Mulroardayn (O Molbardayn, *alias* Obroche) was dispensed by papal authority as the son of a Cistercian monk to be promoted to all even holy orders and to hold a benefice even with cure.[1] He was provided with a canonry in the diocese of Cashel and the prebendary of Fennor (Fynnowyr)[2] and was also made a canon of Ossory.[3] He was eventually received as a monk of Kilcooly and in due course was professed.[4] On the same day that the pope sent his mandate to the archbishops of Benevento and Cashel and the abbot of St Bernard without the walls of Valentia to receive O Mulroardayn he addressed a second mandate to the same abbot to the effect that learning recently of the death of Philip O Mulwardayn alias O Brothe, he had made a grant of provision therof to Malachy O Mulrian, a Cistercian monk of Holy Cross. The said Malachy having this day resigned to the pope the said grant before the letters thereabout had been drawn up, and the said monastery being still void as above, the pope, recapitulating the preceding mandate to cause William O Mulwardayn, *alias* O Brothe, to be received as a monk of Kilcooly, orders the above abbot, if he finds the said William (who was lately dispensed by papal authority on account of illegitimacy as the son of the said Philip, then professed of the said order, and an unmarried woman,) to be promoted to all, even holy orders, and hold any compatible benefices of any number and kind, and to resign them, simply or for exchange, as often as he pleased to be fit, to make provision to him of the said monastery, value not exceeding 16 marks sterling. The pope hereby grants him an indult to be blessed by any Catholic bishop, and dispenses him to rule, etc. the monastery, notwithstanding the said defect and that the said Philip was his father and in the church of the monastery ministered in the sacrifice of the altar, etc.[5]

Such were the circumstances in which William O Mulbardayn succeeded his father in the abbacy of Kilcooly. The mandate of 3 May 1464

1 CPR, xi, pp 344-5. 2 Ibid., p. 355. 3 Ibid., pp 355 and 505. 4 Ibid., p. 505, and vol. xii, p. 656. 5 Ibid., pp 505-6.

was the first step. The next is evidenced in a document dated the 26th of the same month recording the fact that[6]

> William O Mulwardayn alias O Brothe, principal, bound himself to the papal treasury for the annates of the monastery of the Blessed Virgin Mary of *Arvicampo* (Kilcooly) of the Cistercian Order in the diocese of Cashel, the fruits of which do not exceed sixteen marks sterling, vacant by the death extra curiam of Philip, and given to the same at Siena on 3 May of the sixth year of the pontificate, that is to say, 1464.

Another entry in the *Calendar of Papal Letters*, under the year 1468, noted that William Milwardayn (*sic*), canon of Ossory, had entered and made his profession as a monk of St Mary *de Arvicamp*.[7] On 7 March 1498, a papal mandate[8] was issued to the dean of the church of Ossory in favour of a John O'Mulwardayn alias Obroche, dean of the diocese of Cashel who had asserted that he was twenty three years of age and was a son of an unmarried man and an unmarried woman and 'marked with clerical character, otherwise however duly'. The pope had learned that Kilcooly abbacy was vacant and this mandate states that a Donat O'Mulwardayn alias Obroche had claimed, to have been lawfully elected abbot, which was confirmed by Kilcooly's mother-house, Jerpoint, but 'short of a two-year period'. Seemingly John wanted to become a monk and become abbot of Kilcooly and prior of St Nicholas. However there was an obstacle to overcome before he could achieve his ambitions. As a student John had stolen some money from a fellow-student and to make matters worse he perjured himself by swearing a denial 'even on a certain image'. The pope asks the dean to absolve John, to admit him to the monastery, give him the habit, and eventually appoint him abbot and prior. The pope also allows John to receive the abbatial blessing from any bishop of his choice.

A papal mandate of 11 April 1505[9] records that the Pope was informed 'that the monastery of Holy Cross, [*sic*] *de Arvicampo* (Kilcooly), O Cist, d. Cashel, was vacant *certo modo*, although John O'Mulnaidaio (also spelt O Mulnardayn, O'Muluadion) alias Obroche, who claims to be a monk, has detained the monastery'. The mandate instructs the recipients to convey the monastery to a Philip Gras, a cleric of the diocese of Ossory who claimed, 'to be of noble and baronial birth', if they find the monastery to be vacant. Another papal mandate of the same year,[10] 25 June 1507, seems to recognise 'John Y Mollundayn alias Ybroche, as abbot of the monastery de Arvicampo alias Kylcule, O Cist,' Seemingly the abbot in a petition to

---

6 *Obligations pro annatis* (Cashel); Costello MSS, in Maynooth. **7** CPR, xii, p. 656. **8** CPR, xvii, pt. 1, p. 574. **9** CPR, xviii, p. 20. **10** Ibid., p. 504.

Rome, accused a certain cleric, Edmund Mares, junior, a cleric of the diocese of Cashel of falsely representing the period of his taking the fruits of
a canonry of the church of Cashel and the prebendary of Croachan. The
mandate goes on to state:

> Abbot John alleges that he was provided by apostolic authority to
> the said monastery, then vacant *certo modo* after he had been other-
> wise duly given clerical tonsure notwithstanding his illegitimacy as
> the son of unnamed parents, and that he was dispensed by the same
> authority to have charge of the same and to exercise the govern-
> ment and administration of the monastery and that he is at present
> litigatory over it against a certain adversary of his.

In 1507, we find that on 10 July 'John Imollwardayn alias Ybroche'
bound himself to the papal treasury for the annates of the Blessed Mary of
Kilcooly (and two parish churches besides).[11] Here we have the record of
the accession of a new abbot to the monastery but no mention is made as
to whom he succeeded. It is likely enough, although, considering the
length of time that had elapsed, by no means certain, that at least one
other abbot interposed between William and John who was evidently
another member of the same family. There is no evidence to show that
John was a son of William as William was of Philip. We do not know how
long John remained in office. He was undoubtedly the abbot of Kilcooly
summoned to do suit at the court of liberty of Tipperary in 1508,[12] and we
find him witnessing an indenture made between Piers Butler,[13] earl of
Ormond, and his cousin, Edmund Butler fitz Thomas, lord of Cahir, in
1517 where the abbot's name is rendered John Ambardayn.[14] This is the
last mention we find of Abbot John.

In the *Calendar of Ormond Deeds*[15] one of the witnesses to an indenture
of 1530 is described as Brother Nicholas, son of the abbot of Kilcooly. On
the evidence it is impossible to say whether this Nicholas was a son of
Abbot John O Mulbardayn or of Abbot Thomas Shortall, the last of the
abbots *de regimine* of Kilcooly. On 5 April 1540, Abbot Thomas Shortall surrendered the abbey 'with the consent of the convent' to the representatives of Henry VIII.[16] Our knowledge of the state and size of the community
at that time is not merely meagre; it is practically nil. We know, indeed,

---

11 *Obligationes* (Costello MSS). 12 This is the Piers Butler whose tomb occupies what Canon
Power describes as the 'Founder's niche' in the presbytery. Piers Butler was not, of course,
the founder of Kilcooly abbey, but he was, like others of the Butler family, a generous benefactor and patron of the community. The tomb, which is of the altar type, is most beautifully
sculptured, bearing panels containing figures of the twelve apostles. Piers Og Butler died in
1526, but with his body there reposes in the same tomb the body of one of his descendants,
Visount Ikerrin, who was lieutenant-general of the Confederates a generation later. 13 COD,
iii, p. 332. 14 Ibid., iv, pp 45 and 50. 15 Ibid., p. 141. 16 Morrin, p. 59 (no. 38).

that Thomas Shortall was abbot, that John Brytte was parson[17] and that one other monk, John Colton by name, received a pension payable out of the monastic possessions. It is possible that these three men formed the entire monastic community at that time. John Colton's pension for a half year was twenty shillings Irish,[18] as was also John Brytte's,[19] but the former abbot received a pension of five pounds.[20] Like most of the suppressed monastic houses in the counties of Tipperary and Kilkenny, the abbey and its lands, its spiritualities and its temporalities, were granted to Thomas Butler, earl of Ormond and Ossory, by their Majesties, King Philip and Queen Mary.[21]

After the suppression of the abbey the regular succession of abbots came to an end. During the first half of the seventeenth century, however, there was widespread activity on the part of the Cistercians throughout the area. Kilcooly abbey as well as that of Holy Cross was occupied by a small community of monks at least for a time. The names of only two seventeenth century abbots of Kilcooly are known to us. The first of these two is Thomas Bernard O Leamy who seems to have been the first aspirant admitted into the partially restored abbey of Holy Cross by Abbot Bernard O Foulow on 3 March 1603. In 1606 he was sent to Clairvaux to obtain a more perfect training in the Cistercian life under the rule of Abbot Denis Largentier who, ten years later, was to introduce the reform known as the Strict Observance. Thomas Bernard O Leamy was appointed abbot of Kilcooly by papal provision in 1622 and continued to hold that office until his death in the Cistercian house of refuge set up by Abbot Luke Archer of Holy Cross in Kilkenny city. Dying on 25 July 1636, he was buried in his monastery of Kilcooly amid a great concourse of the clergy and many of the laity.[22]

A passing reference in a seventeenth-century Cistercian manuscript belonging to Holy Cross abbey[23] indicates the existence of a Cistercian community at Kilcooly abbey during the period 1641-50. This information is given quite incidentally by the writer who states that the first novice who presented himself to the community of Holy Cross 'amid the ravages of war such as Ireland had never seen before' was the Revd Fr John Stapleton. He goes on to say that this postulant received the habit of religion on 19 July 1645, and made his novitiate in the monastery of Kilcooly with another brother.[24] This statement is the only contemporary evidence we have of the existence of a community at Kilcooly during this period. It appears from this and other references in the manuscript history of Holy Cross that the professed members of that community lived then in the old

17 Ibid., p. 61. 18 IMED, p. 258. 19 Morrin, p. 61. 20 Ibid., p. 63. 21 Ibid., pp 384-6. This grant included the monasteries of Athassel, Jerpoint, and Kilcooly; and the friaries of Callan, Thurles, Carrick and Tullaghphelim (Tullow in Co. Carlow). It was made on 13 September 1558. 22 Hartry, pp 74f. 23 Hartry. 24 Ibid., pp 74f.

abbey by the Suir in a building erected in the midst of the ruins, celebrating divine worship in the church of the monastery the roof of which they had repaired for the purpose,[25] while the abbey of Kilcooly was used as a house for the novices. Indeed it is possible that the central novitiate formerly at Kilkenny had been set up at Kilcooly after the return of the monks to Holy Cross, and that novices for the various houses or missions throughout Ireland were trained at the abbey of Kilcooly. In the case of John Stapleton we have the evidence of Fr Malachy Hartry that after he had completed his novitiate at Kilcooly he returned to Holy Cross for his profession and later proceeded to Paris to enter on his studies.[26]

Thomas Bernard O Leamy was succeeded as abbot of Kilcooly by James Tobin whose name is found among the prelates who signed the declaration in the ecclesiastical congregation at Waterford on the 18 August 1646 condemning the peace made by the supreme council at Kilkenny with the earl of Ormond in that year.[27] The next mention of Abbot James Tobin is in a register of letters written by Cardinal Pamphilii to Monsignor Rinuccini, then nuncio in Ireland.[28] In this register there is a letter dated Rome, 6 April 1647, which contains the petition of Brother James Tobin (Fra Giacomo Tobia) of the Cistercian Order described as Abbot Kilcoull or Aruicampo to be allowed the use of the mitre and crozier. We do not know whether or not his petition was granted. What we do know for certain is that with the advent of Cromwell and the collapse of Irish resitance he, with his fellow abbots Cantwell of Holy Cross and Fitzharris of Inishlounaght, was thrown into prison where he languished for some time before being banished from the kingdom.[29] He never returned to Ireland for he died on the continent.

20. POST-DISSOLUTION

On 8 April 1540 the possessions of the abbey of Kilcooly were detailed as follows:

> The abbot was seized of this abbey containing a church and belfry, a cemetery, hall, dormitory, four chambers, a kitchen, two stables an

25 Ibid., p. 219.   26 Ibid., p. 115.   27 M.J. Brenan, OSF, *An Ecclesiastical History of Ireland* (Dublin, 1864) p. 459.   28 Vatican Archives: Secretariat of State: Inghilterra 9: 'Registro di Lettre scritte dal Signor Cardinal Pamphilij a Monsignor Rinuccini Nuncio in Hibernia', f. 28v; cf. Padraig Eric Mac Fhinn, 'Scribhinní i gCartlainn an Vatican', *Analecta Hibernica* 16 (1946) 1-280. The reference to Abbot James Tobin is to found on p. 44.   29 C. Ó Conbhuidhe, OCSO, *Studies in Irish Cistercian History* (Dublin, 1998), pp 163, 197.

orchard, two gardens, and sundry other closes, containing eight acres of land, within the precincts; also ten messuages, twelve gardens, two hundred acres of arable land with their appurtances, one hundred acres of pasture, ten of meadow, one hundred of moor, with an orchard and a water-mill in Kilcowley of the annual value of ...; six messuages, one hundred and forty acres of arable land, and one hundred of pasture and moor, with their appurtances in Grangeheise, annual value besides reprises, £3. 5s. 6d.; and six messuages, six gardens and forty acres of arable land, with the appurtances in the grange of Kilcowle, annual value besides all reprises, 9s.; the Rectory of Kilcowley, with its appurtances, annual value besides reprises, £8; the church or rectory of Ballylacken, with its appurtances, annual value besides reprises, ..., and the church or rectory and grange of Heishe, with its appurtances, annual value, besides reprises, £3 13s. 4d.; the said rectories being all appropriated to the said abbot and his successors, and with the before-mentioned lands, lie and are situate in this country. (Chief Remembrancer, quoted in Archdall's *Monasticon Hibernicum*, pp 664-5.)

A more detailed list of the possessions is given in the extent made at Kilkenny, 11 January 1541. This has been printed by Newport B. White in his *Extents of Irish Monastic Possessions, 1540-41*[1] and differs in many particulars from the details given above. The jurors, who were all (nine) 'true and lawful men of the county' found that 'the monastery church has from time immemorial been the parish church. There are no superfluous buildings, but only what are necessary for the farmer. These with two gardens and other accomodations contain 2 acres (lesser meaure), and are worth nothing above repairs.'

Much of the rent was in kind but money was evidently substituted in many cases. Amongst the customs to which the monks were entitled from the various vills and granges of Kilcooly, Graigehesse, Kilcooly Grange and Graigahesse village as well as the village of Grange were: 114 gallons of beer (a gallon of been being the equivalent of 2d.), 96 candles (a candle being the equivalent of 4d.), 114 cakes (a cake being the equivalent to 1d.) and 33 hens. The customs included 10 ploughdays, 6 cartdays, 14 boondays and 14 weeding-days, some tenants giving only two ploughdays, others four; none gave more than two cart-days; some gave ten boondays and 10 weeding days, others gave only four. Every farmer having seven or more sheep gave one (8d.), and similarly for pigs (20d.) but this last custom being uncertain was not reckoned. The church bell was stated to belong to the parishioners. A chalice and some old vestments were given by the

1 IMED, p. 323.

commissioners to the parish church and a silver cross was sold. This cross was one of the two crosses called 'holye crossys' which were sold for 67s. 6d., the other belonging to the abbey of Inishlounaght. The net total of the extent was £30. 18s. 3d. The rents were £28. 6s. 8d. with the deduction of 40s. for a pension to John Colodan (Colton), a monk of the monastery, the net total being thus £26. 6s. 8d. The sum realised by sale of the chattels of the monastery was £21. 11s. 6d.

The above named John Colton, one of the pensioned-off monks, remained as the first curate of the parish for which he was allowed the alterages i.e fees for marriages and baptisms.[2] In the Ormond Deeds, Colton describes himself in a receipt for the pensions as Sir John Colton, following an English medieval custom of claiming priesthood is the equivalent of knighthood.[3]

Dr D. Murphy sj is reported to have stated that two large bells, which tradition say belonged formerly to Kilcooly abbey, had recently (1875) been found and that they were in the possession of the then archbishop of Cashel, Dr Croke.

The parish became a crown living without royal provision. The tithes became the property of the earl of Ormond who leased them to Edmund Butler and John Walshe on 28 September 1583.[4] During Queen Mary's reign an attempt was made to restore the abbey to Cistercian hands but the earl of Ormond defeated it.[5] Queen Elizabeth granted the tithes of the parish to the Viscount Netterville, an old English Catholic peer.[6] In 1636 the earl of Ormond sold Kilcooly to Sir Jerome Alexander from Norfolk, England for £4,200. He had a stormy career, both as a judge and landowner.

Following the 1641 rebellion, the Cistercians returned to Kilcooly only to be dispossessed once more by Cromwell's army in 1650. Alexander recovered the Kilcooly estate in 1660 after the restoration of King Charles. He died in 1670 and is buried in St Patrick's Cathedral in Dublin. He left Kilcooly to his unmarried daughter, Elizabeth. In 1676 she married an Englishman, Sir William Barker of Essex (1676-1719). His son, another Sir William Barker (1677-1746), refurbished the monastic estate and made it habitable for the Barker family. The fourth Sir William Barker (1737-1818) built the Palladian house in 1762 to the north of the abbey. In 1789 he added an artificial lake, stocked with specially imported wildfowl. The third Sir William Barker's (1703-70) daughter, Mary, married a Chambre Brabazon Ponsonby and their son Chambre Brabazon Ponsonby (1762-1834) inherited the Kilcooly property from his uncle, the fourth Sir William. The Ponsonby connection still persists. Chambre Ponsonby

2 D. Seymour St John, *The Succession of Parochial Clergy in the United Diocese of Cashel and Emly* (Dublin, 1908), p. 58. 3 W.G. Neely, *Kilcooly* (Belfast, 1983), p. 12. 4 R.G. Hayes, *Manuscript Sources for the History of Irish Civilisation* (Boston, 1979). 5 B. Bradshaw, *Dissolution of the Religious Orders in Ireland under Henry VIII* (Cambridge, 1974), p. 130. 6 TCD MSS 566-15.

(1839-84) inherited Kilcooly in 1880 and married Mary Plunkett, daughter of Lord Dunsany. This effected a connection with Horace Plunkett, the founder of the co-operative movement.

APPENDICES

ABBOTS OF KILCOOLY

Thoman O'Rourke fl. 1341.[1]
Thomas Bovill d. before 1450.[2]
Philip O'Mulbardayn (O Mulwanyan *alias* O Brogaidor O Brothe) 1430-63.[3]
Odo O Grada, intruded *c.*1448-50
Malachy O'Mylryan elected 1463, retired 1464.[4]
William O Mulbardayn (alias Obroche) elected 1464.[5]
Danat O Mulwardayn (alias obroch) 1498.[6]
John O'Mulbardayn (Imollwardayn alias Ybroche) 1507-17.[7]
Thomas Shortall 1517-40,[8] last pre-reformation abbot.
Thomas Bernard O'Leamy 1622-36.
James Tobin fl. 1647.

LANDS OF KILCOOLY

Kilcooly abbey may be bracketed with Baltinglass and Maigue as one of the few houses whose landed possessions diminished instead of increasing with the passage of time. It was never a very rich house nor were its possessions very extensive. The only document remaining from the former archives of this house is the charter granted by Dómhnall Ó Briain, king of Limerick which has been calendared by Curtis (COD, i, p. 2). It is clear from the charter that this abbey was founded on ancient monastic lands belonging to the Comharb of St Colman with whose co-operation the foundation was made. It is possible that, like Jerpoint, its mother house, this abbey was of Benedictine origin and that the foundation date (1184) given in the official Cistercian *tabulae* marks the date on which it became affiliated to the Cistercian Order. Curtis conjectures that the charter was issued about 1182.

1 HC, 376. 2 CPR, x, pp 511-12. 3 Ibid.; tombstone inscription quoted in Carrigan, *History and Antiquities of the Diocese of Ossory* (Dublin, 1905), iv, p. 395. 4 CPR, xi, p. 505-6. 5 *Obligationes pro annatis diocesis Cassellensis*, 3, transcript by M.A. Costelloe OP, St Patrick's College, Maynooth. 6 CPR, xvii, pt. 1, p. 574. 7 Costelloe, *Obligationes*, 24. 8 Fiant (Hen.) no. 115.

TABLE OF LANDS OF KILCOOLY (TOTAL ACREAGE 5,629 ACRES, ALL IN CO. TIPPERARY).

Barony	Townland	Acreage	Parish and diocese
barony of Slieveardagh	Bawnlea	259-2-23	Kilcooly, Cashel,
	Crossoges	204-1-15	5629-0-36. The
	Deerpark	164-0-10	detached part of the
	Garransilly	321-2-00	parish near Lickfinn,
	Graigaheesha	496-3-13	including Derryvella,
	Grangecastle	214-3-26	Glengoole, Ballinunty
	Grangecrag	138-2-28	and Kilbrannell, may
	Grangehill	208-1-26	have formed part of
	Kilcooly (Abbey)	1455-1-15	the original monastic
	Knockatooreen	427-1-38	estate.These lands do
	Lisduff	638-1-01	not seem to have been
	Newhall	105-0-10	monastic at the time
	Newpark	307-0-34	of the dissolution of
	Renaghamore	364-3-14	the religious houses,
	Sallybog	204-1-26	though the rectory
	Springfield	118-0-37	was impropriate.
While forming part of the original lands granted to Kilcooly, they are not included in the 1540 extent and had probably been previously alienated.	(Clonamicklon	(310-0-08	
	Clonamondra	299-2-36	
	Foilacamin	372-0-33	Boulick,
	Gorteenrainee	149-3-22	Cashel, 1930-2-37
	Kilbraugh	651-1-32	
	Knockanglass)	147-1-26)	

A comparison of the lands listed in the extent of 1541 with the bounds of the monastic estate as described in the charter shows that not a little of the original lands had passed out of the possession of the Cistercians prior to the dissolution of the monastery. The charter names a number of places which cannot now be identified. It lists not only lands granted to the monks but also the lands which bounded the monastic possessions. Although most of the names are long obsolete it is apparent from those that can be identified that the abbey lands included not only that part of Kilcooly parish lying on the borders of Cos. Kilkenny and Tipperary and bounded on the north by the parish of Fennor and on the south by the parish of Ballingarry, but also the greater part if not the whole of the adjoining parish of Boulick. The two separate divisions of Kilcooly parish lying some miles from the part just mentioned do not seem to have formed part of monastic lands; they probably represent churches which were impropriatew in the abbey. The lands with which the abbey was endowed by the king of Thomond amounted to about twelve thousand, five hundred acres, but before thr close of the twelfth century the Anglo-Norman invaders had begun to settle in the area and by the year 1200 a certain Manner Arsic had acquired large tracts of land in this barony. Among the lands thus acquired it is probable that there were some which had been included in the grant made by King Domhnall to the monks of Kilcooly. Certain it is that at the dissolution of the monasteries the monks held no land in the parish of Boulick and the total extent of the abbey land as revealed by the survey then taken and corrected by the Civil Survey, the Down Survey and the modern ordnance survey maps, was 5,370 acres all told. Thus more than half the original land had been lost to the monks before the end of the middle ages.

Sources

The foundation charter is preserved among the Ormond Deeds and an English summary has been printed by Curtis in COD, i, p. 2. This charter, besides naming the bounds of the abbey lands, names also certain of the lands themselves. Among the identifiable lands are *Kilmoischy* (Graigaheesha, parish of Kilcooly), *Kilchule* (Kilcooly, same parish), *Kilwracha* (Kilbraugh, parish of Boulick) and *Clonomylchon* (Clonamicklon, same parish). It is possible that the *Chuilinhuir* of the charter is represented today by Clonourha in the detached part of the parish of Kilcooly while *Cnokelegayn* may be the modern Ballinlacken lying in the same detached part of the parish. The extent made at Kilkenny on 11 January 1541 shows that the rectory of *Ballyenlakyng* was held by the monks. The ruins of the church can still be seen, From the meagre list of placenames noted in the extent it would appear that many of the lands named in the charter had ceased to belong to the monastery before the dillolution. The lands of *Ballylacken* were held by the Hospital of St John the Baptist without the New Gate, Dublin, at the time of the dissolution. Other sources for the Kilcooly lands are: IMED, 322-4 and. MH, 664-5; Fiants Elizabeth, Nos. 504, 3074, 4012, 6132, CPR, 2 Jas. I (p. 52); DS & OS maps; Composite Map of Tipperary; Civil Survey (Tipperary) 1654, i, pp 131-4 (parish of Kilcooly) and pp 126-8 (parish of Boulick). The principal sources for the history of the abbey are the statutes of the general chapter, the Register of Stephen of Lexington and the Calendar of Papal Letters. Other sources: Extents, Fiants Hen. VIII; HC, xiii; Morrin, i; Tax.I.Cist

NOTES ON THE ARCHITECTURE OF KILCOOLY ABBEY

The abbey lies south-east of Urlingford and is in private hands.

J. O'Donovan in his Ordnance Survey Letters covers the parish of Kilcooly but does not describe the abbey because perhaps it was in the private ownership of Sir William Barker, Bart. O'Donovan just remarks that 'the great abbey remains in tolerable preservation'.[1]

Canon Power, in his Mount Melleray manuscript, gives us a detailed description of what he found in the 1920s:

> Kilcooly, in the parish of the same name and barony of Slieveardady, Co. Tipperary, stands within the enclosed Kilcooley demense close to the eastern boundary of the county and on the remote edge of the pleasant Cashel plain. On the west of the site, for some distance, is a wide stretch of turbary and bounding the view on the other, or Kilkenny side are undulating uplands along the foot of which flows the river Munster, a tributary of the Nore. The face of nature immediately around the abbey has been gently changed by landscaped gardening and planting since the monks' days. A hundred perches or so to the north-east of the ruin lies an ornamental lake or fish pond of some ten acres but whether the water represents the monastic fish-pond the writer is unable to say.
>
> The abbey ruin here, it is pleasant to record, is very well cared for and preserved by the owners of the demesne, who have set a headline for all Ireland to copy. Chancel and south transept are still roofed over but the present is not apparently the original roof. Kilcooley was considerably smaller than its parent house of Jerpoint but what it lacks in size it makes up for in architectural detail. It has much rich stonework and the exquisite carved stalls in the choir are unique.
>
> As usual the monastic church is the part of the building best preserved, although its aisles have disappeared. This measures one hundred and twenty three feet in total internal length with a breadth, at the transepts, of seventy seven, and, in the nave, of twenty three feet. Lines of pent roof dripstone show that the nave was not always aisleless as at present; the same is also indicated by two bays of nave arches, now built up, over the great west dooor. Now also closed up by masonry is a fine decorated window beside the doorway, on the inside and set in the wall, is a holy water stoup of most unusual pattern; it is furnished on front with two Gothic opes, to admit the hand. At present there is no trace of screen (of wood or stone) across the nave, but the former existence of such a feature is almost postulated, as in the neighbouring Holy Cross and Hore, by the two beautiful carved seats set into the piers of the tower arch. These are the choir seats of the abbot and prior respectively, and there is nothing at all like them in any other Irish abbey.

1 OSL, Co. Tipperary, RIA,i, p. 436.

The abbot's *sedile*, on the south side of the choir. is the more elaborate: it has above an ogee headed canopy with moulding and foliage
ornament and altogether, it is a delightful piece of work worthy of
comparison with the sedilia and arcade of Holy Cross and possibly
it is by the same hand as the two latter. Overhead are carved two
shields one charged with a chief indented in base and three spearheads, points upwards, and the other chief indented only. On the
east side of the seat is another shield bearing the passion emblems.
The tower is low-even when the comparatively small size of the
church is considered. It springs from round arches and it has four
opes, underneath, for the bell ropes. The chancel, with its stone
altar still in position, is now lighted by a rather ambitious window of
decorated type, very similar to the corresponding window of Holy
Cross. The windows, or at least its lowest part, is divided into six
lights, a very unusual number and the whole emposition, or at least
its lowest part, is divided into six lights, a very unusual number and
the whole emposition must be about twenty feet in height by nine
feet wide. A circular window, about a foot in diameter, and quatrefoil on the outside, lighted the altar from the south and splayed
widely inwards. Within the chancel are many ancient tombs and
grave-slabs. Occupying the place of the founder's monument is a
large altar tomb commemorating Pierce FitzJames Óg Butler who
died on the feast of St Benedict 1526. This Pierce Óg was ancestor
of the lords Ikerrin and Carrick. On top of the monument rests an
effigy in armour. In the same tomb rests Pierce Óg's grandson, the
first Viscount Ikerrin who, as Lieutenant General of the Irish Army,
took a prominent part in the Confederation war. He directed in his
will that he should be buried in Kilcooly. Around the sides of this
fine monument are sculptured panels with figures of the twelve
apostles reminiscent of similar figures on the McGrath tomb in
Lismore and an unnamed tomb in Cashel. A floor-slab commemorated Philip O Molwanagh, abbot of Kilcooley, who died in 1463,
and another similar slab marks, or marked, the grave of Donald O
Hedyan who died in 1452. Of the remaining inscribed tombstones
in this place three commemorate members of the Cantwell family.
Some of these inscriptions are plainly from the chisel of Rory
Macpatrick O Tunny who also worked at Jerpoint and another is the
work of Patrick O Tunny. In each transept are two chapels, or rather
two altar separated by graceful stone columns. The transepts themselves are of unequal size, the northmost being square (about
twenty four feet) and the other measuring twenty six feet by sixteen.
They have ribbed vaulting and are lighted by late decorated windows. In the north transept there now stands a heavy square font of

stone on a circular leg; this may have been the baptismal font of the old parish church of Kilcooly closeby. The night stairs in the south transept are not in their normal position nor are they of normal character; they start from the north west angle of the transept whence they are carried upward through the thickness of the wall to the dorter which here lies over the transept. This arrangement left the gable of the transept blank except for the doorway to the sacristy and of this fact advantage was taken to decorate the wall by a series of interesting carvings in panels on stone tiles. One panel represents the Crucifixion with Mary and John beside the cross and underneath are a couple of emblematic pelicans. Another panel represents St Christopher and, again, another St Malachy. Above these inserts a kind of raised dado, also in stone, a really beautiful composition. It would be very interesting if we could connect the O Tunneys with our dado or with the Holy Cross arcade and *sedilia*! Examination of the north wall of the church will suggest why the aisles (the north aisle, at any rate) were removed, to make way for the heavy buttresses which had to be erected on account of subsistence and of the dangerous condition of the wall in question. Note also, in this connection, the massive buttresses at the external angles of the chancel. Over the chancel is a commodious and airy apartment entered from the dormitory. It has two windows facing east and is furnished with stone seats in their deep embrasures.

The chapter-room and refectory are small and neither seems ever to have been enlarged, modified or rebuilt. At the south east angle of the cloister are the abbey kitchens with capacious chimneys reminiscent of Boyle, Finally the cloister is of very limited area, only fifty feet square. Everything suggest that the community was ocmparatively small.

A few perches to the north east of the ruin is a detached circular structure, somewhat resembling a bee-hive hut, only that is taller. This is undoubtedly a *columbarium* and neither a hermit's cell nor an accountant's office as fanciful writers have claimed,. The little structure is, like the abbey itself, built of the local limestone; it is a rather small example, no more than half the size of the well preserved columbariam at Ballybeg, now Buttervant. Nearer than the *columbarium* to the main than building, and at the south-east angle to the latter, are extensive vaulted remains, the abbot's quarters and the great house. In another direction, hundred perches or so beyond the *columbarium* is an ancient cemetary enclosing some remains of an old church; from analogy we conclude that it is the site of the early old-Irish religious establishment which the abbey replaced.

Roger Stalley gives us a present-day picture of the abbey[3]

> The buildings continued to be inhabited until relatively recently, and
> it is possible that Cistercian monks returned to the abbey for a short
> time in the 1640s, when one named John Stapleton is said to have
> served his novitiate there. About 1790 a large winged house was build
> east of the medieval buildings by Sir William Barker, whose family
> had previously resided in the old abbey. He erected 'a study or
> summer house' in the ruins, and when his own house was burnt in
> 1840, the family again lived in the medieval abbey for a short while.
>   Little remains of the earliest phase of the monastery's existence.
> The church apparently had a orthodox Cistercian plan, with two
> chapels in each transept, and an aisled nave, with plain piers and
> arches. The arcades were blocked in the fifteenth or sixteenth cen-
> tury as part of a wholesale reconstruction of the monastery. The
> barrel-vaulted presbytery has a large window with uncusped cuvilear
> tracery and the low, narrow transepts have an interesting range of
> ribbed vaults. The arches of the crossing tower are supported on a
> series of well-cut corbels. Built into the piers of the tower at the
> entrance to the nave are two elaborate stone sedilia for the abbot a
> prior. The wall which divides the south transept from the sacristy is
> decorated with several sculptured panels, executed in hard polished
> limestone. The night stair is built within the wall of the transept and
> gives access to a pleasant domestic chamber immediately above.
> The cloister buildings have been so much altered since 1540 that it
> is hard to disentangle their medieval form. The cloister garth was
> clearly used as a bawn, reached through a gateway in the south
> range. Some fragments are left of a late medieval cloister arcade. To
> the south-east is a large semi-fortified hall, built over a vaulted base-
> ment, and to the north-east is a well preserved columbarium. The
> Protestant church to the north-east was built on the site of an old
> chapel, which may have served as a 'capella ante portas'. Within the
> church is a fine group of tombs, including the sculptured slab of
> Abbot Philip O Molwanayn (d. 1463) and the magnificient effigy og
> Piers Fitz Oge Butler (d. 1526), carved by Rory O'Tunney.

Stalley points out that Kilcooly was the only monastery to introduce
major innovations into the plan of its church. The burning and destruction
of the abbey in 1445 enabled the monks to innovate in the rebuilding and
to cater for falling numbers. Stalley describes some of these innovations:[4]

2 Canon Power, Mount Melleray MSS.   3 R. Stalley, *The Cistercian Monasteries of Ireland*, p. 247.
4 Ibid., p. 66.

using flamboyant tracery and lierne vaulting. The south transept was rib vaulted in two bays at a low level and the two easter chapels were replaced by shallow altar recesses. The north transept was also rib vaulted, this time in four irregular bays, with an octagonal pier in the centre. The narrow dimensions of the transept resulted in an awkward, oblong crossing, which had repercussions on the design of the tower above. The western walls of the transept contain stair-cases. That to the south was the successor to the old night stairs, but it was completely enclosed and hidden from view. The north transept stair was reached from outside the building, from a door-way in the west wall, and it led up to the vault spaces and the cross-ing tower. (After the armed raid of 1445, it is strange that the doorway was not more discreetly located.) In the nave the arcades were blocked and the twelfth-century aisles demolished. The recon-structed church was smaller but more intimate that its predeccessor and the crudity of the alterations in the nave were in part compen-sated by the attractive spatial effects of the transepts.

Stalley states that the style of Kilcooly is closely related to Holy Cross and in both there is a similar focus on curvilinear tracery and ribbed vault-ing.[5] He also throws doubt concerning a rather substantial outbuilding at Kilcooly, which many regarded as the infirmary. Stalley thinks[6] that it was either a powerful lodging built for the abbot shortly before the reforma-tion or a residence erected by one of the post-dissolution occupants of the abbey.

5 Ibid., p. 126.   6 Ibid., p. 175.

PART FIVE

The abbey of Hore (Cashel)

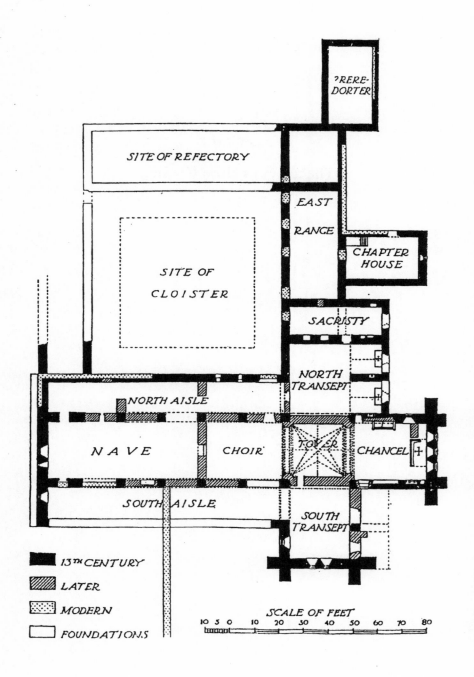

Plan of Hore abbey, made by the Royal Archaeological Institute

21. HORE ABBEY

In or about the year 1270, David Mac Cearbhaill, archbishop of Cashel, resolved to bring the Cistercians into his cathedral city, and for this purpose proposed to endow the monks with the buildings and lands of a Benedictine foundation which had at one time flourished near Cashel, but had in the course of the years gradually declined and appears to have been at this time unoccupied. The traditional story informs us that the archbishop dreamed that the Benedictines of Cashel cut off his head, for which reason, we are told, he expelled the Black Monks and introduced the White Monks in their stead. This story, like many another picturesque legend of medieval times, may be dismissed as apocryphal, even though it is vouched for by a fourteenth-century jury! The first official mention of the foundation at Cashel in Cistercian records occurs in the Statutes of the general chapter for the year 1271. From Statute 55 of that year[1] it appears that the chapter committed to the abbots of Duiske and Maigue the charge of proceeding to the place in which the lord archbishop of Cashel intended to found an abbey of monks, to inspect the said place on the authority of the general chapter and, after due and careful consideration of all those factors which before God ought to be considered, they were to report their findings to the next general chapter.

The statutes of the following year make no mention whatever of the project, but the best authorities are agreed that the actual foundation was made in 1272 and that it was made from Mellifont. It was, in fact, the eighth and last colony to be sent out from that house and thus marked the end of an epoch in Irish Cistercian history. Owing to its situation near the famous Rock of Cashel the new foundation was named the abbey of the Rock (de Rupe) and it is sometimes called in medieval documents the abbey of the Lower Rock to distinguish it from another religious house known as the abbey of the Upper Rock.

The archbishop amply endowed the new foundation with lands, churches and gardens and at least four mills. Among the lands named in the grant were those of Grydhcethoragi, with their spiritual and temporal appurtenances, the townland of Ballymoylan, the townland of Ballysinnath, twelve acres in Cloncath, forty acres near the gate of the abbey, all the land in Kelkalrath or Kilkabrath then in the tenure of Thomas of Fythard with all the appurtenances, ecclesiastical and civil, the church of Glankyn and the chapel of the Burgage Milath with its appurtenances in Oleyhath (Ui Luighdheach,) the two mills of Camus situated near the old bridge, the moiety of the mill of Ballytarsna and free commonage in

---

1 Canivez, 1271: 55.

Camus for all their cattle. This charter, which was granted between 1272 and 1275 was confirmed later by king Edward I and again by king Edward II.[2]

The bulk of the lands mentioned in the foregoing grant, situated in the vicinity of Cashel, formed what was later known as the parish of Hore abbey. The forty acres near the gate of the abbey may perhaps be equated with the forty acres of arable land mentioned in the grant, made by Queen Elizabeth to Sir Henry Radcliffe in 1561, of this abbey with its appurtenances.[3] The land donated by Thomas of Fethard is probably to be equated with the grange near Fydarte listed in the monastic extents of 1541.[4] The Burgage Milath mentioned in the charter I take to be Borrisoleigh in the parish of Glenkeen (the Glankyn of the charter), but the church of Glenkeen must have reverted to the archdiocese at some undetermined period, for in 1485 the then archbishop of Cashel, David Creagh, 'annexed, appropriated and perpetually incorporated' the church of Glankyn in the Cistercian abbey of the Holy Cross of Uachtarleamhan.[5]

To the original endowment were added at various intervals other lands and churches. In 1290 William, the son of Thomas of Fethard, is said to have made a considerable grant of lands to the abbey including some of the lands of Kiltinan, but this grant was not a pure benefaction, for in his charter the said William states that he received from the abbot for this grant a sum of 'money with which I am well satisfied'.[6] At a later period the abbey acquired the grange of Erry in the barony of Middlethird, as well as Littlegrange. The situation of the latter grange does not appear clear from the references in the documents, but it may have been Grangebeg, which formed part of Erry. Besides this landed property, the abbey also held the rectorial churches or chapels of Hore abbey (this was really the abbey church which served also as the parish church), Grange Erry, Little Grange and Lismalin, with their appurtenances, and the vicarage of Railstown, all these being in Co. Tipperary.

Annexed to the abbey was a house for lepers which had been founded originally by Sir David Latimer, seneschal of the Cistercian archbishop, Maelmuire O Briain. Latimer had a daughter who feared lepers. One day, as she was serving the poor, a leper appeared among the beggars. The girl dropped her alms and ran back into the house. The leper, angered by her behaviour, prayed that she might be afflicted with leprosy and this, it is reported, happened. The father built a 'lazar-house' with fourteen beds and enhanced it with four plough lands. The burgesses of Cashel granted it two gallons of ale out of every brewing of ale intended for sale, *de quali-*

---

2 MH, p. 649, quoting King's *Collectanea*, p. 404. 3 Ibid., p. 650, quoting auditor general. 4 *Extents*, p. 326. 5 IMED, Deed no. 55, pp 48-9. 6 MH, p. 649; King's *Collectanea*, incorporated in the HC, xiii (p. 407).

bet Bructiana cerevisiale bructiatae ad vendendum. This was called the 'May flagon', as it belonged to St Mary's abbey of the Rock.

There would seem to have been more than one hospital in Cashel, one, the Hospital of St Nicholas, is believed to have been located on Main Street, a second one, one mile south of the town, on the Cahir road, marked leper hospital on the O.S. maps, and a 'spittle' or hospital for infectious diseases on the eastern vicinity of St Francis' Friary. When Archbishop David Mac Cearbhaill introduced the Cistercians into Cashel, he endowed them not only with the buildings and lands formerly held by the Benedictines but also with the hospital for the lepers and poor persons. It is to be presumed that the monks looked after this hospital and cared for the poor therin, as indeed was done in the hospitals for the poor attached to many of the Irish Cistercian houses in medieval times.[7] Basing his claim on the above-mentioned donation, the abbot of the Rock of Cashel in 1313 demanded two flagons of ale out of every brewing made by the thirty-eight brewers of the city of Cashel for sale in that city. This would give the monks seventy-six flagons of beer out of every brewing, no small or unwelcome addition to the monastic table. For some time the brewers of Cashel paid the two flagons out of every brewing but finally they objected to the custom saying that they were not bound to such a service. The abbot thereupon brought a suit in court against the thirty-eight brewers of the city of Cashel in the seventh year of Edward II. The decision was adverse to the abbot's claim. The jury declared that the beer-tax formed no part of the services required from the burgesses of Cashel by Archbishop Maelmuir's charter, but that the later successor of Maelmuire, that is to say, archbishop David Mac Cearbhaill, had compelled them to pay the beer-tax to the monks of the new Cistercian monastery founded by himself.[8]

One gathers from the foregoing that the citizens of Cashel had no great reverences for the memory of Archbishop Mac Cearbhaill. They were for the most part men of loyal and true English or Anglo-Norman stock. He was an Irishman, and an Irishman who was noted for his resolute opposition to the pretensions of the Crown in regard to ecclesiastical appointments and other infringements of the rights of the Church. When in 1275 the English sought to have a prison erected in Cashel the archbishop absolutely opposed the project, and when the justiciar, carrying out the command of the king, caused the work of construction to be begun, the archbishop fulminated sentence of excommunication against all who took part in the work or aided, counselled or approved of it. Hence we find it stated in a contemporary document[9] that 'while he lives he will do all the harm he can do to the king, his officers and all his land of Ireland'.

7 Registrum, Letter civ, nos. 63 and 87. 8 HC, xiii, pp 406-7. 9 Ibid., i, p. 289.

Naturally enough those whose animosity was thus aroused against the archbishop were also opposed to his works, and so the unfortunate Cistercians of the new foundation at Cashel came in for a share of their vituperation. Referring, apparently, to the Cistercian monastery founded by the archbishop in 1272, a certain Margaret le Blunde in a petition accusing the archbishop of various outrages, declares among other matters that the bishop had lately built an abbey in Cashel town on the king's inheritance and filled it with robbers who kill Englishmen and rob the country; and when the king's council say anything about this he fulminates sentence of excommunication against them.[10]

Archbishop David Mac Cearbhaill was a true friend of the Cistercians, and in the year 1255 had petitioned and obtained from the general chapter the privilege of having dwelling with him in his service two Cistercians whom he might choose from any abbey in Ireland on condition that he employed them only in offices befitting their state (*honestis officiis*).[11] Two years after the foundation of the abbey at Cashel the Cistercian general chapter granted his petition that the anniversary of his father and mother should be celebrated in the abbeys of Jerpoint and Cashel which he and his ancestors founded, provided that the abbots and convents of the said houses agreed to this. Moreover, the general chapter agreed that, after the death of the archbishop himself, his anniversary might be celebrated in all the Irish abbeys of the order if the abbots and convents of those houses so wished.[12] Archbishop Mac Cearbhaill's relations with the Cistercians had, indeed, commenced long before the foundation of the abbey at Cashel. We have seen that, as early as 1255, he had obtained from the general chapter the privilege of having two monks employed in his service and dwelling with him. The very fact that the general chapter agreed to this arrangement is proof of the cordial relations then existing between the archbishop and the Cistercian Order. Indeed, his love and esteem for the order were so great that in the year 1269 he received the Cistercian habit himself and made profession of the rule while continuing, nevertheless, to act as archbishop of Cashel. There was a precedent for this in the archdiocese, for one of the archbishop's predecessors, Donnchadh Ó Lonnargain, had become a Cistercian monk at Citeaux where he had been taken ill on his way to Rome. Having concluded his business with the pope, had returned to his archdiocese clothed, to use the words of the pope (Honorius III), with 'the habit of a monk and the dignity of a pontiff', which two states, the Holy Father pointed out, in a letter addressed by him to the people of Cashel, were not repugnant. The letter was written on 3 August 1220, almost half a century before Archbishop Mac Cearbhaill became a Cistercian in his turn.

10 Ibid., 296.   11 Canivez, 1255:50.   12 Ibid., 1274:56.

The Cistercians had, in truth, a long and honourable connection with the archdiocese of Cashel, four monks of the order having occupied the see in succession between 1182 and 1237. This meant that for more than half a century the most important see in Munster was ruled by a succession of Cistercian monks. The Cistercian succession was interrupted for fifteen years while the Dominican, David Mac Kelly, ruled the archdiocese, to be succeeded in 1254 by David Mac Cearbhaill who, almost immediately after his accession sought and obtained the assistance of the Cistercians in the administration of the diocese. He did not, however, take the Cistercian habit himself until he had been fifteen years a bishop; but during the last twenty years of his episcopacy he was a Cistercian in the fullest sense of the word. As such, he naturally interested himself in the affairs of the order whose welfare he had so much at heart, and one of his first cares after receiving the habit was to found an abbey of the order in his archepisco-pal city. The abbey is thought to have been founded in 1272; it was certainly in existence by 1274,[13] in which year also we find the archbishop proposing to the general chapter that the abbey of Bective in Co. Meath should be transferred to a new site.[14] Although the general chapter was not unfavourable to the project it did not materialise.

Archbishop Mac Cearbhaill was present in person at the general chapter of 1274, having come to Citeaux on his way back from the General Council of Lyons. He had many petitions to make to the chapter, but one in particular, must be mentioned here. Forty-six years earlier the general chapter on the recommendation of Stephen of Lexington, then abbot of Stanley, later to be abbot in succession of Savigny and Clairvaux, had deprived the abbey of Mellifont of her entire *filiatio*, subjecting the daughter houses of the disgraced Mellifont to new mother houses in England and Wales. At the instance of the archbishop of Cashel[15] this decree was now revoked and the long-alienated daughter houses were restored to Mellifont.[16] On this occasion also the archbishop obtained official recognition of the feast of St Patrick, which, for the future, all the Irish abbots might, if they so wished, celebrate with two masses, as on the feast of St Martin. They were also reminded by the chapter that, in accordance with the definitions of the order, they were bound to celebrate the principal feast of the cathedral church in the individual dioceses.[17]

The monastery of the Rock of Cashel was Mellifont's last foundation, and, in fact, the last Cistercian monastery to be founded in Ireland prior to the dissolution of the monasteries in the sixteenth century. Its history is for the most part unknown. There are no references to it in the annals, and only three references in the statutes of the general chapters. Although

---

13 Ibid. 14 Ibid., 1274:60. 15 *Chronicles of the Reigns of Stephen, Henry II and Richard*, ed. R. Howlett (London, 1885), ii, p. 567. 16 Canivez, 1274:11. 17 Ibid., 1274:27.

amply endowed by the archbishop at the time of the foundation, the community were to find that the king and his ministers, instead of aiding and protecting them, rather contributed to their impoverishment. Morover, the archbishop, in augmenting their endowments had, unwisely as it appears, bestowed on them certain lands and possessions, formerly held by the religious of the Upper Rock and of St Nicholas of Cashel, a proceeding which did not commend itself to the good citizens of Cashel who,[18] 'while two of their monks and a brother were in their church of St Nicholas ... came, killed one monk before the altar, beat the other to death, drove the brother from the church and threw him into the water'.

The Cistercians of Cashel, declaring that as 'men of religion' they could not prosecute the trespass recorded above, prayed the king to provide a remedy. On the same occasion they complained to the king that

> Having been endowed by David Mac Kervyl archbishop of Cashel of divers lands and tenements in free alms, they are harassed and impeded by escheators, sheriffs, and other ministers of the king against their feoffments. They thereupon pray the king to confirm the archbishop's feoffments so that they may remain in peace and be no longer harassed.[19]

The king heard their appeal and though he did not there and then confirm the archbishop's feoffments, being advised not to do so at the time, he commanded that a writ should be issued to the justiciar of Ireland to call before him the escheator and the other parties concerned. Since a man had suffered death the justiciar was also commanded to call before him the Justices of the king's bench and others of the council, and to do full right so that no further complaint might be made to the king. Shortly after this the king confirmed

> to the abbot and convent of the Cistercian Order of the Lower Rock of Cashel, the assignment which David, archbishop of Cashel had made to them, in augmentation of their living, of lands and possessions formerly held by the religious of the house of the Upper Rock and of St Nicholas of Cashel, and which they had surrendered to the archbishop; and also of other lands which the archbishop had acquired from divers persons of those parts.[20]

Though the official title of our abbey was the abbey of the Rock of Cashel, it was generally known as Hore abbey. This last designation has been a puzzle to most writers. Some think it means 'grey' so that they would make

---

18 CDI, iii, no. 622. 19 Ibid. 20 Ibid., no. 745.

Hore abbey equivalent to the Grey abbey. John O'Donovan in his Ordnance Survey Letters adopts this view, saying that the name of the abbey in Irish is *Mainistir Liath,* signifying Grey abbey, and he adds that according to this explanation Hoar abbey would be more correct that the form now generally adopted.[21] The English form appears as 'Hoore' in a letter written by Queen Mary to the lord deputy in 1553.[22] In the extent of 1541 it is called the monastery *de Rupe, alias* Hore.[23] This is the earliest mention I have been able to find of the abbey under the form of Hore abbey. If we take the Irish name (presumably the name applied to the abbey by the Irish speakers of Cashel and the surrounding district at the time O'Donovan's letter was written) as representing faithfully the English form, we shall conclude that this was a name that came in among the people during the course of the centuries and was applied to the abbey as a descriptive name from the fact that it had grown old and hoary with the passing of the years. The Very Revd Professor Power, on the other hand, suggests that the word 'Hore' comes from the Irish *iubhar* meaning a yew tree, as in the case of Newry.[24] Against this theory is the fact that we have no evidence that the Irish word *iubhar* was ever applied to the abbey by any Irish speaker of the neighbourhood, while we have O'Donovan's testimony to the use of the Irish phrase, *An Mhainistir Liath.* In the absence of any more convincing evidence to the contrary it is safer to accept the explanation given by O'Donovan as the most probable one. Finally it may be mentioned that in one of the statutes of the general chapter of the Cistercian Order the abbey is referred to by the name of *B.M. de Rupibus coeli,*[25] that is of the Rocks of heaven! The *coelum* is here perhaps based on the name Cashel while the rocks refer to what the documents term the Upper and the Lower Rock. The term 'Rock of Cashel' in many of these ancient documents refers, not to the actual rock on which the Cathedral and other buildings stand, but rather to the parish named from the rock and divided into two districts, an upper and a lower, called respectively the Upper and Lower Rock, the Cistercian abbey being situated in the latter district, that of St Nicholas in the former.

The abbot of Cashel is mentioned only twice in the Statutes of the general chapter, and on neither occasion is his name given. At the chapter of 1276 he was directed to announce to the abbots of Boyle, Maure, Corcumroe, Assaroe and Moycosquin sentence of deposition passed against them by the general chapter for an absence of twelve years without legitimate excuse or explanation.[26] In 1279 the abbot petitioned the general chapter for permission to remain away for one occasion, which petition the chap-

21 OSL, Co. Tipperary, i, p. 110 (ms, p. 296). 22 Morrin, i, p. 300. 23 Extents, p. 325. 24 'The Cistercian Abbeys of Munster,' *Journal of the Cork Historical and Archaeological Society,* 13, no. 157, p. 6. 25 Canivez, 1276: 23. 26 Ibid.

ter was pleased graciously to grant.[27] The abbot was in trouble with the secular authority in the year 1290, as has already been related, suffering much
at the hands of the king's officers, but for this he received satisfaction from
the king. Three years later he was again in trouble, being fined 50 shillings
for not coming to court when attached, and a half mark because he did
not prosecute.[28] Richard, the second abbot whose name has been
recorded, was sued in court in the year 1300 by John, the son of Richard
for the sum of eighteen marks; the abbot defended himself by pleading
that he was not bound to answer because the action was laid for eighteen
marks while John in his pleadings sued only for seventeen marks, six
shillings and four pence! The abbot won out on this point of law and the
plaintiff himself was amerced by the court.[29] This was probably the abbot
who was ruling the monastery when, in 1302, the sheriff was commanded
to enquire whether it would be to the damage of the king, or any other, if
the king should grant leave to John Gregori to give to the Friars Minor of
Cashel 3 acres of land with appurtenances in Cashel, to hold to them and
their successors for ever. He was also to inquire of whom John held the
land and by what service and how much the land was worth yearly, and if
the remainder of the lands held by John was sufficient for doing suit and
other services due to the chief lords of that fee. Inquisition having been
taken by the oath of good and lawful men, the jurors found that it was not
to the damage or prejudice of the king or any other that John Gregori
might give the friars the said land, This land was stated to be held of the
archbishop of Cashel, no services being due, while the remaining lands
held by John were sufficient for the suit and services due to the chief lords
of the fee since neither suit nor service was owed to any one save six
shillings yearly rent in free alms to the abbot and convent of the Rock of
Cashel.[30]

　　We next find notice of the monastery in the ecclesiastical taxation of
Ireland (1302-3) where the monastery of Cashel appears under the diocese to that name together with the monasteries of Kilcooly and Holy
Cross. It is interesting to note and compare the temporalities and rents of
these houses as revealed in the figures there given. The temporalities of
the abbey of Kilcooly were 30 shillings, the rent of the monastery being
estimated at 19 marks, thus making a total of £14. 3s. 4d. The taxation of
the monastery of Holy Cross in spirituals and temporals everywhere is said
to be £17. 0s. 8d. The temporalities of the monastery of Cashel are set
down as 14s. while the rent of the same monastery at Herich (probaly
Erry?) is given as 100s., making in all £5. 14s.[31] Thus we see that the abbey
of Cashel was far poorer than either Kilcooly or Holy Cross at that period..

27 Ibid. 1279:74.　28 CDI, iv, no. 21.　29 HC, xiii, 261.　30 *Calendar of Justiciary Rolls Ireland,
1295-1303* ed. James Mills (Dublin, 1905), p. 449.　31 CDI, v, no. 718.

The position improved, however, with the passing of the centuries so that in 1458[32] and in 1466[33] the value was estimated at 24 marks (£16), which by 1486 had fallen to 20 marks.[34] The extent made at Cashel on the occasion of the suppression of the monastery shows that in 1541 the total value was £21. 4s. 10d., the net total after various annual charges had been deducted being £15. 13s. 2d.[35] The modern equivalent would be in the region of one thousand pounds sterling.

Very few of the names of the abbots of this house have been recorded or, if recorded, very few of the records have come down to us. We have no record, for instance, of the name of any abbot before the year 1289 at which date it was already seventeen years in existence. Between the years 1300 and 1398, the name of only one abbot has been recorded, namely Abbot Thomas, who flourished in the year 1313. We meet with an Abbot John in 1398 in the record of Essoins, taken before William son of Peter le Botiller, seneschal of the Liberty of Tipperary, in assizes at Clonmel on Tuesday next after the Epiphany in the 21st year of Richard II. The information conveyed in the document regarding the abbot is meagre although it is evident that he was either the defendant or the plaintiff in certain suits for the entry records that 'John, Abbot of the House of the B.V.M. of the Rock of Cashel, puts in his place ... de Loundres and John son of Fulc Mauncell, to win or to lose in all assizes, etc.'[36] During the fifteenth century our list of abbots grows so that eight names are added, six of which are contained in mandates dating from the year 1458 while two appear in other documents. Among the abbots named is an Abbot Nicholas who was ruling the monastery in 1494.[37] There is, in the collection of Ormond Deeds now housed in the National Library of Ireland, a certificate of absolution for homicide granted by Nicholas, abbot of the Rock of Cashel, of the Cistercian Order, to a certain Peter Omorra, the document unfortunately being undated. If the editor of the volume of *Irish Monastic and Episcopal Deeds* is correct in his surmise that this document belongs to the earlier part of the fifteenth century, there must have been two abbots bearing the name Nicholas, one at the end of the century, the other in the early part of the same century. The document, which is of no small interest, certifies that the abbot has absolved Peter Omorra who had slain Donald Fitzmaurice, the absolution being given in virtue of powers received from the Holy See or indulgences granted by certain pontiffs. The reasons for the absolution were that according to the declaration of the said Peter and of many others he was not a cleric, and furthermore that he was guilty of infringing the rights of a church or churches. The certificate reads:

32 CPR, xii, p. 12. 33 Ibid., p. 510. 34 Costelloe, *Obligationes pro Annatis Diocesis Cassellensis* (Maynooth, 1909). 35 Extents, p. 327. 36 COD, ii, 233. 37 Costelloe, op. cit.

Jhus Nasarenus

Pateat omnibus per presentes quod nos Nicolaus abbas monasterii Beate Marie de Rupe Cassel Cisterciensis ordinis absolumimus Petrum Omorra a pena homisidi illius Donali filii Mauricii autoritate sedis apostolice siue indulgentiarum nostrarum concessarum per non nullos pontifices, istis racionibus tum quia non fuit clericus secundum relacionem prefati Petri nec non et alliorum plurimorom hominum tum quia fuit invasor ecclesie siue ecclesiarum, ideo absoluimus eum et per presentes eum absolutum denunciamus racionibus prefatis saluo iure curie episcopi.[38]

A mandate dated 2 January 1458/9 shows that the abbey was then void by the death of William Ockyll (O'Cahill?). The succession list would include the following names beginning with the abbot just mentioned and going back from the year 1458 – William Ockayll, Odo Ygrada (O'Grady), Thomas Yllent and Denis Ychonnillin. The Odo Ygrada of this list is probably the Oda Ograda or O'Grady of Holy Cross who is said in a mandate of 1448 to have been transferred to Kilcooly. I have elsewhere[39] given reasons for holding that Odo never actually functioned as abbot of Kilcooly or, if he did, could only have held the abbey for the briefest space and could not then have been the lawful abbot since there was an abbot there already. We may, however, accept the probability of his becoming abbot of Cashel as early as 1449 if not actually in 1448. If he succeeded Thomas Yllent as the list given above suggests it follows that there must have been two abbots ruling Hore abbey during the decade 1448-1458 but except for the fact that Odo O'Grady was the first of these and William O'Cahill the second we have no means of determining on the available evidence how many years each of them actually held the reins of office.

The mandate of 1458 from which the foregoing names are taken indicates that William Ockayl's successor in the abbacy was a monk of Holy Cross abbey, one William Ikilichan (Yckilichan, Okilichan, Ykilchan – possible O'Callaghan). At any rate the mandate, addressed to the abbot of Owney, commands him to make provision to the said William Ikilchan, if found fit, of the Cistercian monastery of St Mary de Rupe in the same diocese.[40] As we hear no more of Hore abbey until 1466 at which date it is said to be ruled by a certain Denis alias Doncuan Ofaula (O'Foulow or O'Foley) we may conclude that William Ikilchan had provision made to him of the monastery and was later succeeded by Doncuan. How long the latter ruled as abbot we do not know. In 1466 very serious charges were made against him by a monk of Owney named William Seymour. Not only

38 IMED, no. 22, p. 232.   39 See Part 3, Holy Cross Abbey.   40 CPR, xii, p. 12.

was he accused of serious moral lapses but it was furthermore stated that he had dilapidated many of the goods of the monastery, turning them to his own evil purposes, so that in consequence of his negligence the monastery and its buildings had become ruinous and divine worship therin had been greatly diminished, and that it was indeed to be feared that unless a remedy were speedily provided the monastery would fall into such desolation that divine worship would wholly perish and the buildings would fall to the ground. Naturally the best remedy for this deplorable state of affairs was to have the abbot replaced by one who would be zealous to set all those evils right, and who could better do this than the monk whose zeal led him to bring this sad state of affairs to the notice of the pope? Needless to say this was not actually set forth in so many words, but there can be little doubt that the monk who made the complaint sought the abbacy himself, and in the event had provision made to him, having first received a dispensation *super defectu natalium*, from which it appears that he was himself the son of a monk of the same Order.[41]

William Seymour was provided in 1466. In 1486 the abbey was again vacant *per devolutionem ad sedem apostolicam*.[42] This time it was given *in commendam* to David Creagh, archbishop of Cashel but by 1494 we find a new abbot, Nicholas by name, binding himself to pay the *annates* for Peter Butler, a cleric of the diocese of Cashel.[43] Yet another document of the same year states that the abbey has now been so long void that its collation has come into the pope's hand![44] Raymond Stapleton was provided and the entry states that there was an intruder in the abbey. The 'intruder' was probably the Abbot Nicholas already mentioned. All this is, no doubt, very confusing. We have similar instances in the case of Holy Cross and of some other Cistercian abbeys. It appears however from a study of the state of the Order at this period that much of this confusion was due to the struggle then being waged between the regular abbots of the Order and the men who impetrated provisions from the Holy See. These provisors were the cause of much trouble in the Order and, with the commendatories, played a prominent part in causing the collapse of regular discipline and bringing many of the houses into disrepute. It was unfortunately true that the constitutions and usages of the Order of Citeaux were flouted by these provisors, and that this led in not a few cases to more than one claimant to the abbacy at the same time, he abbot who obtained his office in the regular way by election followed by the confirmation received from the abbot of Citeaux or by his authority, and the man who had provision made to him of an abbey by papal authority over the heads of all the monks and in despite of the constitutions of the Order. Many of these latter were not even Cistercians when so appointed. Many of them too, did not recognise

41 Ibid., pp 509-10. **42** Costelloe, op. cit. **43** Ibid. **44** Ibid.

the right of an abbot to rule a house unless he had been appointed by papal provision, and represented to the Holy See that certain houses were void which at the time were actually ruled by abbots elected, confirmed, and installed in the regular manner, according to the usages and constitutions of the Cistercian Order. In such cases the monasteries had to bear the heavy burden of supporting both the provisor and the regular abbot, as we learn from a report sent to Citeaux by the abbot of Mellifont.[45]

From 1494 to 1508 the history of Hore abbey is a blank page. An entry in the Calendar of Ormond Deeds records that the abbot of the Rock of Cashel was among the prelates summoned to the court of the liberty of Tipperary in 1508 but the name of the abbot does not appear in the record.[46] An indenture made between Pierce Butler, earl of Ormond, and his cousin Edmund Butler FitzThomas, lord of Cahir, on the Vigil of the Assumption, 1517, was witnessed, among others, by Patrick Stackpole, abbot of the Rock of Cashel (Patricio Stacopoll abbate de Rupe Cassel).[47] Thus we meet for the first time him who was to be the last regular abbot of the Cistercian convent of Cashel, the man who, twenty-three later, was to surrender into the hands of King Henry VIII with the consent of his convent as the saying went, the abbey of Cashel, its lands and possessions, its spiritualities and its temporalities, as well as the sacred trust he had received when he acquired the abbatial office and dignity. Seven years before the suppression he had been one of three Cistercian abbots who set their seals and their signatures to a notarial instrument relating to the claim of Pierce Butler, earl of Ossory, to the lordship of Ormond.[48] Of the three, William O'Dwyer, abbot of Holy Cross, had resigned the following year and so was out of office if not actually dead when the suppression took place. Patrick Stackpool lived to surrender his monastery and accept an annual pension of £4 from Henry VIII. Only one monk is recorded as receiving a pension, Maurice Mannan, who received 13 5s. 4d. John O'Mulryan, abbot of Owney, saved his house at the expense of his honour and his religion by divesting himself and his monks of the habit of their order, accepting Henry VIII 's changes in ecclesiastical polity, and forming the late abbey of Owney into a provostry of secular priests obeying the regulations of Henry's national church and becoming himself provose for life. It was a sorry ending.

An extent made in 1541 noted that 'The abbey church has from time immemorial been the parish church. There are no superfluous buildings, all being suitable for the farmer. These with gardens and other accomodations contain two acres and are worth nothing above repairs' The extent

45 Edited by C. Ó Conbhuidhe, OCSO 'The Irish Documents in Octavian's Register', in *Seanchas Ardmacha*, 2 (1957) 269-74. 46 COD, iii, 332. 47 Ibid., iv, pp 45 and 50. 48 IMED, 249. 49 Extents, p. 325.

also reports the sale of chattels £9. 15s. 4d. and notes that 'The church bell belongs to the parishioners.' There were c.600 acres, two granges, several messuages and cottages, unmeasured gardens and the rectories of Hore abbey, Raylestan and Lismalin. Edmund Heffernan was occupier. The buildings then consisted of a church and belfry with a cemetary, a hall, dormitory, four chapels, kitchen, stone, etc.[51]

In 1561 the abbey and its lands were granted to Sir Henry Radcliffe by Queen Elizabeth. In 1576 a lease of both, specifying no precise term, was gone to James Butler. The 1561 grant numbers two additional rectorial churches Grangegerry and Little Grange.[52]

The last mention of the Cistercians and Hore abbey is that of 1620 when one of the monks, Fr James Hedin, a native of Cashel, was professed for the monastery of St Mary of the Rock of Cashel, in the presence of the Revd Lord Luke Archer, abbot of Holy Cross.

There is a reference to Hore abbey reported in *Bealoideas*,[53] the journal of the Irish Folklore Society. It concerns a certain Joseph Damer (1630-1720) who was a money lender and banker of Fishamble Street, Dublin. He was also a sheep farmer, wool exporter and candle manufacturer. It was told that 'one day while buying some barrels of tallow in Cashel, he noticed that one of the barrels was unusually heavy and so saying nothing, he purchased the barrel. When he opened it he found that it contained church plate in gold with the monks of Hore abbey had hidden from Cromwell's men'.

APPENDICES

ABBOTS OF HORE

Laurence fl. 1289-91.[1]
Richard fl. 1300.[2]
Thomas fl. 1313.[3]
Walter fl. 1367.[4]
William fl. 1387.[5]
John fl. 1398.[6]
Nicholas fl. in the early part of the fifteenth century.[7]

50 Ibid., pp 325-7. **51** MH, citing chief remembrancer. **52** MH, citing auditor general. **53** *Bealoideas* 4 (1934) and *Dublin Historical Record* 1 (1941). **1** TCD MSS F. 4. 23, fo. 93r. **2** Ibid. and see also MH, p. 649, quoting KC, p. 261. **3** MH, p. 649, quoting KC. **4** TCD MSS. F. 4. 23. **5** Ibid. **6** COD, ii, p. 233. **7** IMED, p. 232: Deed no. 22(C6). There is no date, but White is of the opinion that it was issued in the earlier part of the fifteenth century.

Denis O'Connellan (Ychonnillin)and Thomas Yllent fl. before 1448.[8]
Odo O'Grady (Ygrada) fl. 1448.[9]
William O'Cahill (Ockayll) d. before 1459.[10]
William O' Callaghan (Ikilichan), monk of Holy Cross, 1459.[11]
Donocuan O'Foulow or O'Foley (Ofaula) deprived in 1466.[12]
William Seymour provided in 1466.[13]
David, archbishop of Cashel, held the abbey *in commendam*; provided in 1486.[14]
Nicholas provided in 1494.[15]
Raymond Stapleton, dean of Cashel, was provided in 1464, probably *in commendam.*
Patrick Stackpole[16] provided before August 1517. Surrendered the abbey in 1540.

LANDS OF HORE ABBEY (TOTAL ACREAGE 2948 ACRES, ALL IN CO. TIPPERARY)

Barony	Townland	Acreage	Parish and diocese
Middle Third	Ballinamona		Parish of Hore abbey, Cashel
	Deerpark		
	Farrabamanagh		
	Hore Abbey		
		1520-0-07	
	Grangebeg		Erry, Cashel
	Grangemore		
		978-0-00	

Sources

The foundation charter is no longer extant but a summary of the posses-sions listed therein may be found in KC and MH, p. 649. For grants made by William, son of Thomas of Fethard, see MH, p. 649 and HC xiii, 407. IMED, the Fiants, and the Patent Rolls show clearly that the Grange of Erry was quite distinct from the Grange near Fethard. In some of the documents the designation Grange of Fethard is replaced by that of Little Grange. In view

8 CPR, xii, 12.   9 Ibid.   10 Ibid.   11 Ibid.   12 Ibid., p. 509.   13 Ibid.   14 *Obligationes pro Annatis Diocesis Cassellensis*, 15 (from the transcript made by M.A. Costello OP, now preserved in St Patrick's College, Maynooth). I am indebted to the authorities at Maynooth for allow-ing me to make a copy of those parts of the transcript relating to the Cistercians in the dio-cese of Cashel.   15 Ibid., 19.   16 Patrick Stackpole was provided before August 1517 (COD, iv, 45 and 50). He surrendered the abbey to Henry VIII's commissioners on 6 April 1540 (see Morrin, i, p. 58, no. 35). For grant of pension to the former abbot, see *Fiants* Henry VII, no. 109, and Morrin, i, p. 62 (no. 31).

of the fact that William, son of Thomas of Fethard, in confirming the grants made by the latter to the abbey gives this grange as being in the tenement of Killeyan (Kiltinan, Co. Tipperary) I think that the Grange of Fethard (or the Grange near Fethard) *alias* Little Grange is probably the townland of Grangebeg in the parish of Kiltinan which lies about three miles south east of the town of Fethard. But there are other reasons for thinking that this grange belonged to the monks of Osney in England. Other sources: IMED, 325-7; Fiants: Henry VIII, 109, 542; Elizabeth, nos. 293, 2968, 5160, 6026, 6386, 6423; CPR: 42 Eliza. (Morrin, ii, pp 561f, 564f); 1, 2, 3, 9, 11, 14, 16 Jas. I (pp 12, 41, 57, 70, 208, 214, 257, 265, 317, 365); CS Tipperary (vol. i), DS & OS maps and Composite Map of Tipperary. Other sources are A.H., xxviii; Brady; COD; CDI; *Extents*; HC xiii; MH;

Morrin, i; Rot.Pat; Tax.I Cist; TCD MSS F. 4, 23, f.93r.

NOTES ON THE ARCHITECTURE OF HORE

In his Ordnance Survey Letters (1840) John O'Donovan discusses Hore abbey in two places On page 144 (Flanagan, RIA reproduction, 1932) O'Donovan's first description, which follows on from his account of the findings of the inquisition, does not make clear whether it is his own observation or not. He does not indicate a source.

> The noble ruins of this erection still remain and are for the most part entire. The steeple is large and about twenty feet square on the inside, which is supported by a variety of ogives from each angle, some meeting in an octagon in the center and others at the key stones of the vault, and the structure is supported by two fine arches about thirty feet high. The choir or Chapel which adjoins the east side of the Steeple is about twenty nine feet in length and twenty four in breadth on the inside; the east window is small and plain and in the sidewalls are some remains of stall etc. The nave is sixty feet in length, twenty three in breadth and on each side was an arcade of three gothic arches, the north side whereof is levelled, with lateral aisles which were about thirteen feet broad; between this and the steeple is a part but we are equally ignorant as to its name and the use it was applied to. It is thirty one feet in length, of the same breadth with the nave and divided from the steeple by a plain wall. On each side are similar arcades of two arches only and this opens with the west arch of the steeple. On the south side of the steeple is a small door leading into an open part, about thirty

1 OSL, Co. Tipperary, vol. 1.

feet long and twenty four broad; the sidewalls are much broken and
in the gable end is a long window; there is a similar division on the
north side of the steeple. Here is a small low-arched apartment
which seems to have been a confessionary, as there are niches in the
wall with holes etc.

J. O'Donovan's second description is as follows:

The Abbey is a building of considerable extent but now much
ruined. Its nave is ninety seven feet in length and twenty four feet
five inches in breadth on the inside and its choir thirty feet inches
in length and twenty four feet in breadth. The arches from which
the tower springs are nineteen feet five inches in width, and about
thirty feet in height and twnety nine feet in depth (thickness) from
east to west.

The east gable of the choir contained three pointed windows
extending to near the top of the roof (where the roof was) but they
are now partly built up with modern masonry. There are also two
pointed windows in the sidewalls also partly built up with rough
masonry. The choir and a part of the nave of this abbey would
appear to have been fitted up for a modern Protestant Church.

There are five large pointed arches on the south wall of the nave
and there was an equal number on the north wall but only two of
them now remain. The side aisles into which they led are now
nearly all destroyed.

The tower does not look at all graceful, being too low for its
length and breadth and for the great arch on which it rests.

Canon Power,[3] nearly one hundred years later, describes (in his Mount
Melleray manuscript) the ruins, as he found them:

The abbey site is low lying, in an alluvial meadow on the west side of
the famous Rock and within a couple of hundred yeards of the
latter, in the barony of Middle Third, Co. Tipperary. On its north
side flows a small stream driving various small mills and filling dams
in its progress towards the Suir. The site, on the whole is hardly of
typical Cistercian character and, in this connection, it is to be
remembered that the place was adopted, not selected, by the
Cistercians.

The ruins of the abbey are of considerable extent and are mod-
erately preserved. They derive a special interest from the abbey plan

2 Ibid., pp 110 and 144.   3 Power, Mount Melleray manuscript.

which is unique in Ireland; the cloisters lie on the north side of the church instead of on the south as everywhere else. The present may have been the plan of the Benedictine abbey which the Cistercians took over only in the second half of the thirteenth century, in the year 1272, to be exact. On the other hand we have to remember that many English Cistercian houses are on the plan of Hore. The existing remains comprise the ruin of the Church and tower with basement on the eastern range, all much dilapidated. The church, of only moderate size, had aisles, transepts, and, as already stated, a tower, in addition to the nave and chancel. Total internal length would be about one hundred and twenty feet, by twenty three accross the nace and forty nine feet over the nave and aisles. As at Holy Cross the choir extends back a great way to the west of the transept crossing, again, as at Holy Cross, a stone screen pierced by a narrow doorway in the middle, separates it from the cut of western nave. There is portion of a second stone screen across the chancel arch buit this is a very late erection -probably post Suppression. The nave is separated from its aisles by arcades of five bays, each twelve feet across and now built up; the only ornament here is a slight chamfer on the pier. Small quatrefoil clerestory windows above, and a late window in the west gable lighted the nave and the aisles extended back the whole way from the transepts to the western gable of the church. In the chancel the sedilia are ruined. There is a sacrarium and, beside it, communicating with the earth by two drains, an ogee-headed alcove, four feet high by two feet wide, which was fitted with a door. This cupboard recess may have been an ambry or, more probably, a safe for the sacred vessels. The alcove, by the way, is divided by a stone shelf into two parts. On the north side of the chancel the founder's tomb is completely ruined. The fine original early English East window has survived; it is of three lights about twenty feet high & two feet ten inches (centre) and one foot nine (sides open) in width. The south side wall of the chancel had also an early English window, of one light, but this was shortened at a later date and, on the north side, a corresponding ope was transformed and partly built up. A doorway to the west of sedilia led into the adjoining transept chapel and another doorway, on the opposite side, gave access to the sacristy. Though the central tower has partly fallen the four tower arches, about twenty feet in height, are complete, and the ceiling is richly groined. The visitor will notice an escutcheon in slight relief on the (?) of one of the piers and on a detached block of limestone lying on the floor at the crossing he will see a coat of arms charged with three spearheads. Each of the chapels has two chapels-the more usual number-but these are in very ruinous state; it is evident they had beautifully groined ceilings. At the external angles are the usual heavy Gothic buttresses. The material of the building throughout is the local limestone.

In the reverse of the usual arrangement we have the general sacristy next to the north transept and, adjoining this, the chapter room, which shows evident marks of alteration at a date later than the original foundation. Projecting to the east some fourteen feet beyond the general (north-south) line of the range this important apartment was the tour de force of the monastic architect. Not a trace of the cloisters is visable; the cloister area was small, only one hundred and twenty feet square overall at the utmost Remains of a considerable building such as existed in the corresponding place, at Baltinglass, Shrule and elsewhere, are to seen at the north-east cloister angle.

Roger Stalley in *The Cistercian Monasteries of Ireland* describes the present situation:[4]

The church and sections of the east range survive and they provide a good indication of Cistercian attitudes to design in the later thirteenth century. There is little decorative embellishment and the buildings are distinguished by their austere dignity. The church follows the usual Cistercian plan in Ireland, with two chapels in each transept, those to north still partly intact. The presbytery was not vaulted and was lit by three graded lancets in the east wall. The nave is exceptionally plain, with clerestory windows of quatrefoil form (cf. Bective) sited over the piers. The original design did not include a tower, so the roof must have run unbroken from east to west. The existing tower is a mid-fifteenth century addition and, with its fine limestone dressings and lierne vault, it is a typical example of Ormond architecture of the time. Many of the windows in the church were remodelled following the dissolution. The cloister lay to the north, the only Cistercian example of this in Ireland, and some fragments of cloister arcade remain. The walls of the church are characterised by a regular sequence of unfilled scaffolding holes. The overall design of Hore is a remarkable testimony to the conservative approach of the Cistercians, containing as it dows several features of twelfth-century Burgundian origin.

Stalley describes the church at Hore:[5]

---

4 Stalley, *The Cistercian Monasteries of Ireland*, p. 246. **5** Ibid., p. 110.

The architecture of Hore is extremely conservative and its chaste early English style is more compatible with a date of 1210 than 1280. The austere chancel is reminiscent of Dunbrody, for the lancets are devoid of mouldings and, like Dunbrody it was not vaulted. The retrospective character of the design is continued in the transepts, where the chapels were covered by pointed barrel vaults, a testimony to the persistence of Burgundian tradition. The church is distinguished by a dearth of ornament and the colourless design represents Cistercian asceticism at an extreme. The numerous scaffolding holes, apparently left unfilled when the building was finished, confirm the impression of a community preoccupied with function rather than beauty. The late thirteenth-century design of Hore reveals no knowledge of contemporary developments in England and the monks were apparently satisfied with a church that looked much like other Irish abbeys.

Stalley points out that Mellifont was not a prototype for Hore, which like other Irish houses adopted the standard 'Bernardine' or 'Fontenay' plan with two square chapels in each transept. Stalley speculates that perhaps Inishlounaght may have been the model for Hore.[6]

6 Ibid., p. 58.

EPILOGUE

A reform movement inaugurated at Clairvaux in 1615 grew into what became known as the 'Strict Observance' and was formed into a congregation in 1623. This Congregation of the Strict Observance had the approval of the then abbot of Citeaux, Nicholas Boucherat II, but the general chapter withheld its approbation, looking upon all such congregations with a certain amount of suspicion. The reform, nevertheless, continued to make headway so that by the year 1660 no less than sixty-two houses were following the Strict Observance.

After the death of Denis Largentier, abbot of Clairvaux, in 1624, relations between the two groups rapidly deteriorated. The main body of the order, now known as the Common Observance, opposed the attempts of the more extreme members of the Stict Observance to force the reform on the rest of the Order. In this aim the Strict Observance had the support of the powerful Cardinal Richelieu who, in 1633, declared himself abbot general of the whole Order and, dispersing those members of the abbey of Citeaux who were not willing to adopt the Reformed Observance, placed in the archabbey a community drawn from the latter group and thus attempted to impose his will on the Order. When he died in 1642 he left the Order in a state of complete turmoil.

The 'war' between the observances continued, and it was only in 1666 that the Constitution *In Suprema* of Pope Alexander VII put an end to the dispute. This constitution was intended to restore peace and unity to the Order. It allowed the Strict Observance to continue in existence, subject to the authority of the abbot of Citeaux and the general chapter. Its abbots were to have equal rights with the abbots of the Common Observance, both in the general and intermediate chapters as well as in the system of visitation. It was forbidden, however, to use pressure of any kind in order to force monks into the Strict Observance. While the houses of the Strict Observance were to keep perpetual abstinence, according to the ancient usages of the Order, those of the Common Observance were allowed the use of flesh meat three times a week, except during Advent and Lent and on certain other specified days.

Though the Constitution of Alexander VII was said to have 're-established the Cistercian Order in its ancient splendour,' it was not well received by the Strict Observance who claimed, that it was to a great extent the result of intrigue. Their spokesman at the stormy general chapter of 1667 was the redoubtable Abbot de Rance who had the unanimous support of the abbots of that observance. The struggle between the two observances went on as before, an angry and bitter one it was too, until Alexander's successor, Clement IX, was forced to intervene with another

Brief confirming that of Alexander.

Meanwhile the abbot of La Trappe, Armand-Jean le Bouthillier de Rance, had undertaken an even stricter reform in the house which he ruled. This reform had as its aim a return to the primitive observance of Citeaux. One link between the Irish Cistercians of the seventeenth century and the reformator of La Trappe must be mentioned here. We have mentioned already in passing Abbot Patrick Plunkett, titular abbot of St Mary's abbey, Dublin. This abbot, who became first president of the Irish Congregation of SS. Malachy and Bernard, was later made bishop of Ardagh and later still transferred to Meath; he was an exile in France during the Cromwellian regime. Here it was that he met de Rance who received at his hands the abbatial blessing in 1664. The Cistercian Order was then on the eve of extinction in Ireland, while in little more than a century it was to be wiped out in France itself by the Revolution. Little did Patrick Plunkett then realise that in blessing the new abbot he was blessing the man who, under God, was to be the means of preserving the Cistercian institute through the reform he was soon to establish and which was to survive in a wonderful manner the secularisation of the monasteries in the eighteenth century. Little did he think, as he imparted that blessing, that one day the spiritual children of the new abbot would restore to Ireland the Cistercian Order after it had ceased to exist in that country for the best part of a century.

Abbot de Rance died in 1700 but his reform lived. In 1784, the Cistercian houses in Austria and Belgium were suppressed. In 1790, the monasteries of France met with a like fate, Common and Strict Observance alike being swept away. Some effort was made to save La Trappe but it was in vain. The community, however, foreseeing the coming dissolution, had established a house in Switzerland. There they settled after their expulsion from France and in 1793 were able to found new houses in Spain and Germany. In 1794 a house was founded in England, the first in that country since the suppression of the monasteries by Henry VII.

With the invasion of Switzerland and other countries by the French republican armies the Trappists had to take to flight and for the next few years the community wandered from place to place and from country to country until at the restoration of peace they were able to return to France. Not only was La Trappe restored to the Order but other ancient houses were brought back including that of Melleray in the diocese of Nantes in Brittany. To this abbey came the little community which had been established at Lulworth in England but which had to leave the latter country owing to an outburst of bigotry.

There were at this time three congregations of Trappists, for those who had settled in Belgium had formed a group of their own under the leadership of Westmalle, while those in France had broken into two sections known respectively as the Congregations of Sept-Fons and La Trappe. Besides these was the Common Observance, in Austria, Hungary and Italy for the most part. This Observance consisted of a number of independent congregations. All those congregations, including the various Trappist ones, were under the authority of the abbot general of the Order, who was, however, no longer abbot of Cîteaux except nominally. That house had ceased to exist, having been auctioned at the time of the French Revolution and not yet restored to the Order.

In 1831 the British subjects among the monks of Mellerary were expelled from France and sought refuge in Ireland, for the majority of these 'Britishers' were, indeed, Irishmen. The story of Mount Melleray has been told elsewhere and need not be entered into here. It will suffice, then, to give here a brief resume of the history of the Irish Cistercians from 1831.

In December 1831 the Cistercians from Melleray to the number of sixty-four reached the Cove of Cork on the French battleship, *Hebe*, and, having remained a few days in the city, proceeded to Rathmore in Co. Kerry where a house had been prepared for their reception. In May 1832, the prior of the new community took up his abode in a little cottage on the bleak mountainside at Scrahan, near Cappoquin, and was followed soon after by his brethren who arrived from Rathmore in batches.

Not until 1833 had the whole of the Rathmore community been transferred to their new home at Scrahan, thenceforth to be known as Mount Melleray. In the spring of that year the work of reclaiming the mountain for cultivation was begun. God's blessing attended the labours of the monks from the beginning, and, on 20 August, the feast of St Bernard, the foundation stone of the new monastery was laid in the presence of the bishop, the clergy and about twenty thousand people.

When the new buildings were ready for roofing the community petitioned the pope to raise Mount Melleray to the dignity of an abbey. This was done, and the election of the prior, Fr Vincent Ryan, as abbot was duly confirmed. Though Mount Melleray belonged to the Congregation of La Trappe, which was actually governed by the abbot of La Grande Trappe, as vicar general of the Congregation, it was also under the jurisdiction of the abbot general of the Sacred Order of Cistercians, whose right it was to bless all the abbots of the Cistercian Order, either personally or through his delegate. Before the new abbot could be blessed as a Cistercian abbot, therefore recourse had to be had to the abbots general of the Order of which the various Trappist Congregations formed part.

In February 1835 two letters were received from the Most Revd Abbot General, Dom Sextus Benigni, one of which was addressed to the abbot-elect and the other to the community of Mount Melleray. The letter to the abbot-elect conferred on him 'all the privileges and honours, powers and prerogatives, possessed by the other abbots of the Order, as well as the plenitude of abbatial jurisdiction.' It also delegated the bishop of the diocese to give the abbatial blessing. By this important document the monks of Mount Melleray with their abbot were recognised as true children of the Cistercian family. Soon after the foundation of Mount Melleray, its founder Fr Vincent Ryan helped to re-establish the Cistercians in England in Mount St Bernard, Leicestershire.

Despite the hardships and difficulties which confronted the monks in their early years in Ireland, the new community made very great progress and, in July 1849, made a new foundation in the United States of America. The new monastery, which was named New Melleray after its parent house, was situated in the diocese of Dubuque, in the state of Iowa, and is today one of the most flourishing houses in the Order. In 1878, a second foundation was made at a place called Mount Heaton, near Roscrea and the place was renamed Mount St Joseph.

The abbots of Mount Melleray and Mount St Joseph were present at the historic general chapter held in Rome in October 1892, when, at the invitation of Pope Leo XIII, the three Trappist Congregations were united into one Order. The pope, who had at heart the reunion of the whole Order, invited the monks of the Common and Middle Observances to join with the Trappists in one family, but left them free to follow their own wishes in the matter. They preferred, however, to remain as they were. The new Order, thus formed, was separated completely from the Cistercians of the Common Observance, given its own abbot general, and named the 'Order of the Reformed Cistercians of Our Lady of La Trappe'. When, in 1898, the ancient abbey of Citeaux was restored to the Order and became the mother house of the Reformed Cistercians, whose abbot general was henceforth abbot of Citeaux, the allusion to La Trappe was dropped from the title of the Order. It is now known as the Order of Reformed Cistercians, or more usually, the Cistercians of the Strict Observance.

Despite the fact that Cistercian convents for nuns outnumbered Cistercian abbeys for monks throughout Europe in the early years of the Order, it seems as if there were only two convents in Ireland, one in Down and the other in Derry. Little is known about them. In the nineteenth century two abortive attempts were made at restoring Cistercian convents in Ireland. One of these was to be in Newry, Co. Down, to be founded from Stapehill, Dorsetshire in the 1820s. The second failed attempt was in Myross, Co. Cork, to be founded from Vaise, France in 1860. However, 1932 saw the establishment of St Mary's abbey, Glencairn, Co. Waterford, founded from Stapehill.

The year 1938 was a historic one for Irish Cistercians with their return to Mellifont. After World War II, with flourishing vocations, both Mount

Melleray and Roscrea made foundations both at home and abroad. First to come was the Roscrea foundation in Nunraw, Scotland in 1946. Then came the foundation of the monastery of Our Lady of Bethleham in Portglenone, Co. Antrim, from Mount Melleray in 1948. This was followed by a foundation in New Zealand in 1954, Southern Star abbey from Mount Melleray. Roscrea followed with a foundation in Victoria, Australia, Tarrawarra abbey, also in 1954. Finally Roscrea founded Bolton abbey, Moone, Co. Kildare, in 1965.

Irish Cistercian nuns also made foundations abroad, in Wrentham, USA, in 1949 and in Abakaliki, Nigeria, in 1982. Thus Irish Cistercians are spread over the continents of Europe, Africa, North America and Australasia.

We have told something of the Order, as well as of Inishlounaght, Holy Cross, Kilcooly and Hore abbeys in these pages and, in the interests of truth, have not attempted to hide the many blots which disfigure the fair pages of its history. No good purpose could be served by seeking to conceal the faults of those who failed to live up to the high ideals demanded by the life to which they had freely vowed themselves. Yet we must remember that if the Cistercian institute failed in medieval Ireland that failure was due in no small measure to circumstances outside the control of the Order. The lot of the medieval Irish Cistercians was unhappy for it was cast in unhappy and unpropitious times. What might have happened, had there been no invasion, we do not know. The past, however, has its lessons for us, and if we profit by those lessons, plain to be read in the pages of history, we shall avoid the pitfalls into which our predecessors fell.

INDEX